101 Techniques watercolor

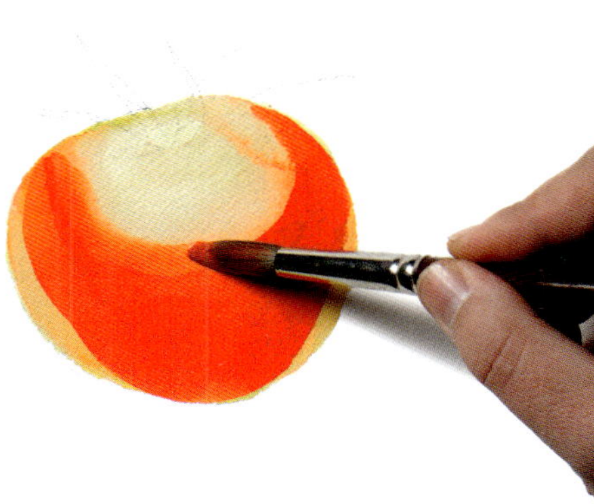

BARRON'S

101 Techniques: **Watercolor**

All specific activities lead to conclusions of a general character. This means that particular things are what help you make progress in an apprenticeship. If we extend these ideas to the world of art, we can say that practicing an artistic technique comes before all theory, and the true way that one learns to paint is by painting. This book is designed to make the reader paint, that is, so that he or she will learn and come to their own conclusions.

The lessons contained in this book are essentially practice. After a presentation of the materials used by watercolorists, the reader is given numerous examples of how to complete the different techniques that are required for painting watercolors. There could be many more or many fewer than the 101 examples that are shown here. Many fewer, because in essence, a brush, some sheets of paper, some paint, and a few simple notions are enough for beginning to paint, discovering new possibilities at every turn. There could also be many more, because as any experienced painter knows, each theme, each moment of the day, and each object in the world that surrounds us suggests a new approach to the old problem of how to paint a watercolor. The light, the colors, our mood, and our disposition all change. The true artist never stops discovering and learning. The 101 techniques gathered here are the most complete compendium of possible techniques for approaching the thematic and stylistic factors with the resources of watercolor painting. Here each exercise is a meeting of a characteristic technique, a particular style, and a specific theme.
The order of the sections is merely functional and responds to the need to organize the lessons in agreement with the nature of each exercise. It is not necessary to follow the suggested order and the readers are welcome to choose another approach, moving forward or backward in the book at their convenience.

Each exercise is a step-by-step sequence that takes up one or two pages. Its difficulty has nothing to do with how long it is. This is indicated by the use of one or two stars. One star means that the technique is rated for the beginning artist, while two stars mean that the exercise is intended for painters with a bit more experience. But beginners are encouraged not to skip the exercises with two stars, because they can learn as much or more from them than from the simpler exercises. The golden rule for all apprentices is to always attempt something that is just out of their reach. It is certain that artists who know watercolors well will be surprised more than once at discovering simple solutions (with "one star") to themes that may seem complicated at first glance.

This book was written by a team of professionals with vast experience in teaching drawing and painting. This experience has guided us to results that we can confidently say will be of great use for beginning artists as well as experienced ones. At every step we have strived to offer clear, direct, and accessible educational material that is varied, attractive, and purely esthetic. And we are sure that all these values will not go unnoticed by the reader.

Contents

beginner level ★ advanced level ★★

Watercolor Paint

Available in both tubes and cakes, watercolor paints are made of a finely ground pigment and gum arabic, an adhesive agglutinate whose job is to fix the paint to the paper and to keep it from separating as it dries. Gum arabic is a water-soluble resin that is sold in small solid blocks. Its special transparency is the reason that the watercolors are so transparent. Watercolors, then, are composed of pigments agglutinated with gum arabic with some special additives that give the paint a creamy texture.

Color Cards

The major companies make color cards with 80 to 100 different colors. They include fourteen yellows, nine reds, eleven blues, ten greens, etc. Of course, so many variations are not required for painting, and each artist chooses the ones that work best for them. That is precisely what the color cards are for. All of them indicate the level of permanence of each color, pointing out the most impermanent and the most stable ones.

Recommended Range of Colors

A plausible range for most work should include the following colors: cadmium yellow, cadmium red medium, yellow ochre, burnt sienna, carmine, ultramarine blue, cobalt blue, cerulean blue, emerald green, permanent green, and sap green. With this palette you can create all the other colors by mixing them properly, while you are acquiring the proper experience to enlarge your palette. There is nothing worse than beginning to paint watercolors with too large a palette, because you do not develop the necessary ability to capture the coloration of each model without learning to mix well.

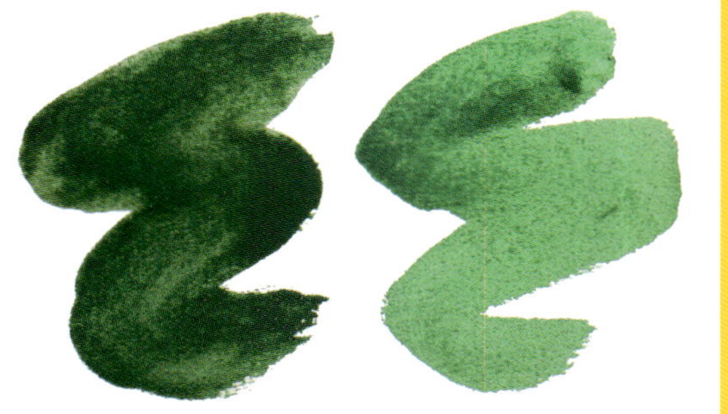

Watercolors applied to paper lose their intensity when the brushstroke dries, that is, when all the water has evaporated. The presence of water brightens the color, although this does not last.

Watercolors lose their intensity when they are dissolved in water. This gives artists the ability to play with the rich tones within each area of color.

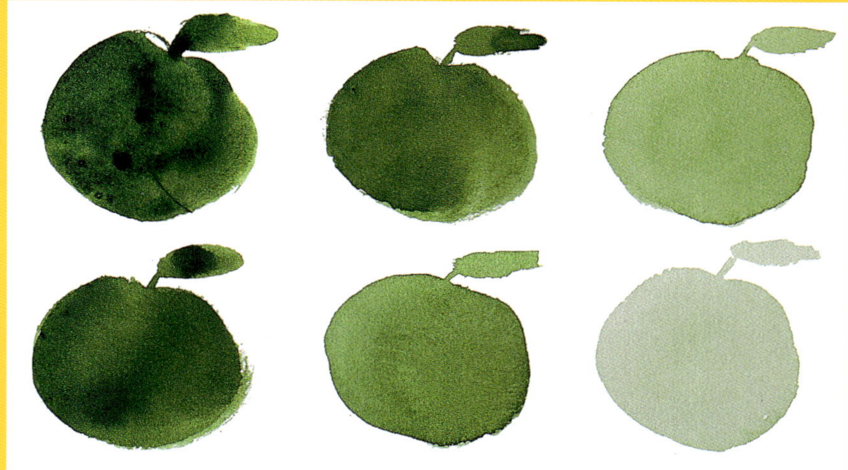

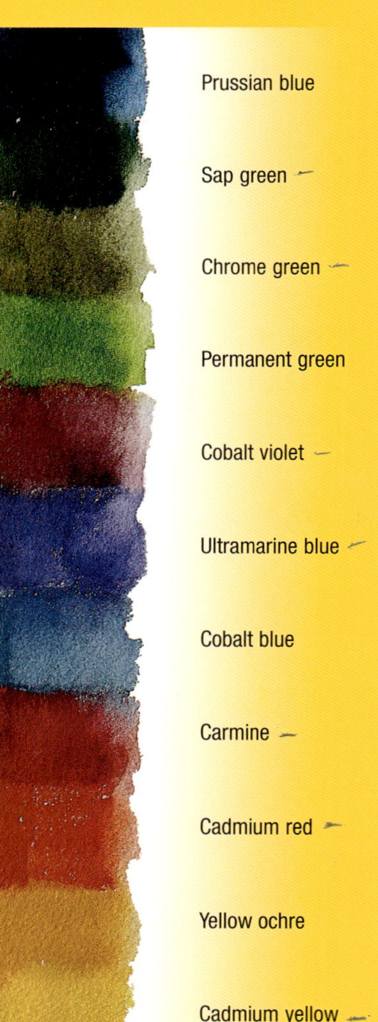

This is a sufficient range of colors for painting any subject that does not require very special tones.

Presentations

Watercolors are sold in pans, small rectangular cakes in white plastic, and in tubes. The pans can be quickly diluted and maintain even colors. The manufacturers use pigments of the highest quality, and for this reason, the prices vary according to color, based on the cost of the pigments that were used. Watercolors in tubes are also of professional quality, and they have a more fluid consistency than the pans. They dissolve very easily when they come into contact with water, and they allow you to work with large amounts of paint. Professional watercolorists use both wet watercolors in pans and creamy watercolors in tubes. Each artist becomes used to one or the other of these presentations, and normally tubes are used by artists that usually work in large formats, while pans are chosen for small formats, notes, and color sketches. Actually, both forms fulfill all the requirements that the watercolorist insists upon for his or her work.

Palettes

Watercolor palettes are used for carrying paint as well as for mixing paint in the metal trays. Special palettes with wells where the paint is deposited are used with watercolors in tubes. Leftover paint dries but can be used by dampening it again, so it is not necessary to clean the wells after each painting session; the material is not wasted.

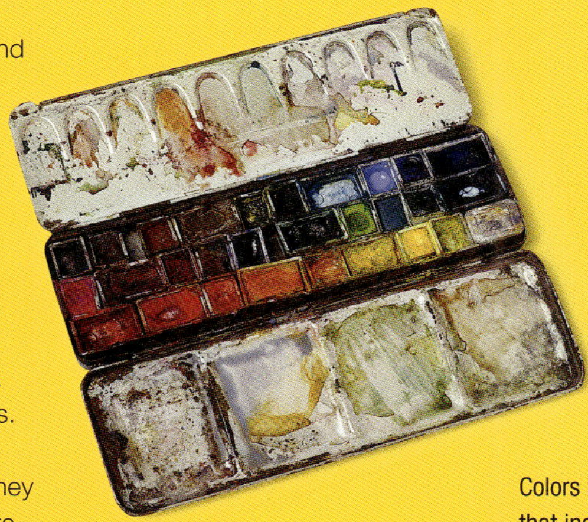

Colors in pans are sold separately or in metal palettes that include mixing areas.

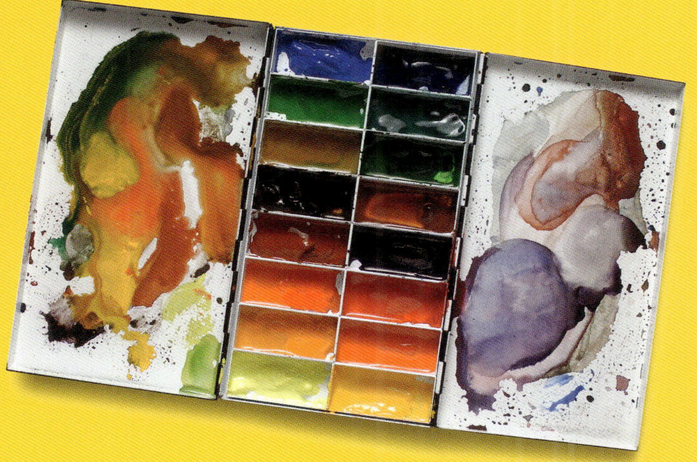

This is the palette that is used by watercolorists who prefer paint in tubes. The paint is deposited in each of the wells. When they are dry the paints can be used again by adding water.

Tubes of paint are sold individually and can be mixed on any surface, although they are normally put in a palette with wells.

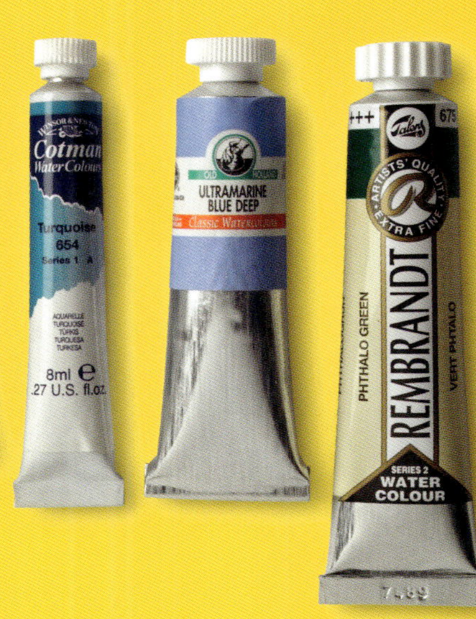

Watercolor pans are carried in metal boxes that are also used as palettes for mixing.

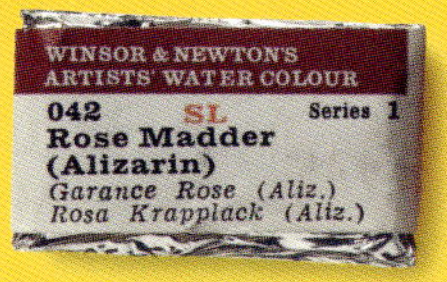

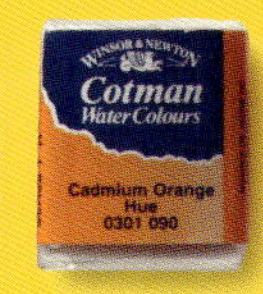

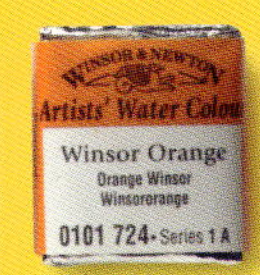

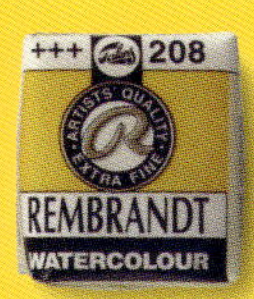

Materials / **Brushes**

Natural Hair

Natural hair brushes are the best kind for painting with watercolors. The ones made from sable hair stand out for their superior quality. They hold a large amount of paint, keep their shape and tension, and their tips are sharp and well formed. Ox hair brushes are less expensive and somewhat softer. The remaining varieties, squirrel, pony, and goat, are much softer and are only good for painting large washes.

Synthetic Hair

These are made of artificial fibers, which do not hold as much liquid and are much stiffer. They are a useful economical alternative for beginning watercolor artists.

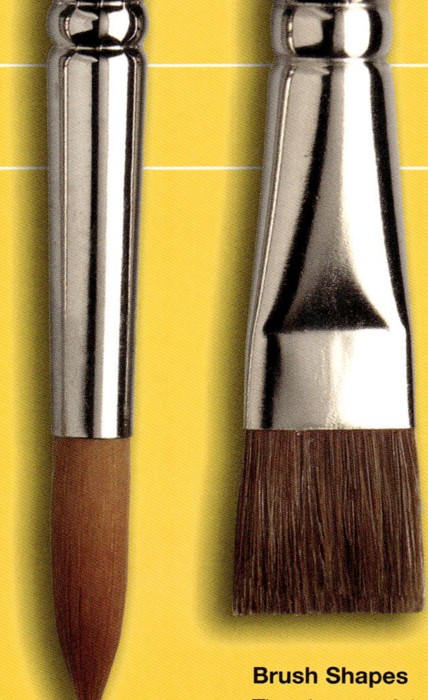

Flat and round brushes are the most commonly used for watercolors.

Brush Shapes

The shapes of the brushstrokes are a crucial factor in watercolor painting. Their form is always determined by the shape of the hair of the brush. Watercolor brushes are basically manufactured in two shapes, flat and round. The round brushes are used more by watercolorists because they can be used both to spread a large amount of paint and to "draw" fine lines with the tip. The flat brushes are also very useful because they can be used to make brushstrokes with sharp edges and make it easy to spread paint (as gradations or not) in the background or in large areas of the paper. It is highly recommended that the round brushes be of natural hair, and at least one of them should be of superior quality with a good tip and stable tension. The flat brushes can be made with synthetic hair, especially if they are large ones.

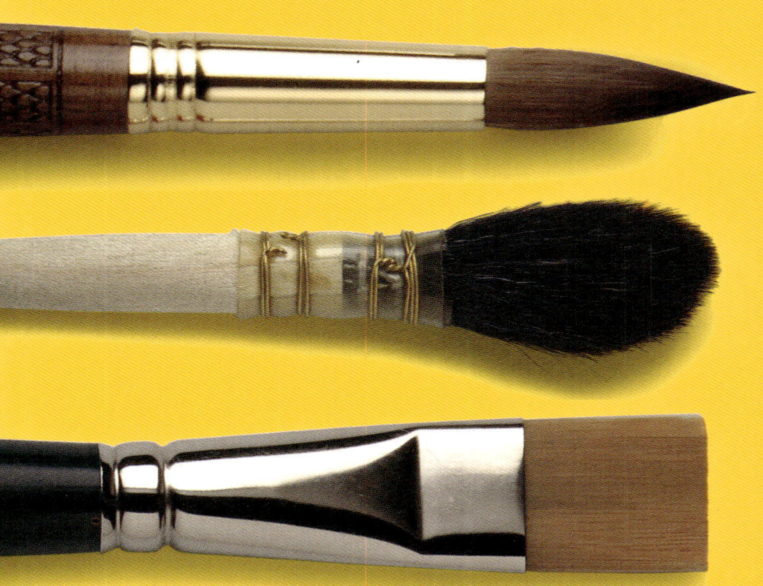

The sable hair brush (above) is the best quality. Its tip is very sharp, it holds a large amount of water, and its tension is just right. Brushes using other natural hair are softer and the tips are not as good, or they cannot form a point, like the squirrel hair (center). Synthetic hair brushes tend to lose their tips easily. For this reason the flat square shapes are mainly used.

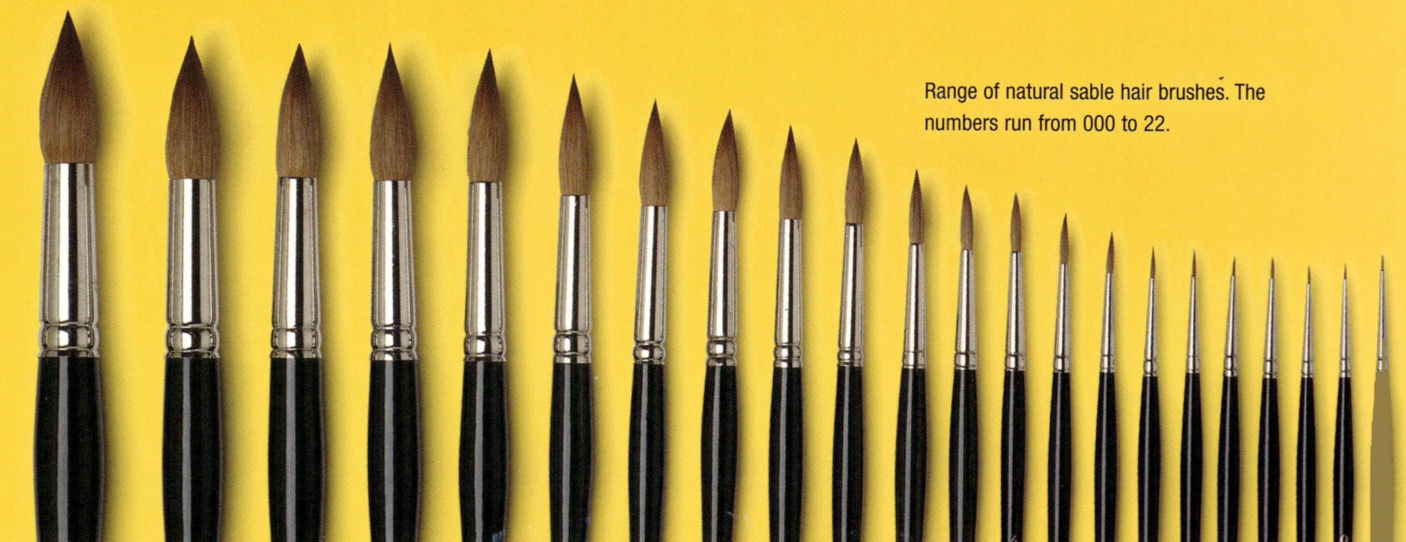

Range of natural sable hair brushes. The numbers run from 000 to 22.

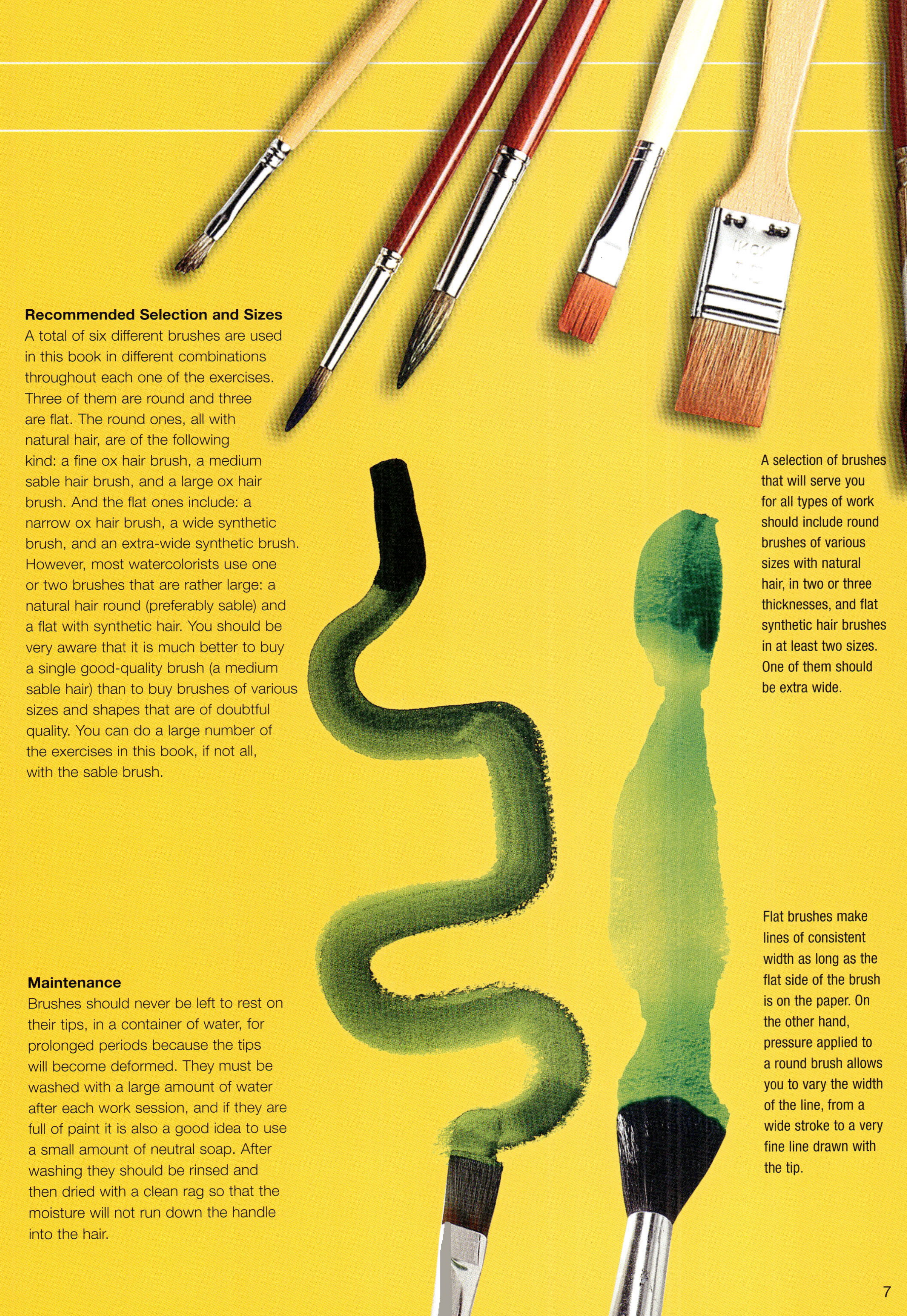

Recommended Selection and Sizes

A total of six different brushes are used in this book in different combinations throughout each one of the exercises. Three of them are round and three are flat. The round ones, all with natural hair, are of the following kind: a fine ox hair brush, a medium sable hair brush, and a large ox hair brush. And the flat ones include: a narrow ox hair brush, a wide synthetic brush, and an extra-wide synthetic brush. However, most watercolorists use one or two brushes that are rather large: a natural hair round (preferably sable) and a flat with synthetic hair. You should be very aware that it is much better to buy a single good-quality brush (a medium sable hair) than to buy brushes of various sizes and shapes that are of doubtful quality. You can do a large number of the exercises in this book, if not all, with the sable brush.

A selection of brushes that will serve you for all types of work should include round brushes of various sizes with natural hair, in two or three thicknesses, and flat synthetic hair brushes in at least two sizes. One of them should be extra wide.

Maintenance

Brushes should never be left to rest on their tips, in a container of water, for prolonged periods because the tips will become deformed. They must be washed with a large amount of water after each work session, and if they are full of paint it is also a good idea to use a small amount of neutral soap. After washing they should be rinsed and then dried with a clean rag so that the moisture will not run down the handle into the hair.

Flat brushes make lines of consistent width as long as the flat side of the brush is on the paper. On the other hand, pressure applied to a round brush allows you to vary the width of the line, from a wide stroke to a very fine line drawn with the tip.

Materials / **Papers**

Paper Quality
Watercolor paper should always be of good quality, and the artist, even if a beginner, would do well to buy only papers that are especially made for watercolor painting. Specialized manufacturers include their mark on each sheet, whether they are watermarks with monograms visible when lit from behind, or dry seals in relief that can be seen in one of the corners of the sheet.

Weight
This corresponds to the thickness of the paper. A paper's weight is measured in grams per square meter (metric) or in pounds per ream of 500 sheets. The most common and recommended weight for watercolor painting should be at least 140 lb (300 gsm). Japanese papers (r ce paper) are much thinner, and handmade papers can be much thicker.

Surface
The texture of the paper can be satin, hot press, cold press, or rough. Cold press is the best for most types of work. Each manufacturer offers a different texture that will create different results. The choice of one over the other will depend on the artist's personal taste.

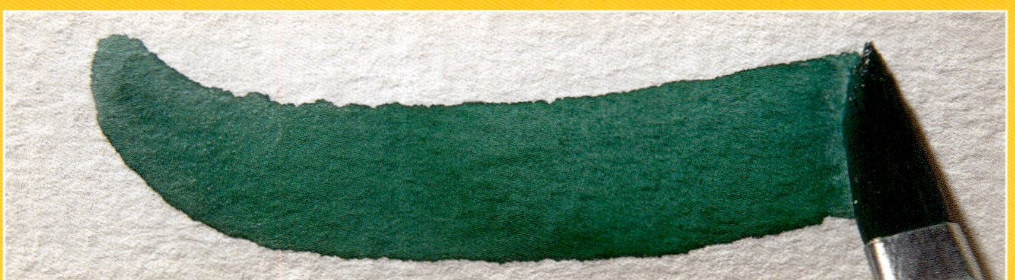

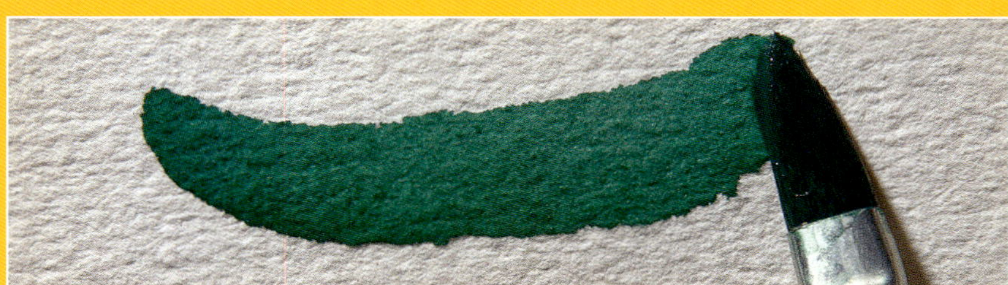

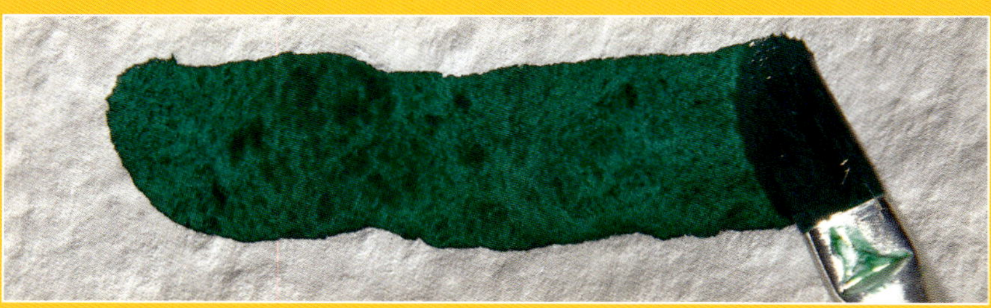

From top to bottom: papers with smooth texture, rough texture, and very rough texture.

Watermarks are a characteristic of most professional-quality papers. In these photographs you can see two of these marks, one accompanied by its monogram, when held up to the light.

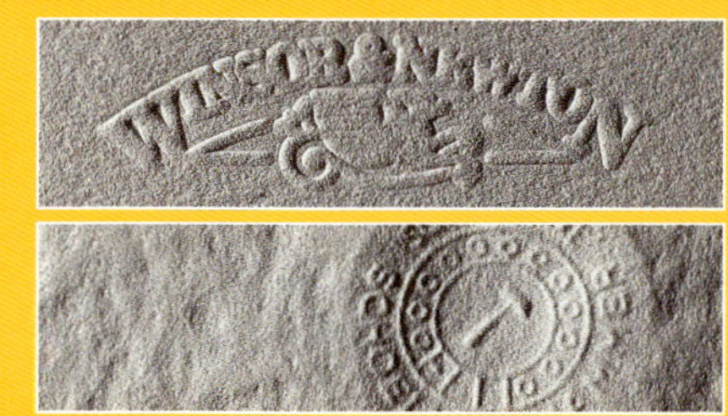

Other manufacturers mark their papers with dry seals, in relief, visible and noticeable to the touch in one corner of the paper.

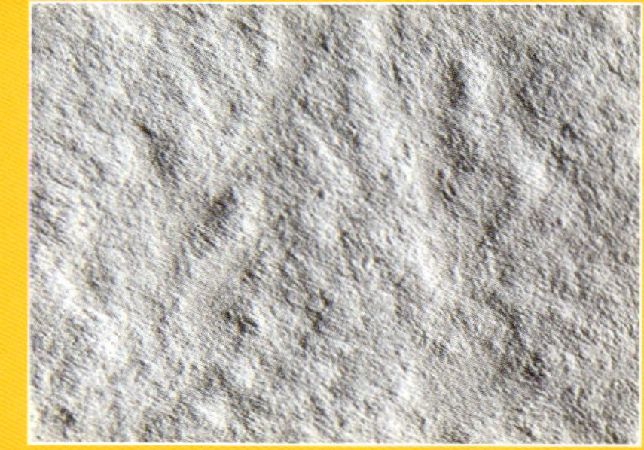

These images reproduce the surface texture of three rough papers from different companies. It is not a matter of differences in quality, but of personal choice of finishes that are more or less irregular.

Presentation

Paper can be bought in blocks of sheets that are bound along the edges. The sheets contained in these blocks have the advantage of not buckling from moisture. After the paper is dry it is easily removed from the block with a letter opener or similar tool. Large sheets 23½" x 31½" (80 x 60 cm) are also available, which can be cut to any convenient size.

Rice Papers

Typical papers of quality are composed of cotton fibers, but Asian papers are manufactured from rice fibers. They are very thin, but also very strong. They require a very light and direct approach and are not recommended for beginners.

Handmade Papers

Handmade papers have a thick and irregular texture. They are very absorbent because they have small sizing, and if the artist does not have a little experience the finished work will have a rather dull, matte finish.

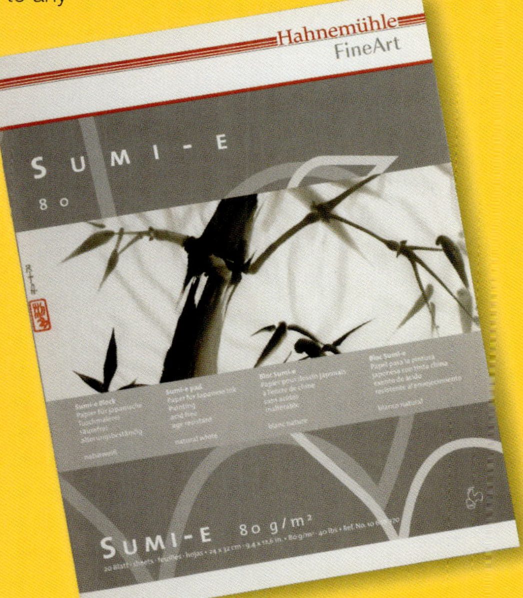

Rice papers are very thin. They are used for ink washes or light watercolors.

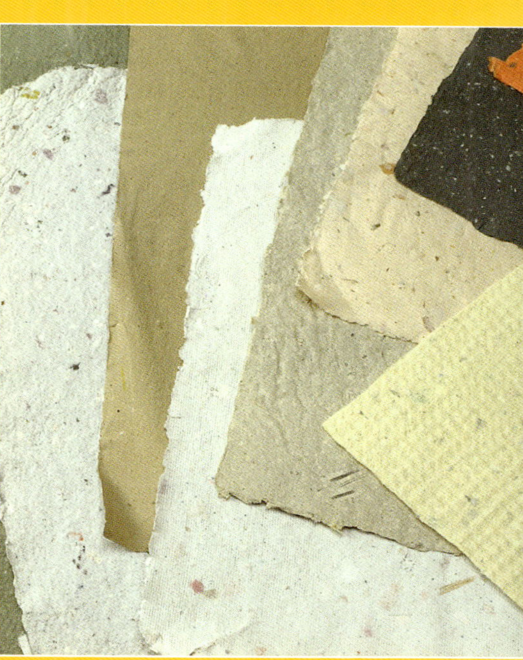

Handmade papers come in many sizes, formats, textures, and colors.

Watercolor blocks keep the wet paper from buckling. When the watercolor is dry the sheet can be removed from the block with a letter opener or a spatula.

The paper is sold in blocks of sheets that are glued along the edges, in small sketchbook sizes. Or you can buy large sheets of paper that can be cut to different sizes.

The Workspace

A watercolorist can work without any problems on top of a normal table. It is even better if he has a wooden board on which he can place the watercolor block or sheet of paper. The board should be slightly inclined to make it easier to see the work. Many watercolorists use tabletop stands or easels. There should be enough surrounding space to accommodate the watercolor box, the brushes, a container of water, a rag, and any other complements. It is important to always have some pieces of the same paper used for the painting at hand to practice and test colors before applying them to the work. Finished watercolors should always be kept in a folder and never rolled up. For easy access, many painters have a folding poster rack for storing the folders.

Rags and Paper Towels

It is very important to have a cotton rag at hand for when you need to dry your brush and for general cleaning purposes. Many watercolorists also use sponge rags in squares or rolls to absorb excess paint and water from the brush hair when it is required by the painting technique.

Sponges

Some watercolor techniques require dampening the paper before painting. A flat wide brush can be used for this, but a sponge makes the task easier. Natural sponges are preferable to synthetic ones, which are rougher and less flexible.

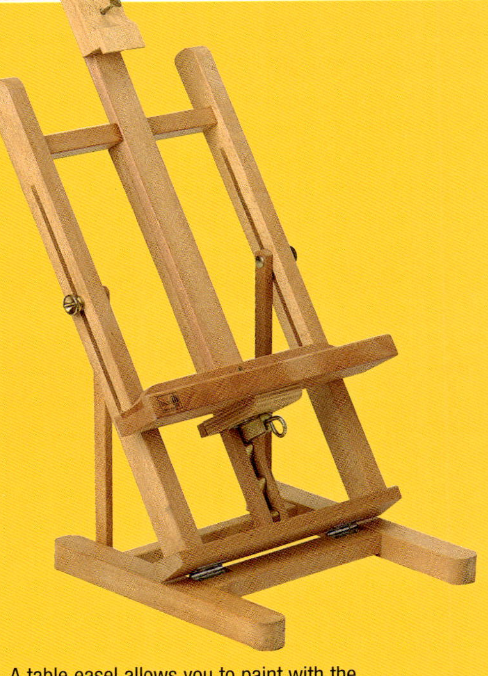

A table easel allows you to paint with the paper at the proper angle. Either a watercolor block or a board with paper attached can be held by it.

An old towel can be used for cleaning brushes and for transporting them.

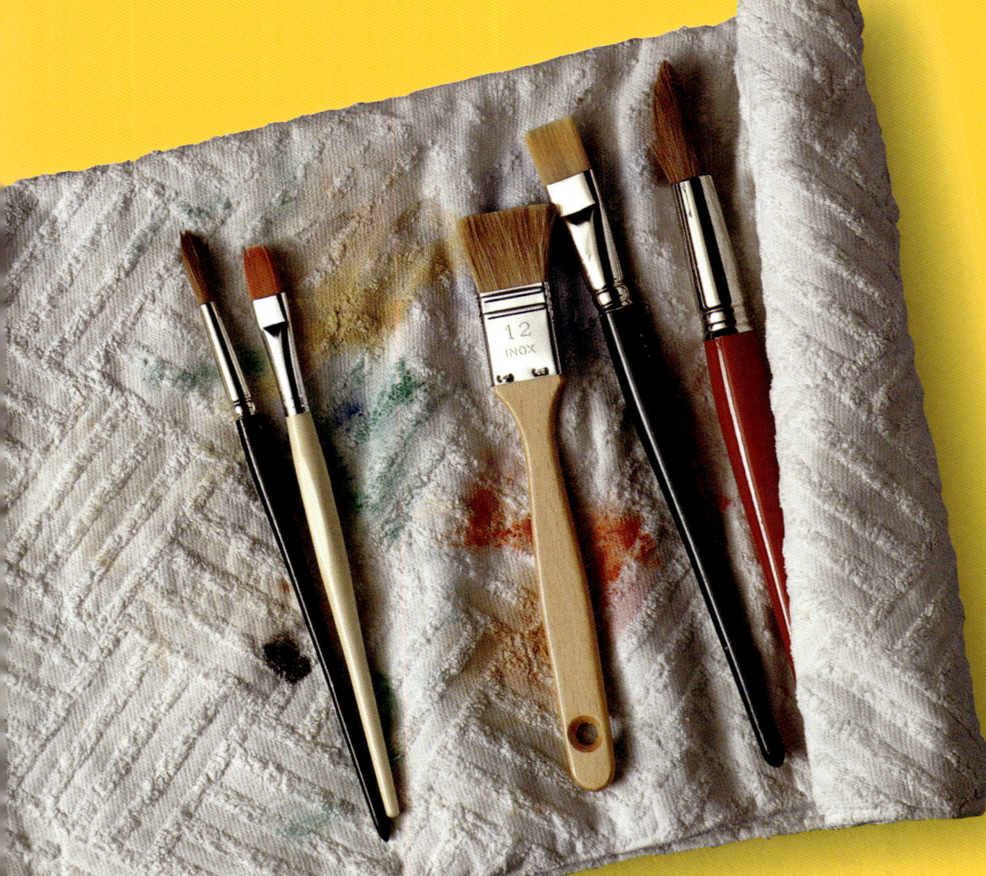

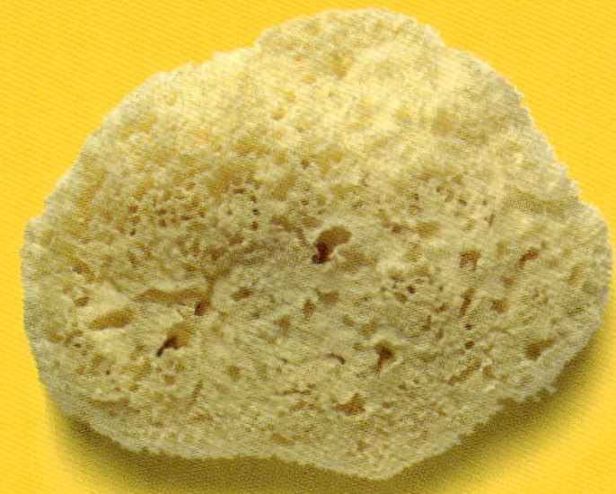

A sponge can be used for easily dampening the paper. Natural sponges work best.

Paper towels can be used to absorb excess water and paint from the brush hair before painting.

Containers

It is necessary to have a plastic or glass container with a wide opening and large enough to hold a good amount of water. If the painting session will go on for several hours, the dirty water will have to be changed once in a while so that it will not affect the color of the paint that is being used.

Other Utensils

If you are going to work with loose sheets of watercolor paper, you will need tacks or masking tape to attach the paper to a board. The best kind of board is made of wood and has a waterproof surface.

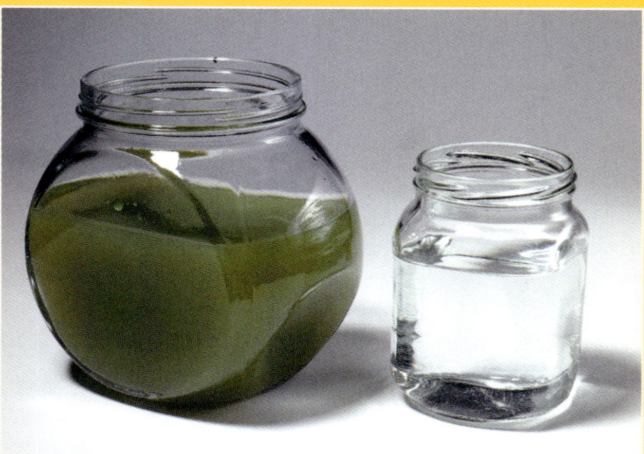

It is helpful to have at least one wide-mouthed container for water.

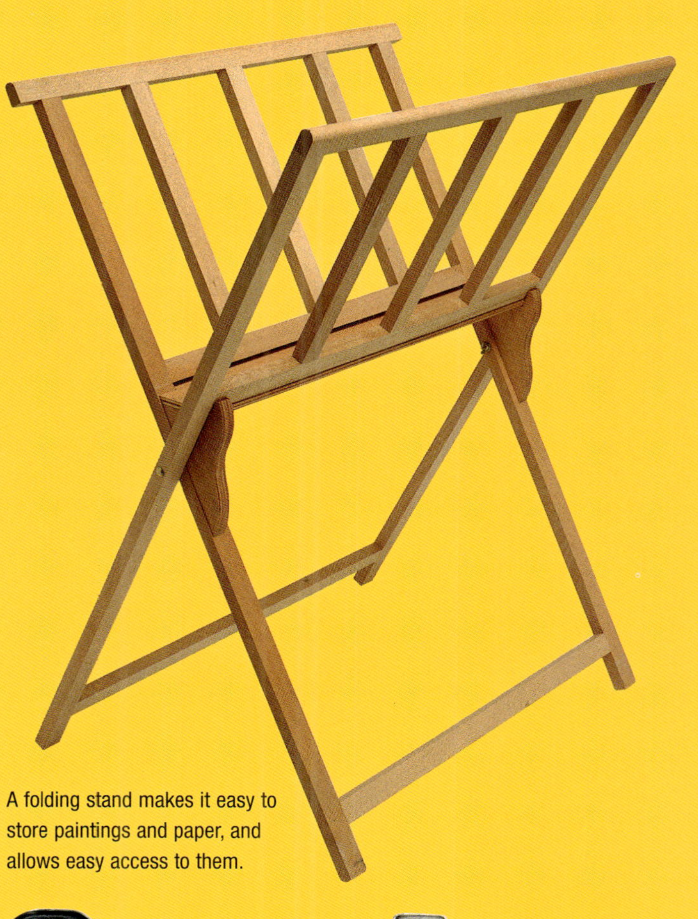

A folding stand makes it easy to store paintings and paper, and allows easy access to them.

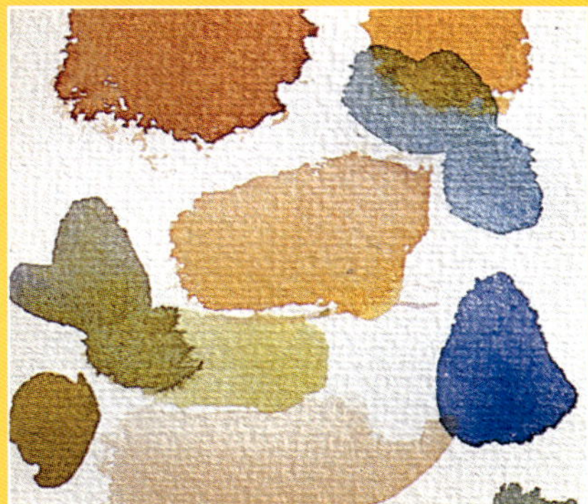

You should always have test paper near the painting in progress so you can check color mixtures and the amount of water in the brush. The paper should be of the same type that is used for the painting.

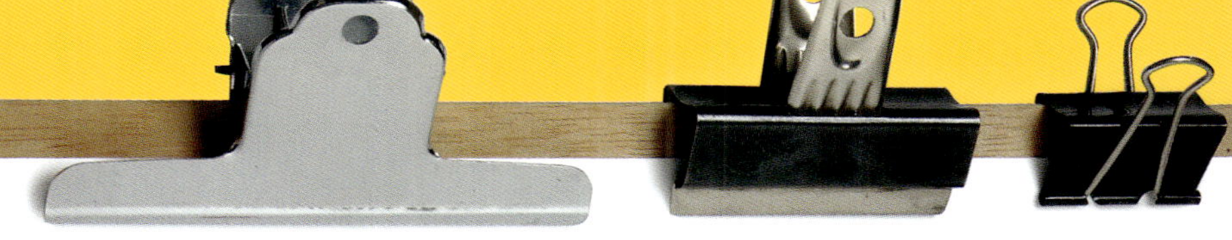

Clips can be used to hold the paper to a board.

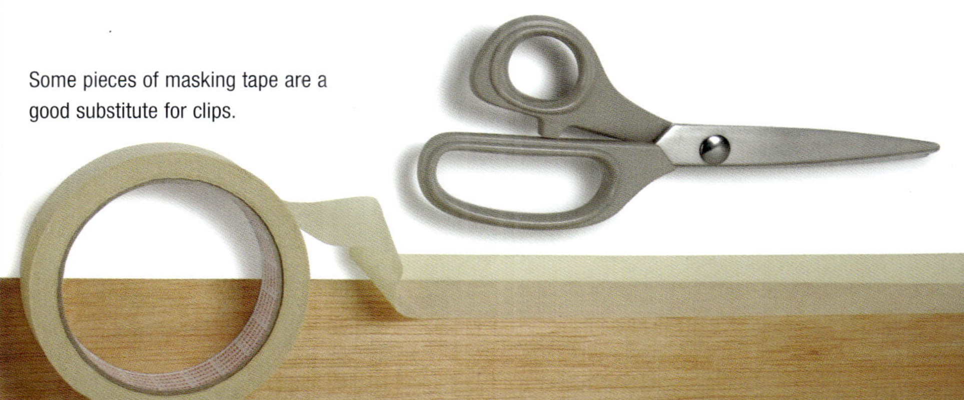

Some pieces of masking tape are a good substitute for clips.

Materials / **Compatible Products**

Additives

There are many products that modify the fluidity, consistency, and drying time of watercolor paints. Gum arabic adds gloss to the colors and increases their transparency. Ox gall helps the paper absorb water and eliminates traces of oil. Alcohol accelerates the evaporation of the water so that the watercolors dry faster, and glycerin slows down the drying time. All of these products should be used in moderation: two or three drops in the container of water are normally enough to achieve their effect. However, in most cases and if good quality watercolors are being used, it is not necessary to use any type of additives.

Gouache

Gouache paints are used just like watercolors, but they are thick and opaque. Although it is not very orthodox, many watercolorists use white gouache for creating spots and small white areas over parts that have been painted.

Pastels

Lines made with pastels do not completely dilute in water, and they can be used to add less conventional textures and chromatic effects. They are sold in sticks and as wooden pastel pencils. The pencils are much harder than the sticks and less soluble in water.

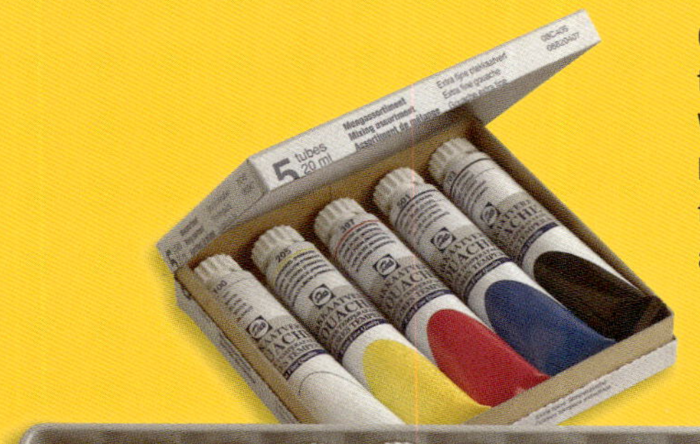

Gouache paint is thick and opaque. White gouache can be used in moderation to restore some white areas.

Pencils

It is important to have a medium-hard graphite pencil for making the preliminary sketches for paintings. Other pencils that can be used with watercolors are charcoal, chalk (sanguine, white, etc.), and water-soluble color pencils, whose lines dissolve in water and create interesting effects.

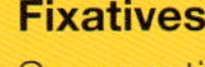

Fixatives

Some artists use fixatives and protective varnish to make their paintings more durable. Most of them use commercial aerosols. But many watercolorists believe that protective substances alter the natural finish because they add stray reflections to the natural appearance of the work.

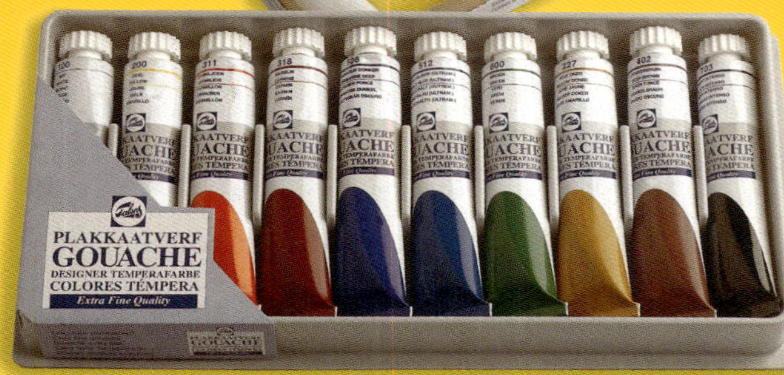

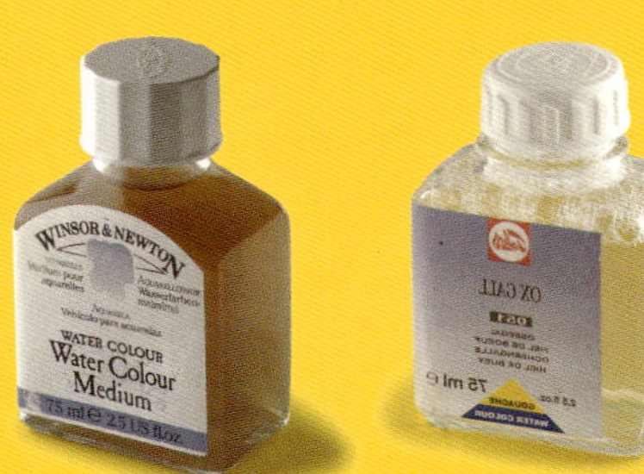

Gum arabic and ox gall are the two most frequently used additives for watercolors.

Hard and soft pastels barely dissolve in water but they combine well with watercolors.

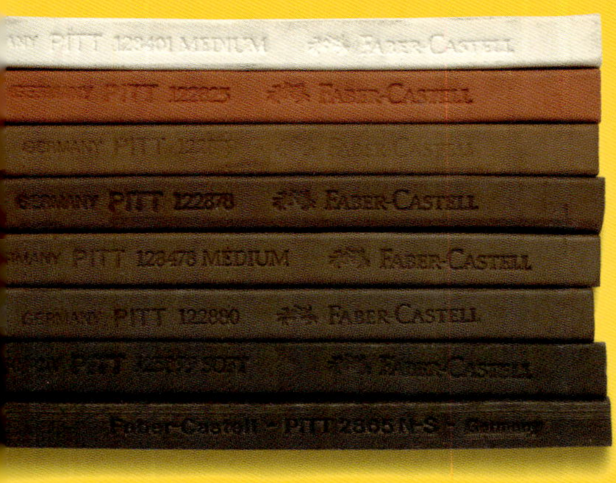

Sanguine pencils are sometimes used for adding marks and lines to the watercolor.

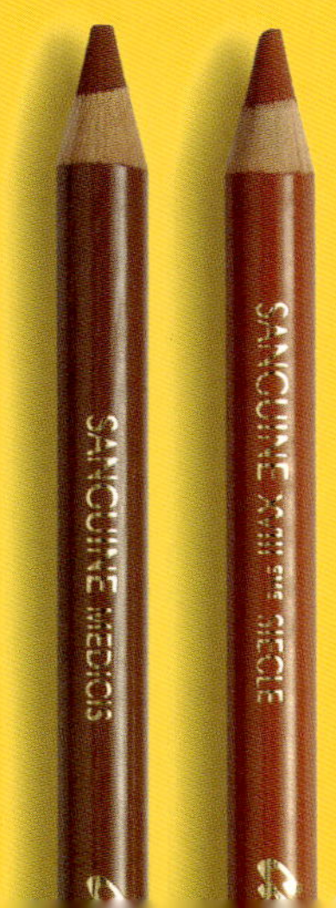

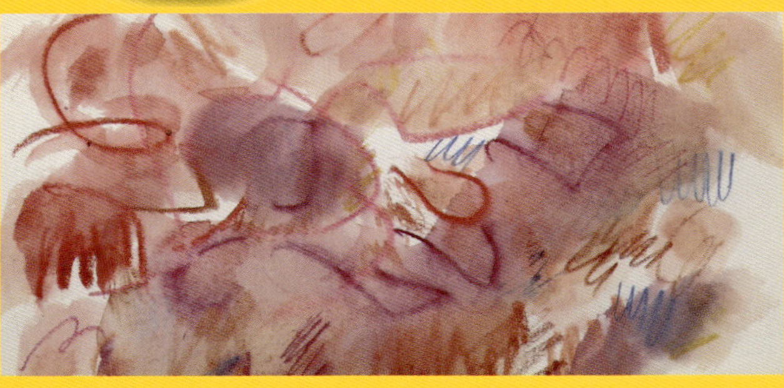

Water-soluble color pencils combine easily with watercolors. Their lines can be maintained or completely dissolved according to the amount of water that is used.

Wax Crayons

These are not soluble in water. White and color wax crayons cannot be altered. This means crayons can be helpful tools for creating colorful effects and original and creative lines. White crayons are used most; all can be purchased in pencil or stick form.

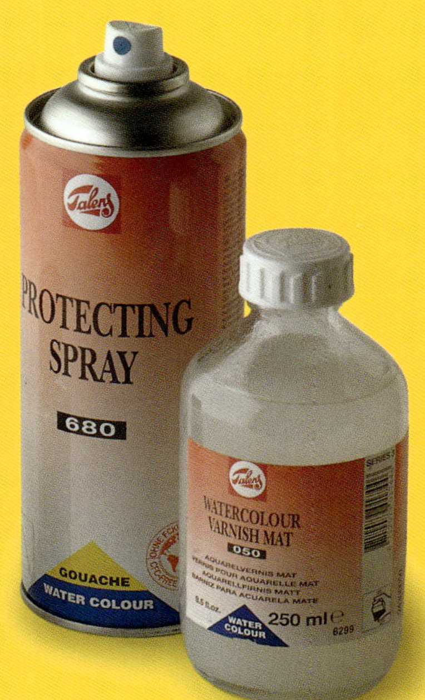

Varnishes and aerosol fixatives protect artwork, but they can become slightly yellow or create random reflections.

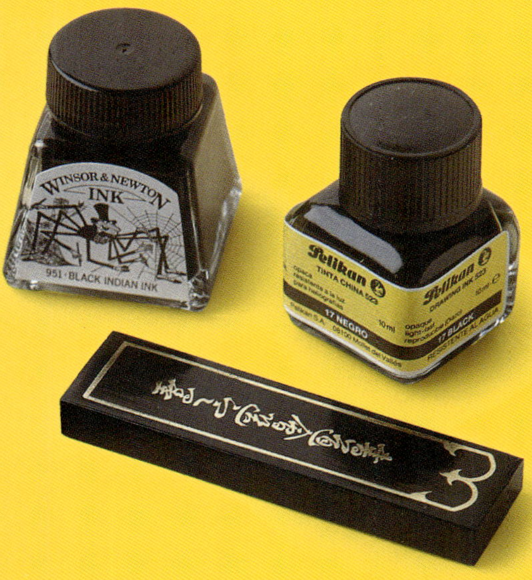

Inks

India ink can be diluted with water but is waterproof after it dries. This creates many possibilities for the watercolorist who likes to experiment with new techniques. Ink can be applied with a brush, nib pen, or reed pen. Colored inks can be very attractive; they are transparent and have bright colors, but they fade quickly if exposed to natural light, so they are not highly recommended.

Other Products

Salt, turpentine, and gesso are some of the complementary products that appear in this book. In each case their nature and use with watercolors is explained, so no more details are required here.

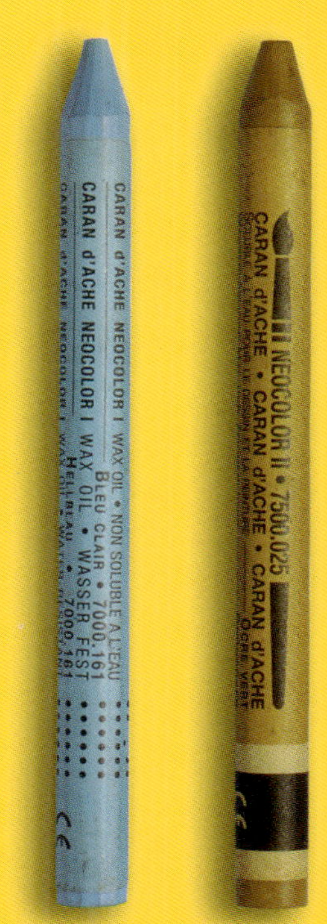

Wax crayons are not water soluble, and they hold their color and the shape of their line under washes of watercolor.

White wax crayons can create effects that are similar to reserves on white paper, but they are more spontaneous.

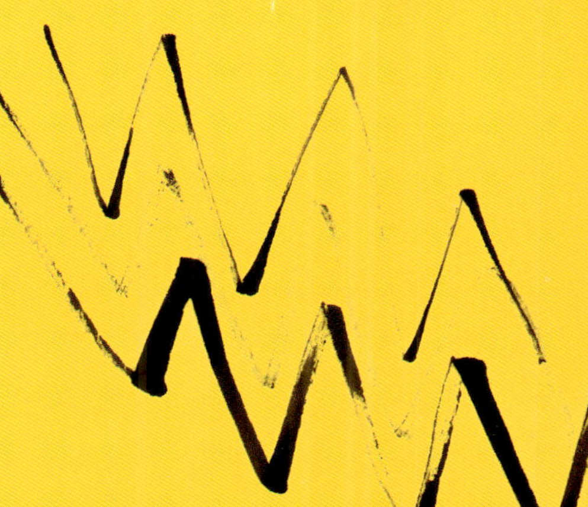

India ink in sticks or bottles can combine very well with watercolors, either diluted or painted over dried brushstrokes.

India ink can be applied with a brush, a nib pen, or a reed pen.

Technique number

Beginning level

Important brushstroke lines

Notes on level and required materials

17 Wet on Wet / **Absorbing with Paper**

LEVEL OF DIFFICULTY
★★
COLORS
Cadmium yellow
Permanent red
Cadmium red
Carmine
Sap green
BRUSH
Medium round natural hair
PAPER
140 lb medium-rough texture

Absorbent paper will create more detailed and intense areas than a rag. Its large number of fibers makes it very efficient and allows it to immediately remove water wherever it is applied. Here you will use it for quickly and easily creating a beautiful bunch of carnations as if by magic.

1. You do not need a preliminary drawing, because applying the paper towel will create the shapes of the flowers. First, add a generous wash of carmine mixed with cadmium red to the dampened paper.

1

Carmine + cadmium red

2

2. Using a piece of crumpled paper towel, absorb different areas of similar size from the wash.

3

Carmine + cadmium yellow

Apply very saturated paint to make dark colors by pressing on the brush to make all the paint flow to the paper. The more pigment deposited on the paper, the darker or more intense the color.

4

3. Highlight the white areas by painting between them with saturated carmine. Add some areas of orange with a mixture of carmine and yellow.

4. The effect produced is a cloud of color where you can barely make out recognizable forms.

5

7

6. Dilute the previous mixture a little and make long brushstrokes to represent some leaves that show through the flowers.

7. The result is spectacular; it just requires confidence in your own abilities and a little bit of daring in the use of the materials.

18 Wet on Dry / **Monochrome Transparency**

LEVEL OF DIFFICULTY
★
COLORS
Cadmium yellow
Permanent red
Carmine
Sap green
BRUSH
Medium round natural hair
PAPER
140 lb medium-rough texture

When you apply one color over another dry color, it produces a transparency; the coloration of the upper tone is affected by that of the lower one. Transparencies always have a special smoothness and luminosity since the colors do not mix physically, but are mixed by your eyes.

1. Draw the fruit (a persimmon) and cover it with a light-yellow wash. When it is very dry, paint another wash of orange over it.

1

2

2. Gradate the orange in the upper part until the tone becomes the same as the underlying yellow. The transparency makes a rich color.

3. Again, when the color is completely dry, cover the fruit with another wash, this time with bright red. Soften its edges so that they blend with the base colors.

Cadmium yellow

Cadmium yellow + permanent red

3

Carmine

5

Sap green

4. The last application of color, over a dry base, will be saturated carmine that shades the middle part of the persimmon.

4

5. The smoothness of the surface and its luminosity are very convincing. They are the result of painting layers of transparent color on a dry base.

Advice and tricks

Step number

Advanced level

19 Wet on Dry / **Accumulated Transparencies**

LEVEL OF DIFFICULTY
★★
COLORS
Cadmium yellow
Yellow ochre
Sap green
BRUSH
Medium round natural hair
PAPER
140 lb medium-rough texture

The accumulation of transparencies can go on nearly without end, but it is important to adjust the use of this technique to the requirements of the subject. Here the transparencies are obligatory, since you will be representing the greenish glass of a bottle. Working within a limited color range allows you to create a large number of different colors and a really painterly effect.

1

Cadmium yellow + sap green

Sap green

Sap green + yellow ochre

2

1. After drawing the outline of the bottle, paint the two large blocks of contrasting color: yellow mixed with a little green in the upper part and green mixed with ochre in the lower. Paint a saturated wash of sap green in the middle.

2. Represent the interior volume of the base of the bottle with a dark-green line in the shape of an inverted V. Then add a more saturated transparency at the top.

3

4

3. Paint the dark colors of the upper part with a mixture of green and yellow ochre over a completely dry base.

4. Add the last dark transparencies to the glass and lightly paint the labels on the bottle with a dark green tone that is very diluted with water.

37

Incorporation of colors into the painting

The 101 Techniques

This section is organized in ten large blocks or monographic chapters, each one consisting of five to twelve practical examples that demonstrate variations and approaches of a typical technique of watercolor painting.

Each exercise incorporates information on the required materials: colors, size, and quality of the paintbrushes, and the kind of paper. In addition, all of the exercises indicate their level of difficulty with one or two stars. One star indicates the basic level: it means that the approach is within the abilities of a beginning painter. Two stars, the advanced level, signify that the exercise is meant for a painter with somewhat more experience.

The development of the watercolor is shown in step-by-step sequences that cover one or two pages, and the explanations of each step are accompanied by information on the colors that are to be used at every moment and in every part of the work, and by arrows that show the correct movement of the brush at important moments.

01 Washes / **Flat Silhouettes**

LEVEL OF DIFFICULTY
★
COLORS
Cobalt violet
Carmine
BRUSH
Medium round natural hair
PAPER
140 lb medium-rough texture

Here you are going to paint silhouettes in a single color without shading, changing the tone according to the object that is being represented. You will use two colors. Sometimes you will apply pure violet, and other times you will mix it with a little carmine. Each silhouette represents a different level of saturation, created by diluting it with more or less water.

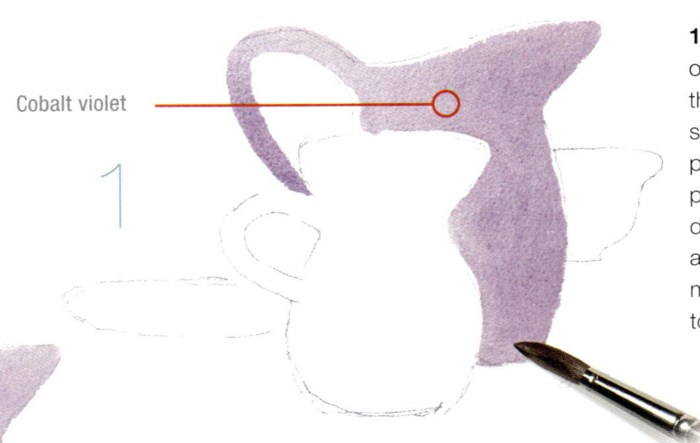

1. Draw the outlines and then fill in the silhouettes. First paint the largest pitcher with very diluted violet, attempting to maintain a uniform tone.

2

2. Paint the small pitcher with pure saturated violet. The paint should not dry on the paper.

3. Spread the "puddle" of violet and carmine paint that was left on the paper. If you have too much liquid it is a good idea to remove some from the brush with a sponge pad.

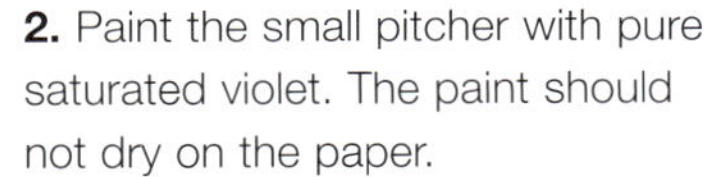

4

4. Paint the rest of the objects following the same procedure, allowing the previous paint to dry before continuing to paint. The result is a mixture of violet with a bit of carmine.

3

Cobalt violet
+ carmine

02 Washes / **Gradated Silhouettes**

LEVEL OF DIFFICULTY
★
COLORS
Cadmium yellow
Sap green
BRUSH
Medium round natural hair
PAPER
140 lb medium-rough texture

In this exercise you will use two colors that will at no time be mixed. The different colors that are created will be the result of the amount that each color is diluted. The differences in dilution create the shades. The brush work is important for defining the form of each mass of color, following the lines created during the preliminary sketch.

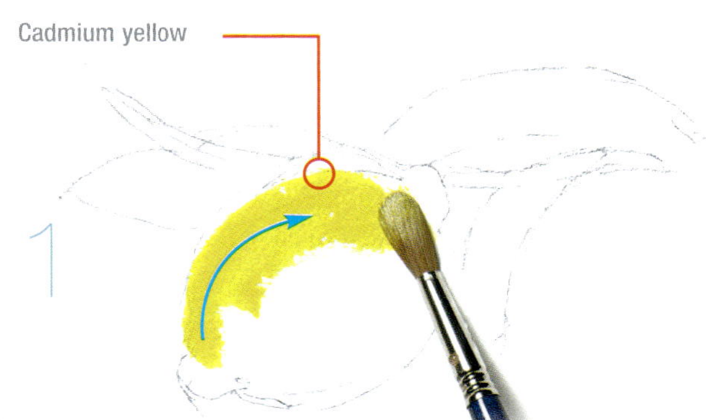

1. The movement of the brush creates the form. The hair follows the inside of the outline of the sketch.

2. Each leaf is a simple brushstroke, thinner at each end than in the middle. The first leaves are of a green that is so diluted it looks gray.

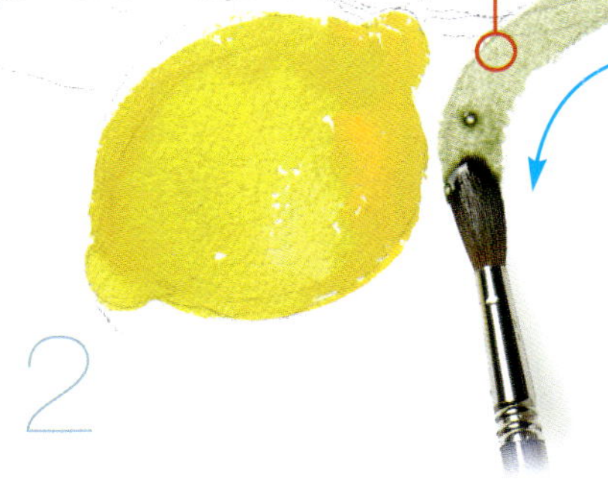

3. Paint this leaf with a single brushstroke, with a much more saturated green, that is, with a smaller amount of water.

4. The different intensities of the leaves suggest distance between them, otherwise it would seem that all of them occupy the same plane.

03 Washes / **Cool Monochromes**

LEVEL OF DIFFICULTY
★
COLORS
Ultramarine blue
Burnt sienna
BRUSH
Medium round natural hair
PAPER
140 lb medium-rough texture

Mixing ultramarine blue and burnt sienna results in a more or less cool gray depending on which color is more dominant in the mixture. To make this wash, graduate the dilution of the mixture and the amount of each component color.

1

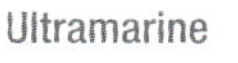

1. Use a very saturated mixture that will later be lightened by adding more water. These first brushstrokes are for the lower branches of the tree.

2

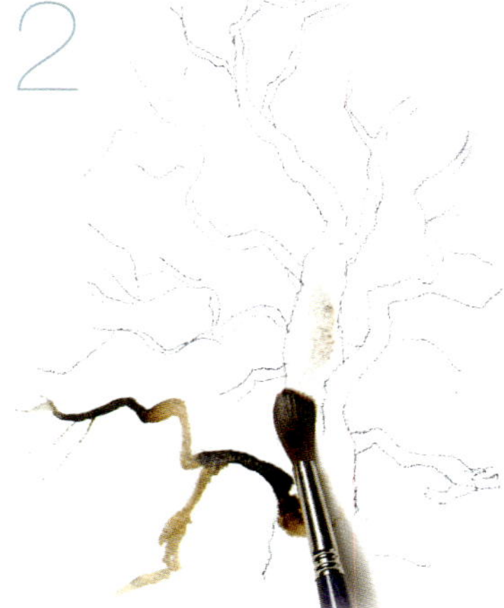

2. Brush very diluted color to extend a part of the previous brushstrokes. Make it follow the damp brush marks.

3

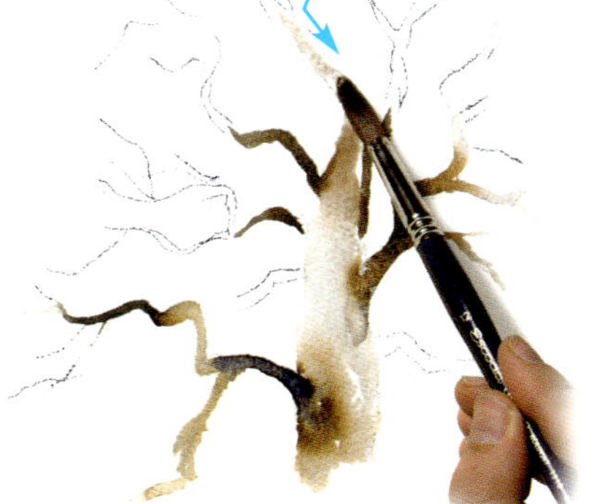

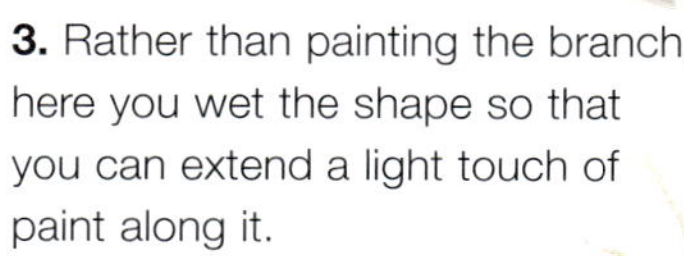

3. Rather than painting the branch, here you wet the shape so that you can extend a light touch of paint along it.

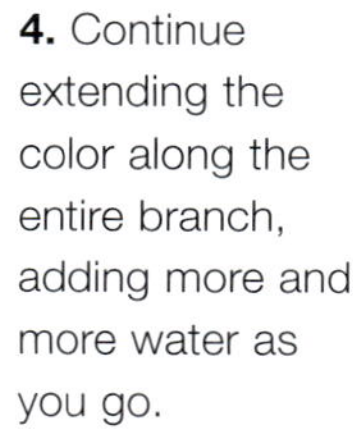

4. Continue extending the color along the entire branch, adding more and more water as you go.

4

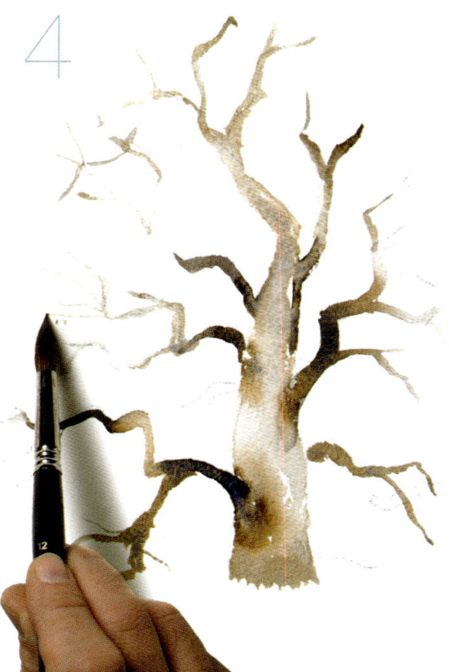

5

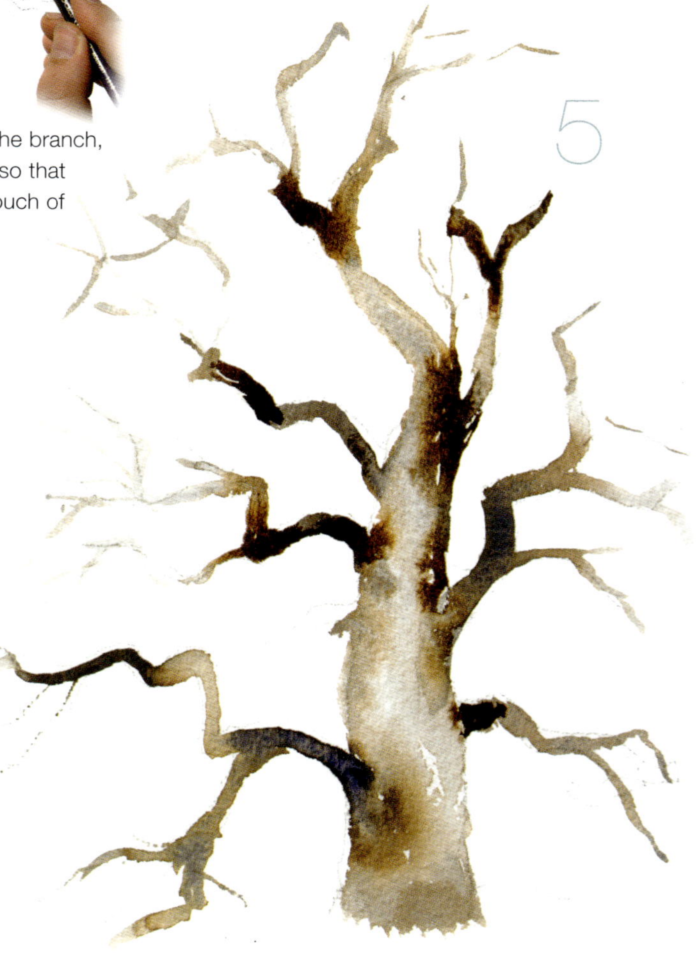

5. The color of the darkest areas varies between blue gray and gray sienna, and the intensity becomes less as it moves toward the ends of the branches.

04 Washes / **Warm Monochromes**

LEVEL OF DIFFICULTY
★
COLORS
Cadmium yellow
Permanent red
BRUSH
Medium round natural hair
PAPER
140 lb medium-rough texture

Red and yellow are the warmest colors on the palette. Here you will use them in combination to create the colors of an autumn leaf. All the shades of orange are the product of mixing these two colors, which also are used straight for creating lively contrasts.

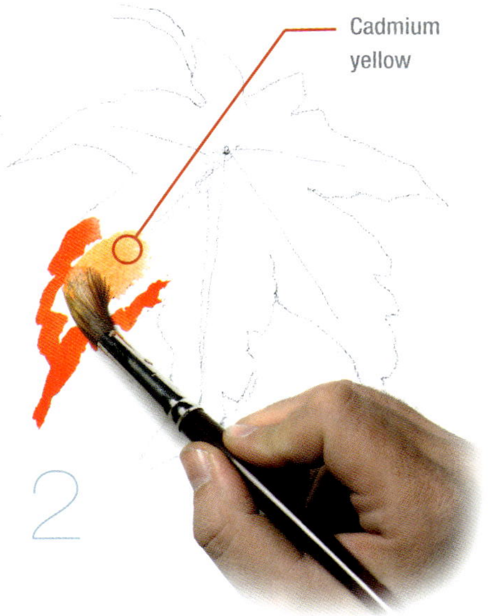

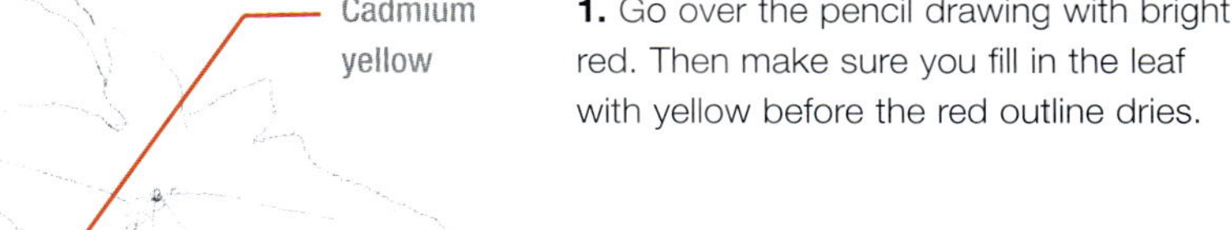

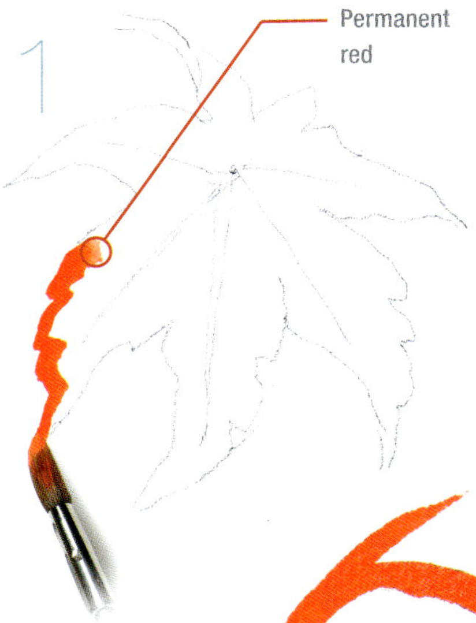

1. Go over the pencil drawing with bright red. Then make sure you fill in the leaf with yellow before the red outline dries.

Permanent red

1

2. Here is how you fill in the leaf: apply diluted yellow and spread it until it makes contact with the red outline and both colors mix with each other.

2

3. Paint each part of the leaf the same way, making sure that the area you are painting does not dry before you complete it.

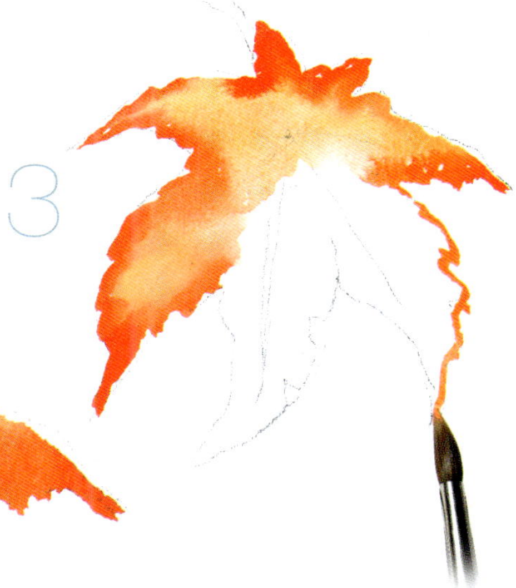

3

4. The wash in the center where the red and yellow tones mix creates a beautiful and very natural visual effect.

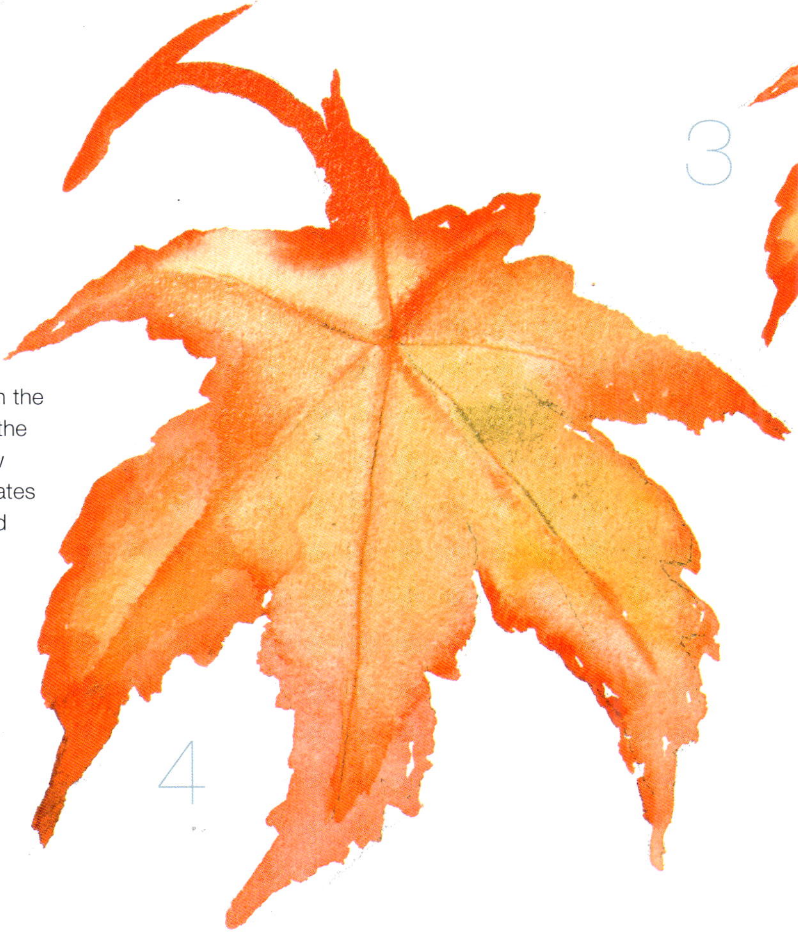

4

05 Washes / **Harmonic Colors, Unmixed**

LEVEL OF DIFFICULTY
★★
COLORS
Cadmium yellow
Yellow ochre
Permanent green
Burnt sienna
BRUSH
Medium round natural hair
PAPER
140 lb medium-rough texture

By overlaying tones from the same color range you can create a handsome, well-articulated object. Although they are from the same range, this does not mean that the colors have to be mixed much. In this case, the different tones are applications of pure color diluted with more or less water to adjust the level of intensity of the modeling and of the light achieved in this exercise.

If the brush is of good quality and sufficiently charged with liquid, the tip will be pointed enough to create a precise line.

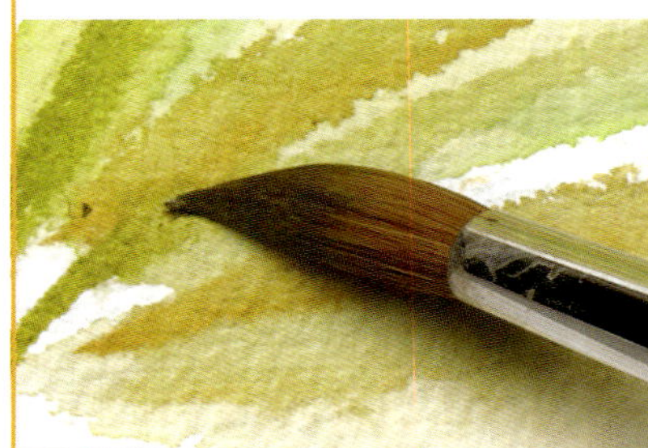

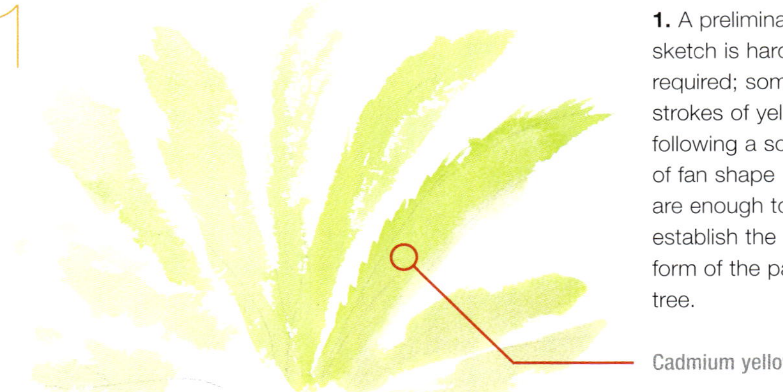

1. A preliminary sketch is hardly required; some strokes of yellow following a sort of fan shape are enough to establish the form of the palm tree.

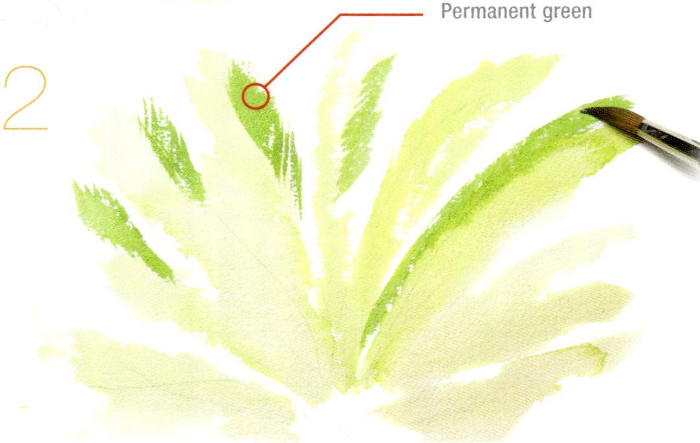

2. A very diluted green makes the ideal tone for shading half of each of the palm leaves painted before.

3. Paint over the previous colors with a stroke of yellow ochre, and the result is a greenish middle tone between the yellow and the green.

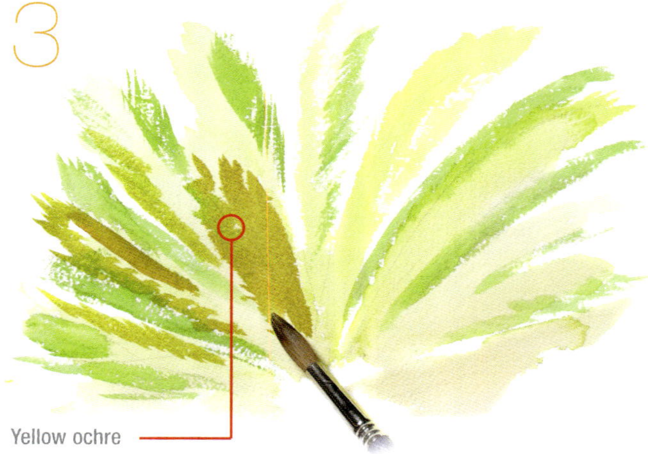

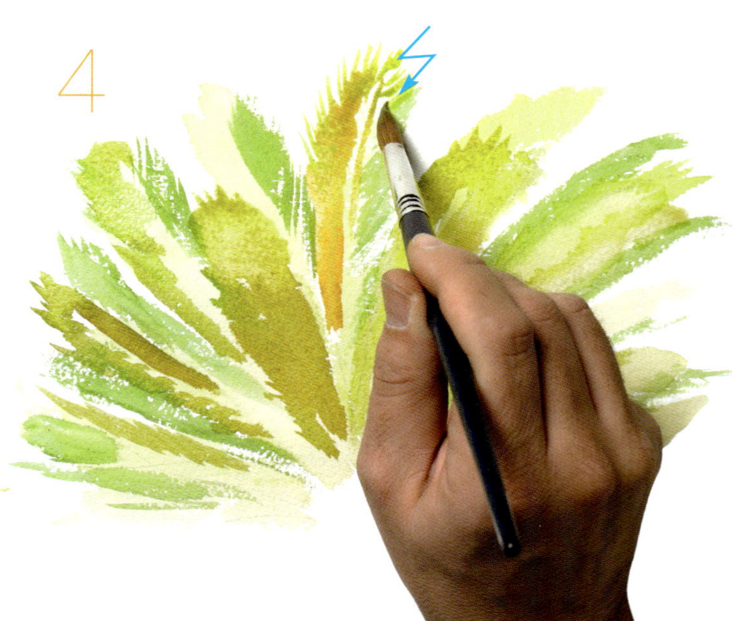

4. Work with the tip of the brush, delicately, to represent the characteristic jagged edges of the palm leaves.

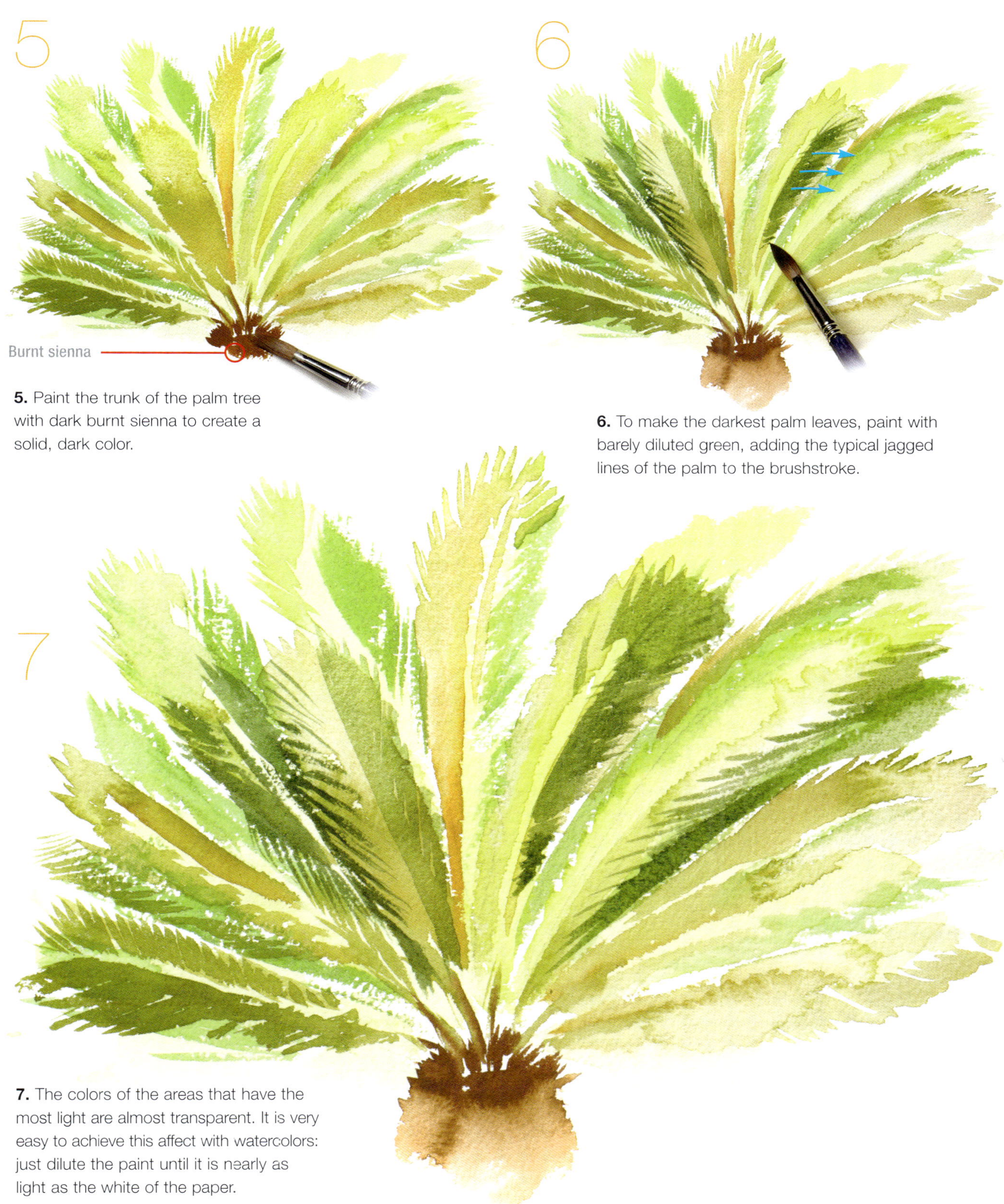

5. Paint the trunk of the palm tree with dark burnt sienna to create a solid, dark color.

6. To make the darkest palm leaves, paint with barely diluted green, adding the typical jagged lines of the palm to the brushstroke.

7. The colors of the areas that have the most light are almost transparent. It is very easy to achieve this affect with watercolors: just dilute the paint until it is nearly as light as the white of the paper.

06 Washes / **Two Harmonic Colors, Mixed**

LEVEL OF DIFFICULTY
★
COLORS
Ultramarine blue
Carmine
BRUSH
Medium round natural hair
PAPER
140 lb medium-rough texture

If you vary the proportions of the colors in the mixture, you can easily modify the brightness and color of the paint. In this example, the purple tones move gently and delicately toward scarlet thanks to the harmonious relationship between the blue and crimson that were used.

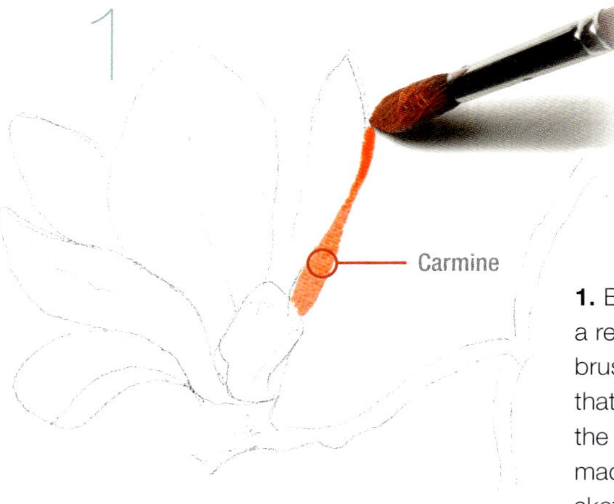

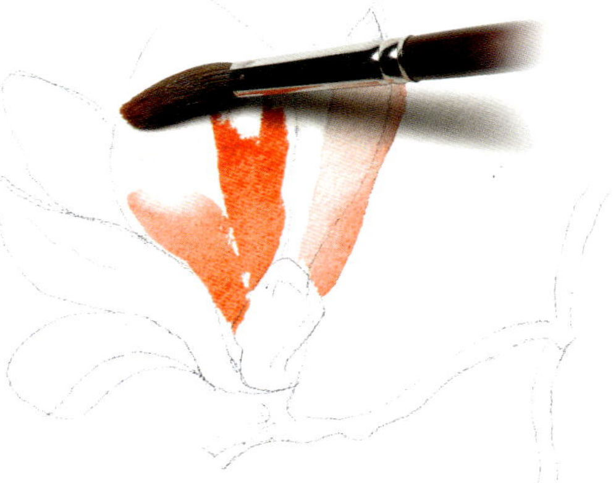

1. Begin with a reddish brushstroke that follows the previously made pencil sketch of the flower.

2. While the brushstroke is still wet, add more water and spread the red over the whole surface of the petal.

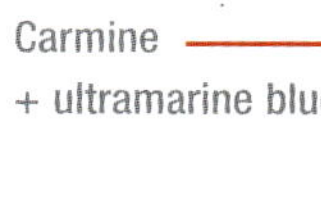

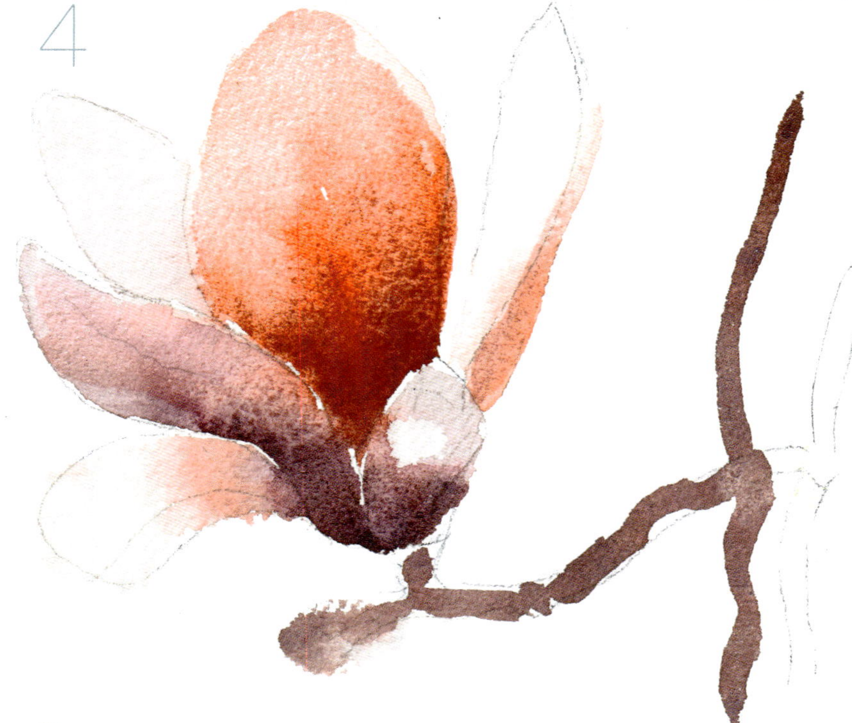

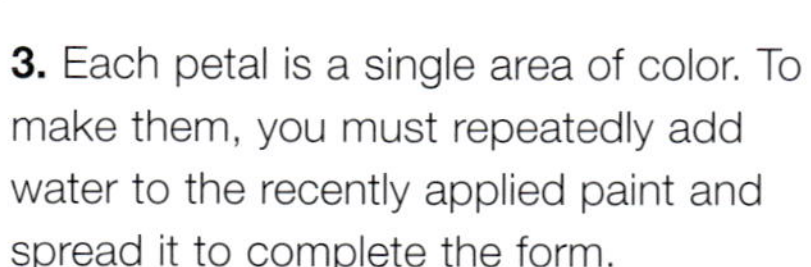

3. Each petal is a single area of color. To make them, you must repeatedly add water to the recently applied paint and spread it to complete the form.

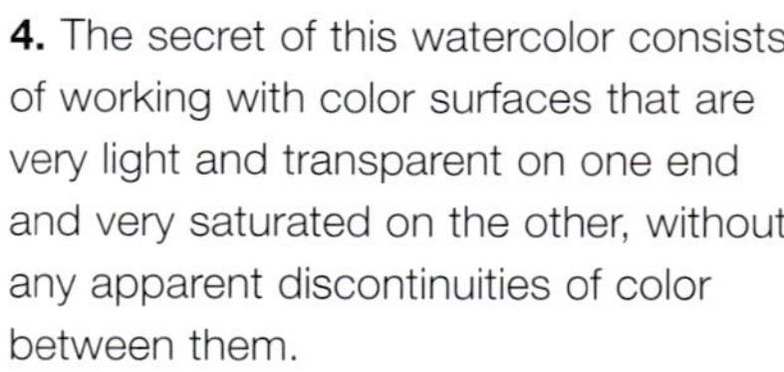

4. The secret of this watercolor consists of working with color surfaces that are very light and transparent on one end and very saturated on the other, without any apparent discontinuities of color between them.

07 Washes / **With Contrasting Tones**

LEVEL OF DIFFICULTY
★
COLORS
Cerulean blue
Cadmium red
Cadmium yellow
BRUSH
Medium round natural hair
PAPER
140 lb medium-rough texture

This subject can seem difficult, but it is not. The watery shades on the fish are the result of painting with a lot of water; they appear by themselves. This is an important lesson: you must take advantage of the technique, following its natural tendencies. The results are always better and easier to achieve.

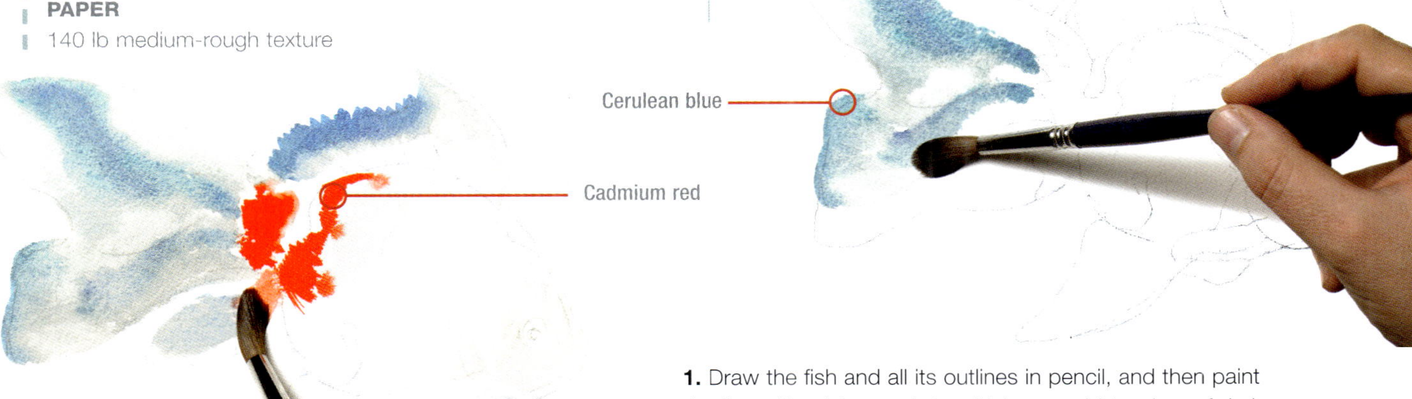

1. Draw the fish and all its outlines in pencil, and then paint the fins with a blue wash to which you add touches of darker blue to create the effect of transparent texture.

2. Paint the red areas using less water than in the blue ones, that is, with more saturated color. Try to keep the brush from coming into contact with the blue to avoid mixing them.

3. Apply a yellow dot in the eye with the tip of the brush. When it is completely dry you can paint a dark dot over it (red mixed with blue).

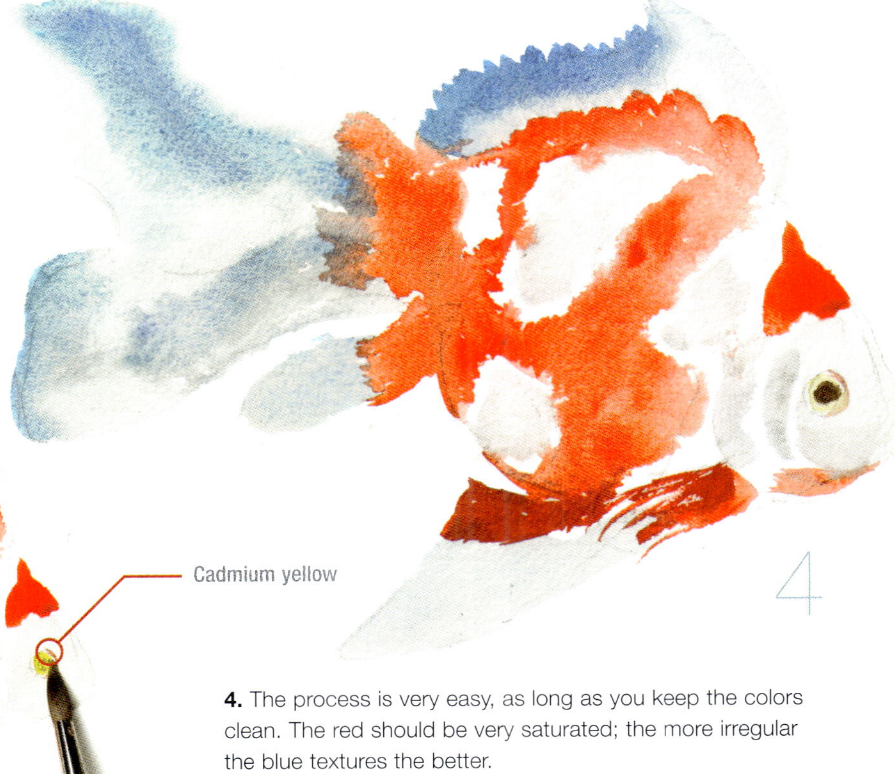

4. The process is very easy, as long as you keep the colors clean. The red should be very saturated; the more irregular the blue textures the better.

08 Washes / **With Several Grays**

LEVEL OF DIFFICULTY
★
COLORS
Burnt sienna
Ultramarine blue
Sap green
BRUSH
Medium round natural hair
PAPER
140 lb medium-rough texture

One of the subtlest joys of watercolor is painting with grays, which are never a mixture of black and white, but a mixture of several colors. In this case, the grays are a product of combining blue and sienna. These two colors are enough (with the help of a green) to suggest the delicate coloring of this bunch of flowers.

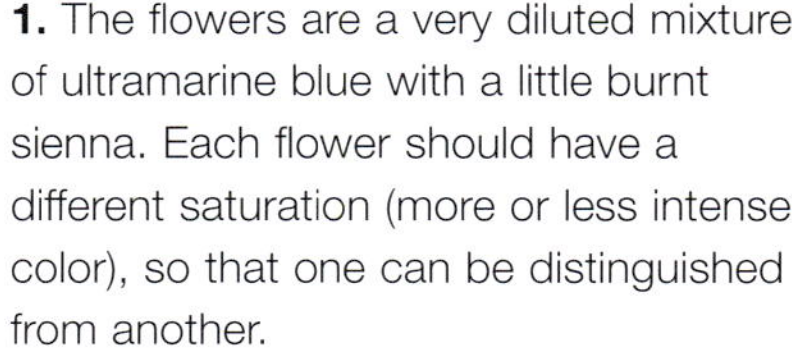

1. The flowers are a very diluted mixture of ultramarine blue with a little burnt sienna. Each flower should have a different saturation (more or less intense color), so that one can be distinguished from another.

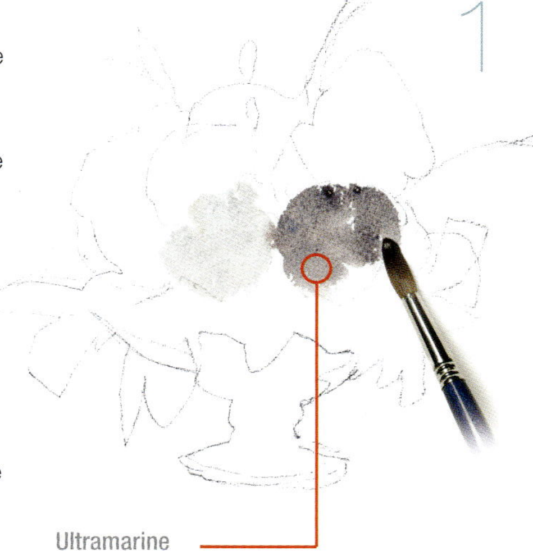

1

Ultramarine blue + burnt sienna

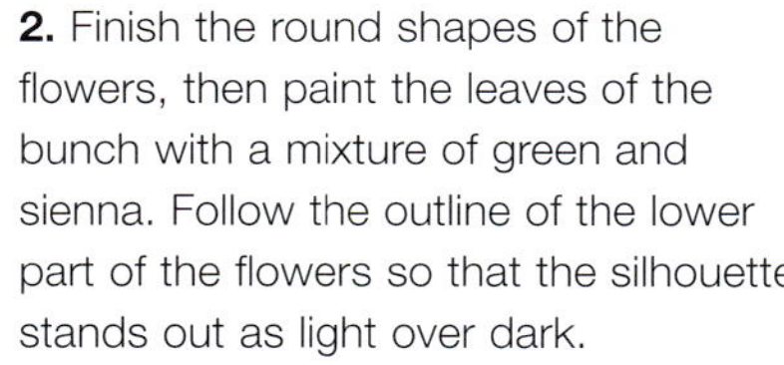

2. Finish the round shapes of the flowers, then paint the leaves of the bunch with a mixture of green and sienna. Follow the outline of the lower part of the flowers so that the silhouette stands out as light over dark.

2

Sap green + burnt sienna

3. The base of the vase is a more saturated mixture of the two colors that were used for painting the flowers: burnt sienna and blue. You can paint this without shading, as a silhouette with a uniform tone.

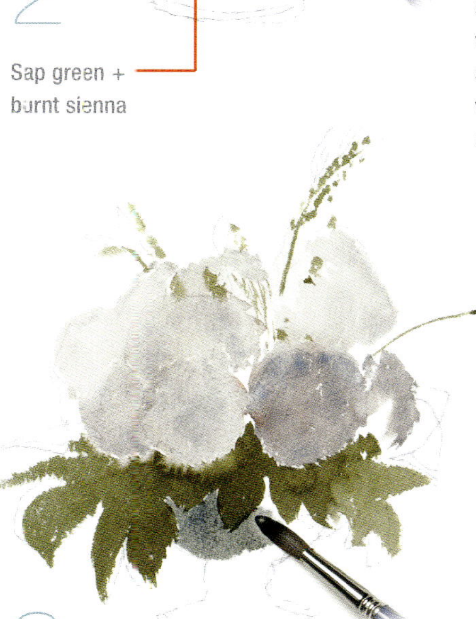

3

4. The frugality of the color does not seem poor, but elegant and harmonious. It is a matter of combining the values or intensities more than the colors.

4

09 Wet on Wet / **Washes on Wet Paper**

LEVEL OF DIFFICULTY
★

COLORS
Cobalt blue
Ultramarine blue

BRUSH
Medium round natural hair

PAPER
140 lb medium-rough texture

This exercise demonstrates the basic approach to working wet on wet, that is, painting over colors that are not dry to cause the paint to spread. You will work with two blue colors applied on wet paper. The result is handsome and colorful.

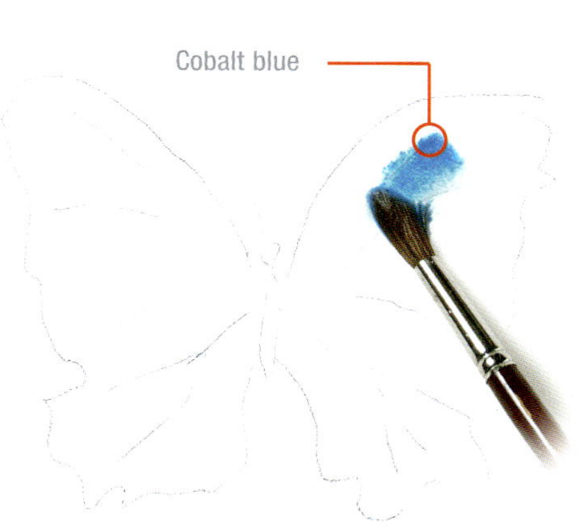

1. Draw the butterfly and wet the entire surface (but not outside of the outline) with clean water. Apply cobalt blue and let it flow freely until everything is covered.

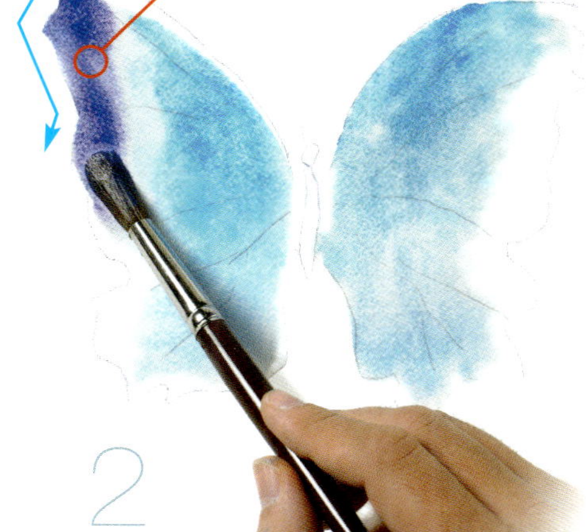

2. While the paint is still wet, paint the outside edges of the wings with very saturated ultramarine blue and allow the color to blend with the cobalt blue inside.

3. Work quickly so the paint does not dry on the paper. Add very saturated blue dots to create the spotted effects on the wings.

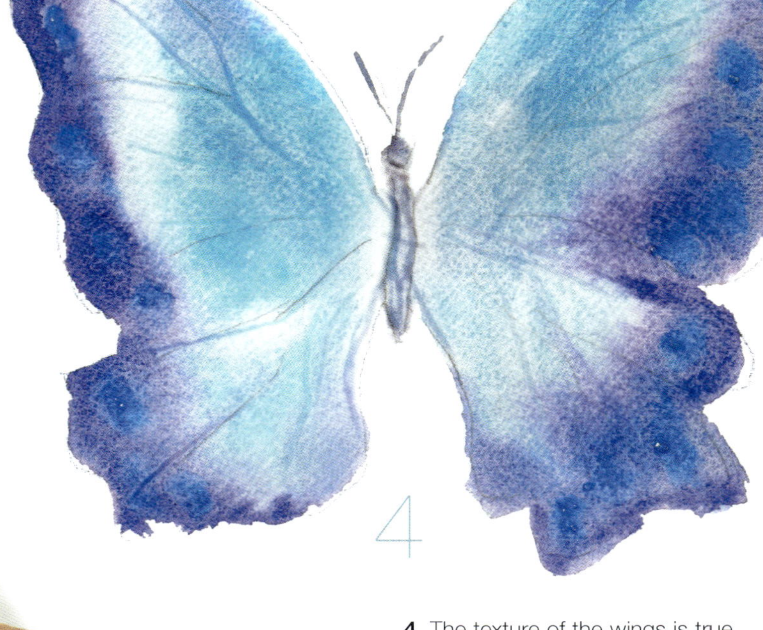

4. The texture of the wings is true and natural because you painted on wet paper.

10 Wet on Wet / **Discontinuous Gradations**

LEVEL OF DIFFICULTY
★
COLORS
Sap green
BRUSH
Medium round natural hair
PAPER
140 lb medium-rough texture

Painting on wet paper results in gradations caused by the dilution of the paint on the paper. You can take advantage of this to create very natural and simple gradations that express some forms from nature. Here you will use this method to paint branches of bamboo.

1. "Paint" a broken line with clean or slightly dirty water over a drawing of the bamboo. Each break in the line represents a segment in the bamboo stalk.

2. Lightly apply a very saturated green with the brush to each segment so that the color will spread and make gradations on the wet areas.

3. Paint the other branches when the first one has dried, following the same method but using more-diluted paint to create lighter tones.

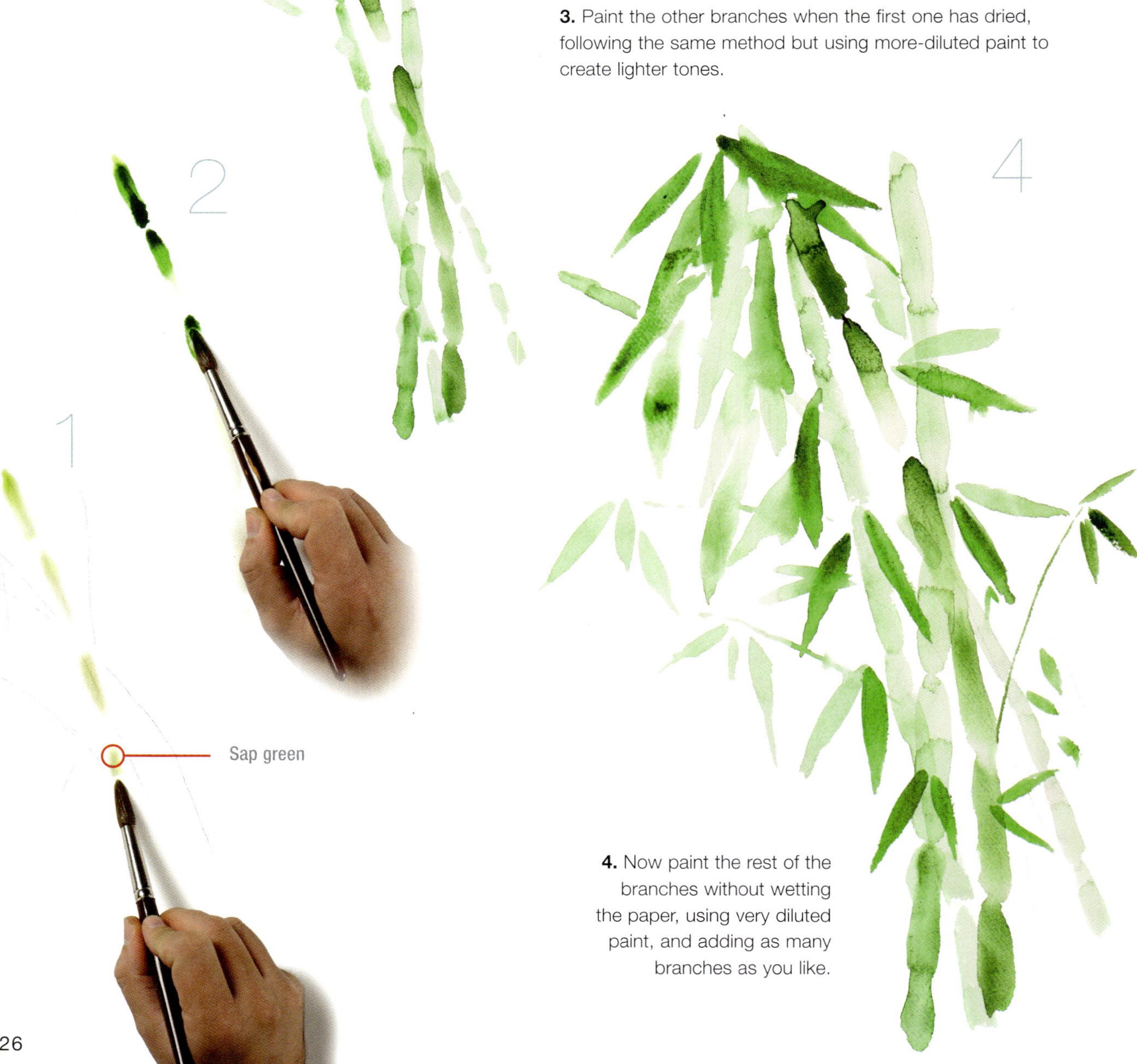

4. Now paint the rest of the branches without wetting the paper, using very diluted paint, and adding as many branches as you like.

11 Wet on Wet / **Expanding Color**

LEVEL OF DIFFICULTY
★
COLORS
Cadmium yellow
Permanent red
Permanent green
BRUSH
Medium round natural hair
PAPER
140 lb medium-rough texture

This is the most direct, free, and spectacular way of painting on wet. The paper should be dampened enough so that the paint will spread in unexpected ways. This can be in your favor if you use saturated colors and distribute them strategically on the paper.

1

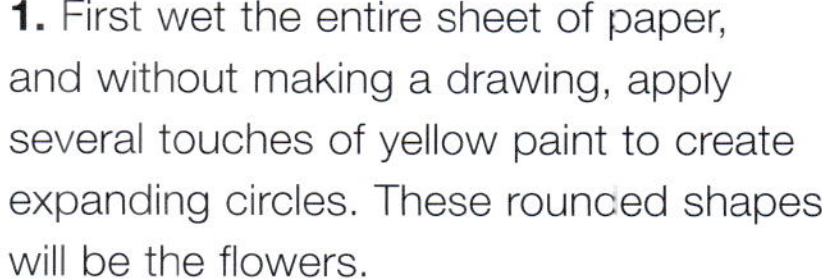

1. First wet the entire sheet of paper, and without making a drawing, apply several touches of yellow paint to create expanding circles. These rounded shapes will be the flowers.

Cadmium yellow

2

Permanent red

2. Apply dabs of orange paint in the centers of the still-wet yellow circles to make the corollas. The paint should be very saturated, and the application on the paper should be quick.

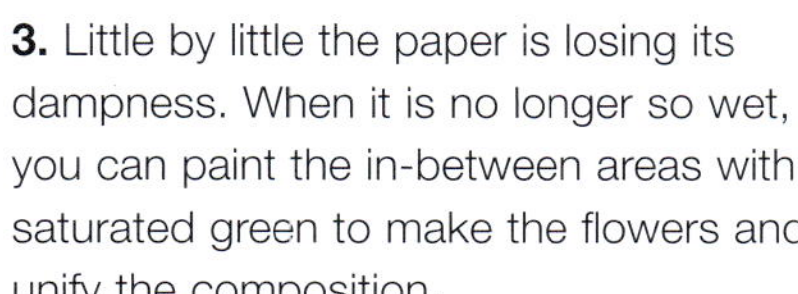

3. Little by little the paper is losing its dampness. When it is no longer so wet, you can paint the in-between areas with saturated green to make the flowers and unify the composition.

3

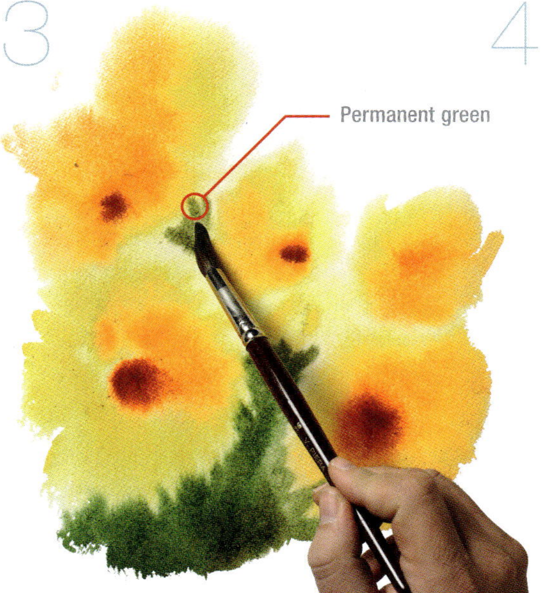

4

4. The result is very free and colorful. When painting this, it is a good idea to work on a large sheet of paper with saturated colors; the water on the paper will take care of diluting them.

12 Wet on Wet / **On Damp Paint**

LEVEL OF DIFFICULTY
★
COLORS
Ultramarine blue
Cobalt violet
BRUSH
Medium round natural hair
PAPER
140 lb medium-rough texture

When the base colors are not completely dry they can be affected by colors that are painted over them, and the new colors are affected at the same time. Experienced artists are familiar with these effects, but beginning watercolorists must pay attention to avoid surprises and stay in control at all times.

1. After drawing the flower, wet the petals first, then paint over the wet areas with cobalt violet in different saturations.

2. When the previous colors are less damp but still have not dried, paint new petals with ultramarine blue.

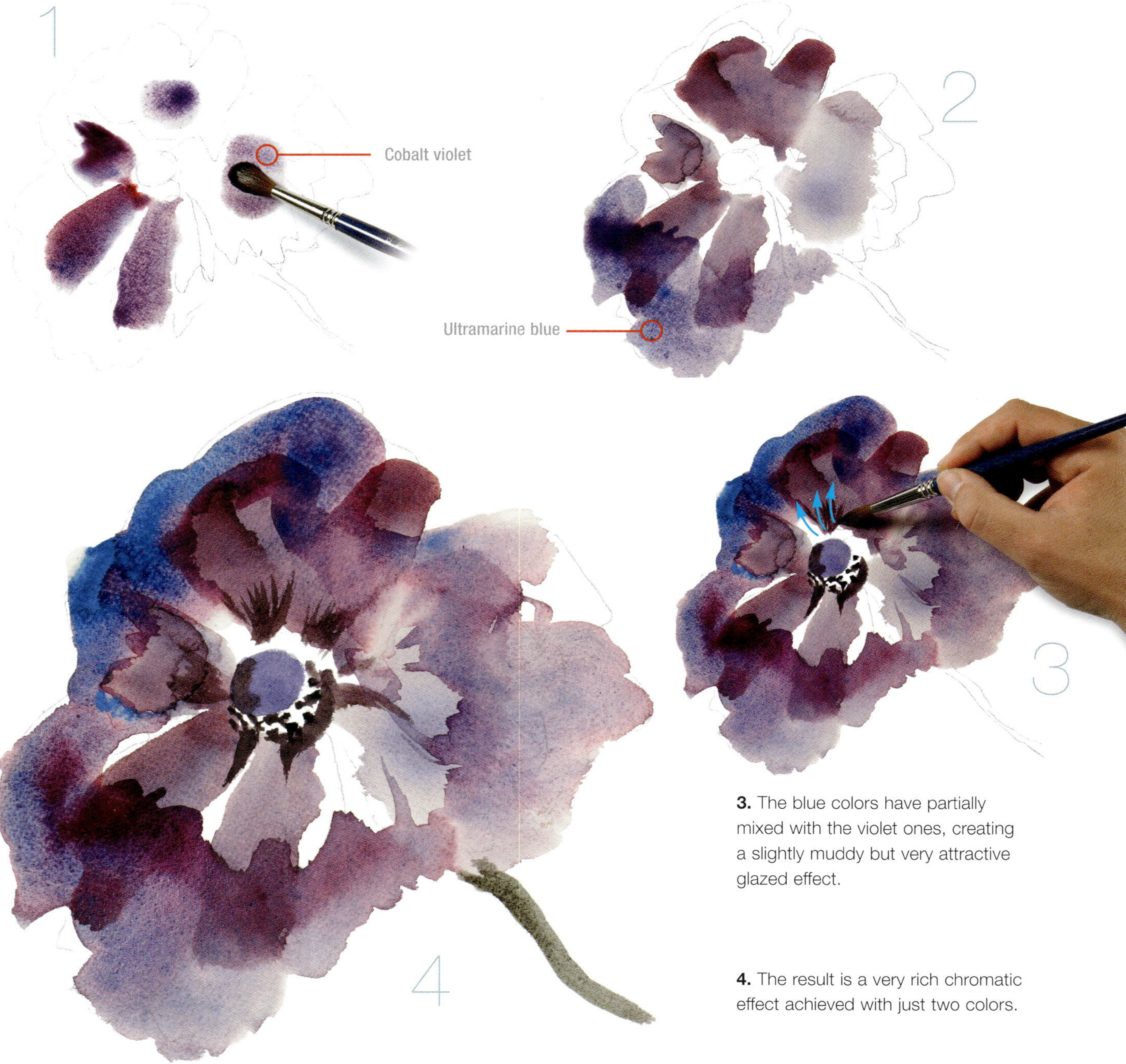

3. The blue colors have partially mixed with the violet ones, creating a slightly muddy but very attractive glazed effect.

4. The result is a very rich chromatic effect achieved with just two colors.

13 Wet on Wet / **Paper Dampened in Areas**

LEVEL OF DIFFICULTY
★
COLORS
Ultramarine blue
Sap green
Yellow ochre
Burnt sienna
BRUSH
Medium round natural hair
PAPER
140 lb medium-rough texture

In this exercise we show you how to control the spreading of paint on a wet area while at the same time controlling the shapes of the areas.

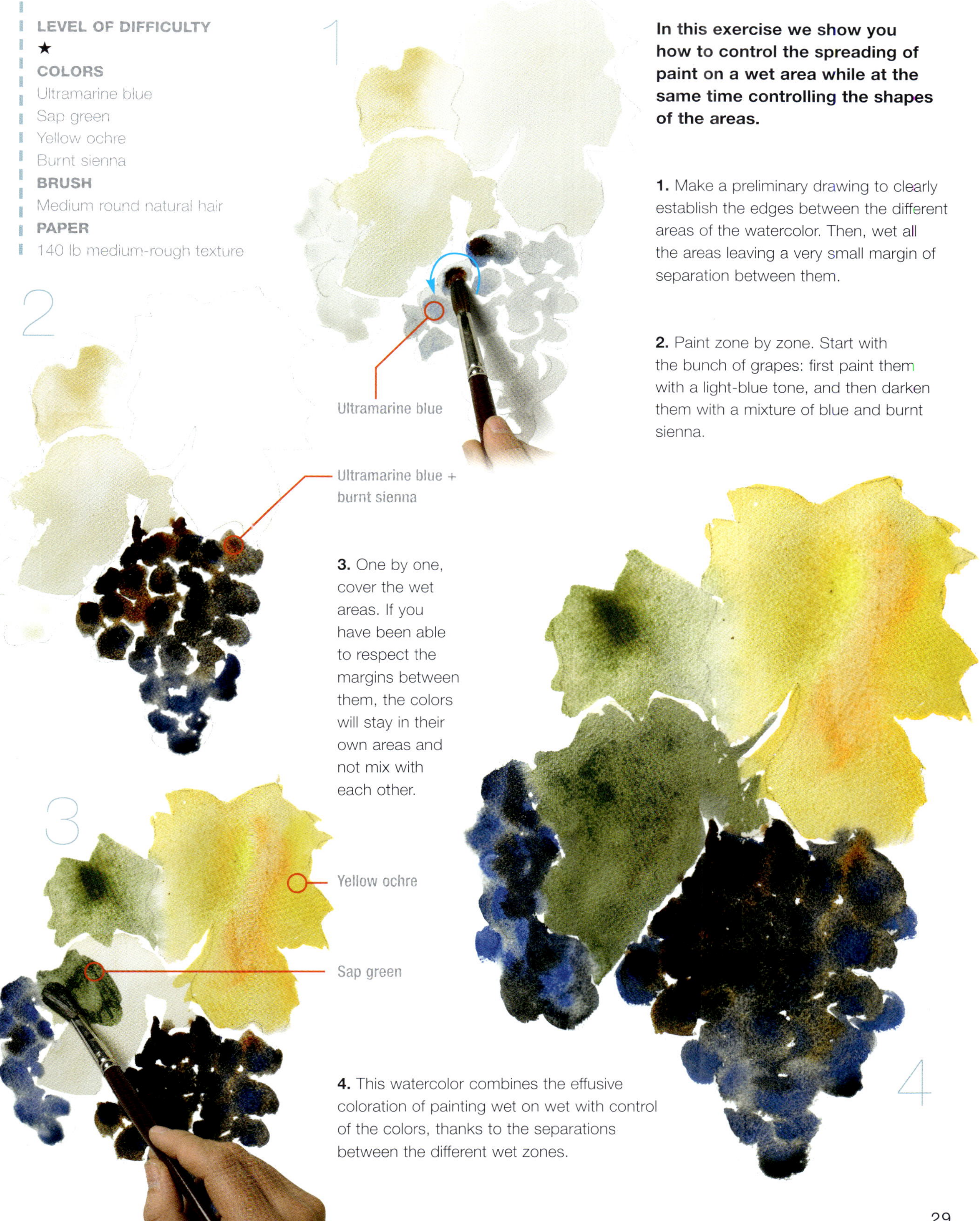

1. Make a preliminary drawing to clearly establish the edges between the different areas of the watercolor. Then, wet all the areas leaving a very small margin of separation between them.

2. Paint zone by zone. Start with the bunch of grapes: first paint them with a light-blue tone, and then darken them with a mixture of blue and burnt sienna.

3. One by one, cover the wet areas. If you have been able to respect the margins between them, the colors will stay in their own areas and not mix with each other.

4. This watercolor combines the effusive coloration of painting wet on wet with control of the colors, thanks to the separations between the different wet zones.

14 Wet on Wet / **Absorbing with the Brush**

LEVEL OF DIFFICULTY
★★
COLORS
Ultramarine blue
Carmine
Permanent red
Cadmium yellow
BRUSH
Medium round natural hair
PAPER

As long as a color is wet you can alter its tones by lightening it, darkening it, and even by eliminating it. The last is a very common approach used by watercolorists to lighten colors to the point that they can almost be confused with the white of the paper.

1. First draw the rooster and wet its interior. Then, apply a small amount of carmine, which will turn into pink because of the water on the paper.

2. Add a dark blue to the middle of the rooster's body, and spread it toward the lower part of the bird to shade it.

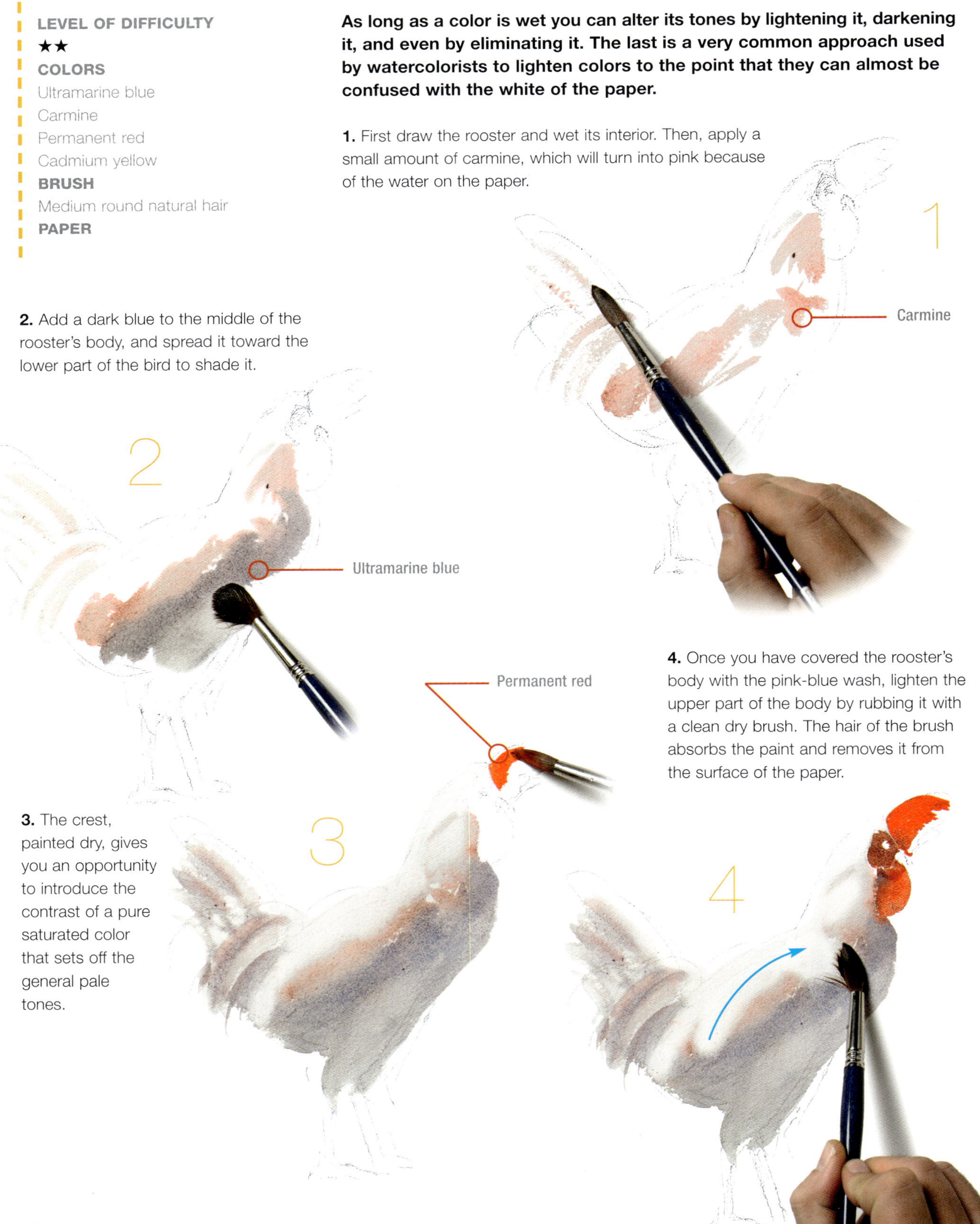

3. The crest, painted dry, gives you an opportunity to introduce the contrast of a pure saturated color that sets off the general pale tones.

4. Once you have covered the rooster's body with the pink-blue wash, lighten the upper part of the body by rubbing it with a clean dry brush. The hair of the brush absorbs the paint and removes it from the surface of the paper.

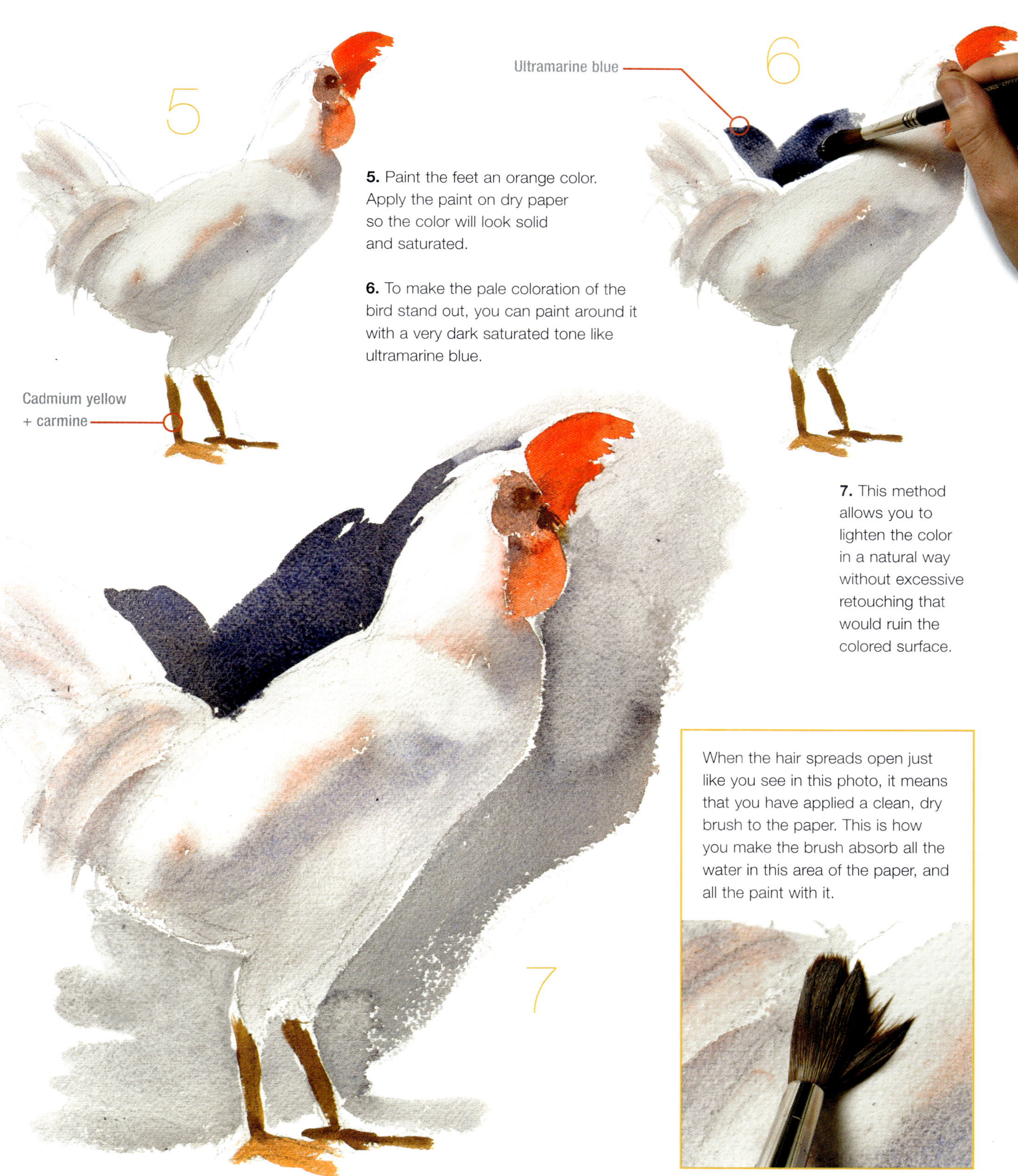

5. Paint the feet an orange color. Apply the paint on dry paper so the color will look solid and saturated.

6. To make the pale coloration of the bird stand out, you can paint around it with a very dark saturated tone like ultramarine blue.

7. This method allows you to lighten the color in a natural way without excessive retouching that would ruin the colored surface.

When the hair spreads open just like you see in this photo, it means that you have applied a clean, dry brush to the paper. This is how you make the brush absorb all the water in this area of the paper, and all the paint with it.

15 Wet on Wet / **Highlights with Paper**

LEVEL OF DIFFICULTY
★
COLORS
Cobalt blue
Carmine
Permanent red
Sap green
BRUSH
Medium round natural hair
PAPER
140 lb medium-rough texture

Cotton rags and absorbent paper towels are indispensable tools for all watercolorists. They can be used for general cleaning and drying brushes but also for creating the effects that are shown in this exercise, where you will attempt to make white highlights of previously painted forms.

1

Cobalt blue

1. After making the pencil drawing, spread a blue wash across the bowl that holds the cherries.

2. While the paint is still wet, apply paper until it absorbs the area of the bowl, leaving it nearly clean.

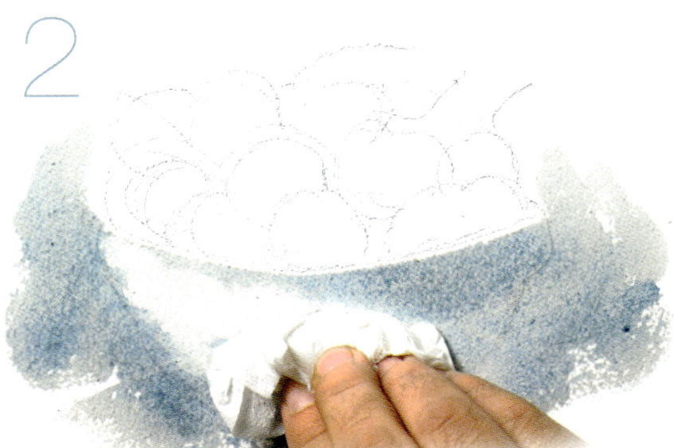

3

Permanent red

Carmine

3. Paint the cherries on wet using repeated applications of red. Add some touches of carmine on each cherry to give the cherries a three-dimensional feeling.

4. Touch each cherry with a corner of a piece of paper towel to make small white areas that create the feeling of highlights or reflections on the fruit.

4

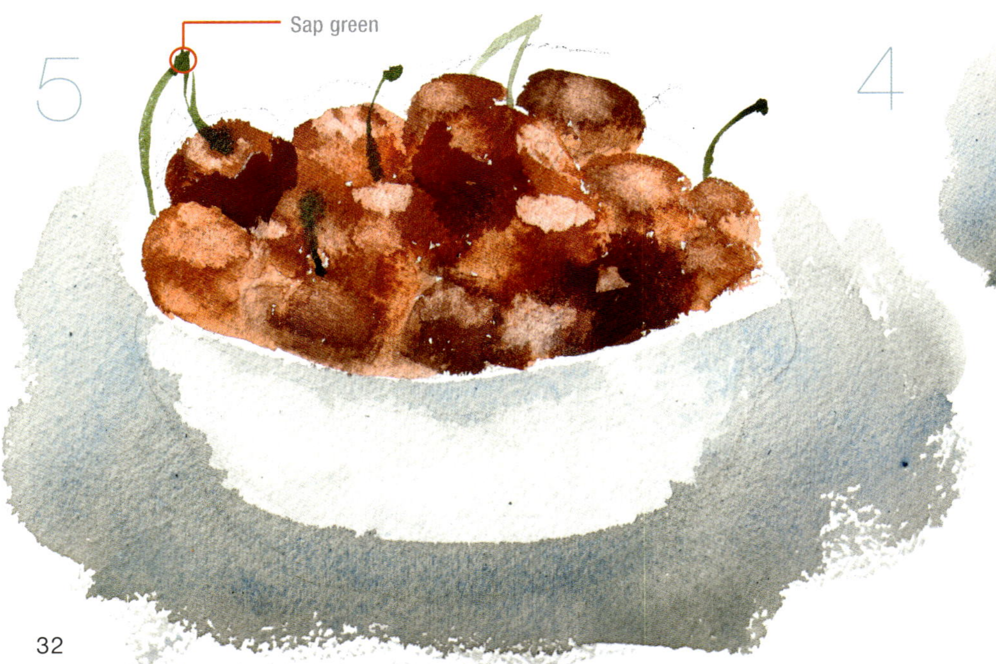

5. Finish by drawing some stems with green. This is a very simple and efficient way to resolve the problem of the highlights, and the results are very lively and attractive.

16 Wet on Wet / **Absorbing with a Rag**

LEVEL OF DIFFICULTY
★
COLORS
Sap green
Burnt sienna
BRUSH
Medium round natural hair
PAPER
140 lb medium-rough texture

A cotton rag can be used in the same way as paper towels to absorb the water and paint of a watercolor that is still wet. This exercise shows a drastic and very efficient way of representing a tree in bloom, perhaps an almond tree, by absorbing recently applied paint.

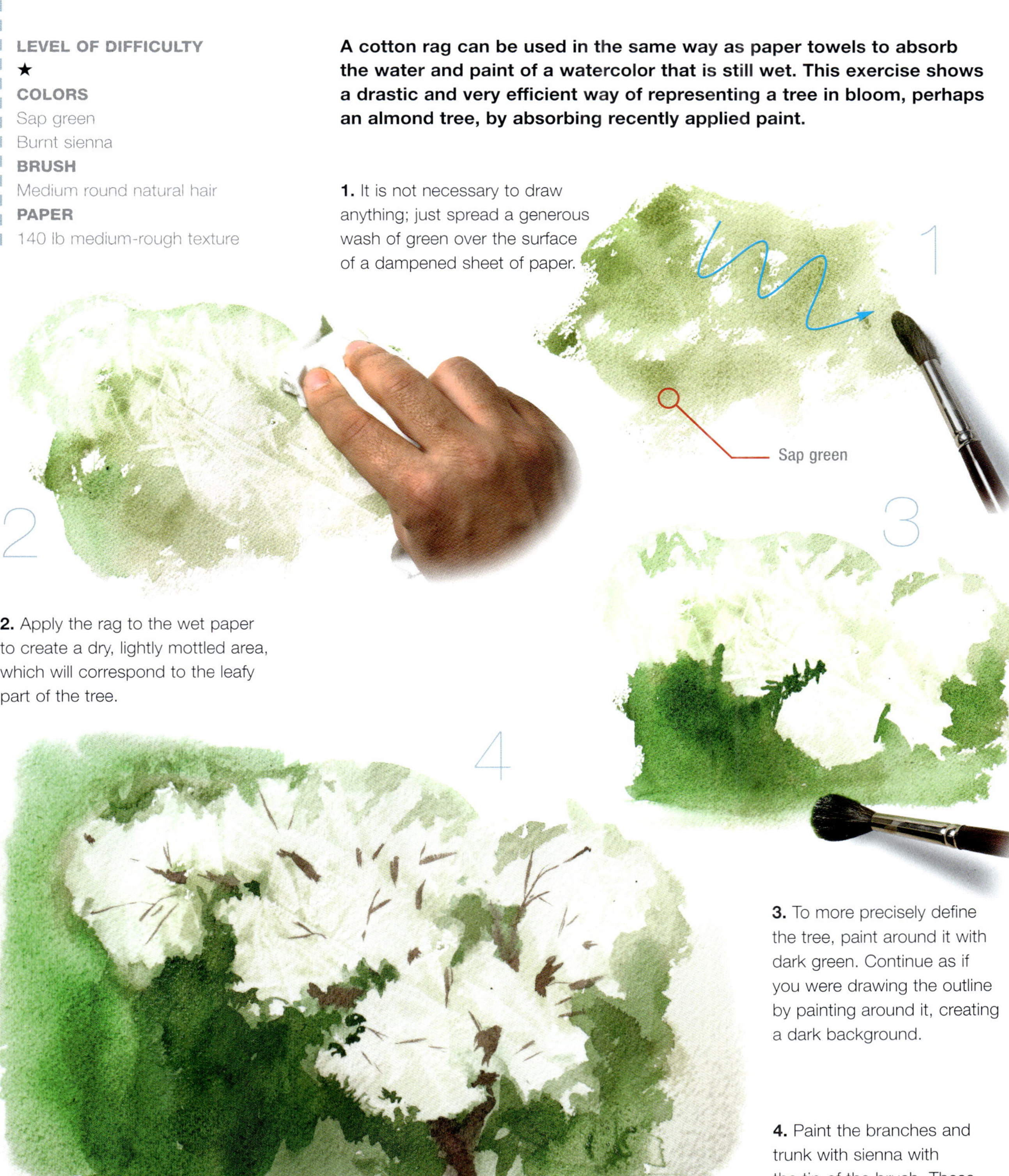

1. It is not necessary to draw anything; just spread a generous wash of green over the surface of a dampened sheet of paper.

2. Apply the rag to the wet paper to create a dry, lightly mottled area, which will correspond to the leafy part of the tree.

3. To more precisely define the tree, paint around it with dark green. Continue as if you were drawing the outline by painting around it, creating a dark background.

4. Paint the branches and trunk with sienna with the tip of the brush. These suggestions will be enough to make the form and size of the tree recognizable.

17 Wet on Wet / **Absorbing with Paper**

LEVEL OF DIFFICULTY
★★
COLORS
Cadmium yellow
Permanent red
Cadmium red
Carmine
Sap green
BRUSH
Medium round natural hair
PAPER
140 lb medium-rough texture

Absorbent paper will create more detailed and intense areas than a rag. Its large number of fibers makes it very efficient and allows it to immediately remove water wherever it is applied. Here you will use it for quickly and easily creating a beautiful bunch of carnations as if by magic.

1

1. You do not need a preliminary drawing, because applying the paper towel will create the shapes of the flowers. First, add a generous wash of carmine mixed with cadmium red to the dampened paper.

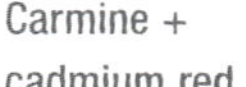

2

2. Using a piece of crumpled paper towel, absorb different areas of similar size from the wash.

Apply very saturated paint to make dark colors by pressing on the brush to make all the paint flow to the paper. The more pigment deposited on the paper, the darker or more intense the color.

3

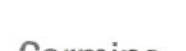

3. Highlight the white areas by painting between them with saturated carmine. Add some areas of orange with a mixture of carmine and yellow.

4

4. The effect produced is a cloud of color where you can barely make out recognizable forms.

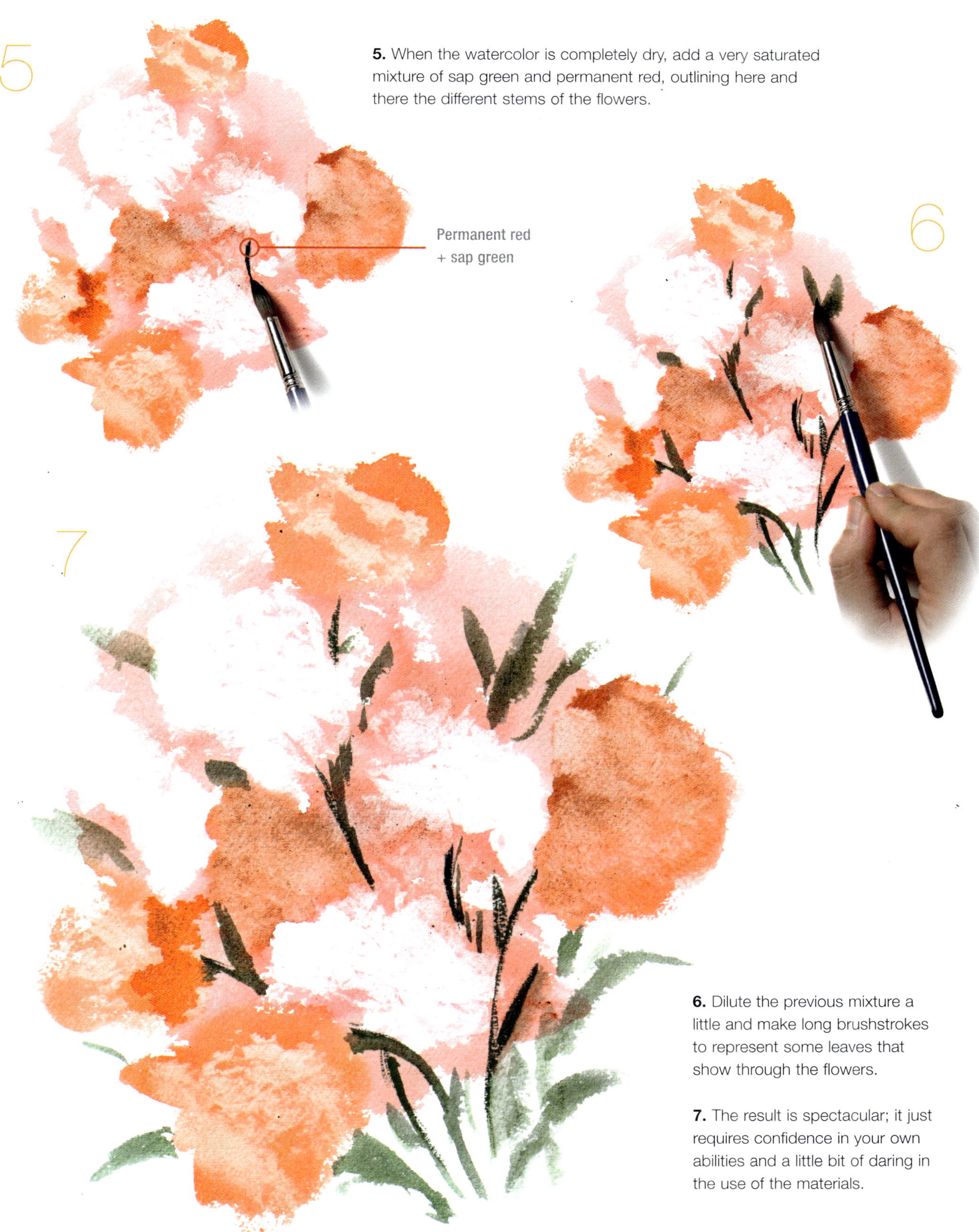

5. When the watercolor is completely dry, add a very saturated mixture of sap green and permanent red, outlining here and there the different stems of the flowers.

6. Dilute the previous mixture a little and make long brushstrokes to represent some leaves that show through the flowers.

7. The result is spectacular; it just requires confidence in your own abilities and a little bit of daring in the use of the materials.

18 Wet on Dry / **Monochrome Transparency**

LEVEL OF DIFFICULTY
★
COLORS
Cadmium yellow
Permanent red
Carmine
Sap green
BRUSH
Medium round natural hair
PAPER
140 lb medium-rough texture

When you apply one color over another dry color, it produces a transparency; the coloration of the upper tone is affected by that of the lower one. Transparencies always have a special smoothness and luminosity since the colors do not mix physically, but are mixed by your eyes.

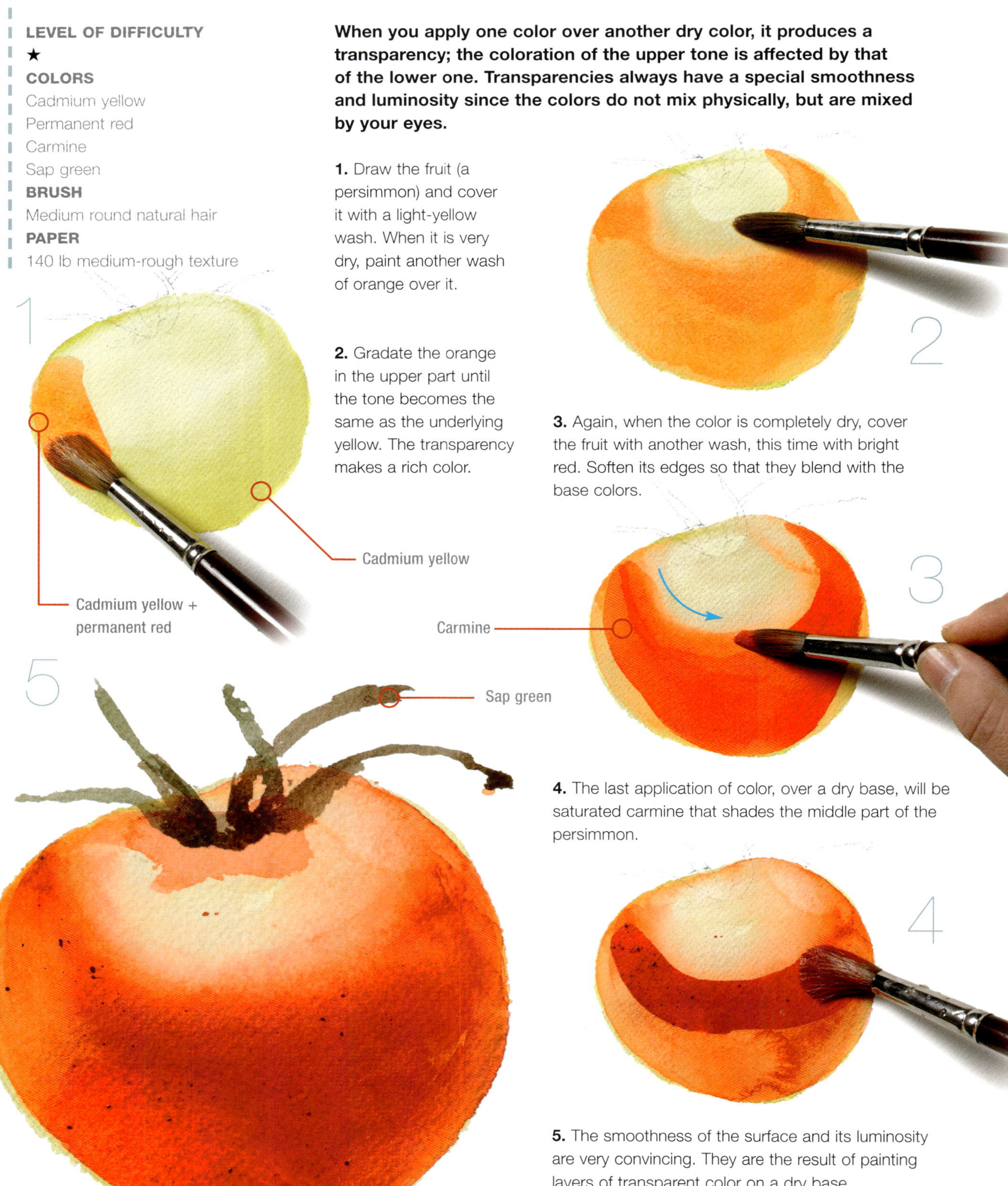

1. Draw the fruit (a persimmon) and cover it with a light-yellow wash. When it is very dry, paint another wash of orange over it.

2. Gradate the orange in the upper part until the tone becomes the same as the underlying yellow. The transparency makes a rich color.

3. Again, when the color is completely dry, cover the fruit with another wash, this time with bright red. Soften its edges so that they blend with the base colors.

4. The last application of color, over a dry base, will be saturated carmine that shades the middle part of the persimmon.

5. The smoothness of the surface and its luminosity are very convincing. They are the result of painting layers of transparent color on a dry base.

19 Wet on Dry / **Accumulated Transparencies**

LEVEL OF DIFFICULTY
★★
COLORS
Cadmium yellow
Yellow ochre
Sap green
BRUSH
Medium round natural hair
PAPER
140 lb medium-rough texture

The accumulation of transparencies can go on nearly without end, but it is important to adjust the use of this technique to the requirements of the subject. Here the transparencies are obligatory, since you will be representing the greenish glass of a bottle. Working within a limited color range allows you to create a large number of different colors and a really painterly effect.

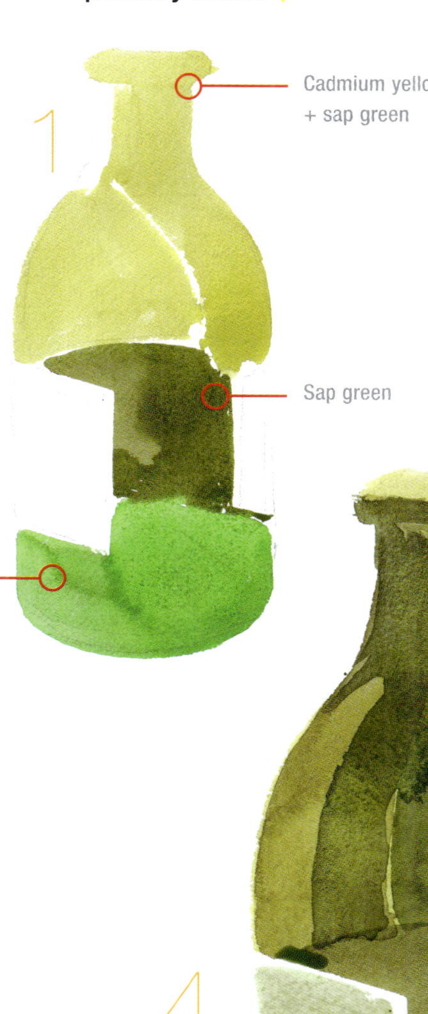

1. After drawing the outline of the bottle, paint the two large blocks of contrasting color: yellow mixed with a little green in the upper part and green mixed with ochre in the lower. Paint a saturated wash of sap green in the middle.

2. Represent the interior volume of the base of the bottle with a dark-green line in the shape of an inverted V. Then add a more saturated transparency at the top.

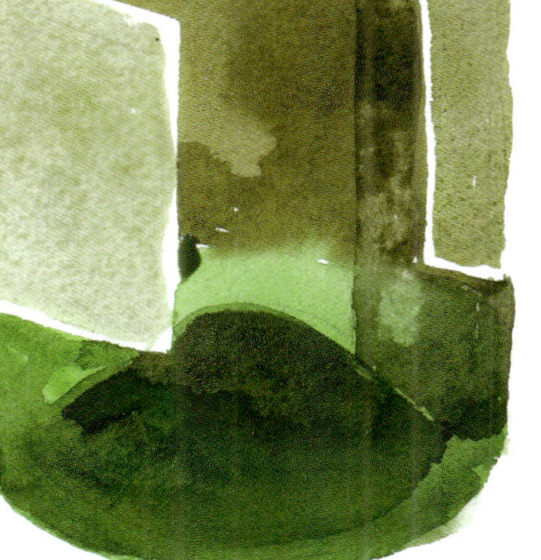

3. Paint the dark colors of the upper part with a mixture of green and yellow ochre over a completely dry base.

4. Add the last dark transparencies to the glass and lightly paint the labels on the bottle with a dark green tone that is very diluted with water.

LEVEL OF DIFFICULTY
★
COLORS
Yellow ochre
Burnt sienna
Sap green
Carmine
BRUSH
Medium round natural hair
PAPER
140 lb medium-rough texture

This exercise illustrates the simplest possible case of the transparency technique. It consists of painting different shapes and colors over completely dry paint. You will use the colors seen on autumn leaves, from green to dark red.

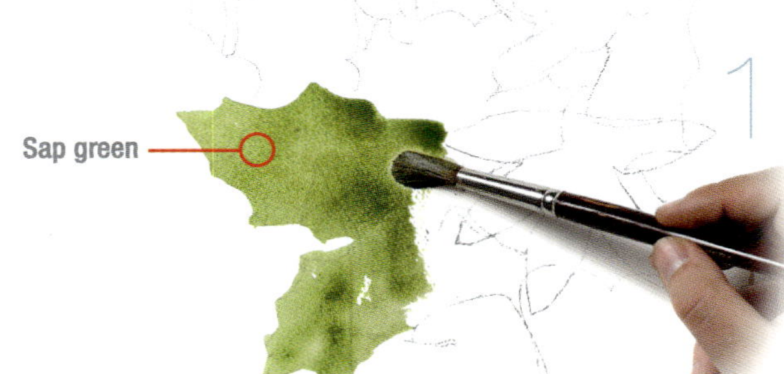

1. Draw each leaf clearly so its outline can be identified under the washes. Each leaf is a single color; you can begin by painting any one you wish, the green one, for example.

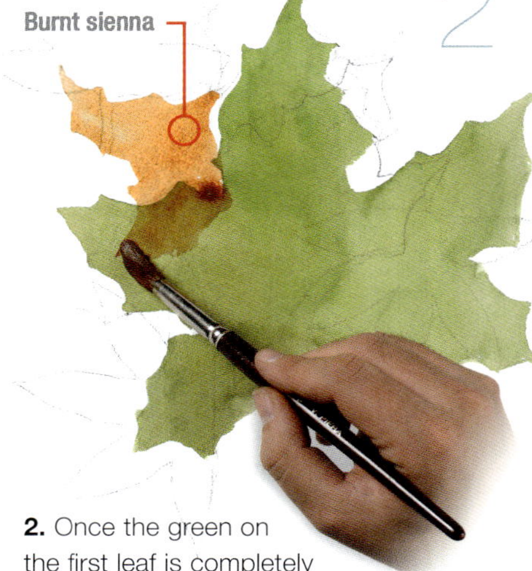

2. Once the green on the first leaf is completely dry, paint the next one with sienna.

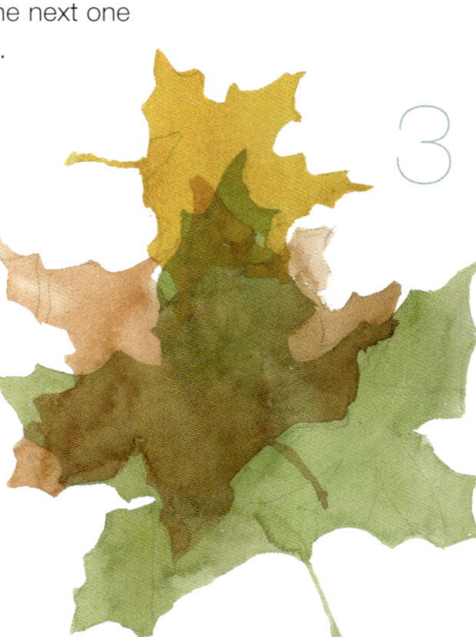

3. The leaves will seem like sheets of colored plastic or glass; their transparency affects their own color and that of the rest. Add a leaf painted with a mixture of yellow and sienna.

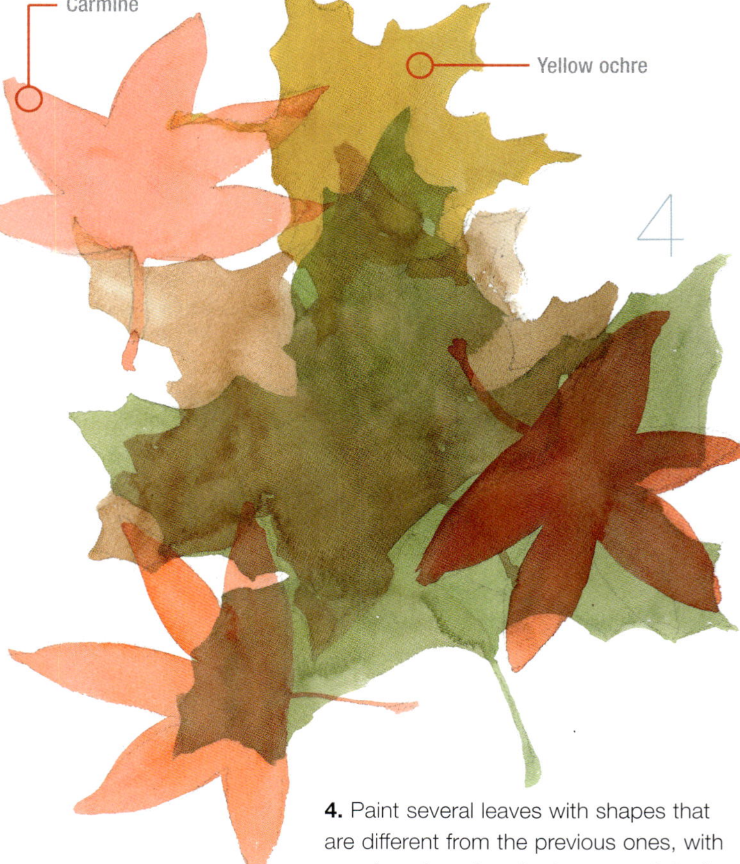

4. Paint several leaves with shapes that are different from the previous ones, with carmine of varying shades on each leaf. The watercolors will work very well for an autumn theme, both for the subject and the colors used.

21 Wet on Dry / **Dark on Light**

LEVEL OF DIFFICULTY

★

COLORS

Cadmium yellow

Burnt sienna

Carmine

BRUSH

Medium round natural hair

PAPER

140 lb medium-rough texture

This is a fantasy theme, an imaginary version of a landscape where you will exaggerate the colors in an arbitrary manner to demonstrate the transparent effect of dark colors over light. You can take all the liberties you wish, as long as the transparencies are extremely luminous.

Cadmium yellow

1. First paint the yellow strokes that form the treetops. Proceed carefully, creating different shapes (like clouds) and sizes.

2. The pink background of the composition is the silhouette of a tree and a bell tower. Leave the silhouette of the farthest tree white. When the pink is dry, paint the foreground with burnt sienna overlapping the previous pink color.

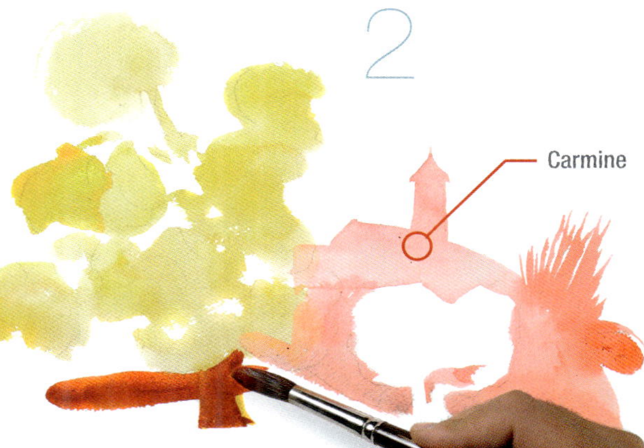

Burnt sienna

3. Paint the tree that was left white with sienna. The tone is lighter than that of the transparency applied over the pink.

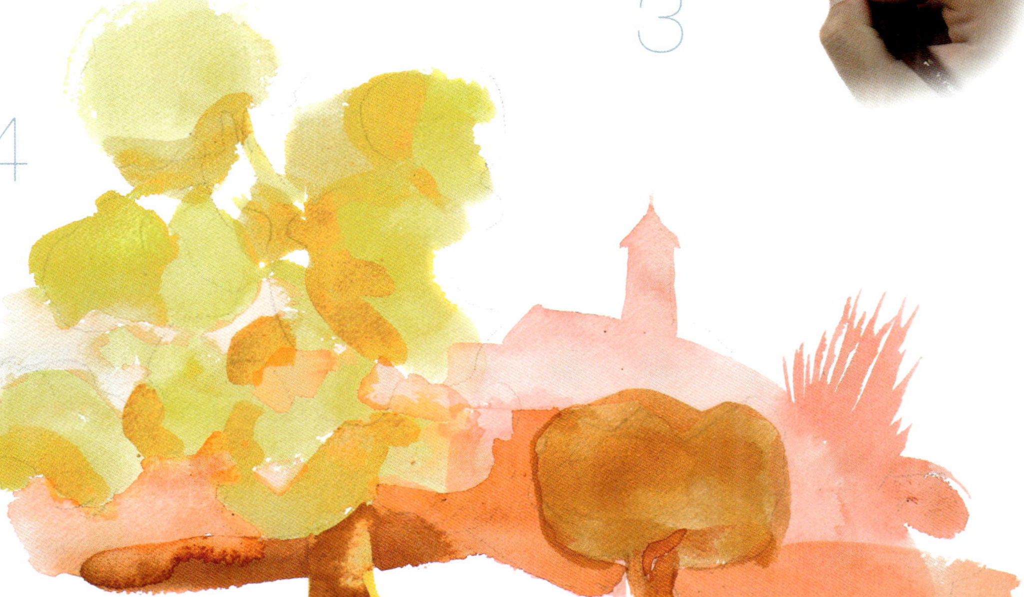

4. Finally, shade the yellows with a few applications of diluted burnt sienna. The unreality of the color focuses attention on the colorful effects of the transparencies.

22 Wet on Dry / **Light on Dark**

LEVEL OF DIFFICULTY
★★
COLORS
Cadmium yellow
Burnt sienna
Yellow ochre
BRUSH
Medium round natural hair
PAPER
140 lb medium-rough texture

The effect of a light transparency over a dark base is less evident than the opposite (dark paint over a light base), but it works well for certain subjects where you might wish to suggest a form rather than describe it in detail. Paint these wheat stalks starting with the darkest, and then add the lighter and more transparent ones over them.

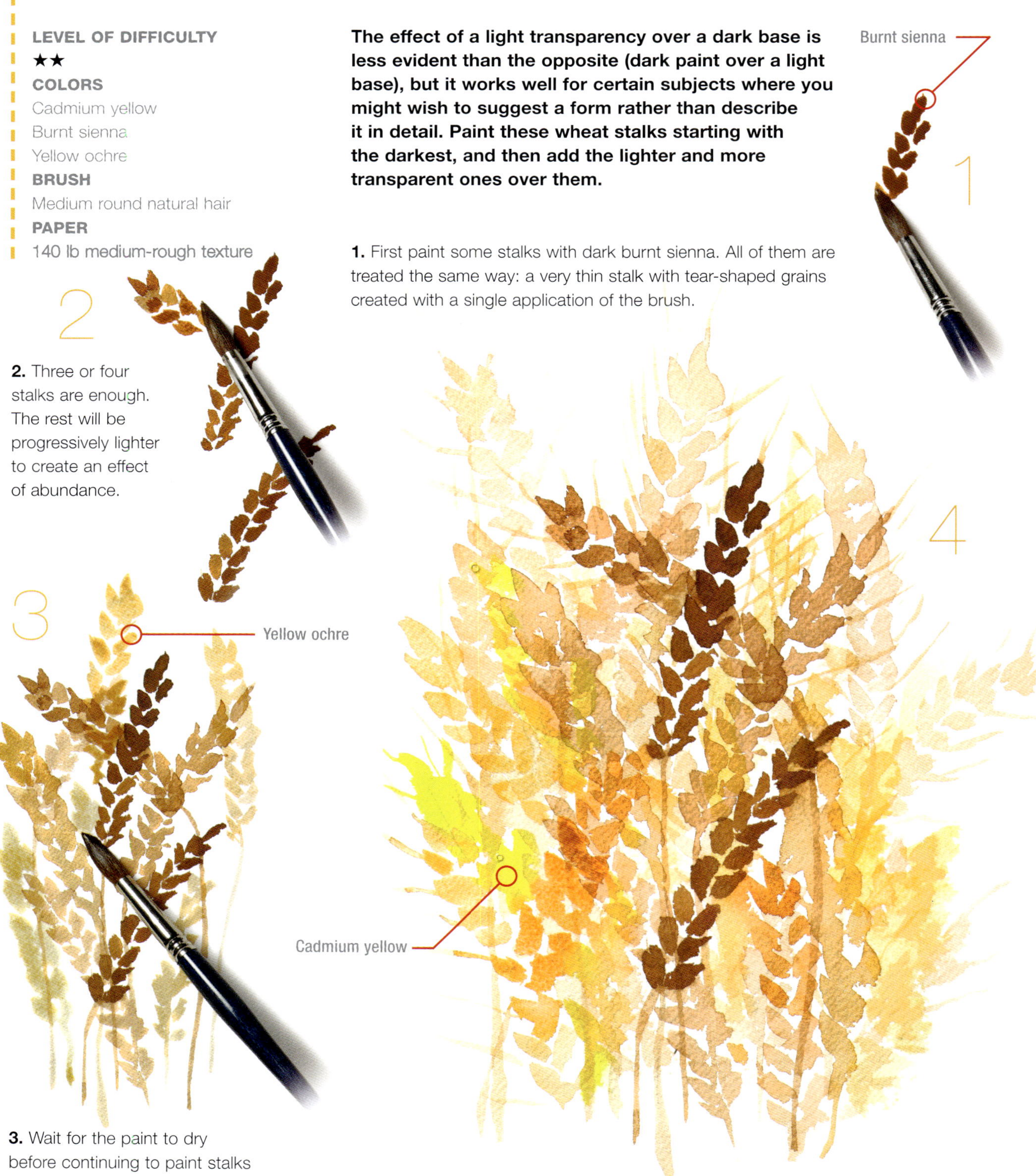

1. First paint some stalks with dark burnt sienna. All of them are treated the same way: a very thin stalk with tear-shaped grains created with a single application of the brush.

2. Three or four stalks are enough. The rest will be progressively lighter to create an effect of abundance.

3. Wait for the paint to dry before continuing to paint stalks in increasingly lighter colors: diluted siennas, ochres, and finally, yellows.

4. Superimposing increasingly lighter colors creates a feeling of light and volume in a group of forms that, in reality, are completely flat and without detail when studied individually.

23 Wet on Dry / **Cool on Warm**

LEVEL OF DIFFICULTY
★
COLORS
Cadmium yellow
Yellow ochre
Raw sienna
Permanent green
BRUSH
Medium round natural hair
PAPER
140 lb medium-rough texture

Warm colors tend to visually move toward the foreground of a painting. But this is a theoretical rule; in practice, nothing keeps you from painting cool colors over warm ones, especially if, as in this case, warm and cool (yellows and greens) combine harmoniously in transparencies.

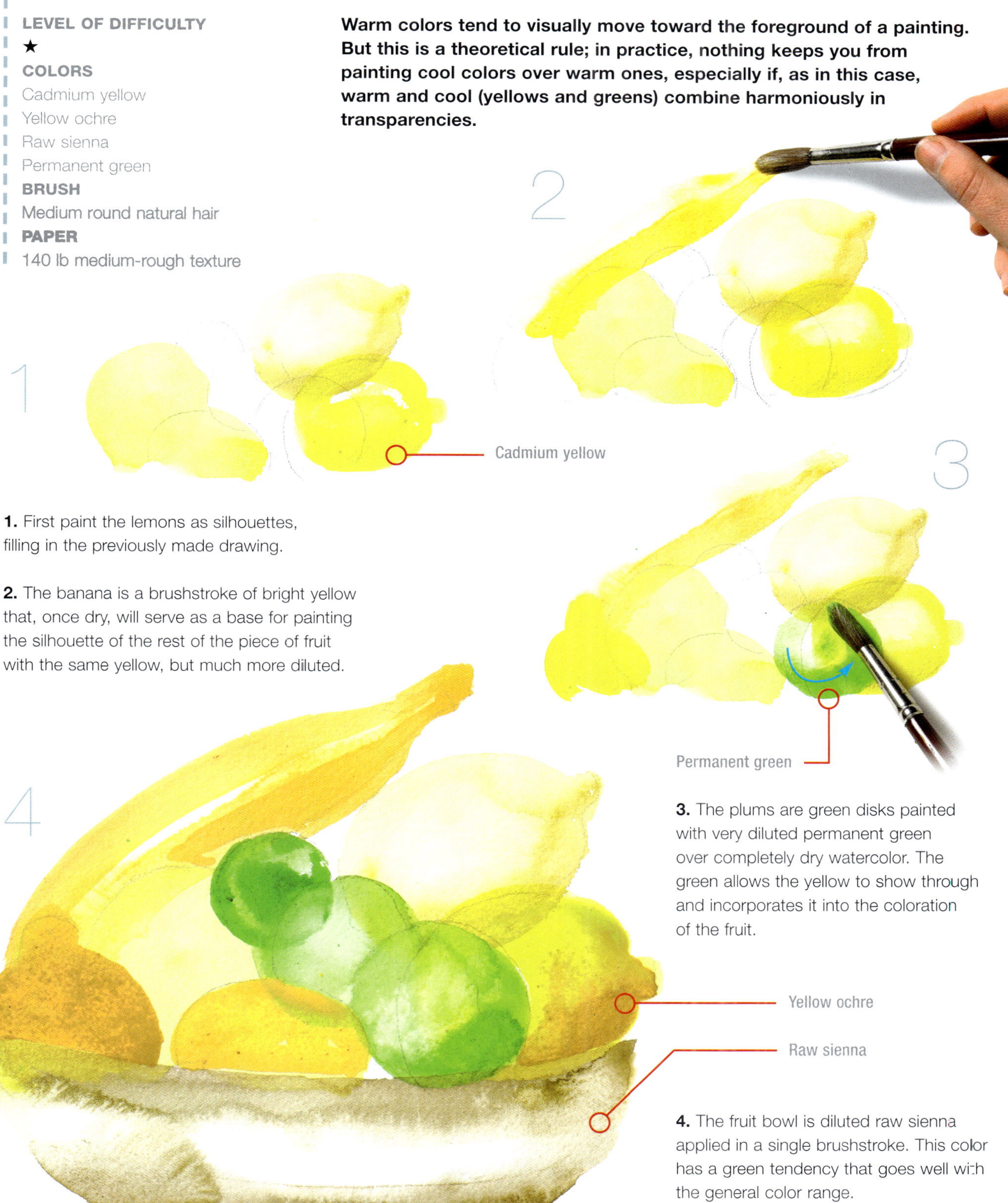

1. First paint the lemons as silhouettes, filling in the previously made drawing.

2. The banana is a brushstroke of bright yellow that, once dry, will serve as a base for painting the silhouette of the rest of the piece of fruit with the same yellow, but much more diluted.

3. The plums are green disks painted with very diluted permanent green over completely dry watercolor. The green allows the yellow to show through and incorporates it into the coloration of the fruit.

4. The fruit bowl is diluted raw sienna applied in a single brushstroke. This color has a green tendency that goes well with the general color range.

24 Wet on Dry / **Warm on Cool**

LEVEL OF DIFFICULTY
★★
COLORS
Permanent red
Ultramarine blue
Raw sienna
BRUSH
Medium round natural hair
PAPER
140 lb medium-rough texture

The red colors of the top of this tree stand out and look brighter when they come into contact with the purples, blues, and grays of the autumn landscape in the background. To this colorful effect is added the characteristic luminosity of multiple transparencies with which you will construct this watercolor. The transparencies create the dense rich atmosphere that dominates the painting.

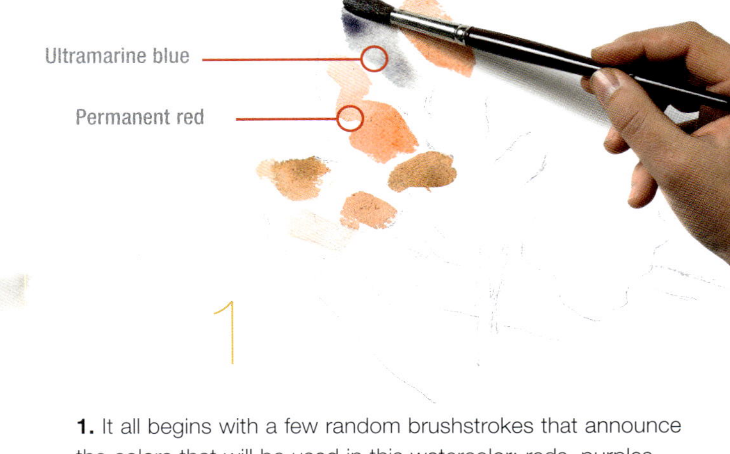

1. It all begins with a few random brushstrokes that announce the colors that will be used in this watercolor: reds, purples, and blues. Paint the sky and the tree at the same time with brushstrokes that do not touch one another, and then wait for them to dry.

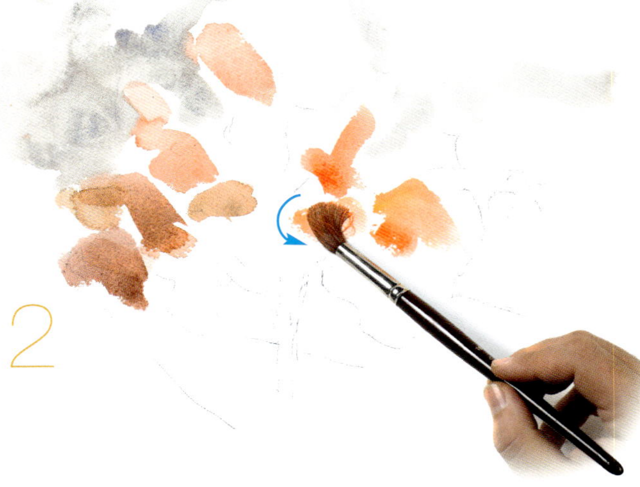

2. The brushstrokes form an increasingly dense fabric, and soon some colors will be painted over others.

3

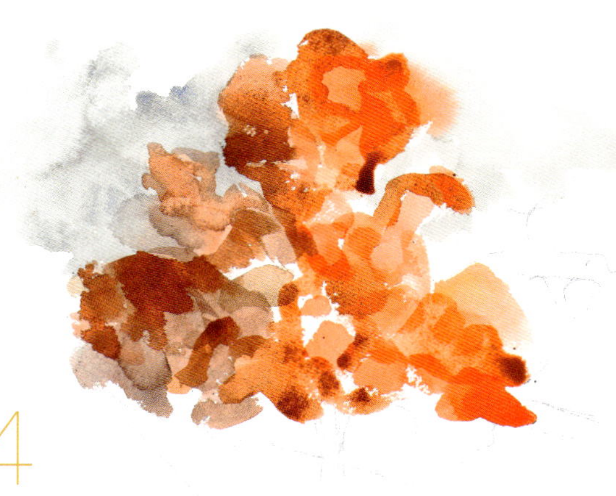

3. Each new application of color is made over dry paint to preserve the transparent effect as much as possible.

4. In the illuminated part of the tree, keep the red pure, while at the left mix in some blue to create a purple tone. Use overlaid transparent purple to represent the shadows.

5. Add blue and gray brushstrokes in the white spaces to intertwine the warm strokes with the cool ones.

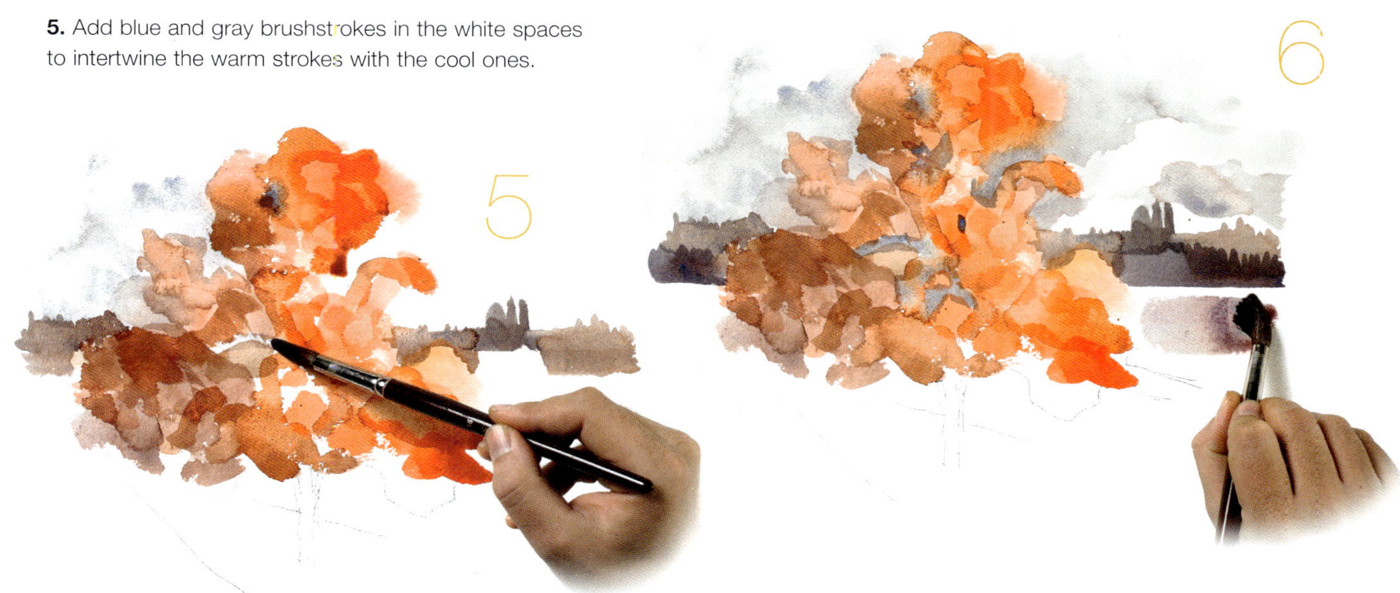

6. The middle ground is resolved with brushstrokes of blue with a touch of red, a violet tone that you must spread in layers of varying densities from light to dark.

7. Finally, paint the foreground with a simple wash of raw sienna to shade the composition and locate the tree in its urban context.

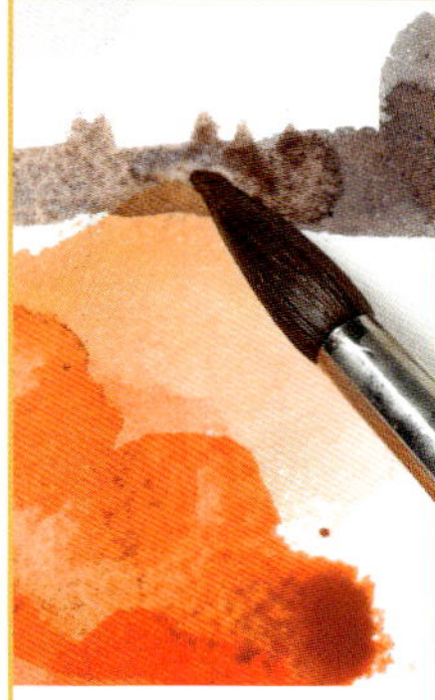

When you wish to work with areas of overlaid transparent paint, you must avoid painting over areas that are still wet. If they are, the colors will acquire a muddy tone that will destroy the limpid effect of the transparency.

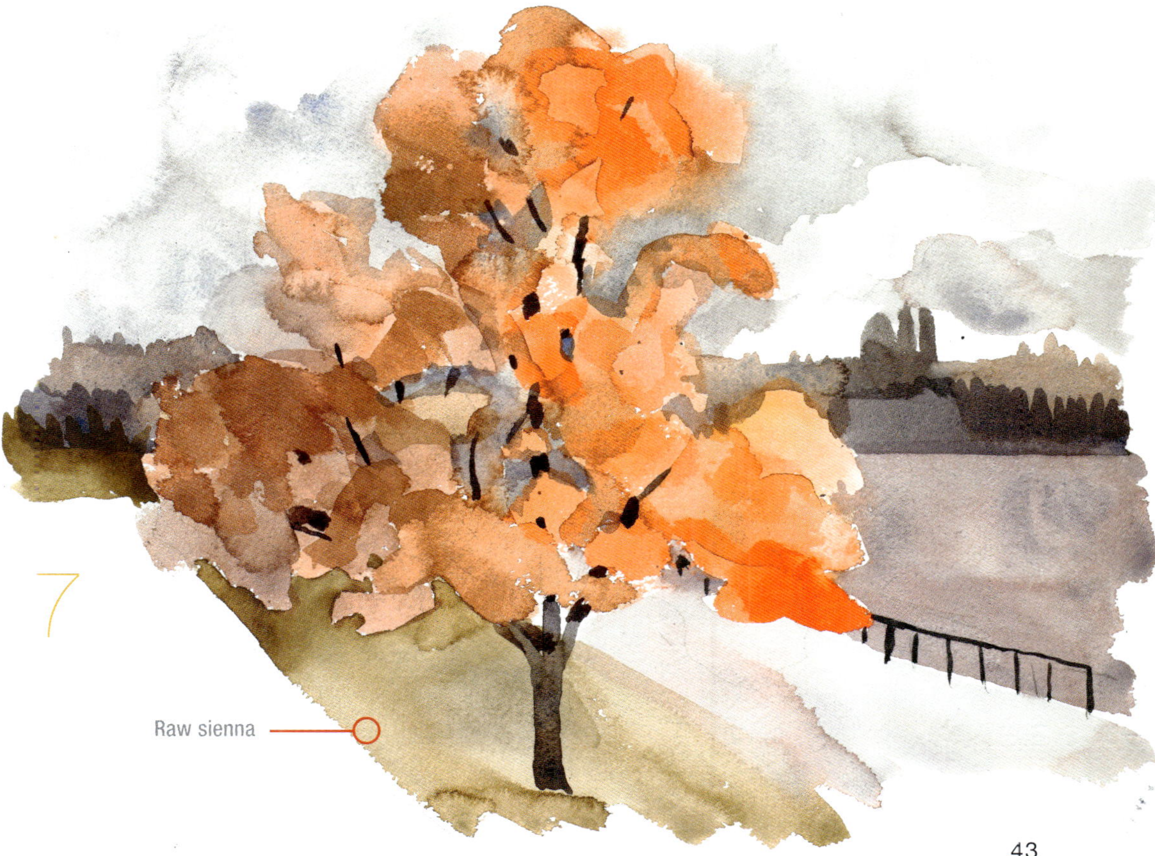

25 Wet on Dry / **Opaque over Transparent**

LEVEL OF DIFFICULTY
★
COLORS
Cadmium yellow
Carmine
Burnt sienna
BRUSH
Medium round natural hair
PAPER
140 lb medium-rough texture

Watercolors are transparent, but it is always possible to create more opaque colors by mixing very saturated ones. In this exercise, you will create a silhouette that looks opaque by contrasting it with a very transparent background that, in addition, was painted on wet paper to accentuate the atmospheric effect.

1

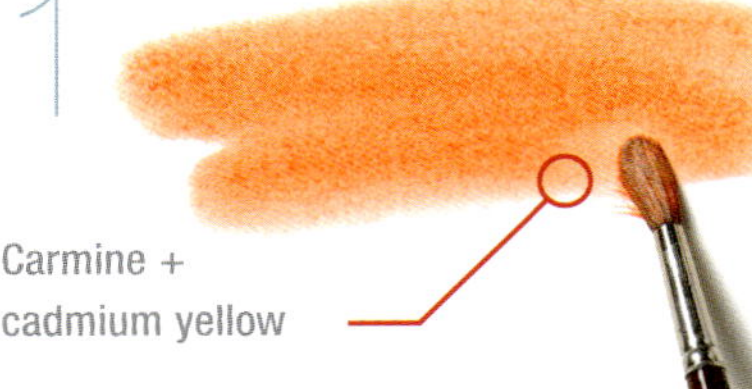

1. First wet the paper, and then spread a wash with a lot of paint—a mixture of carmine and yellow. The wash should create an atmospheric background.

2

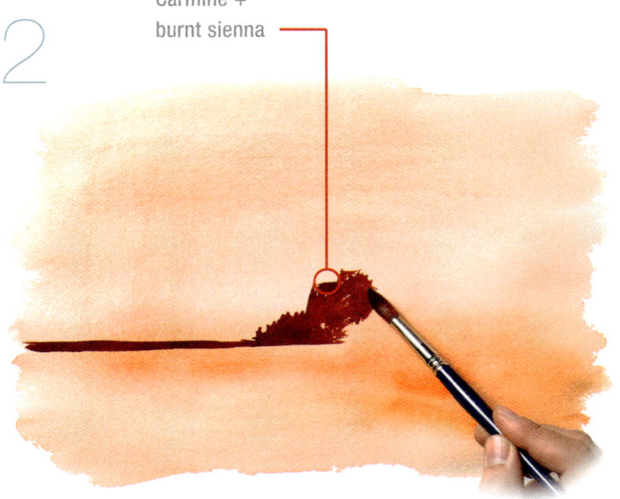

3

2. Paint the silhouette of the castle and the coast with a very dark tone made with carmine and burnt sienna. The tone must be uniform to create a convincing opaque effect.

3. The reflection on the water is painted with the same tone of the silhouette, but a little diluted. Then dilute the paint more and more to represent the waves.

4. The strong colors suggest a fiery sunset. The unity in the coloration of the scene is only broken by changes in the tone and transparency of very similar colors.

4

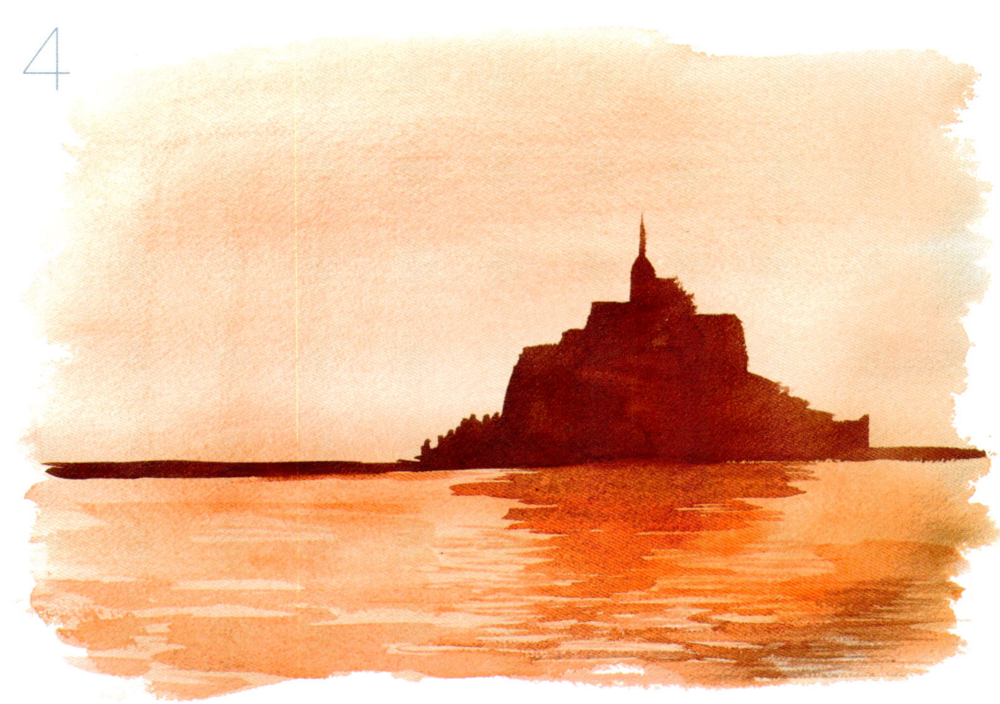

26 Wet on Dry / **Reflections and Opacities**

LEVEL OF DIFFICULTY
★★
COLORS
Cadmium red
Carmine
BRUSH
Medium round natural hair
PAPER
140 lb medium-rough texture

The drawing for this theme requires a certain amount of skill, but painting it is easier than it looks. It is just a matter of filling the shapes with saturated red paint, leaving some white areas to suggest the reflections. The red, in contrast, will look dark, and the strong contrast with the white areas will increase the sense of a shiny and lustrous surface.

1. Draw the lobster with simple outlines using very saturated cadmium red.

2. Separate each red area with white borders, which will express the reflections of the crustacean's shell.

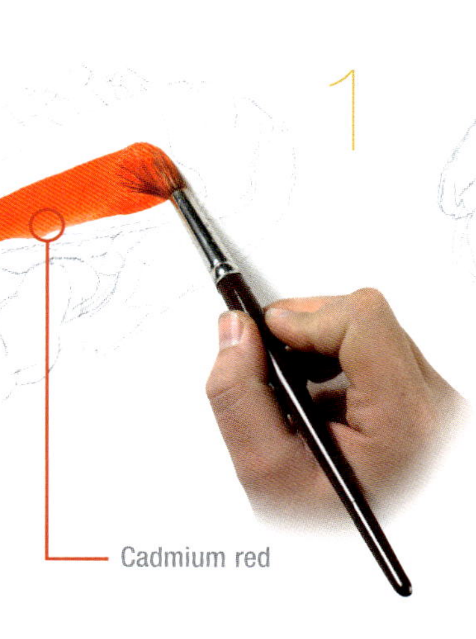

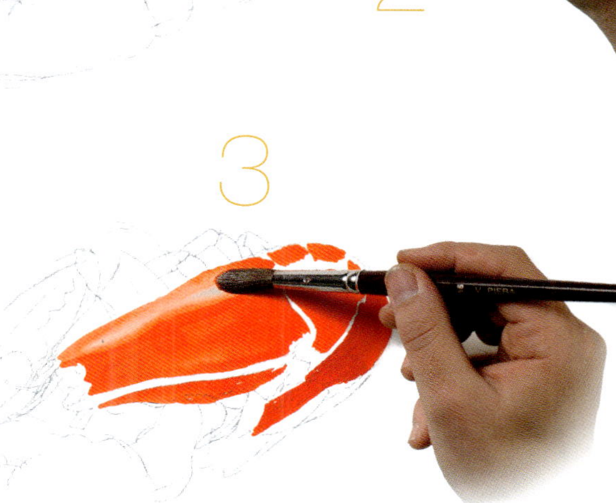

3. Brush the white margins with clean water, which will dilute the paint and blur the transition between the red and white. This will create the effect of a bright area.

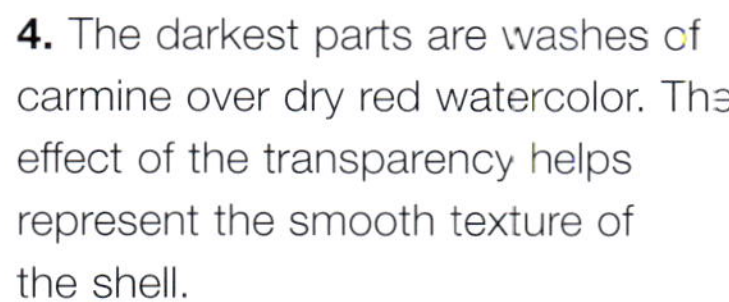

4. The darkest parts are washes of carmine over dry red watercolor. The effect of the transparency helps represent the smooth texture of the shell.

5. The difficult part of this watercolor is the drawing and the care that must be taken around the edges. The reflections must be completely white, and the areas where they border the color must be blended so the paint loses its hard edge.

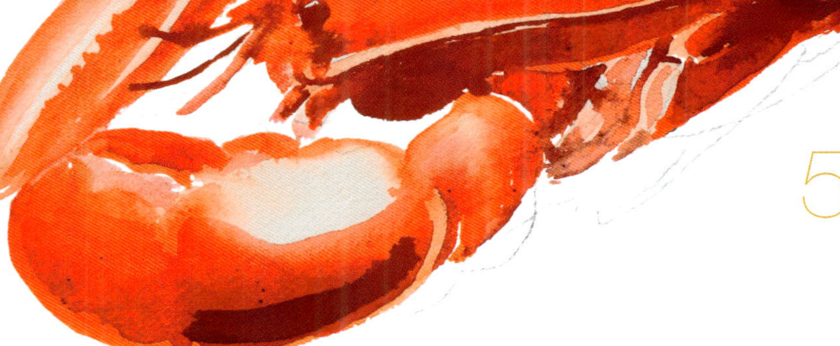

27 Wet on Dry / **Monochromatic Transparencies**

LEVEL OF DIFFICULTY
★★
COLORS
Cadmium yellow
Burnt sienna
Yellow ochre
Cadmium red
Ultramarine blue
BRUSH
Medium round natural hair
PAPER
140 lb medium-rough texture

Burnt sienna + yellow ochre

1

It is not necessary to work with many different colors to achieve interesting effects. Transparent glazes allow you to differentiate and increase the tones you are using, which in this case are very few. The pieces of fruit in this picture are developed by progressively layering transparent colors, usually the base colors themselves.

1. After drawing the subjects, paint the outlines of the pears with a mixture of ochre and burnt sienna. This mixture should be wet on the lighter pears and saturated on the dark ones.

2. Use the same color for shading and darkening each pear; the brush must be a little more saturated. Remember that each new transparency should be painted when the base color is completely dry.

3. The hard-edged dark areas (not blended with the base color) strengthen the feeling of volume rather than weaken it. The silhouettes of the pears should include the stems, which are painted with the tip of the brush.

Sometimes it is helpful to emphasize the effects: a narrow white area increases the sense of volume even though the white zone does not appear on the real object. It is a subtle detail that efficiently contributes to creating a feeling of three-dimensionality.

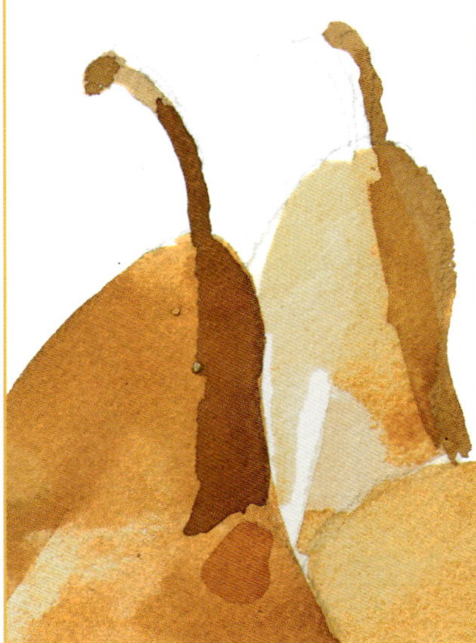

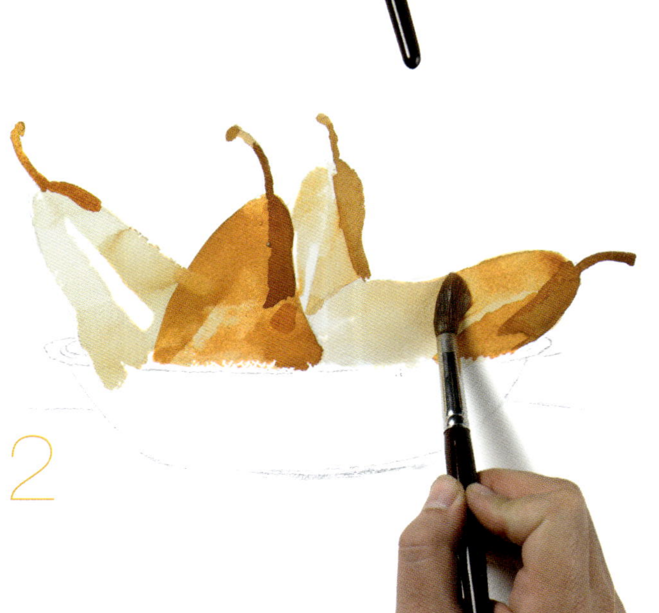

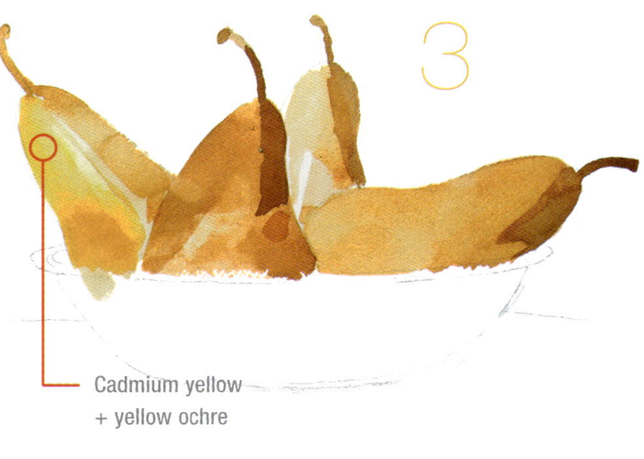

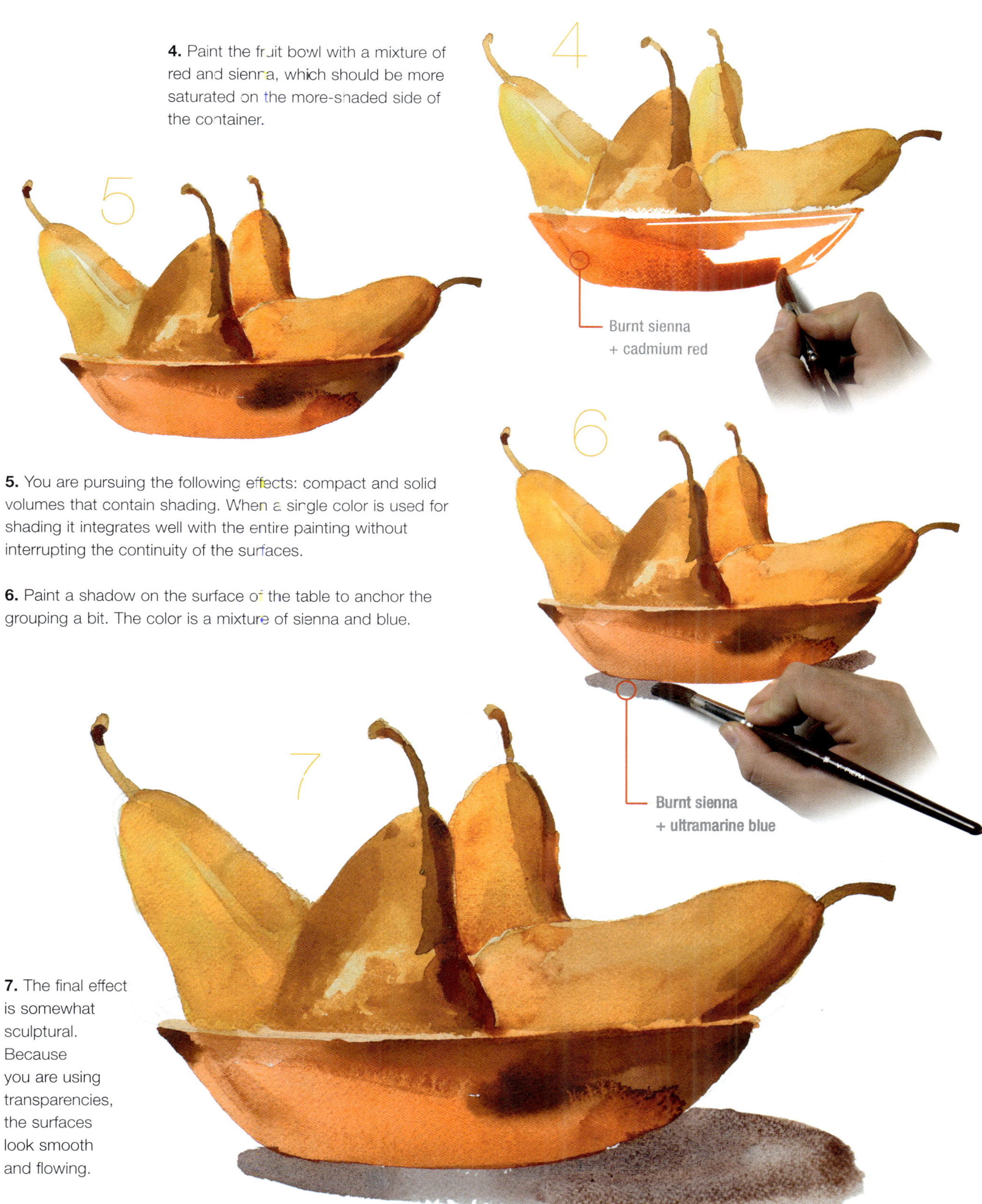

4. Paint the fruit bowl with a mixture of red and sienna, which should be more saturated on the more-shaded side of the container.

5. You are pursuing the following effects: compact and solid volumes that contain shading. When a single color is used for shading it integrates well with the entire painting without interrupting the continuity of the surfaces.

6. Paint a shadow on the surface of the table to anchor the grouping a bit. The color is a mixture of sienna and blue.

7. The final effect is somewhat sculptural. Because you are using transparencies, the surfaces look smooth and flowing.

28 Drawing and Color / Drawing with Pencil and Watercolor

LEVEL OF DIFFICULTY
★
COLORS
Burnt sienna
Yellow ochre
Sap green
Cerulean blue
BRUSH
Medium round natural hair
PAPER
140 lb medium-rough texture

A graphite pencil is the usual medium used for drawing the preliminary sketch for a watercolor painting. In this example, you will use a very soft pencil so that the lines will be very visible in the finished painting. The paint will not closely follow the edges of the drawing; sometimes it will flow over them and other times you will leave white areas on the paper, creating a purposely unfinished look.

1. Sketch a village scene with loose and free lines. The colors of the forms in the foreground, a tree and some bushes behind a wall, are saturated and very contrasting.

2. As you paint the farther buildings, use paint (burnt sienna with a little green) that is more diluted than that of the foreground, and reduce the contrast between light and dark.

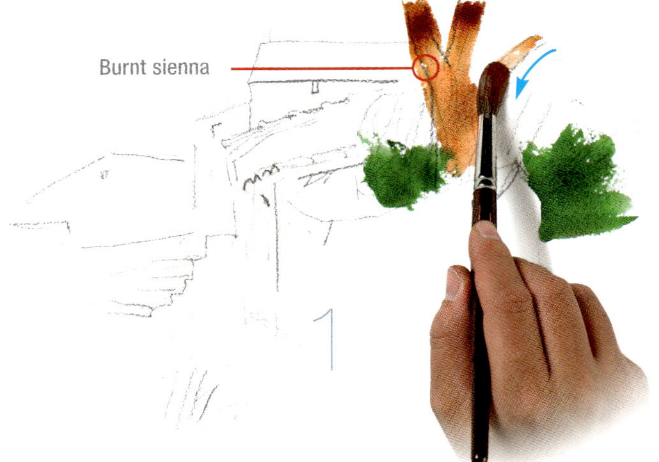

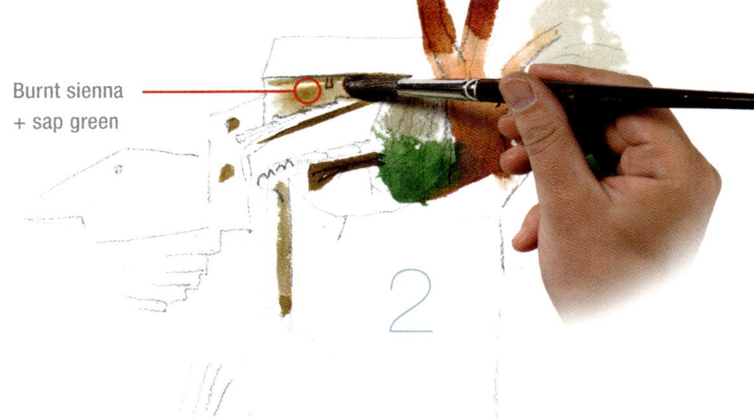

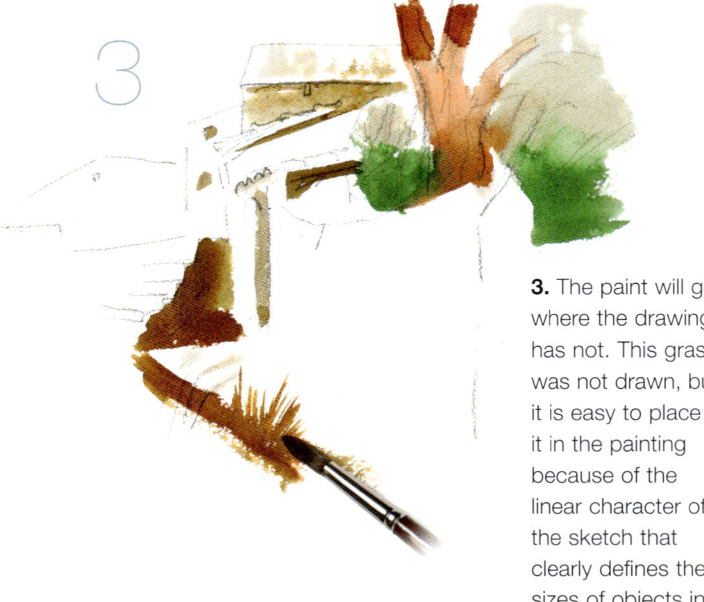

3. The paint will go where the drawing has not. This grass was not drawn, but it is easy to place it in the painting because of the linear character of the sketch that clearly defines the sizes of objects in the foreground.

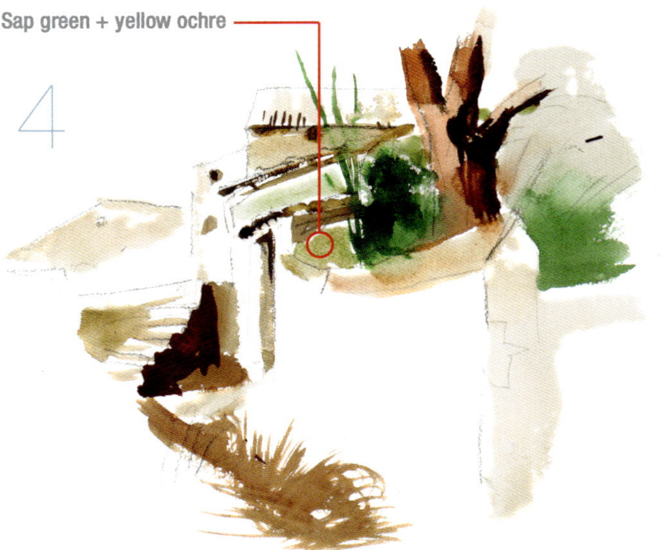

4. It is important not to continually paint over the edges of the drawing. What is illustrated with the pencil lines does not have to be reiterated with the paint. The areas of paint can develop parts of the subject that are just lightly indicated by the drawing.

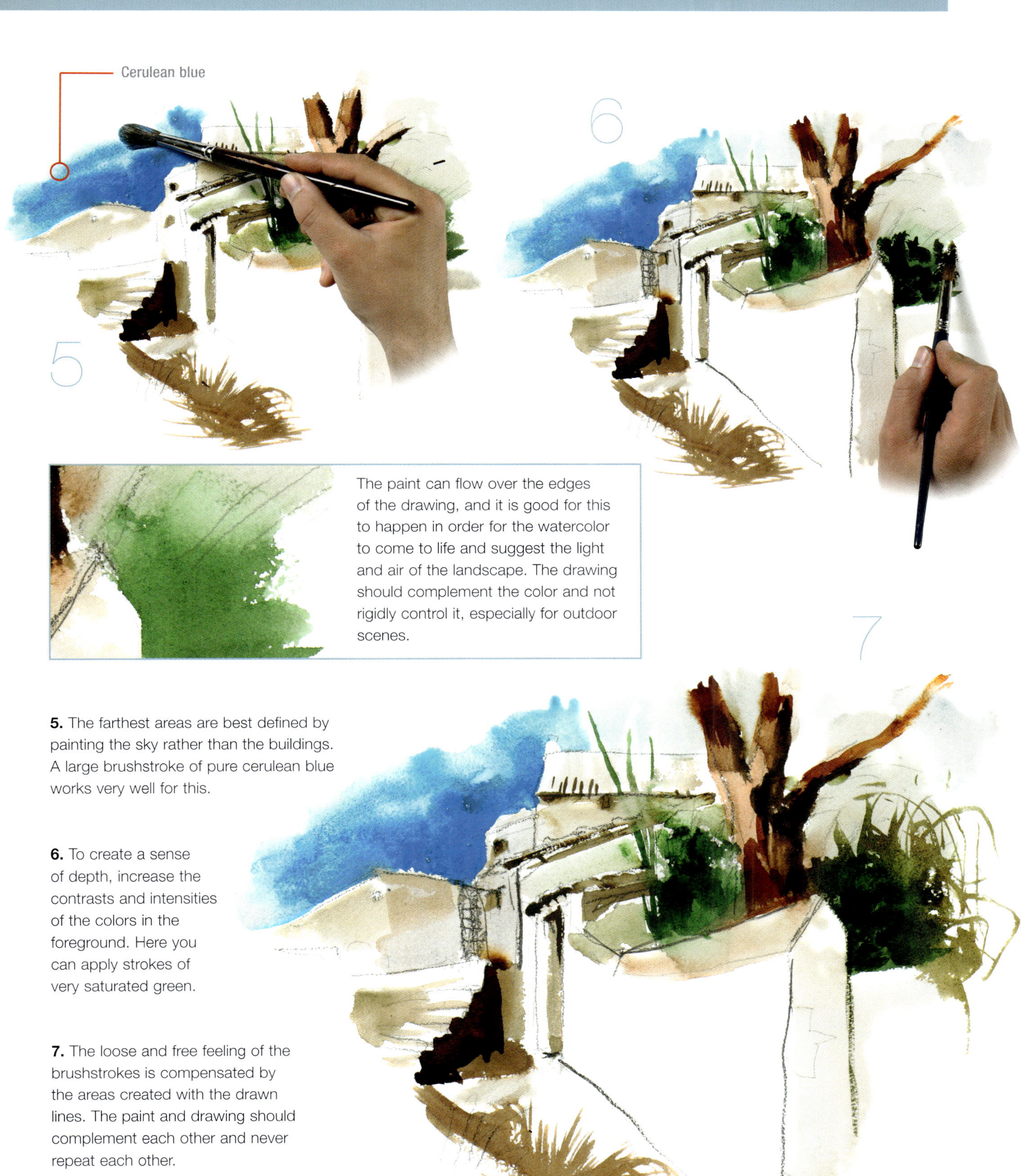

The paint can flow over the edges of the drawing, and it is good for this to happen in order for the watercolor to come to life and suggest the light and air of the landscape. The drawing should complement the color and not rigidly control it, especially for outdoor scenes.

5. The farthest areas are best defined by painting the sky rather than the buildings. A large brushstroke of pure cerulean blue works very well for this.

6. To create a sense of depth, increase the contrasts and intensities of the colors in the foreground. Here you can apply strokes of very saturated green.

7. The loose and free feeling of the brushstrokes is compensated by the areas created with the drawn lines. The paint and drawing should complement each other and never repeat each other.

29 Drawing and Color / **Precision Drawing with a Brush**

LEVEL OF DIFFICULTY

★

COLORS

Burnt sienna
Yellow ochre
Sap green
Cerulean blue
Cobalt violet
Carmine

BRUSH

Medium round natural hair

PAPER

140 lb medium-rough texture

Certain subjects, like these dried flowers shown here, require a linear treatment with a precise and elegant brushstroke. The pencil line should be nearly invisible, so it is recommended that you make the drawing by pressing very lightly on the paper with a hard pencil. You should use a round brush of good quality so that the tip will be as firm and sharp as possible.

1. Make a minimal sketch of the subject, then paint the dry leaves with different tones. The colors should range from light ochre to chestnut to dark brown. Use a mixture of ochre, green, and sienna.

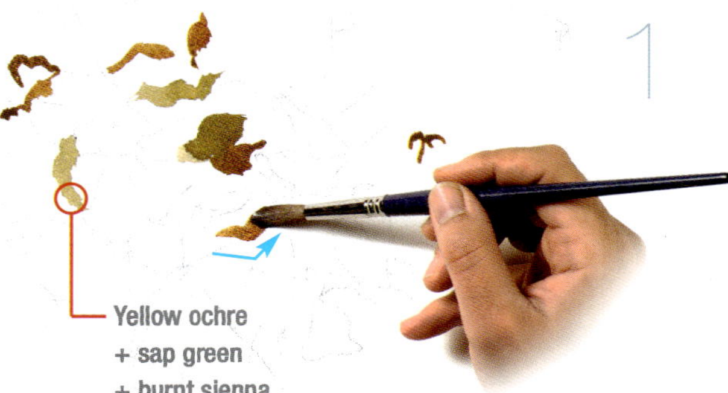

2. The first paintings of leaves have irregular shapes, but some of them should have the same size, form, and placement.

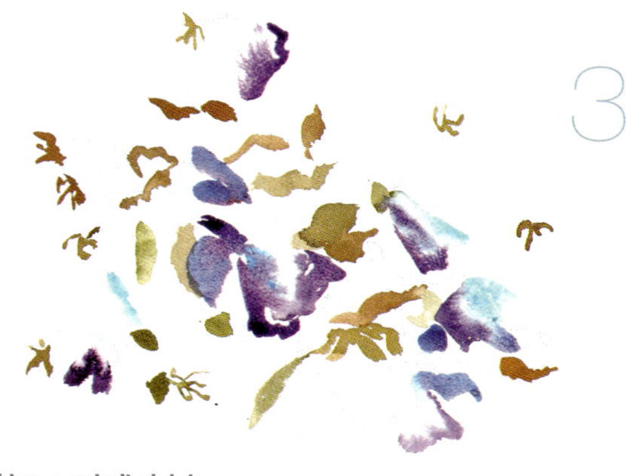

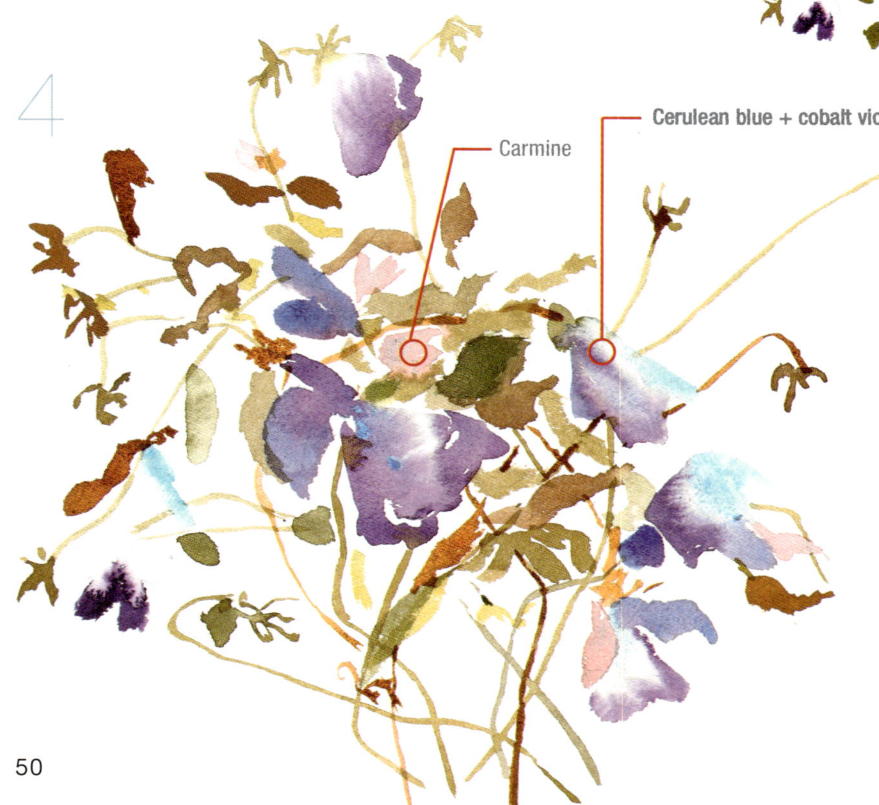

3. The blue flowers are made with strokes of cerulean blue. Add some saturated violet while the paint is still wet, and allow the paint to run over the blue color. Then, using the tip of the brush, draw the stems with precise uniform lines.

4. Add some light pink petals here and there and more brown leaves, until the picture is irregular and dense enough and looks natural.

Drawing and Color / **Schematic Color Drawing with a Brush**

LEVEL OF DIFFICULTY
★

COLORS
Yellow ochre
Cadmium red
Burnt sienna
Raw sienna

BRUSH
Medium flat natural hair

PAPER
140 lb medium-rough texture

One of the strongest ways of creating the drawing for a watercolor is to work with very simple sketches made directly with a brush. Flat brushes make a simple line with no complications or fussy details. The rest of the painting is also schematic and quick.

1. This drawing of a cat is basic, schematic, and with few details. Draw it with a diluted mixture of ochre and burnt sienna. The shapes tend toward a geometric regularity.

2. Add loose sinuous strokes to the cat's body to suggest the fur. For the details on the head, use the point of the corner of the brush on the paper.

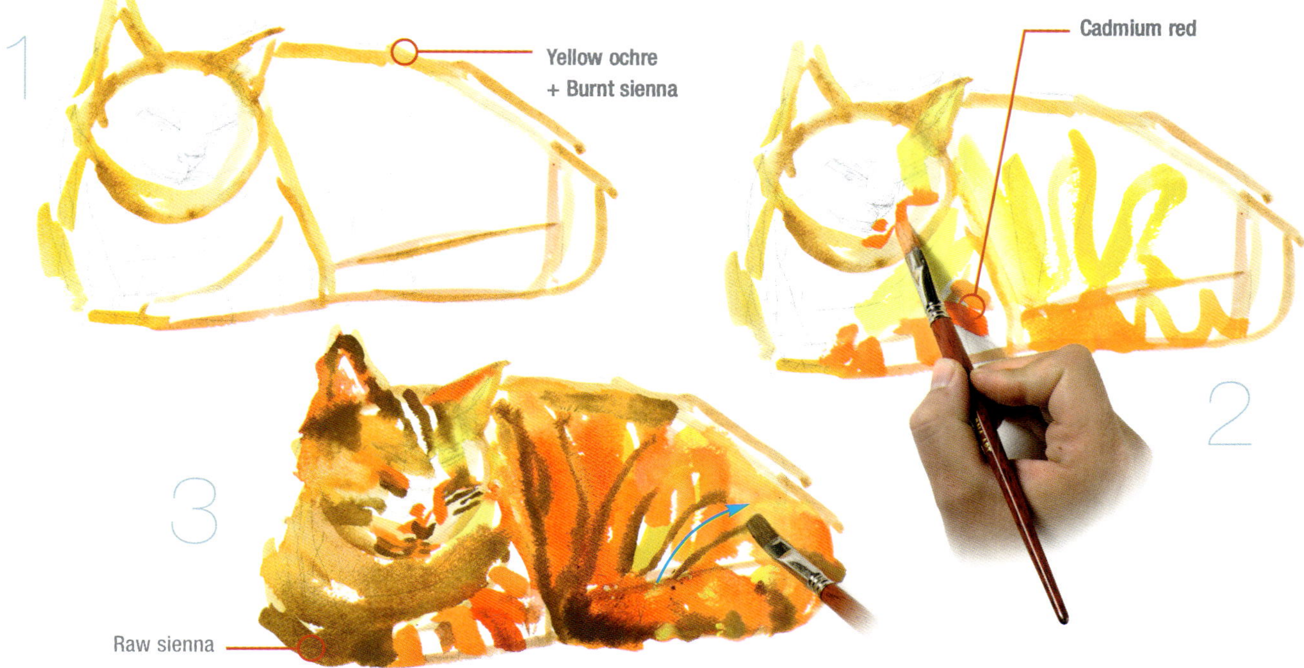

3. Work quickly on wet paper; it is not important if the colors run together. You can retouch the stripes on the fur with lines drawn with the corner of the brush.

4. The color of the cat results from successive applications of red, yellow, and raw sienna. The brushstrokes spread freely because the paint was wet. There is not a clear edge between the initial drawing and the painted color; both applications followed the same rhythm and intention.

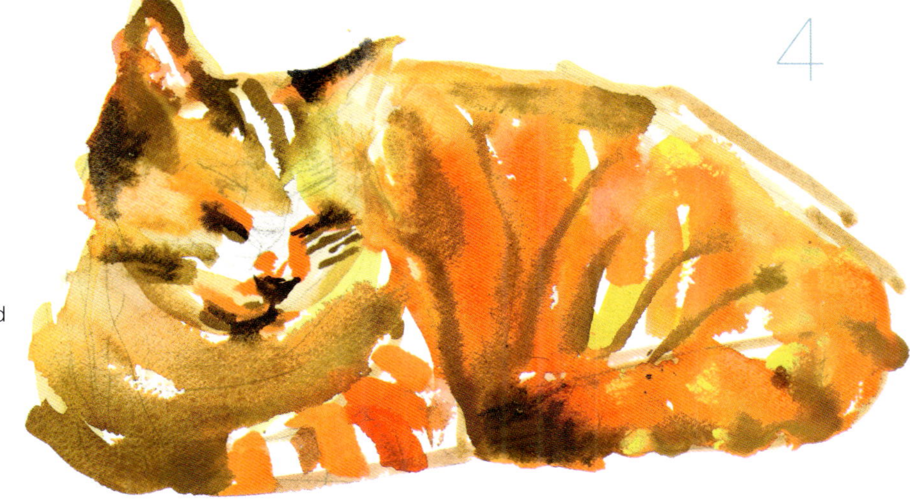

31 Drawing and Color / **Color Drawing Outline**

LEVEL OF DIFFICULTY
★★
COLORS
Cadmium red
Cadmium yellow
Carmine
Permanent blue
Permanent green
BRUSHES
Medium round natural hair
Narrow flat natural hair
PAPER
140 lb medium-rough texture

When the subject does not have any complications regarding color, the forms can be drawn directly with the same color that will be used for painting, using the brush as a drawing tool. If you do not feel sure of your drawing skills, you can begin with a pencil drawing and then go over it with the brush.

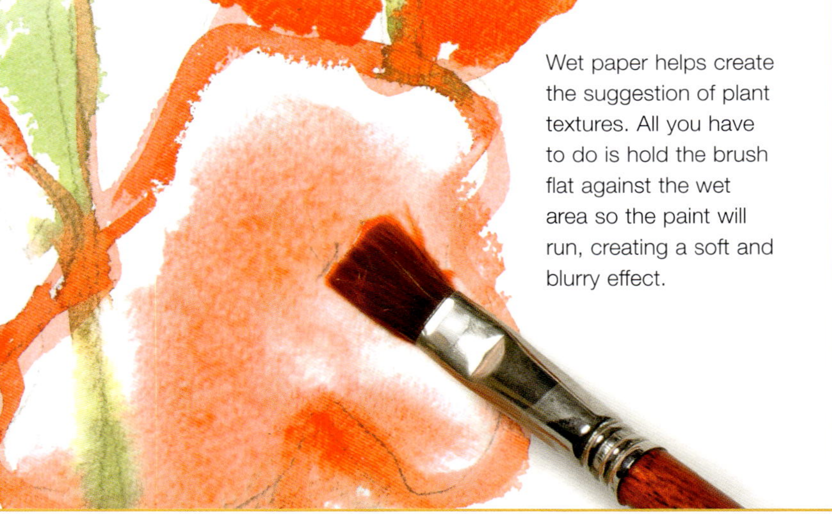

Wet paper helps create the suggestion of plant textures. All you have to do is hold the brush flat against the wet area so the paint will run, creating a soft and blurry effect.

1

1. These red lines, made with the round brush, are the same cadmium red that you will use later to paint the poppies. Use quick cursive strokes. The lines should not be too narrow, because this watercolor does not require a drawing with precise or complicated outlines.

2

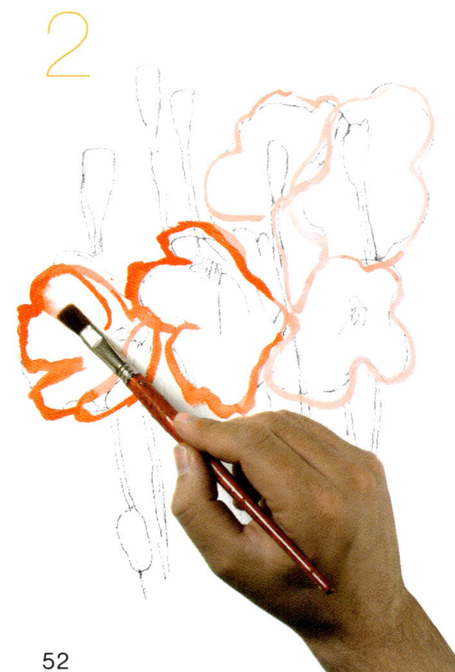

2. Use a very wet round brush with a little blue paint to spread the lines toward the inside of the flower to create a first-color effect.

3. Working on wet paper, retrace some outlines to create a vibrating effect that will break the monotony of a too explicit and uniform outline. The water will cause variations in the intensity of the lines, causing them to fade slightly in some areas.

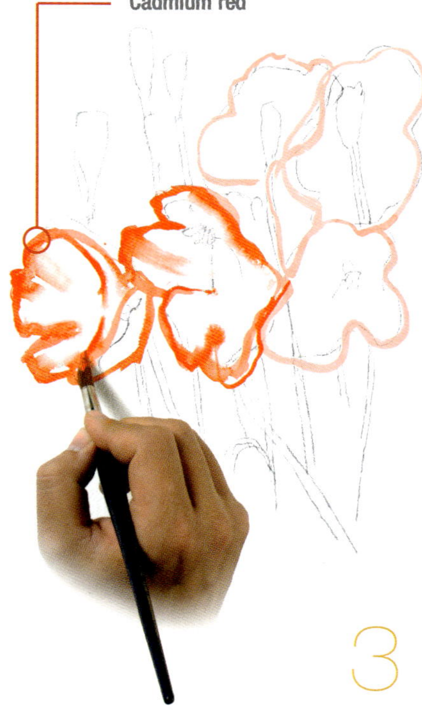

3

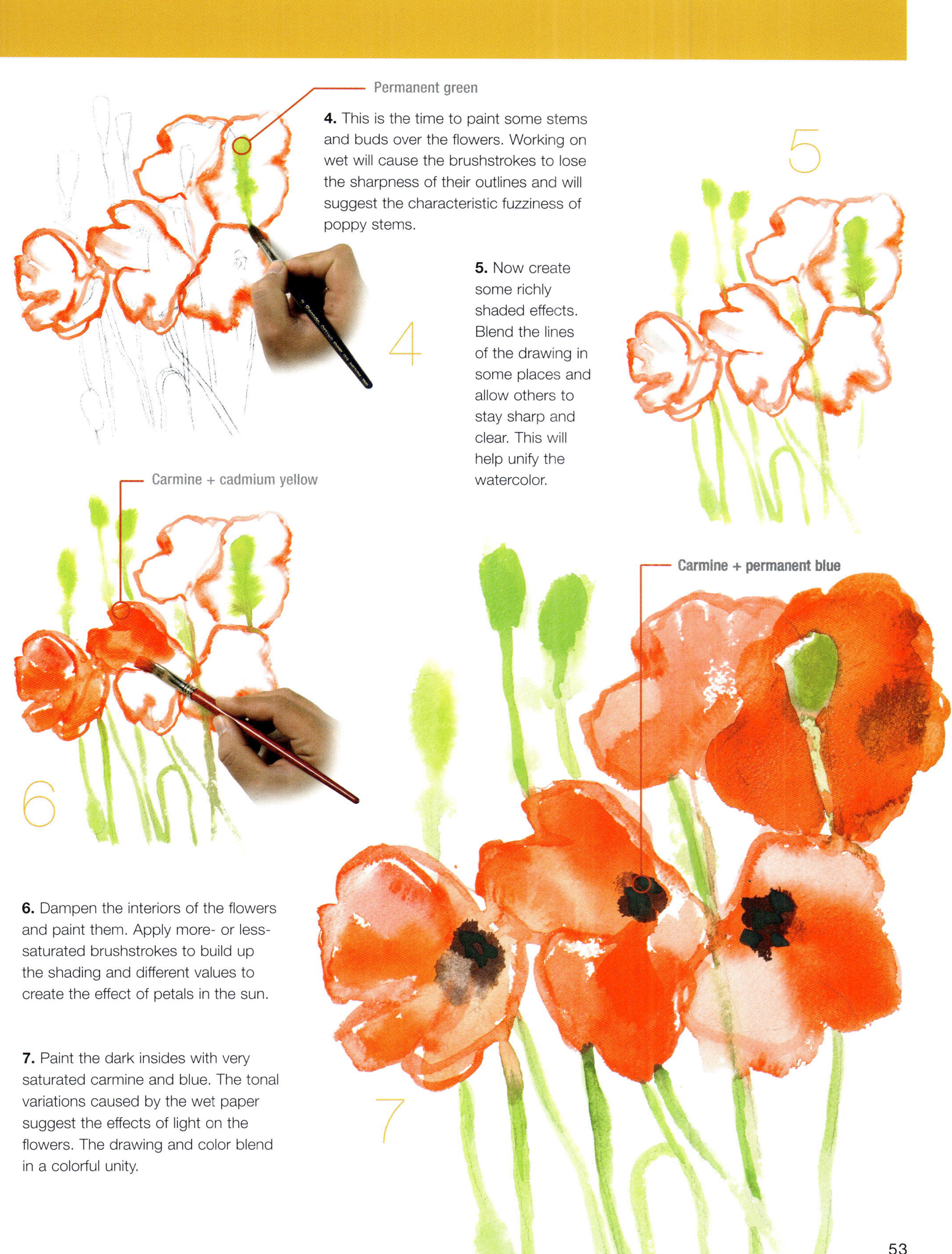

4. This is the time to paint some stems and buds over the flowers. Working on wet will cause the brushstrokes to lose the sharpness of their outlines and will suggest the characteristic fuzziness of poppy stems.

5. Now create some richly shaded effects. Blend the lines of the drawing in some places and allow others to stay sharp and clear. This will help unify the watercolor.

6. Dampen the interiors of the flowers and paint them. Apply more- or less-saturated brushstrokes to build up the shading and different values to create the effect of petals in the sun.

7. Paint the dark insides with very saturated carmine and blue. The tonal variations caused by the wet paper suggest the effects of light on the flowers. The drawing and color blend in a colorful unity.

LEVEL OF DIFFICULTY
★★
COLORS
Yellow ochre
Burnt sienna
Permanent blue
Carmine
BRUSH
Medium round natural hair
PAPER
140 lb medium-rough texture

Plumage is painted with a hatching technique, superimposing lines that create textures and shading. This is typical of pen drawings, but it can be adapted to watercolor when the subject requires. In this case, you will use it to represent the plumage of a duck. Exaggerate the color a little to make the finished painting livelier.

1. Draw the duck with a pencil and begin to work with the tip of a brush, creating curved lines that follow the rounded silhouette of the head. Use permanent blue mixed with a small amount of carmine and sienna. The lines should be of different intensities to suggest volume.

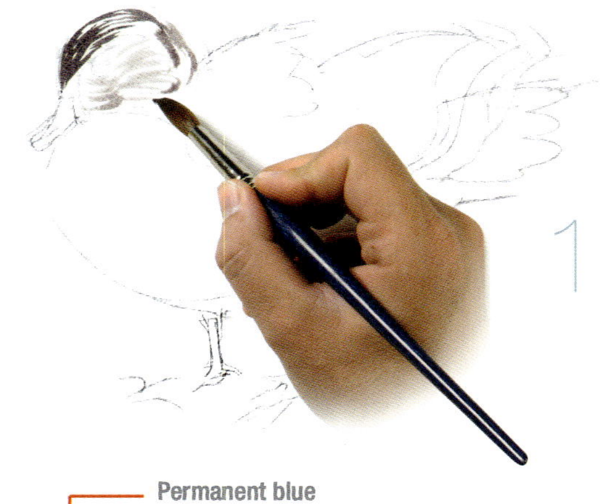

2. Alternate colors in the different parts of the plumage: blue, carmine, ochre, etc. The rhythm of the lines should be agile so the texture of the brushstrokes is unified.

2

Carmine + permanent blue

Yellow ochre

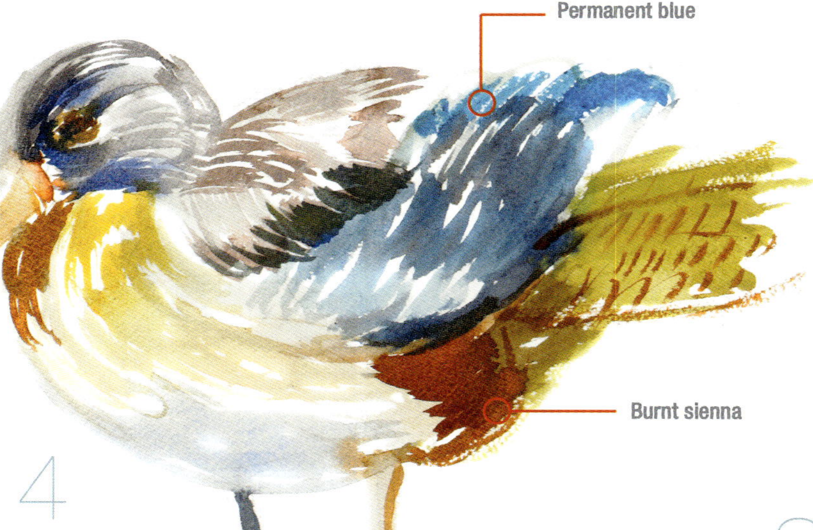

3

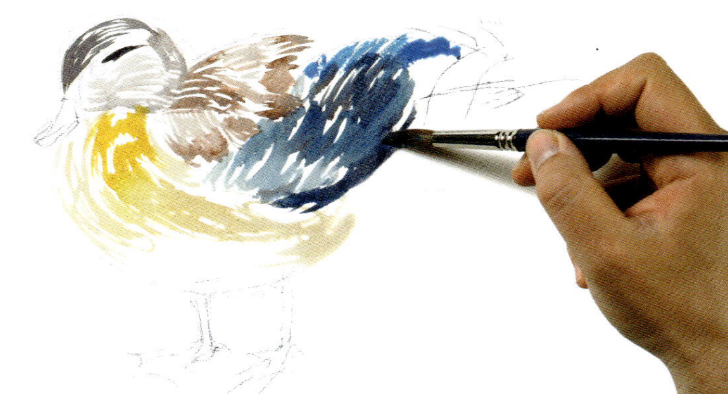

3. Here you can see how many brushstrokes join together, but not completely. This partial fusion makes it so the volume of the duck does not break up into an aggregation of colors with no body or consistency.

4. The different areas of color follow the general form of the bird and suggest the consistency of the plumage. It is not a good idea to fill the form with shading, because it will destroy the multicolor effect of this delightful watercolor.

33 Drawing and Color / **Lines with Color Pencils**

LEVEL OF DIFFICULTY
★
COLORS
Cerulean blue
Permanent green
Water-soluble color pencils
Blues and greens
BRUSH
Medium round natural hair
PAPER
140 lb medium-rough texture

The marks made by watercolor pencils can be diluted with water, and they mix well with watercolors. These pencils are not normal working tools of watercolorists (at least those who are illustrators), but they can be used as a drawing medium that enriches the painting with a graphic look.

1. Watercolor pencils can be used at any stage of the painting. Here you will use them first for defining the forms of the flowers by lightly shading the petals before starting to paint with the watercolors.

2. The lines are very easily diluted with just a wet brush. The color is not as intense as that of watercolors, however their soft transparent effect is nearly identical.

3. As you add green and blue washes, draw lines and shapes with the pencils. As you draw on the wet areas, the lines will dilute slightly. If you then paint over them, the lines will become more diluted and disappear.

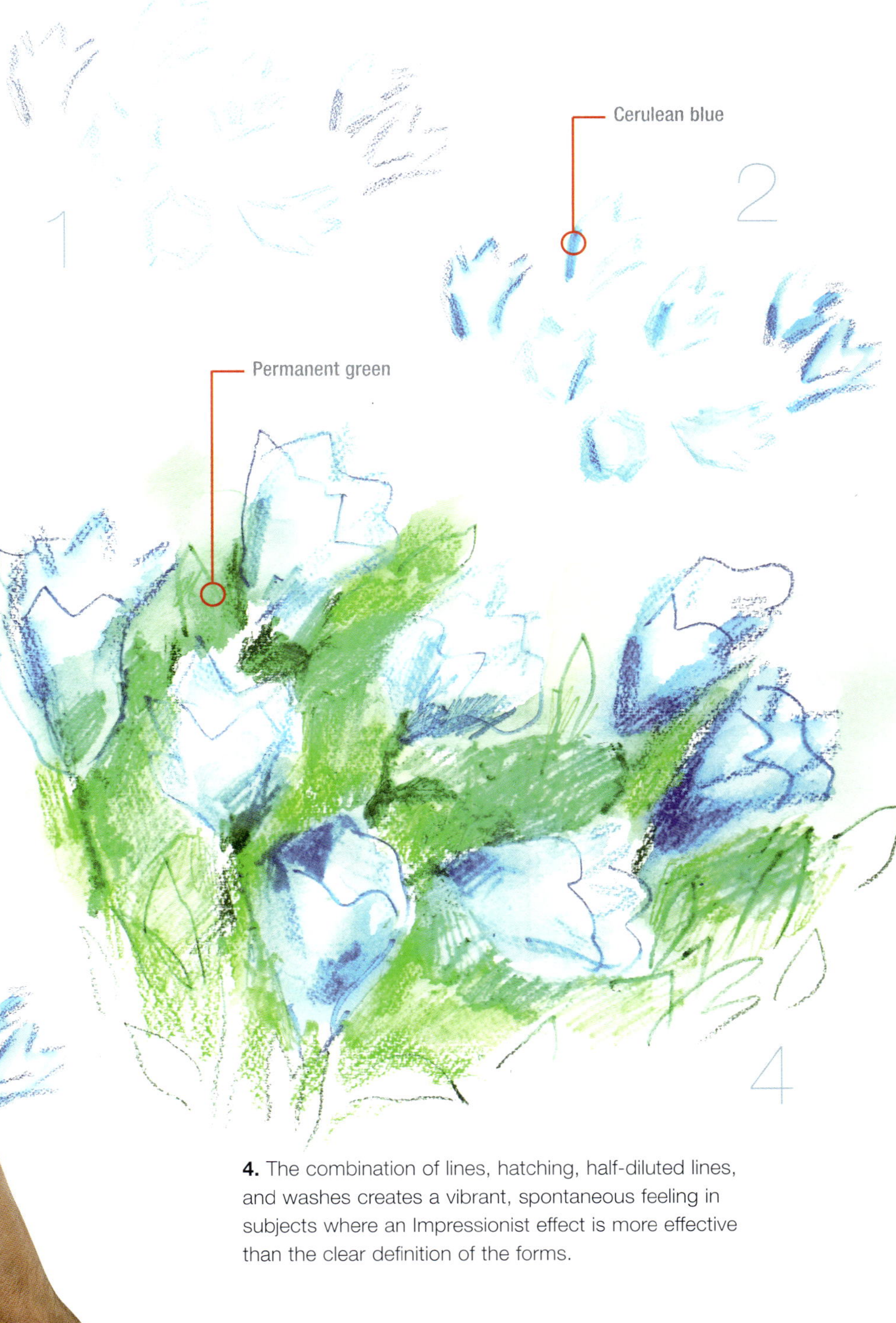

4. The combination of lines, hatching, half-diluted lines, and washes creates a vibrant, spontaneous feeling in subjects where an Impressionist effect is more effective than the clear definition of the forms.

LEVEL OF DIFFICULTY
★★
COLORS
Cadmium red
Cadmium yellow
Cerulean blue
Cobalt violet
Permanent red
Permanent green
BRUSHES
Medium round natural hair
Wide flat natural hair
PAPER
140 lb medium-rough texture

Unconventional methods usually render unexpected results, which can be as interesting as those shown here. It is a matter of drawing not at the beginning but at the end of the process. The drawing, done with a brush, becomes a way of organizing the free and abstract washes that were applied at the beginning.

1

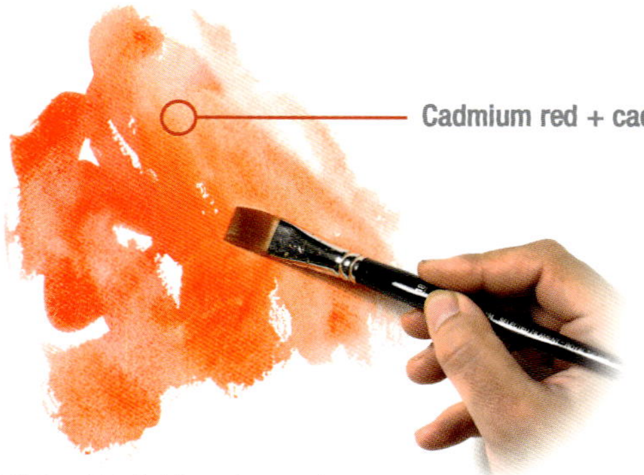

Cadmium red + cadmium yellow

1. With the wide flat brush create a large random area of red paint. Use a lot of paint and water so the wash will be large.

2

Permanent red

2. Spatter the surface with more water, with red paint, then with yellow. Then brush first with paint and then with water on the painted surface. The colors will spread and run freely.

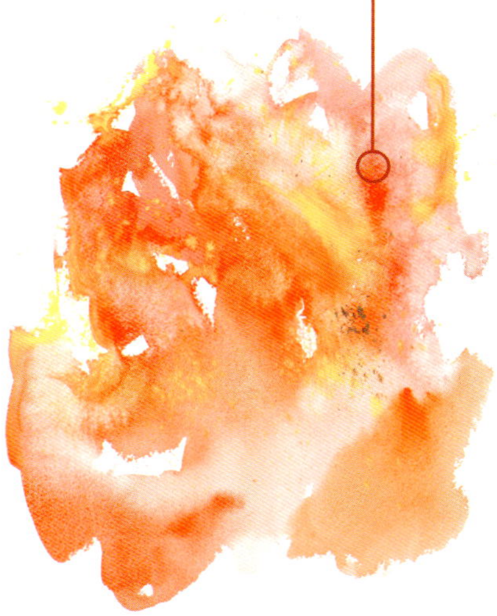

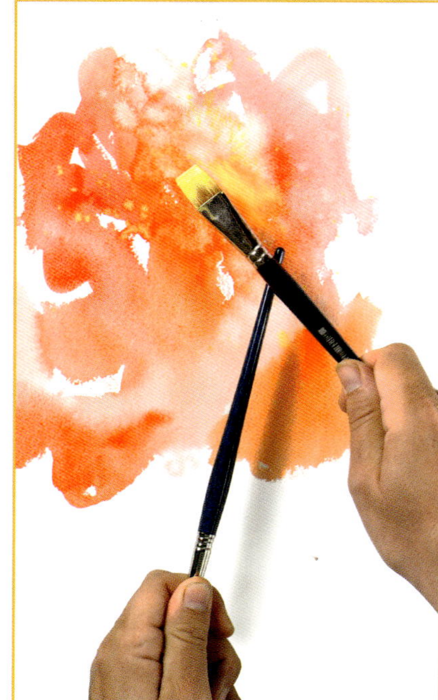

To create and control the spattering, charge the brush well with paint, hold it at the end of the handle, and tap it with the handle of another brush. The closer both of them are to the surface of the paper the easier it will be to control the dispersion of paint.

3

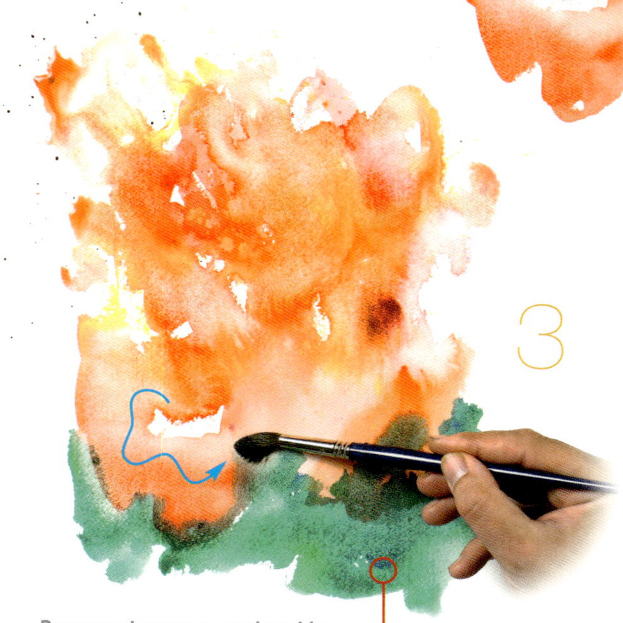

3. Paint around the bottom edge with permanent green mixed with cerulean blue to enliven the large red area. Use a lot of paint and make it as saturated as possible.

Permanent green + cerulean blue

4. In the areas where green has come into contact with the red there will be puddles caused by working wet on wet. This will add color variations and enrich the finished work.

5. Using the medium round brush, draw the outlines of flowers of different shapes and sizes in saturated violet, red, and blue tones. Use a high quality round brush with a good tip.

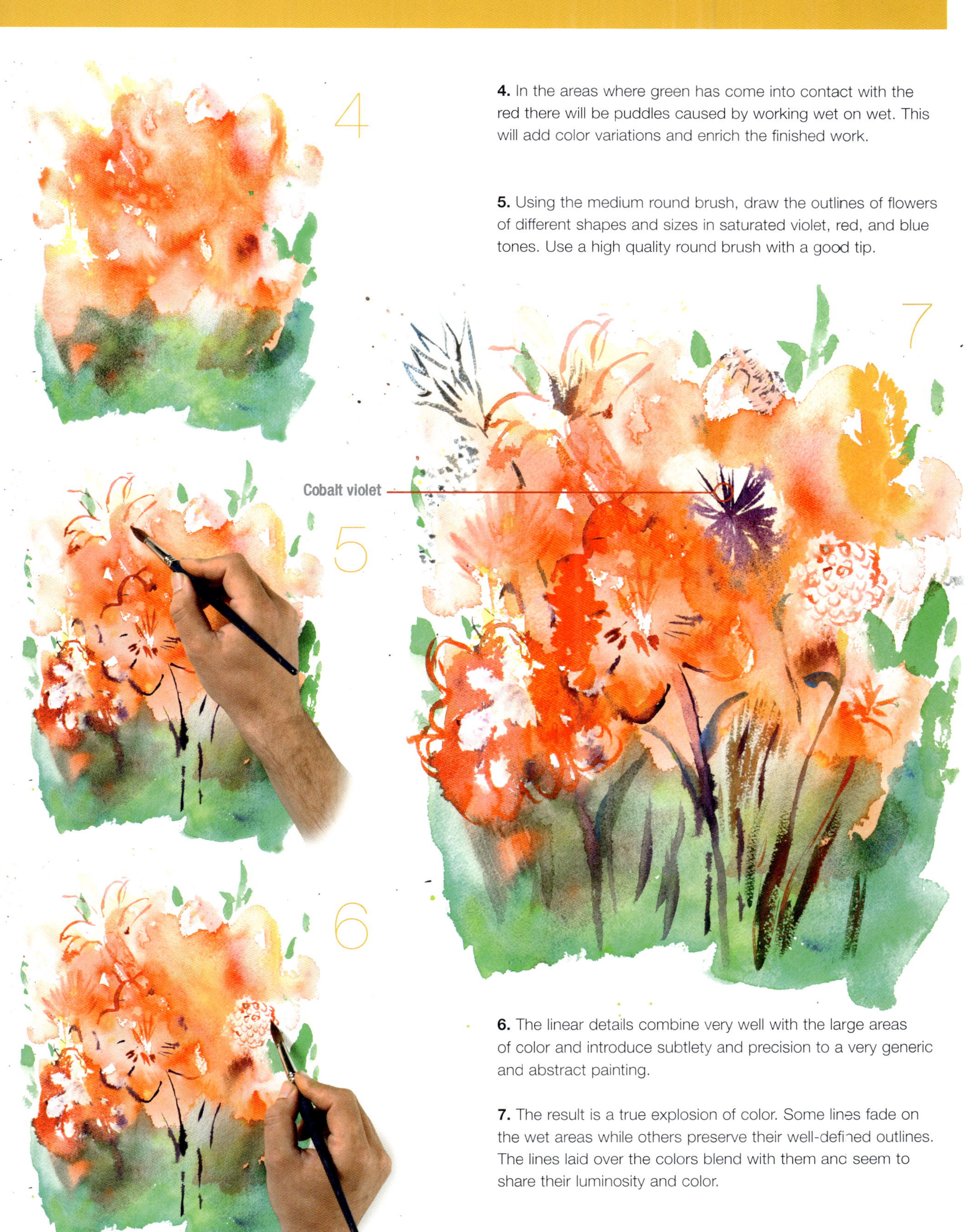

6. The linear details combine very well with the large areas of color and introduce subtlety and precision to a very generic and abstract painting.

7. The result is a true explosion of color. Some lines fade on the wet areas while others preserve their well-defined outlines. The lines laid over the colors blend with them and seem to share their luminosity and color.

Detailed Drawing with a Marker

LEVEL OF DIFFICULTY
★
COLORS
Yellow ochre
Sap green
Ultramarine blue
Black fine-tip marker with waterproof ink
BRUSH
Wide flat synthetic hair
PAPER
140 lb medium-rough texture

Some subjects require the use of other tools. This vase decorated with figurative motifs seems to need a meticulous representation of them. You will use a fine-tip black marker with waterproof ink, like those used for writing.

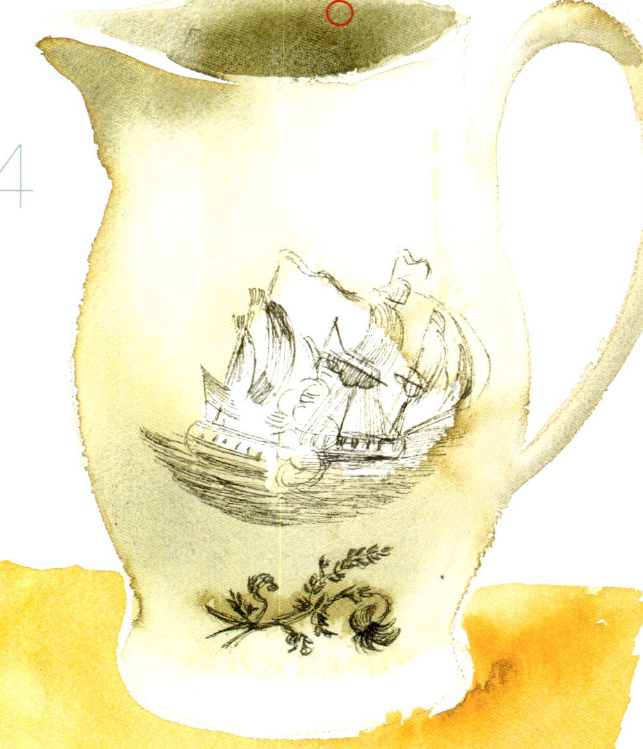

1. First draw the jar. The most difficult part is capturing the symmetrical shape of the container. To do this, draw one side with a single line, and then try to reproduce its curves on the other.

2. With a flat wide synthetic hair brush indicate the modeling with a few strokes, covering the entire container with a mixture of ochre and a little green.

3. Paint the mouth of the jar in a darker tone. Use the same colors, but add ultramarine blue to the mixture.

4. The process is very simple. The detailed decoration is integrated into the modeling of the jar, adding a graphic aspect that has a freshness in the finished painting.

LEVEL OF DIFFICULTY
★
COLORS
Cerulean blue
Cadmium orange
Blue, red, and brown watercolor pencils
BRUSH
Medium round natural hair
PAPER
140 lb medium-rough texture

Watercolor pencils are usually used for small details or decorating objects represented in the watercolor. In this exercise, they are used to resolve the painted decoration on a toy horse.

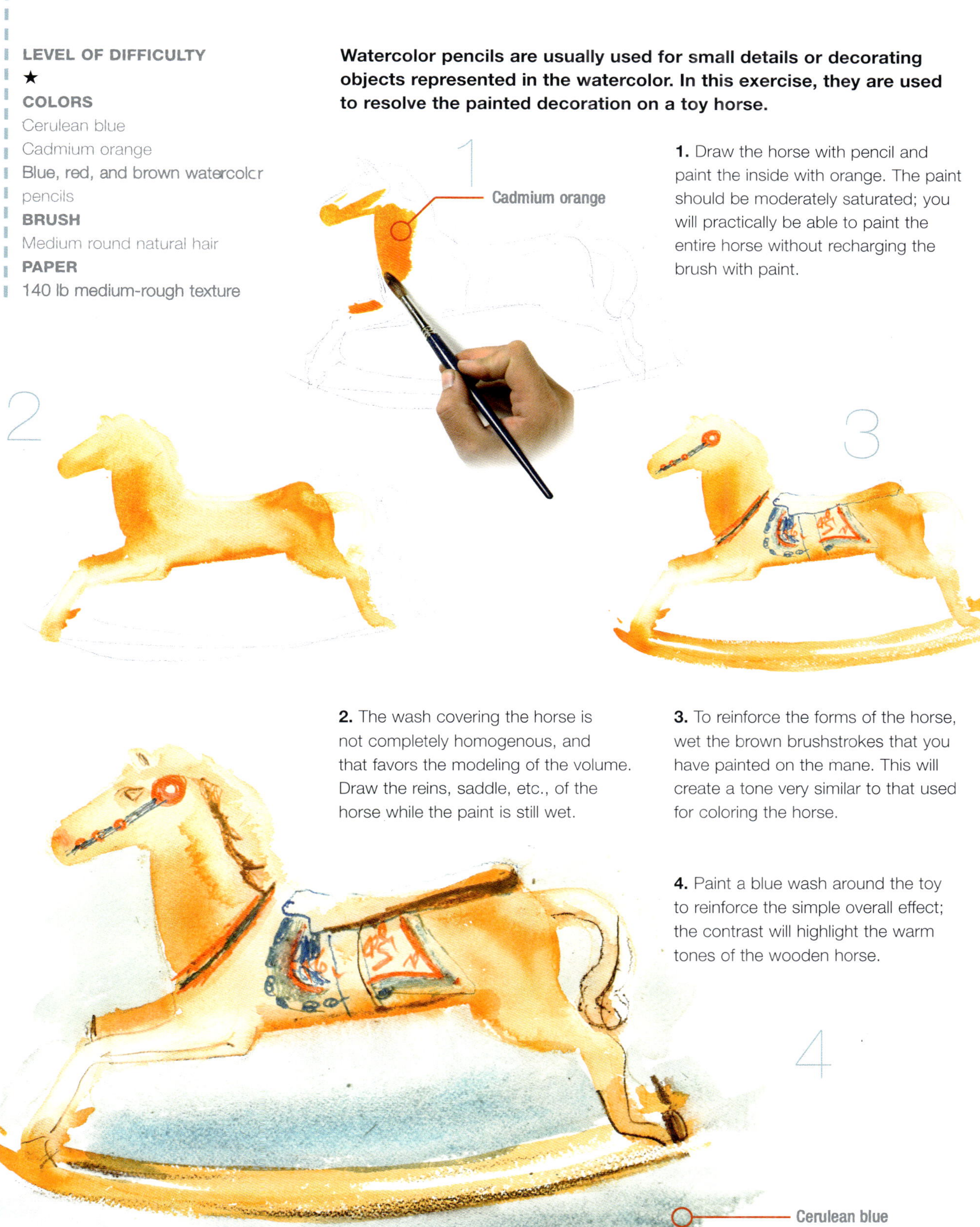

1. Draw the horse with pencil and paint the inside with orange. The paint should be moderately saturated; you will practically be able to paint the entire horse without recharging the brush with paint.

2. The wash covering the horse is not completely homogenous, and that favors the modeling of the volume. Draw the reins, saddle, etc., of the horse while the paint is still wet.

3. To reinforce the forms of the horse, wet the brown brushstrokes that you have painted on the mane. This will create a tone very similar to that used for coloring the horse.

4. Paint a blue wash around the toy to reinforce the simple overall effect; the contrast will highlight the warm tones of the wooden horse.

37 Drawing and Color / **Loose Brushstrokes**

LEVEL OF DIFFICULTY
★★
COLORS
Cadmium yellow
Cadmium orange
Cerulean blue
Permanent red
Permanent green
BRUSH
Wide flat synthetic hair
PAPER
140 lb medium-rough texture

Emphasizing the brushstroke always causes it to be less delicate and subtle, but it gains in energy and liveliness. That is what this exercise is about, where we lay out a simple schematic landscape with a few brushstrokes, using very bright and saturated colors. Here the drawing and the paint are the same thing.

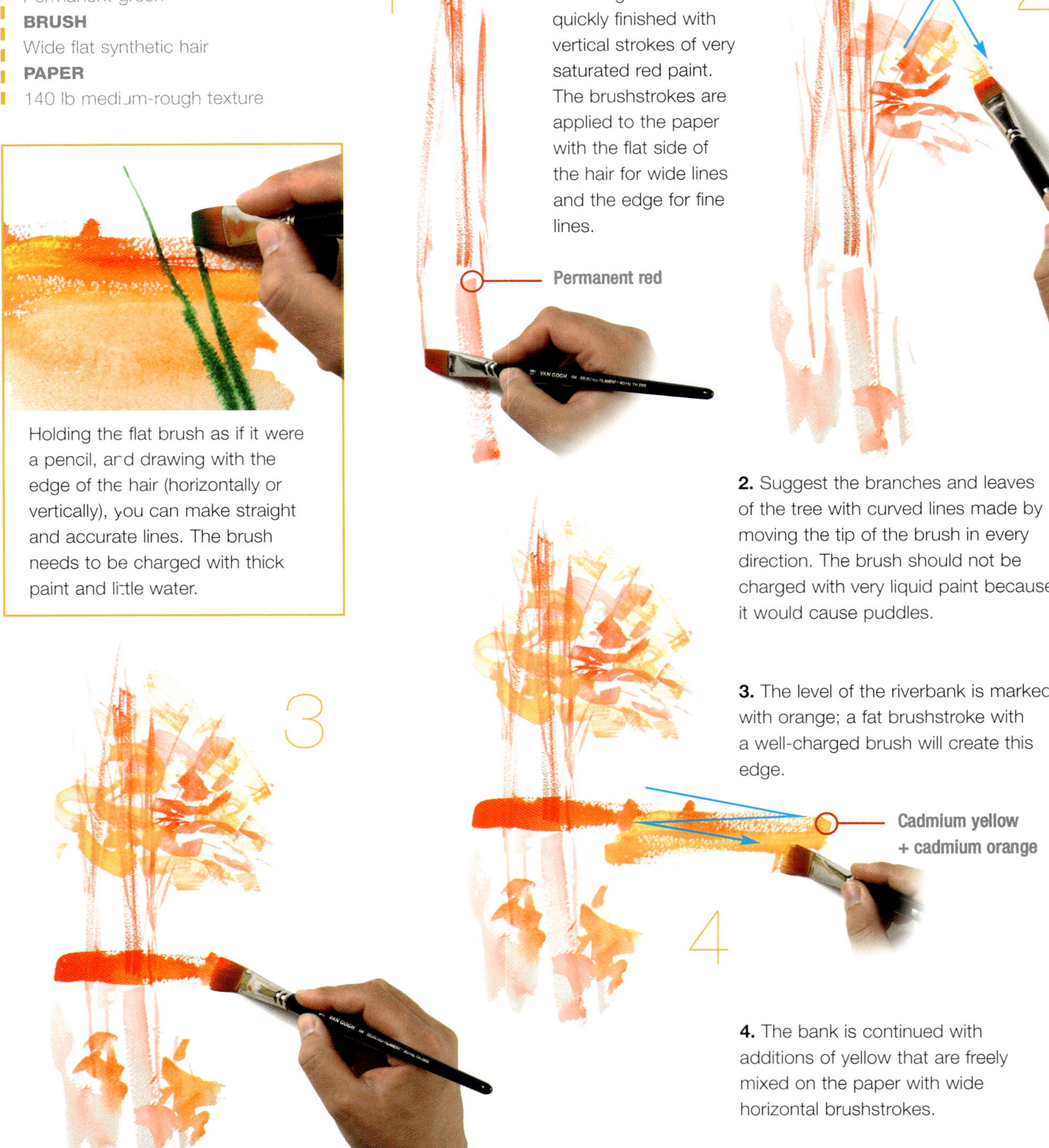

Holding the flat brush as if it were a pencil, and drawing with the edge of the hair (horizontally or vertically), you can make straight and accurate lines. The brush needs to be charged with thick paint and little water.

1. The tree trunks in the foreground are quickly finished with vertical strokes of very saturated red paint. The brushstrokes are applied to the paper with the flat side of the hair for wide lines and the edge for fine lines.

2. Suggest the branches and leaves of the tree with curved lines made by moving the tip of the brush in every direction. The brush should not be charged with very liquid paint because it would cause puddles.

3. The level of the riverbank is marked with orange; a fat brushstroke with a well-charged brush will create this edge.

4. The bank is continued with additions of yellow that are freely mixed on the paper with wide horizontal brushstrokes.

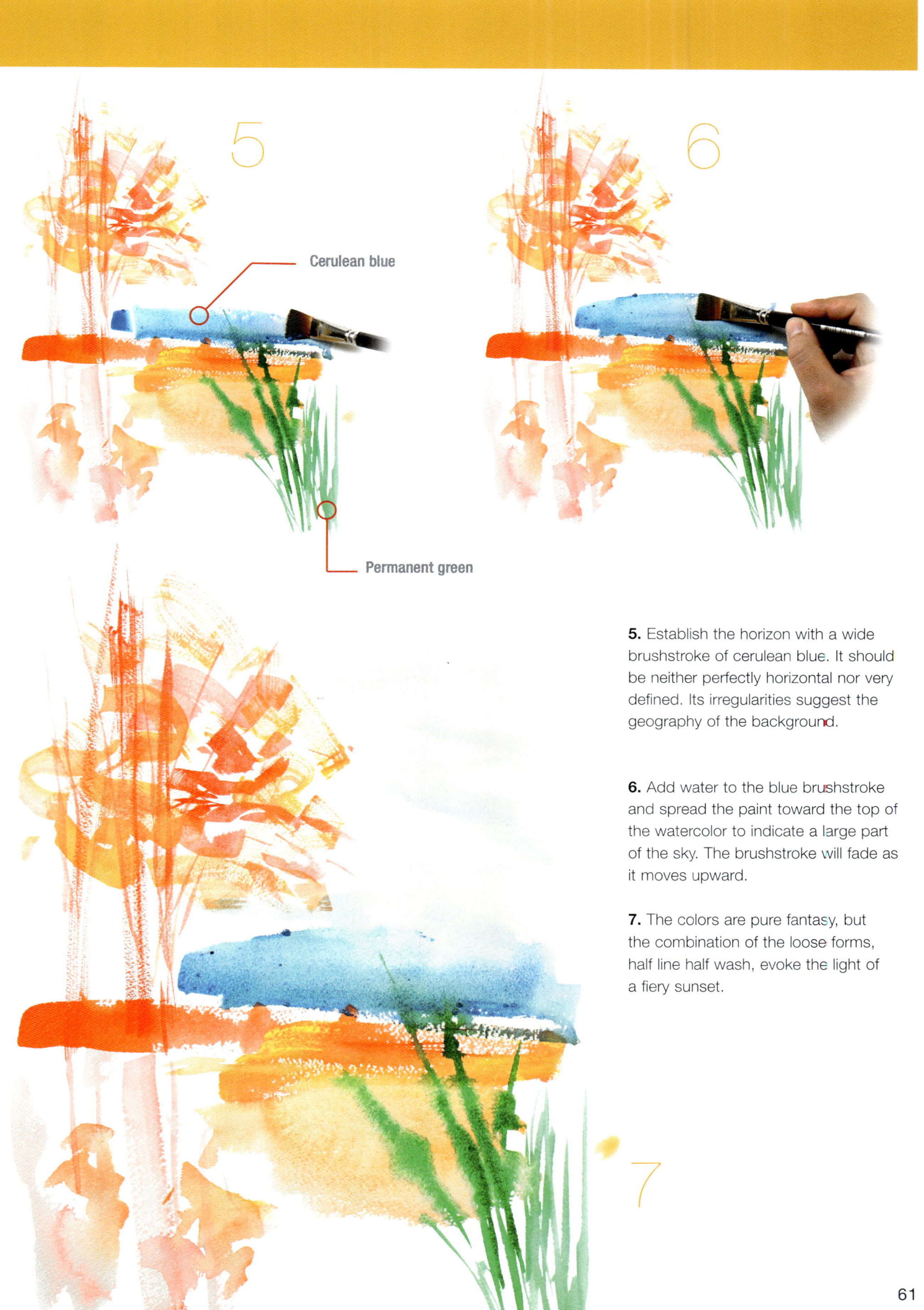

5. Establish the horizon with a wide brushstroke of cerulean blue. It should be neither perfectly horizontal nor very defined. Its irregularities suggest the geography of the background.

6. Add water to the blue brushstroke and spread the paint toward the top of the watercolor to indicate a large part of the sky. The brushstroke will fade as it moves upward.

7. The colors are pure fantasy, but the combination of the loose forms, half line half wash, evoke the light of a fiery sunset.

38 Drawing and Color / **Drawing with a Watercolor Marker**

LEVEL OF DIFFICULTY
★
COLORS
Permanent red
Violet fine-tip watercolor marker
BRUSH
Medium round natural hair
PAPER
140 lb medium-rough texture

Fine-tip markers with water-soluble colors can be combined with watercolors; the results can be very interesting graphically. The color of the watercolors is affected by the color of the marker, and the fine lines are sensitive and very suggestive.

1. Draw the insect as simply as you can, with just a few lines. You can draw with a pencil first if you are not comfortable with using the marker directly.

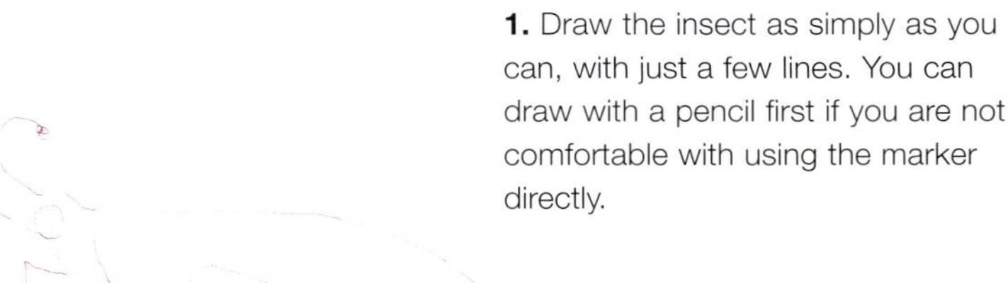

2. Wet the area of the wings, and color them with a brush full of red paint. As you spread the paint to the edges the lines are diluted and affect the red, creating a color that is darker than the red.

3. After painting the entire insect you can retouch some of the outlines, the eyes, and the antennas, to keep it from looking like a solid, compact mass.

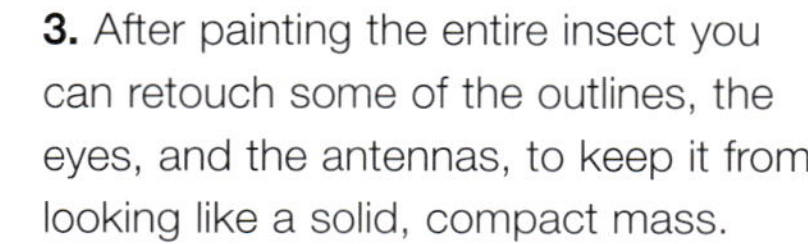

4. Paint the branch with very light red, which will allow the violet lines to be seen clearly and stand out from the red paint.

LEVEL OF DIFFICULTY
★★

COLORS
Ultramarine blue
Burnt sienna
Conventional marker

BRUSH
Wide flat synthetic hair

PAPER
140 lb medium-rough texture

Conventional marker ink is diluted in water, so the lines will be visible. You can use this to the advantage of the watercolor if you work boldly, carrying the washes of color past the edges of the drawing.

1. Make a simple drawing of a pair of tennis shoes, without too many extra lines. You can make the lines with a pencil first if necessary.

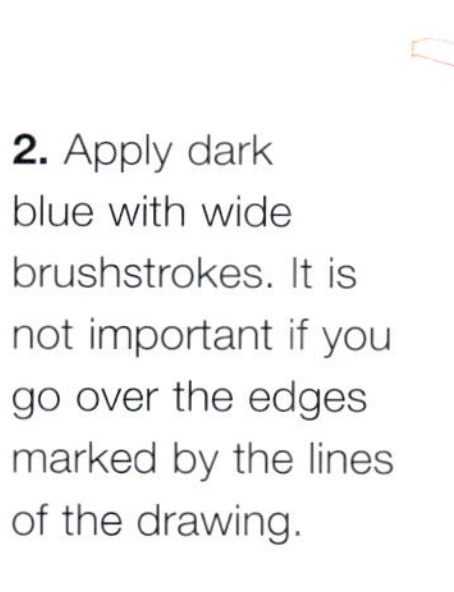

2. Apply dark blue with wide brushstrokes. It is not important if you go over the edges marked by the lines of the drawing.

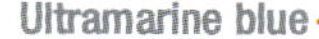

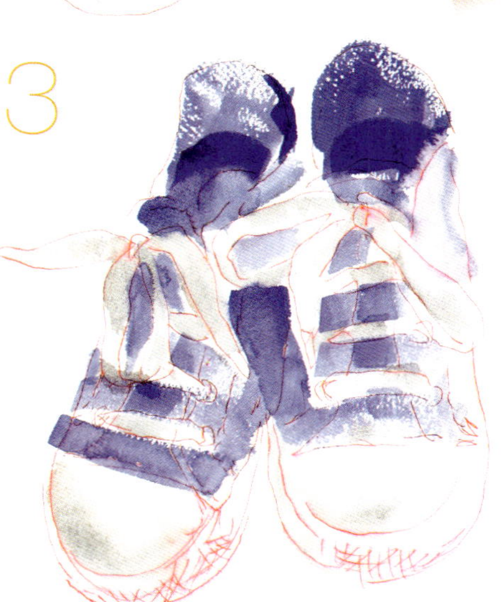

3. Cover the upper area of the tennis shoes with very light blue to suggest light shading.

4. Finally, paint the line that follows the toe with a mixture of dark blue and burnt sienna. This final line can be made with the corner or edge of the brush.

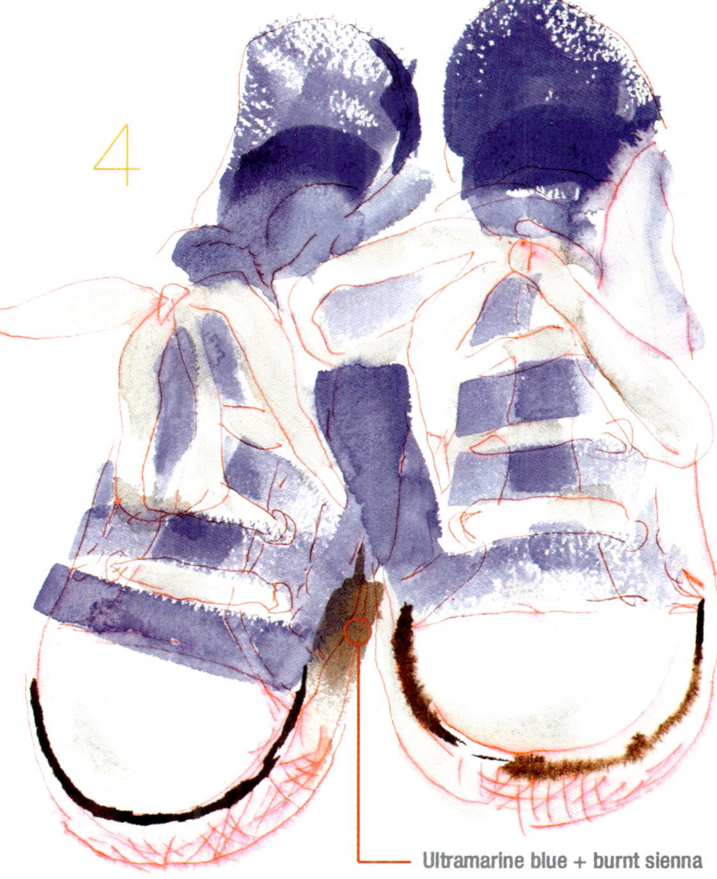

LEVEL OF DIFFICULTY
★
COLORS
Permanent red
Burnt umber
Charcoal pencil
BRUSH
Medium round natural hair
PAPER
140 lb medium-rough texture

When used in moderation, a charcoal pencil combines well with watercolors, although it is easy to muddy the colors if you do not work carefully. In this exercise, the charcoal is used only for the gray and black tones of the bird's plumage.

1. Draw the bird in pencil, and then make a few groups of light lines on the plumage to deposit some charcoal on the paper.

2. Begin diluting the charcoal lines with a wet brush, spreading them along the back of the bird. Draw more lines as you go to reinforce the darkest areas, then blend them with the washes.

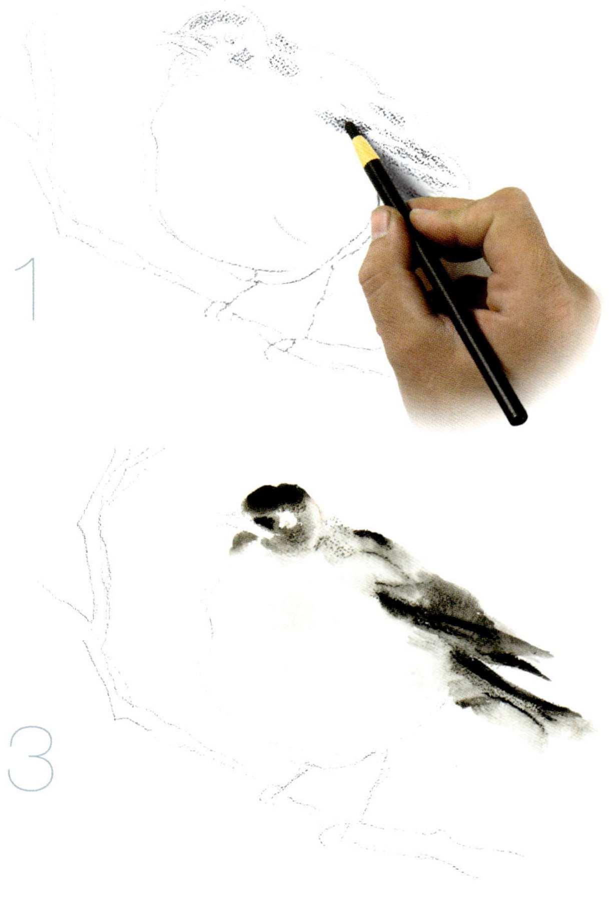

3. When the water dries, the charcoal will be relatively stable on the paper; this is the time to wet the rest of the bird's body before continuing to paint.

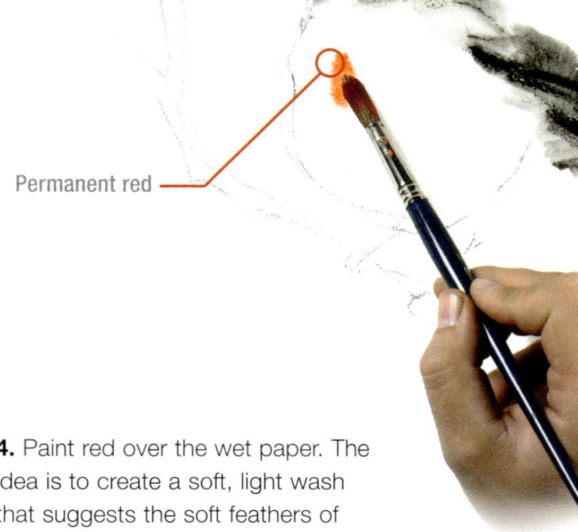

Lines drawn with charcoal on watercolor paper should be light. There are two reasons: by pressing too hard you can make an indentation in the paper that will later produce a mark, and because a mark that is too firm will not be completely diluted and will stay on the paper.

4. Paint red over the wet paper. The idea is to create a soft, light wash that suggests the soft feathers of the bird's breast.

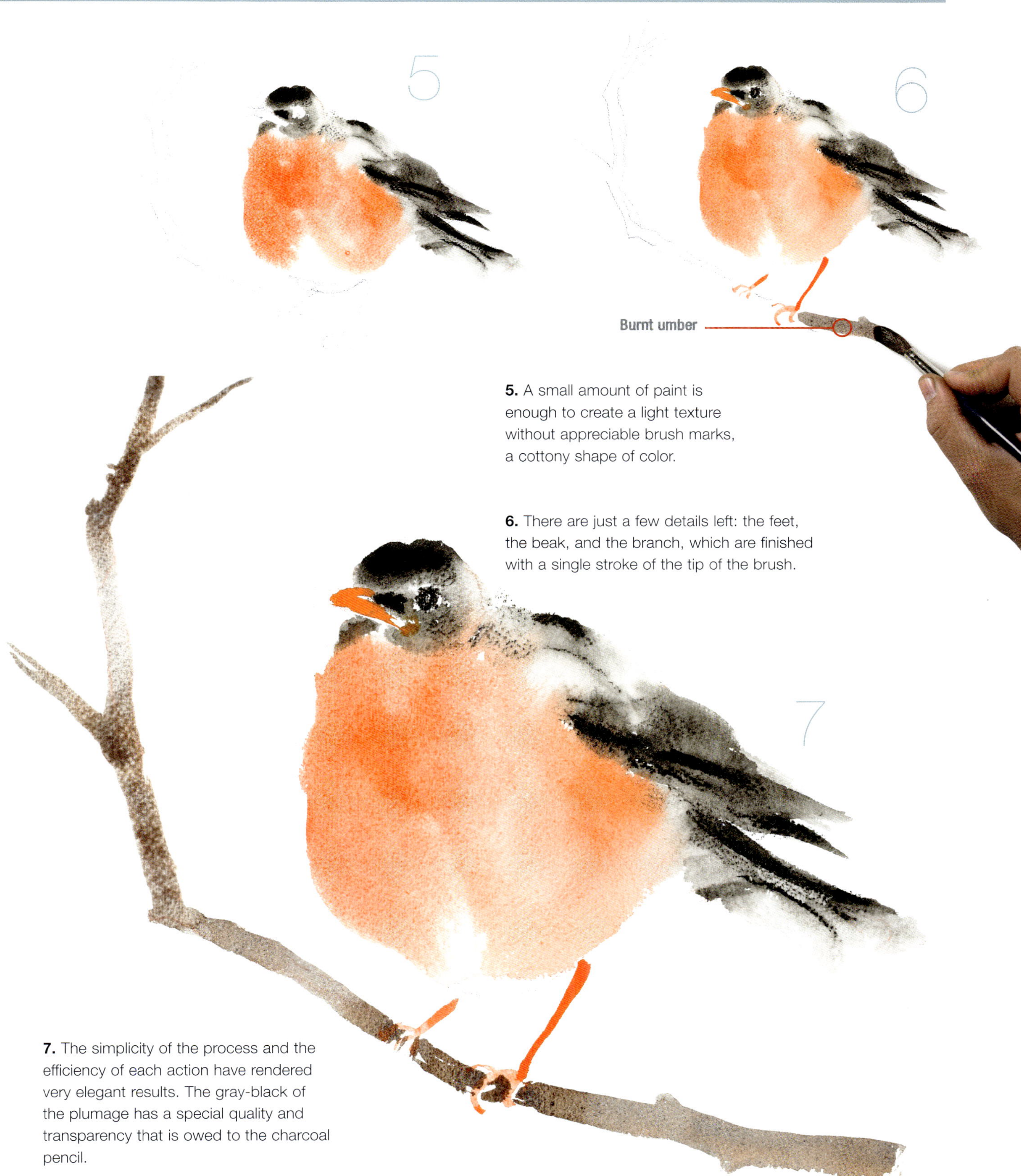

5. A small amount of paint is enough to create a light texture without appreciable brush marks, a cottony shape of color.

6. There are just a few details left: the feet, the beak, and the branch, which are finished with a single stroke of the tip of the brush.

7. The simplicity of the process and the efficiency of each action have rendered very elegant results. The gray-black of the plumage has a special quality and transparency that is owed to the charcoal pencil.

Reserves / Reserves as White Areas

LEVEL OF DIFFICULTY
★
COLORS
Cobalt blue
Burnt sienna
Yellow ochre
BRUSH
Medium round natural hair
PAPER
140 lb medium-rough texture

In watercolor, reserves are areas left unpainted that form an important part of the subject being painted. Here the reserves correspond to the white parts of this panda. The color becomes evident when it is surrounded by the other colors.

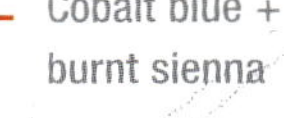

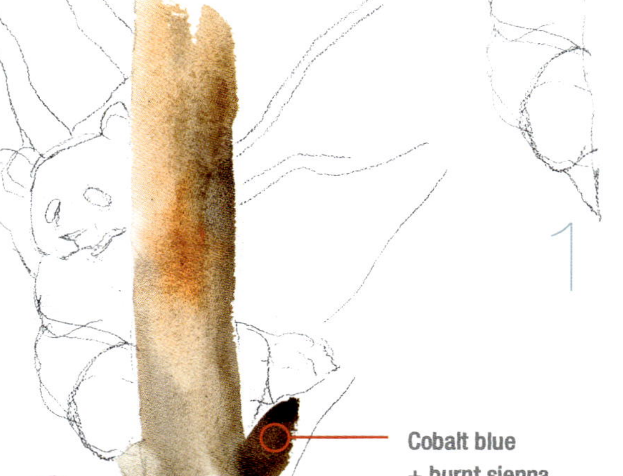

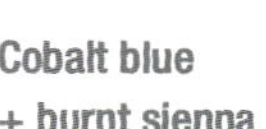

1. After drawing the subject, begin painting the large tree with a saturated mixture of blue and sienna. Apply it first to the center of the trunk, and then spread it toward the edges.

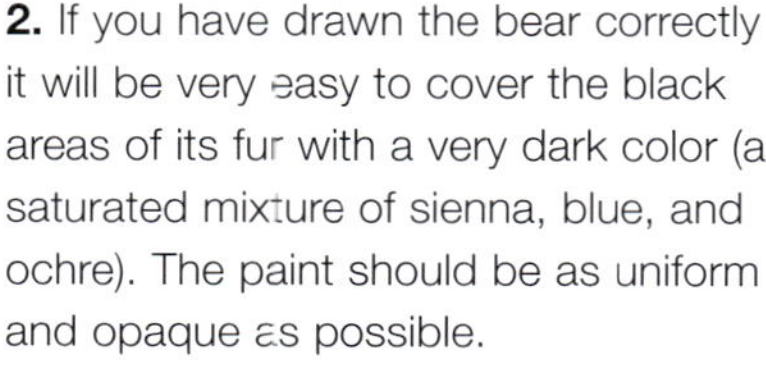

2. If you have drawn the bear correctly it will be very easy to cover the black areas of its fur with a very dark color (a saturated mixture of sienna, blue, and ochre). The paint should be as uniform and opaque as possible.

3. Once the black areas have been painted, it is time to paint the tree branches. Use the brush as if it were a drawing tool.

4. The blue sky makes the reserved white paper stand out. Now there are no unfinished parts, since they can be seen as the areas of white fur on the panda.

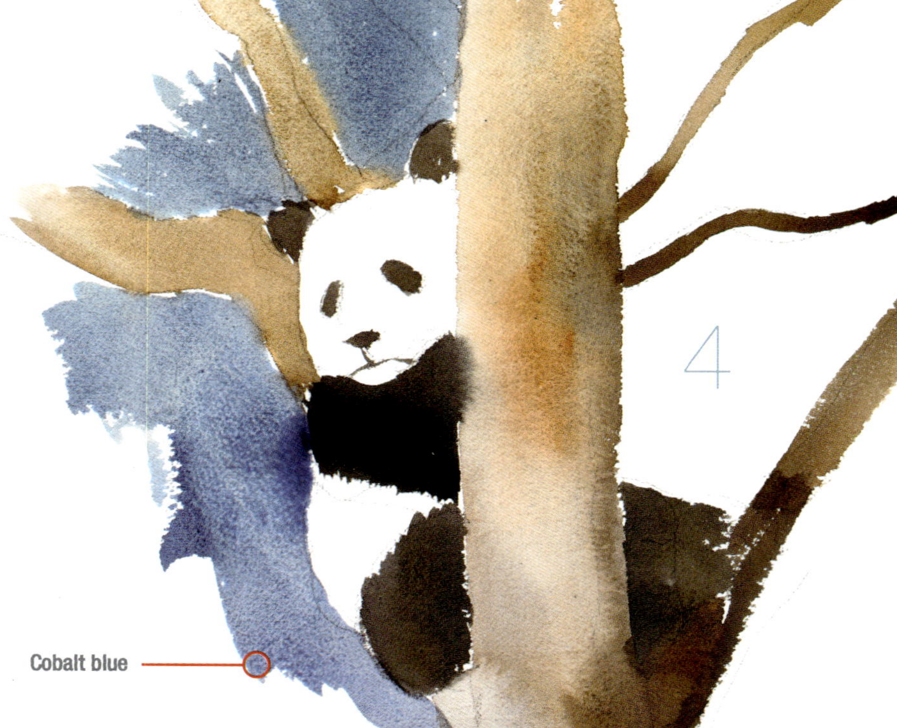

Reserves / **Reserves as Illuminated Areas**

LEVEL OF DIFFICULTY
★
COLORS
Cobalt blue
Cerulean blue
Sap green
Permanent green
Carmine
BRUSH
Medium round natural hair
PAPER
140 lb medium-rough texture

A frequent use of the reserve technique consists of leaving areas that correspond to brightly lit parts of the scene unpainted. In this subject, such areas are the large light-colored stone cliffs facing the light. They are left white until, at the very end of the process, you shade them with some light tones to suggest relief.

1. After drawing the outlines of the cliffs and the line of the horizon, paint the farthest hills with sap green. Apply brushstrokes of different intensities to create the effect of undulating terrain.

Sap green

1

Permanent green

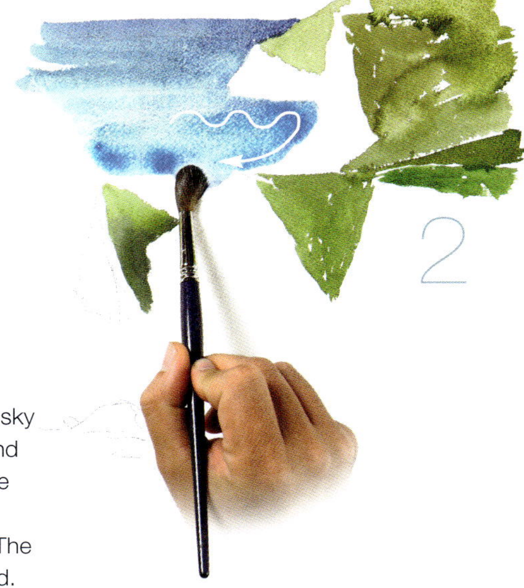

2. When painting the blues of the sea, a mixture of cobalt and cerulean with a large amount of water, leave the large faces of the cliffs in reserve, which are bordered at the top by the green areas.

3. After the sea is painted and the sky covered with a light wash, shade and add relief to the rocks left in reserve using light vertical brushstrokes of cobalt mixed with a little carmine. The brushstrokes should be very diluted.

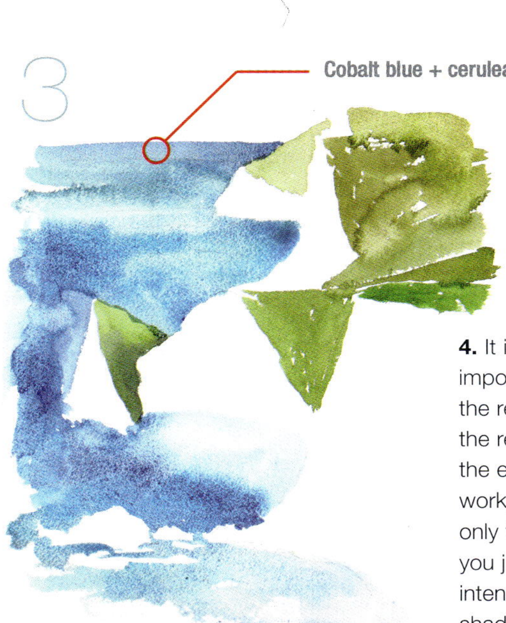

4

4. It is very important to leave the retouching of the reserves for the end of the work, because only then can you judge how intense the shading needs to be.

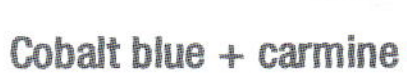

43 Reserves / **Reserves as Forms Against a Background**

LEVEL OF DIFFICULTY

★

COLORS

Cobalt blue
Cerulean blue
Ultramarine blue
Cadmium orange
Cadmium yellow
Permanent red
Carmine
Cobalt violet
Sap green
Burnt sienna

BRUSHES

Medium round natural hair
Wide flat synthetic hair

PAPER

140 lb medium-rough texture

When the motif consists of a series of elements with simple outlines on a background with a more or less uniform color, it is usual to paint the background first and leave the shapes of the objects as reserves to be painted later. The original subject of this watercolor (and the most immediate for any watercolorist) can be painted with this clear and simple approach.

1. This background with the reserved shapes can almost be painted without making a preliminary drawing. All of the shapes are variations of the outline of a tube of watercolor paint: large, medium, long, and short. The color of the background is a very light mixture of ultramarine blue and burnt sienna.

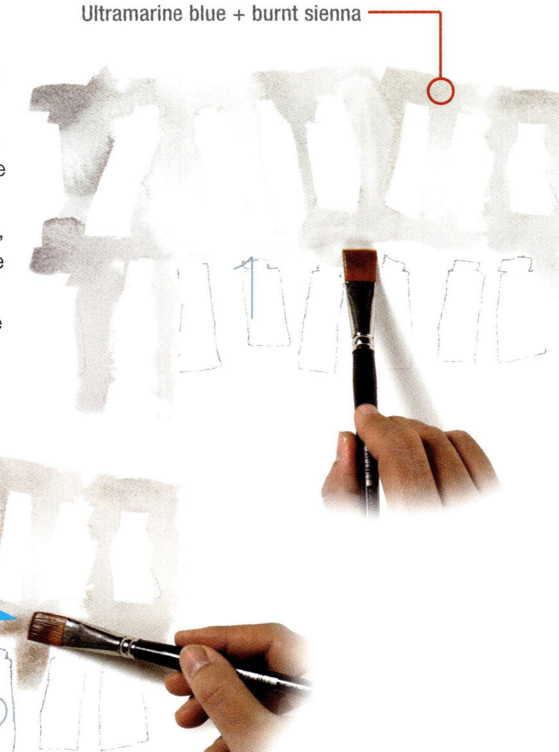

2. To avoid making a totally uniform mass of color, add dark shading in some areas, always with the flat brush, because it is easier to maintain the angled shapes.

3. It is not too important for the shapes of the tubes to be perfect; the deformations and kinks just show that they have been used. Draw the caps and folded bottoms of the tubes with a soft pencil.

4. Paint the colors as you like with the round brush. Most watercolorists use tubes from different manufacturers and of different designs. The variety keeps it from looking like a catalogue color sheet.

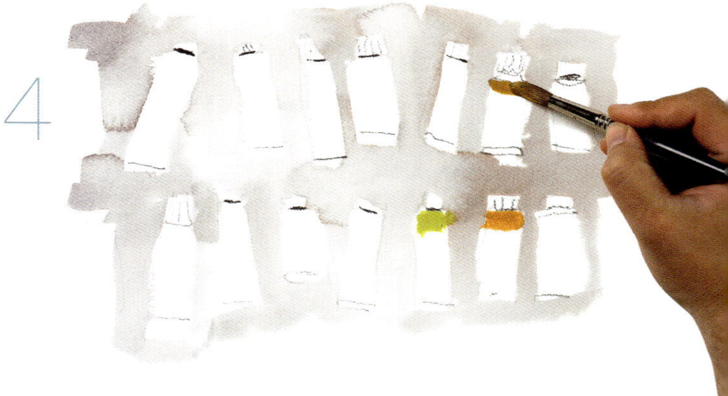

5. Here all the tubes have been painted. In some cases the paint has run when it came into contact with the wet background. The effect is spontaneous and suggests the inevitable disorder of the materials during the work session.

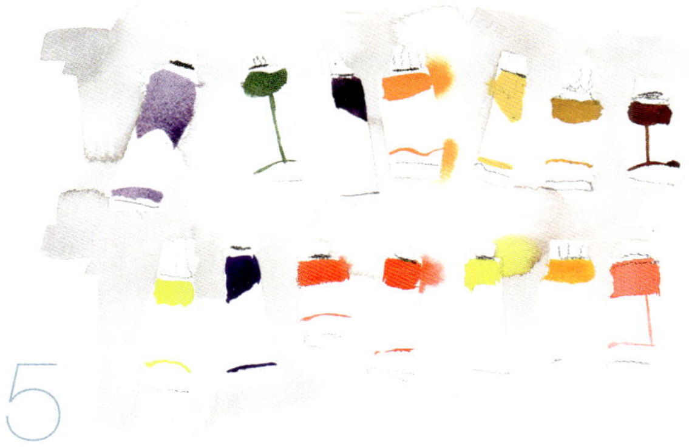

5

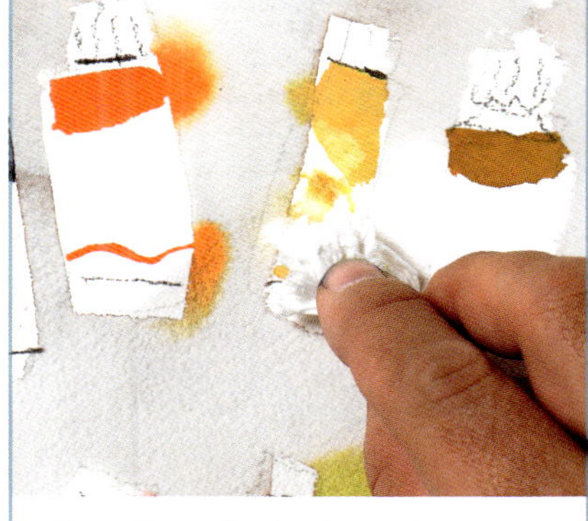

Sometimes the best way to represent a messy surface is to really mess it up. A piece of absorbent paper with nearly dry paint can be applied directly to some parts of the watercolor to create such an effect.

6. Using a more saturated mixture of the colors used for the background, paint small bands alongside the tubes with the tip of the brush to suggest shadows. This will separate the tubes from the background and add relief.

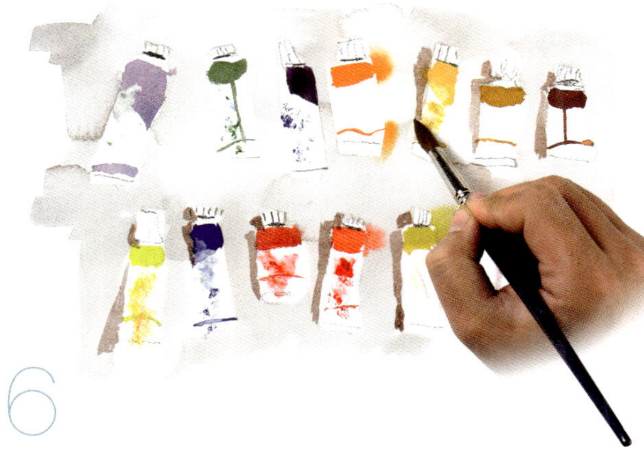

6

7. The shadows and washes spread around the paper emphasize the realism of the representation, while at the same time you have kept the painting as simple as possible.

7

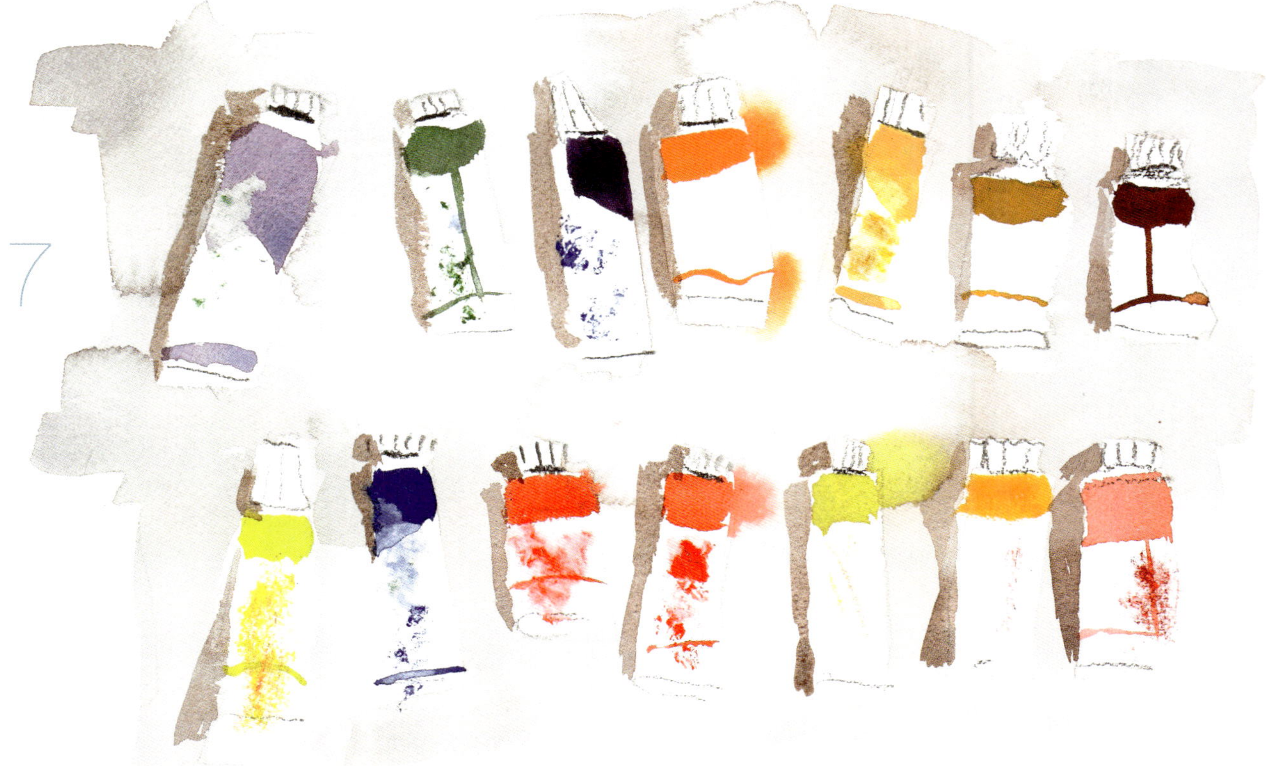

Reserves / **Negative and Positive**

LEVEL OF DIFFICULTY
★
COLORS
Permanent green
Sap green
Yellow ochre
BRUSH
Medium round natural hair
PAPER
140 lb medium-rough texture

In this exercise you will create an interesting effect of symmetry achieved by contrasting white reserves ("negative") with very dark, almost "black" painting ("positive"). This dramatic contrast of light and shadow is balanced with the necessary intermediate tones to create a gradual movement from one to the other.

1. First paint the outside leaves, which will act as a screen against which the reserved grapes will be visible. These are painted "in negative," with permanent green mixed with ochre in the lightest areas.

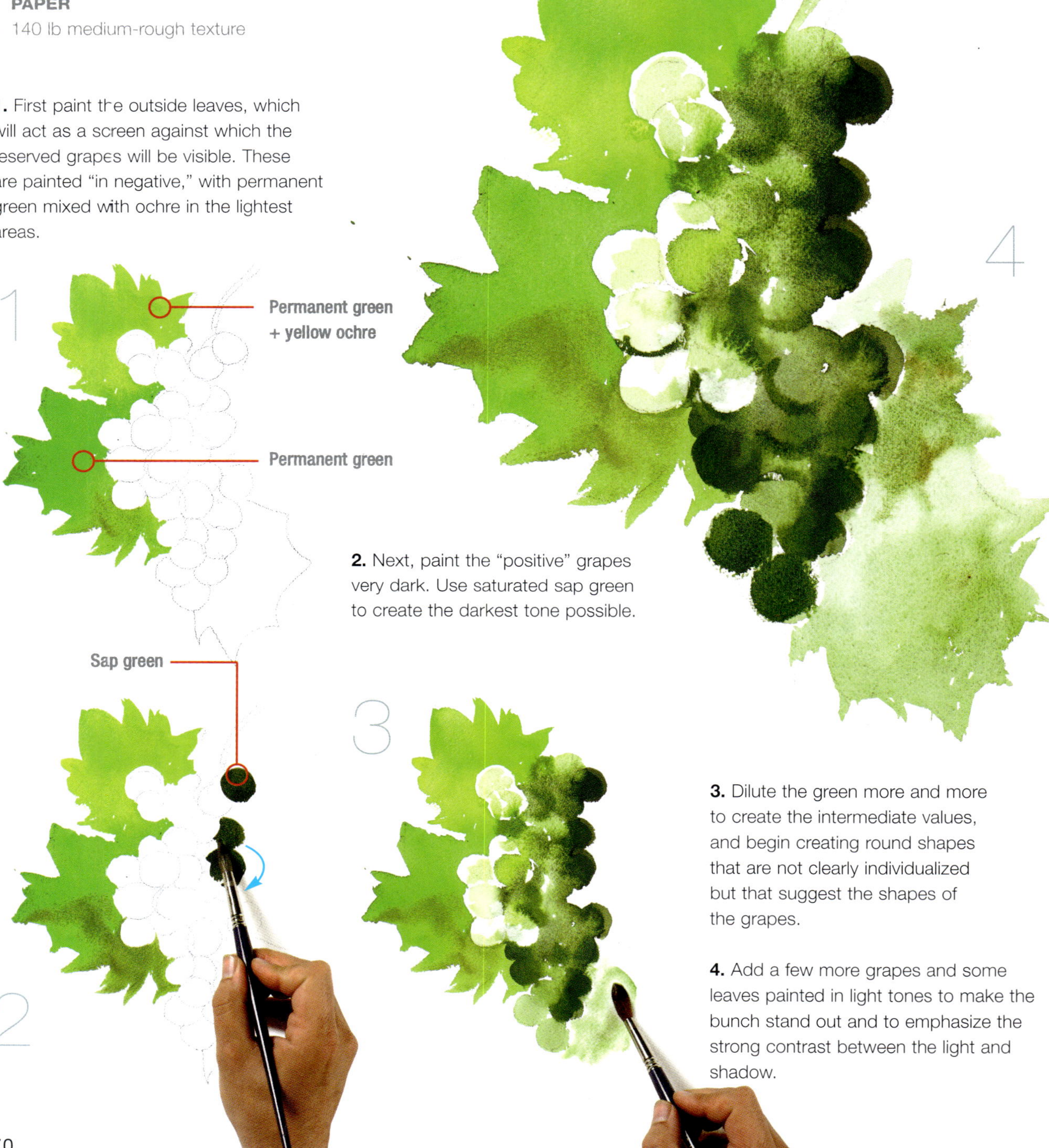

2. Next, paint the "positive" grapes very dark. Use saturated sap green to create the darkest tone possible.

3. Dilute the green more and more to create the intermediate values, and begin creating round shapes that are not clearly individualized but that suggest the shapes of the grapes.

4. Add a few more grapes and some leaves painted in light tones to make the bunch stand out and to emphasize the strong contrast between the light and shadow.

45 Reserves / White for Atmospheric Effects

LEVEL OF DIFFICULTY
★
COLORS
Sap green
Ultramarine blue
Cobalt blue
Cerulean blue
Burnt sienna
Black watercolor pencil
BRUSHES
Medium round natural hair
Medium flat synthetic hair
PAPER
140 lb medium-rough texture

Sometimes the reserves do not define forms or objects, just white "streaks" that fulfill an atmospheric function, like the fog or mist that is seen in some wetlands like those represented here. In this case, they are irregular and arbitrary reserves that appear here and there in the composition.

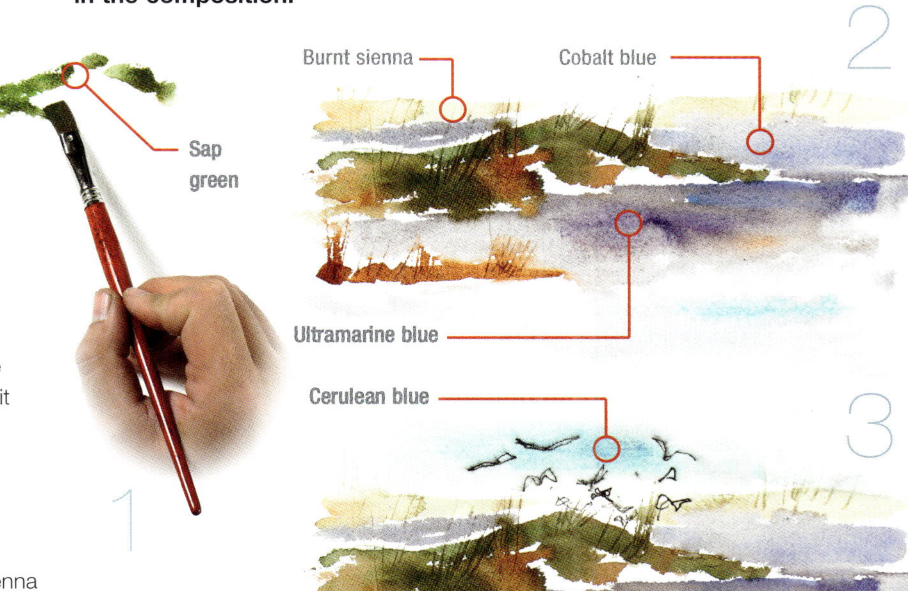

1. Apply some irregular strokes with the flat brush to represent a hill in the wetlands. Do not unify it completely; it is better to leave small separations in white to indicate abrupt irregularities in the terrain.

2. Paint the background very light sienna and draw a few lines with the handle of the brush on the wet paint to represent reeds and grasses. Now resolve the water with several different diluted blues.

3. Cover the sky with a very light cerulean blue, and add scribbled lines that look like birds that are flying and standing on the islands.

4. The reserves can be seen on the shore, and they break the continuity between the land and water, creating an atmospheric feeling.

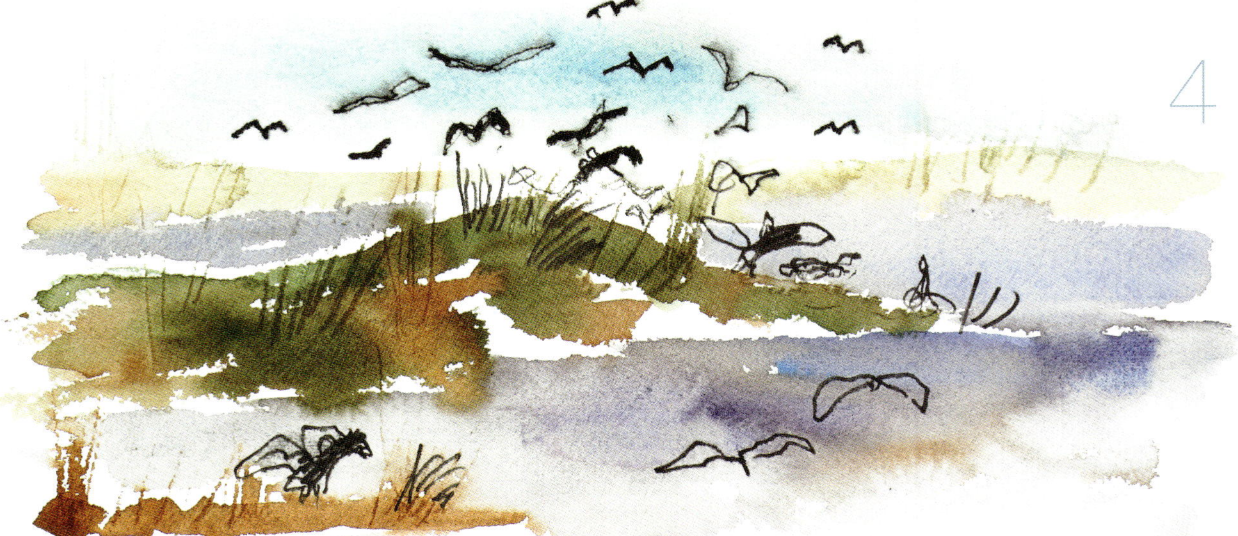

46 Reserves / **Reserves as Unfinished Areas**

LEVEL OF DIFFICULTY
★
COLORS
Cerulean blue
Permanent green
Sap green
Yellow ochre
BRUSH
Medium round natural hair
PAPER
140 lb medium-rough texture

Areas that are left unpainted can have a nonrepresentational function. This unfinished look suggests lightness and simplicity in the treatment, as well as making evident the method used in creating the painting. It is like a silence in a musical piece, a silence that can be as eloquent as sound.

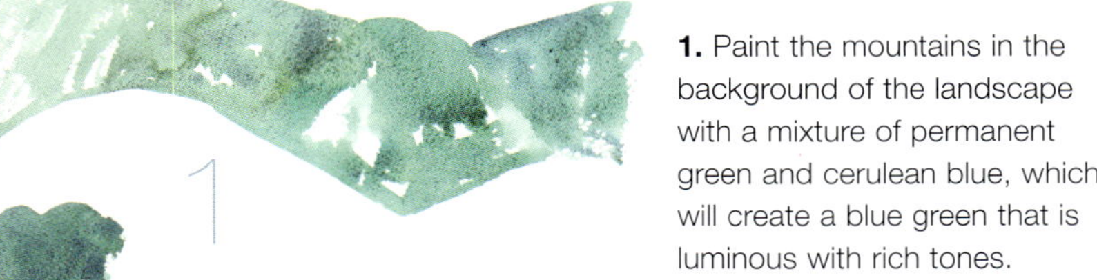

1. Paint the mountains in the background of the landscape with a mixture of permanent green and cerulean blue, which will create a blue green that is luminous with rich tones.

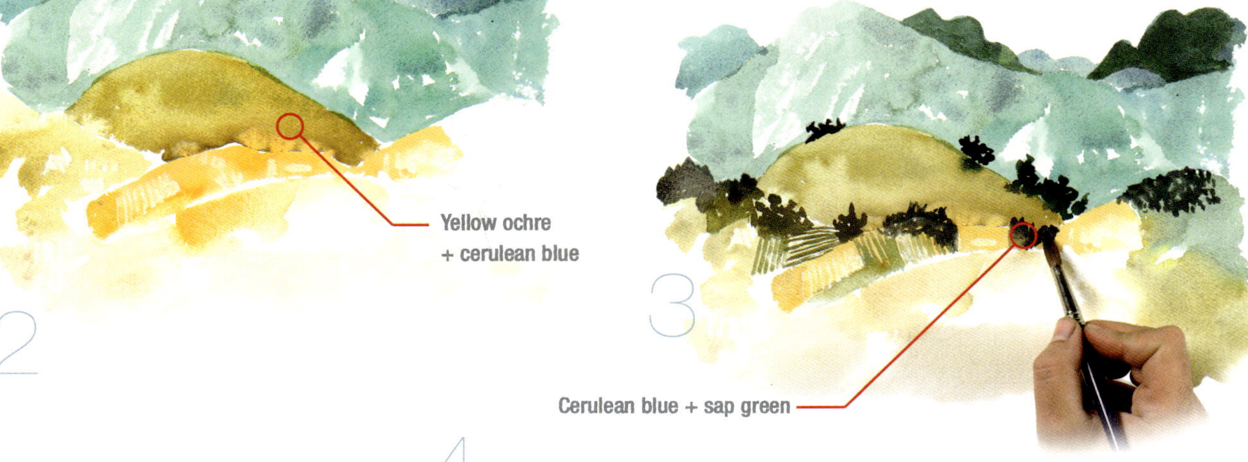

2. Use ochre mixed with a touch of blue to paint the hill, and spread large brushstrokes of pure ochre in the foreground of the landscape.

3. Now work with the tip of the brush to draw trees, bushes, and the edges and borders between cultivated fields. The color is a saturated mixture of blue and sap green. As you paint the nearest areas of the foreground, increase the amount of green in the mixture.

4. After filling the foreground with details, the contrast with the unpainted area becomes more interesting, especially because there is no color there, but there are houses and trees drawn with fine lines.

4

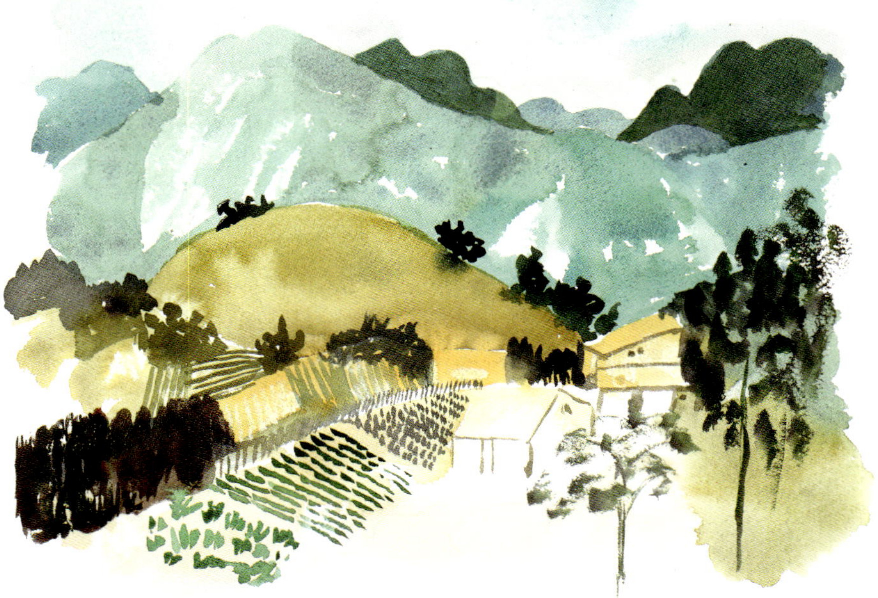

47 Reserves / **Reserves Made by Blotting**

LEVEL OF DIFFICULTY
★

COLORS
Permanent green
Yellow ochre
Cadmium orange
Cadmium red
Black watercolor pencil

BRUSHES
Medium round natural hair
Wide flat synthetic hair

PAPER
140 lb medium-rough texture

Reserves can be created afterward, when the paper has been covered with watercolor. While the paint is still wet you can absorb parts of it with absorbent paper. This effect, already shown in earlier exercises in this book, has the advantage of creating defined reserves on very large areas of paint that maintain the fresh nature of direct applications.

1. Spread a large wash of ochre mixed with a little green. The wash can be very large so that the brush slides easily across the paper.

Permanent green + yellow ochre

1

2. Absorb the paint and water from the wash in three areas of different sizes, and then paint the inside with orange. The irregular edges of the areas result from the irregularities of the paper.

2

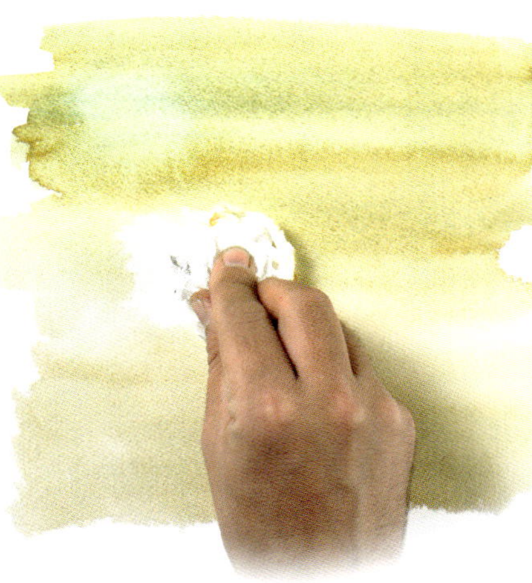

3. Cover the flowers with orange, and then draw some lines with a black watercolor pencil. The lines will spread when they are wet with the tip of a brush.

3

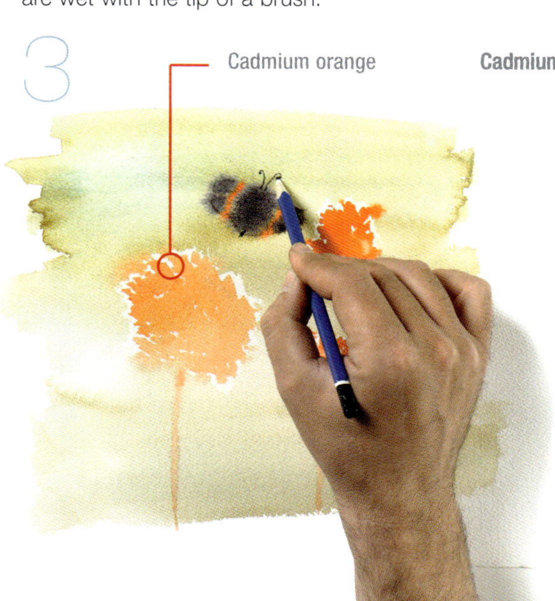

Cadmium orange

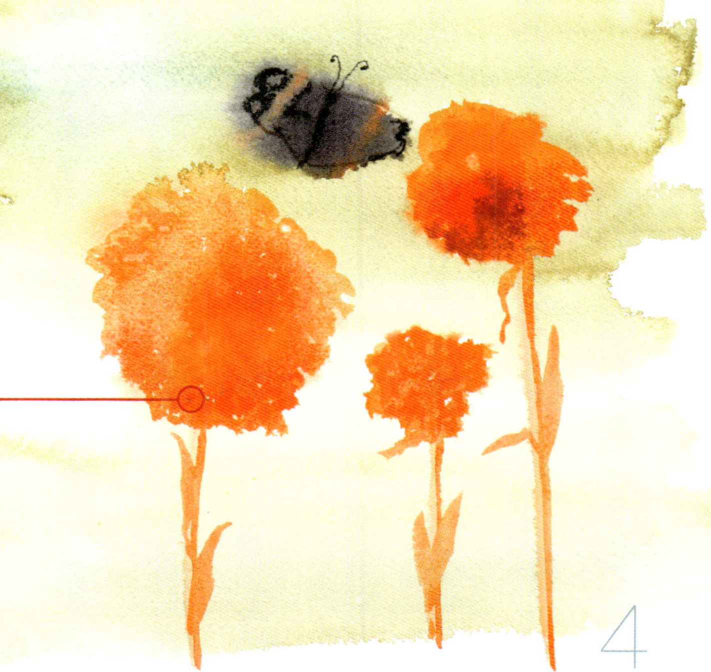

Cadmium red

4

4. Draw the outline of the butterfly making use of the effect of the paint running into the background color. Darken some orange areas with cadmium red, and finally, paint the stems of the flowers.

LEVEL OF DIFFICULTY
★

COLORS
Ultramarine blue
Burnt sienna
Permanent green

BRUSH
Medium round natural hair

PAPER
140 lb medium-rough texture

When you paint a watercolor using the monochromatic wash technique, the reserved areas become the lightest of the light values. If the monochrome is gray, as it is here, the reserve is the lightest "gray" in the scale that goes from black to white.

1

1. Define the table with the folds of the tablecloth. The gray brushstroke determines the angle and perspective of the table.

2

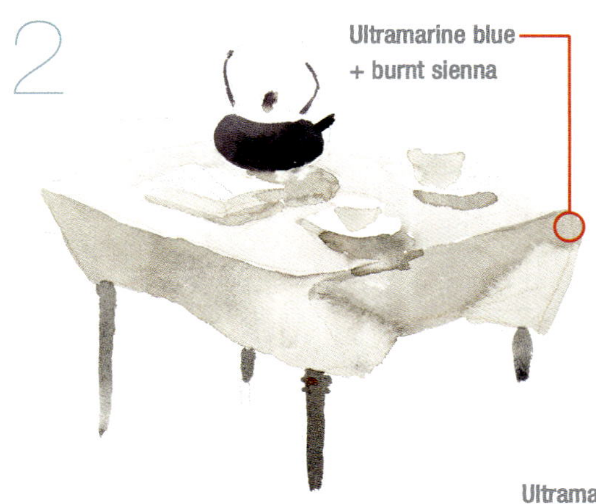

2. Draw the objects on the table with a white pencil. Feserve the cups, plates, and the book, and cover the rest (except for the dark accent of the teapot, which is painted with a darker wash than the tablecloth).

3. Paint the background with light strokes that define the wall, the window, and the long curtain very simply.

3

Ultramarine blue
+ permanent green

4

4. The small white reserves are enough to add relief to the objects and separate them from the light-gray values in the background of the composition.

49 Reserves / **A Large Reserve for the Subject**

LEVEL OF DIFFICULTY
★★

COLORS
Ultramarine blue
Cobalt violet
Permanent green
Burnt sienna
Cadmium red
Cadmium yellow

BRUSH
Medium round natural hair

PAPER
140 lb medium-rough texture

You can use reserves as a way to construct the subject, its lights and shadows, relief and volume. Starting with a large reserve, you will continue to shade with values and add colors. The initial large reserve allows you to preserve the luminosity of the theme to the end.

1

Ultramarine blue + burnt sienna

1. With no preliminary drawing, lay out the essence of the subject directly with large brushstrokes of diluted gray color mixed from ultramarine blue and burnt sienna.

2

3

Ultramarine blue + burnt sienna + cobalt violet

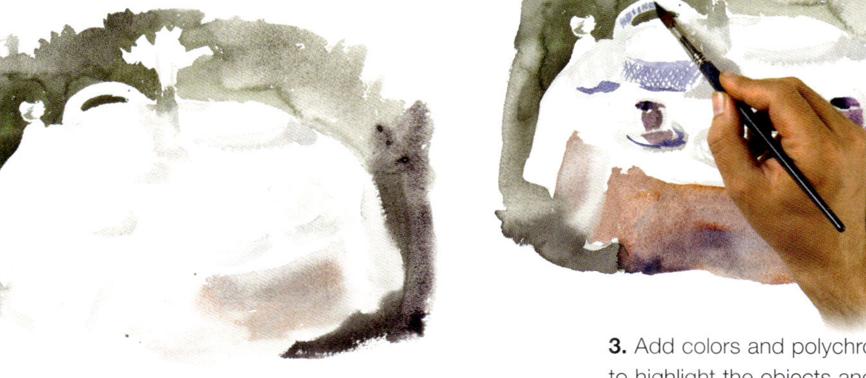

2. Paint a very dark background (ultramarine blue mixed with sienna and cobalt violet) and reserve the silhouette of the subject. The previous brushstrokes now seem like subtle shadows in the white reserve.

3. Add colors and polychrome shadows to highlight the objects and their details with the tip of the brush.

4

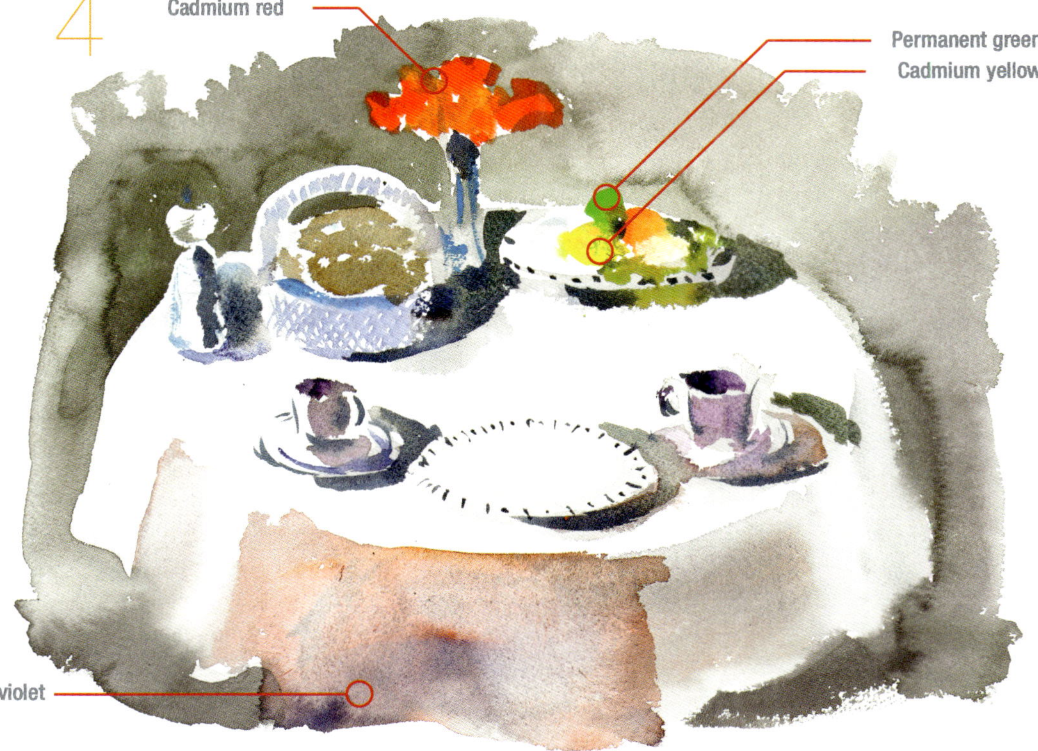

4. The strong luminosity of the grouping is the result of basic chiaroscuro that you created with the large reserve in the beginning and the details and colors you added to it.

50 Reserves / With White Gouache

LEVEL OF DIFFICULTY
★
COLORS
Sap green
Burnt sienna
Permanent red
White gouache
BRUSH
Medium round natural hair
PAPER
140 lb medium-rough texture

Painted reserves, in reality, are not reserves since the paper is covered. But using white gouache creates an effect that is equivalent to reserving unpainted areas, and although some watercolorists consider it a reprehensible practice, it is very useful for making small white areas like those on this tree in flower.

1

1. Paint a wash of light permanent red, and in pencil draw over it the indications of a trunk and braches of a tree. When the wash is completely dry, fill in those lines with saturated burnt sienna.

Burnt sienna
Permanent red

Sap green

2

2. Next to each branch, paint short curved lines of sap green. They should be similar but never the same, expressing the lightness of the leaves of the tree.

3. When the watercolor is completely dry, apply dabs of white gouache to the branches and leaves.

3

White gouache

4

4. Achieving this effect without the use of the white gouache would have been practically impossible. This is not actually a reserve technique, but the result has the same general look.

Reserves / **Informal Reserves**

LEVEL OF DIFFICULTY
★★
COLORS
Carmine
Burnt sienna
Black watercolor pencil
BRUSH
Medium round natural hair
PAPER
140 lb medium-rough texture

When making sketches and notes for color, reserves are always much more informal than when you are making a more ambitious watercolor. This sketch of a child's portrait has unpainted areas that were not previously planned but were the product of the spontaneity of the moment.

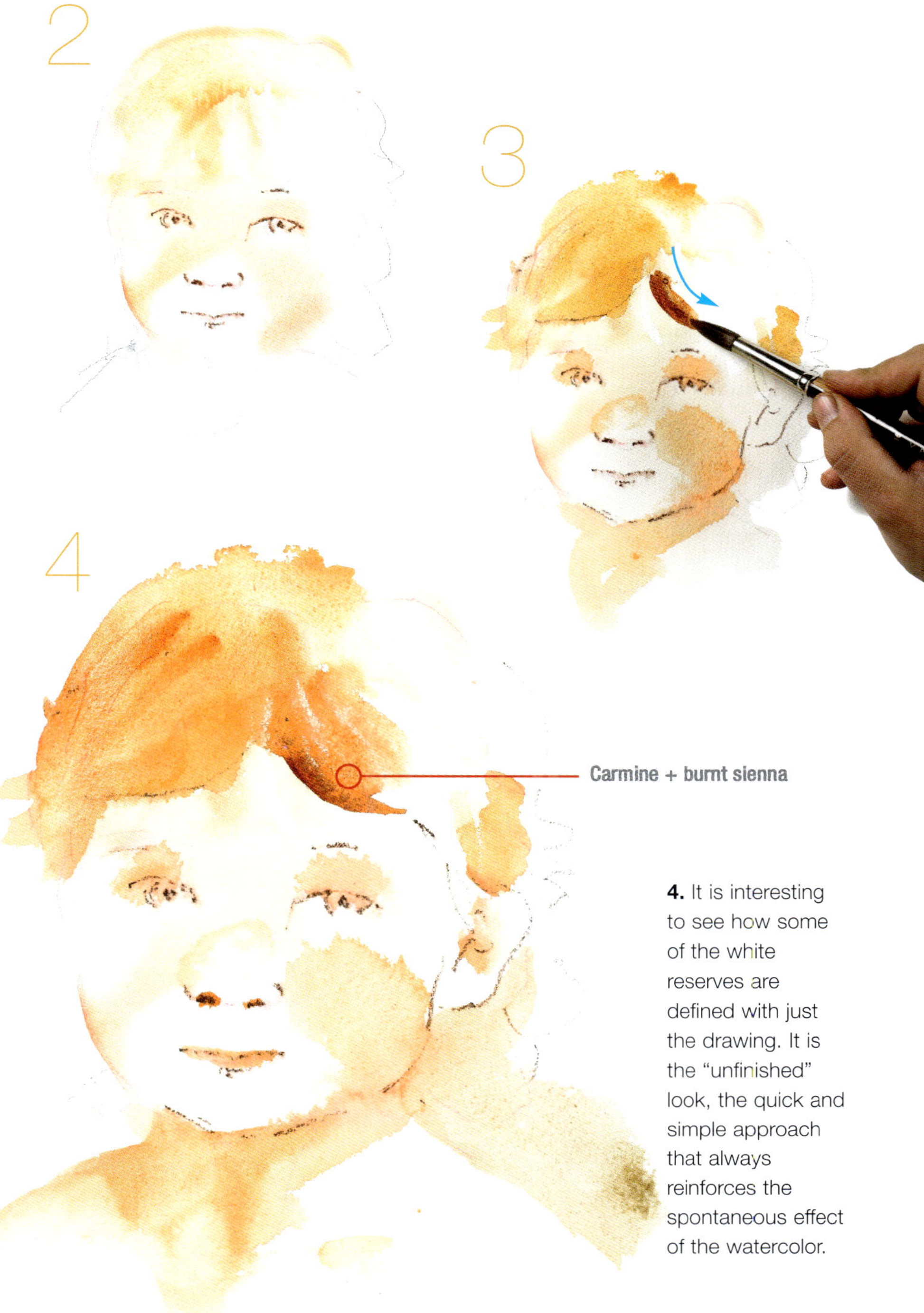

1. Draw the features and the shape of the head, and then apply a light wash of burnt sienna. Leave the nose, the area beneath the eyes, the upper lip, and the chin white to express the effect of the light.

2. Use a black watercolor pencil to define the facial features with very simple lines, without going over them or adding shading.

3. You can darken the more intense values with burnt sienna to reinforce the general contrast. This will give more definition to the volume and expression of the face. These dark values can be seen in the bangs of the hair.

4. It is interesting to see how some of the white reserves are defined with just the drawing. It is the "unfinished" look, the quick and simple approach that always reinforces the spontaneous effect of the watercolor.

Reserves / **Painting Process Based on Reserves**

LEVEL OF DIFFICULTY
★★
COLORS
Cobalt blue
Sap green
Burnt sienna
Yellow ochre
BRUSH
Medium round natural hair
PAPER
140 lb medium-rough texture

In this exercise we explain in detail how to create a theme that is very rich in shading and contrasts. Most of the contrasts result from the use of reserves. Many of the trunks are reserved at the beginning and later painted with shading, but they always maintain the strength and luminosity of the contrasts between the dark tones and the white of the paper.

1. After drawing the theme, paint the central trees with a very light wash of blue gray. When it has dried, begin painting around it as if it were a reserve.

2. Washes of blue gray and green surround the trunks and emphasize their silhouettes. They appear as masses of vegetation located in the middle ground.

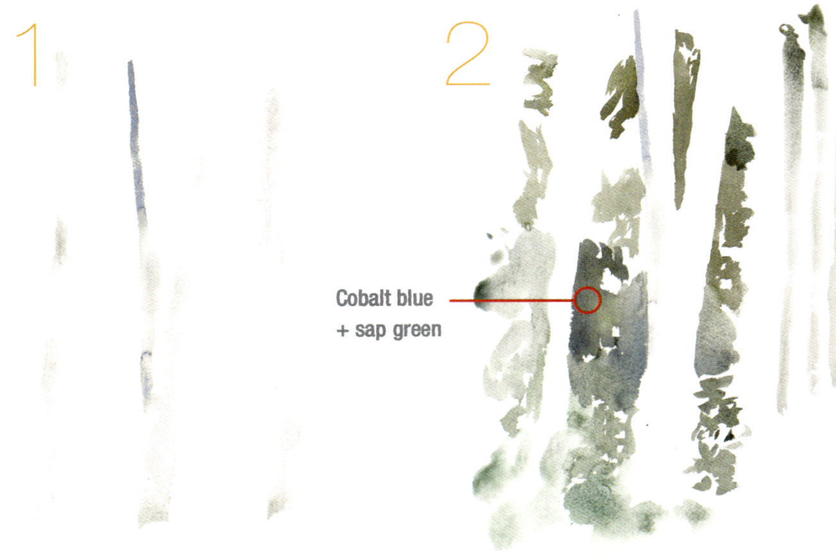

3. Now apply various shades of green and ochre over the dry paint to add variety to the coloration dominated by blue gray, which is a mixture of cobalt blue, green, and burnt sienna.

4. The process should evolve from making large washes to smaller ones. Now is the time to work on the trunks of these birch trees. Draw the characteristic grooves and colors of the bark with the tip of the brush and a mixture of cobalt blue and sienna.

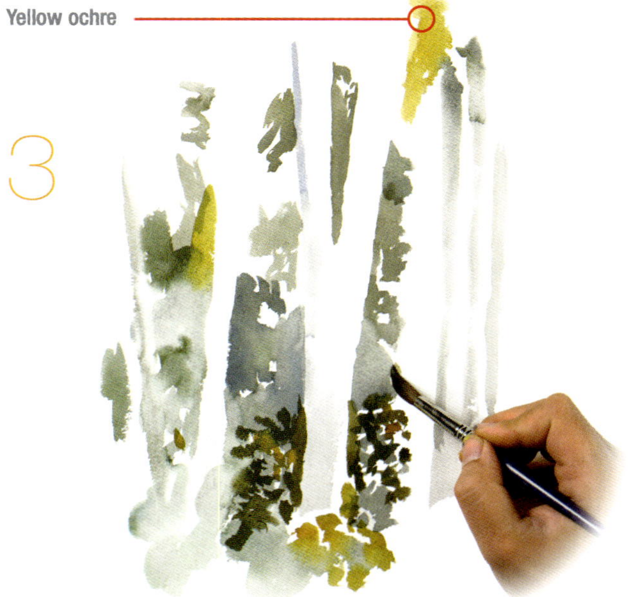

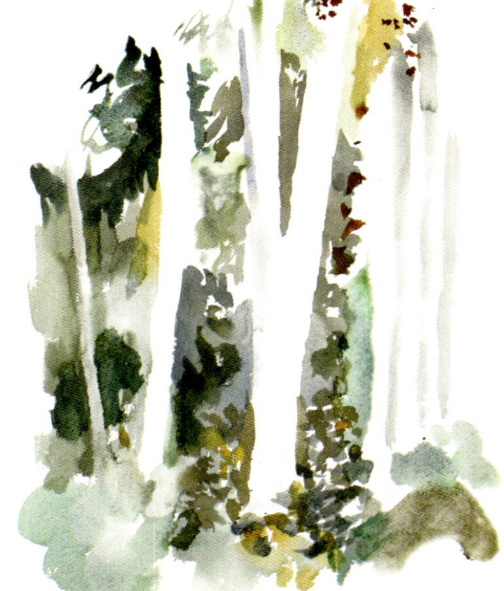

5

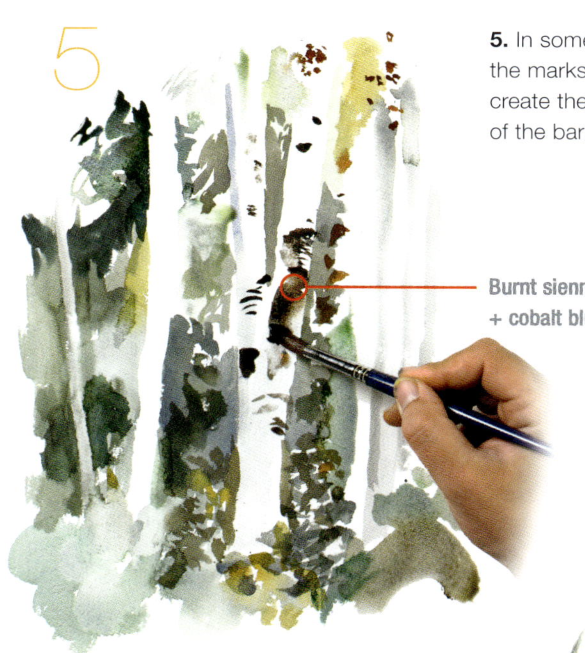

5. In some areas you can spread the marks with a little water to create the effect of the dark parts of the bark.

6

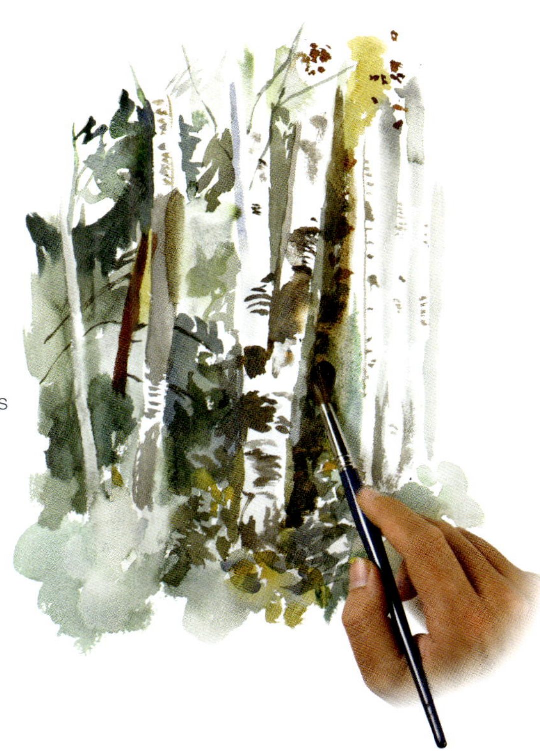

6. For more contrasts, darken some trunks with transparent washes of different colors, such as grays, ochres, and sienna.

7

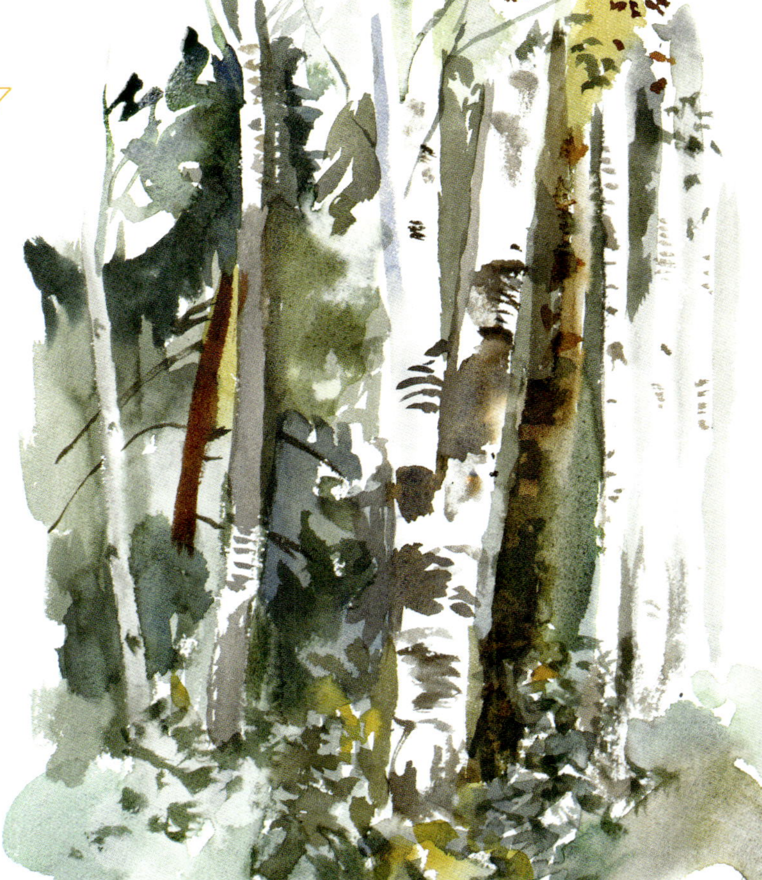

A good round watercolor brush with natural hair will allow you to draw fine unbroken lines with as much precision as your hand allows. This is one of the reasons why it is important to work with high-quality brushes.

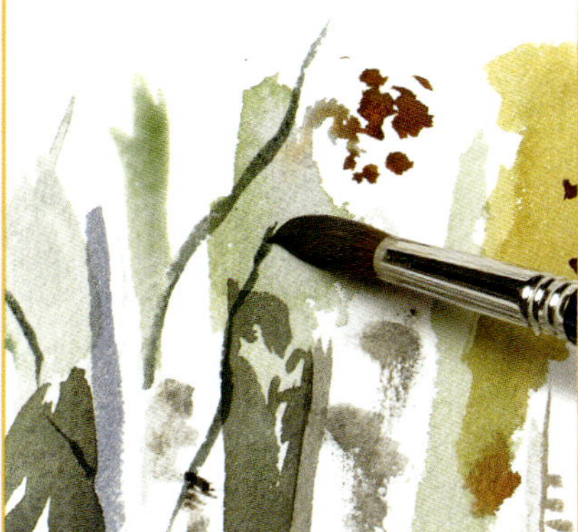

7. The final effect will be very rich in shading, values, and details, really suggesting the density of the forest. But all this richness keeps its unity because of the basic contrasts created at the beginning of the work with the reserves.

53 Color Harmony / **Warm Tonal Harmony**

LEVEL OF DIFFICULTY
★
COLORS
Light cadmium yellow
Permanent red
Cadmium red
Permanent green
BRUSH
Medium round natural hair
PAPER
140 lb medium-rough texture

Tonal harmony is based on tones that are very similar. Here you will use colors that are very near each other on the color wheel to create the flower, and this produces a very pleasant, unifying, harmonic effect.

1. Wet the paper so that the successive applications of color will partially or completely blend and unify the harmony.

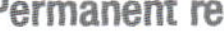

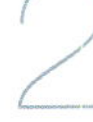

2. You can cover the flower with a preliminary red shade with very few applications.

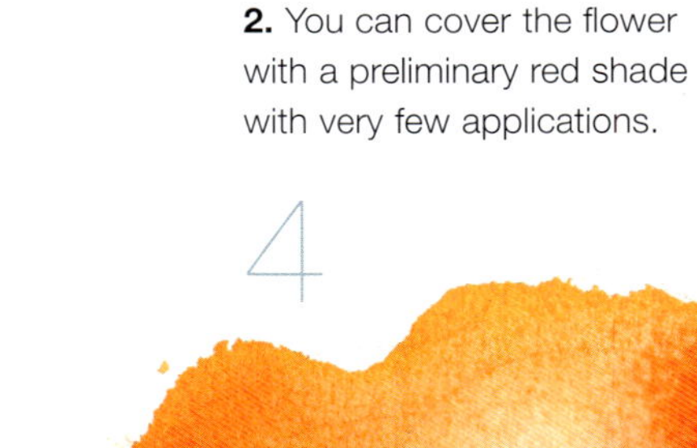

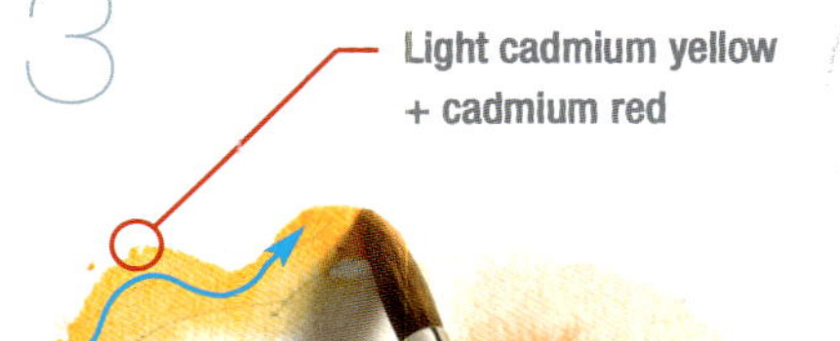

3. Spread yellow along the upper edge of the wash so that it can blend with the red without losing all of its color.

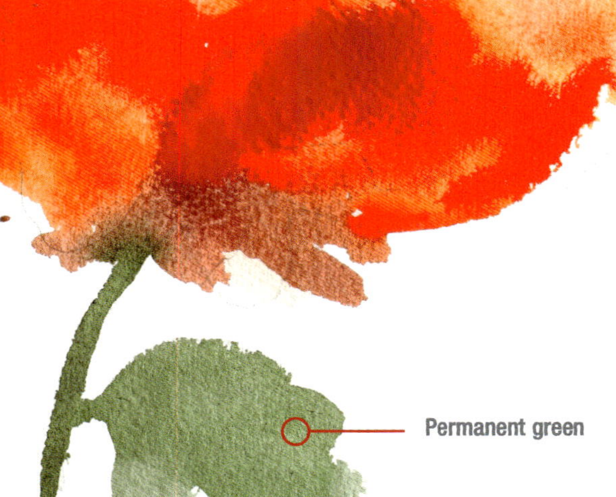

4. The color is very soft and rich in shading. Any possible details are lost in a mass of dense color. Paint the stem and the leaf on dry paper.

54 Color Harmony / **Warm Chromatic Harmony**

LEVEL OF DIFFICULTY
★
COLORS
Burnt sienna
Permanent green
Permanent blue
Carmine
Cadmium yellow
Cobalt blue
Yellow ochre
BRUSH
Medium round natural hair
PAPER
140 lb medium-rough texture

The richness of chromatic harmony resides in the incorporation of contrasting colors. This watercolor has a fundamentally warm harmony, the cool tones only reinforce and enliven it, diversified in many shades united around the reds and yellows that dominate in the chromatic composition.

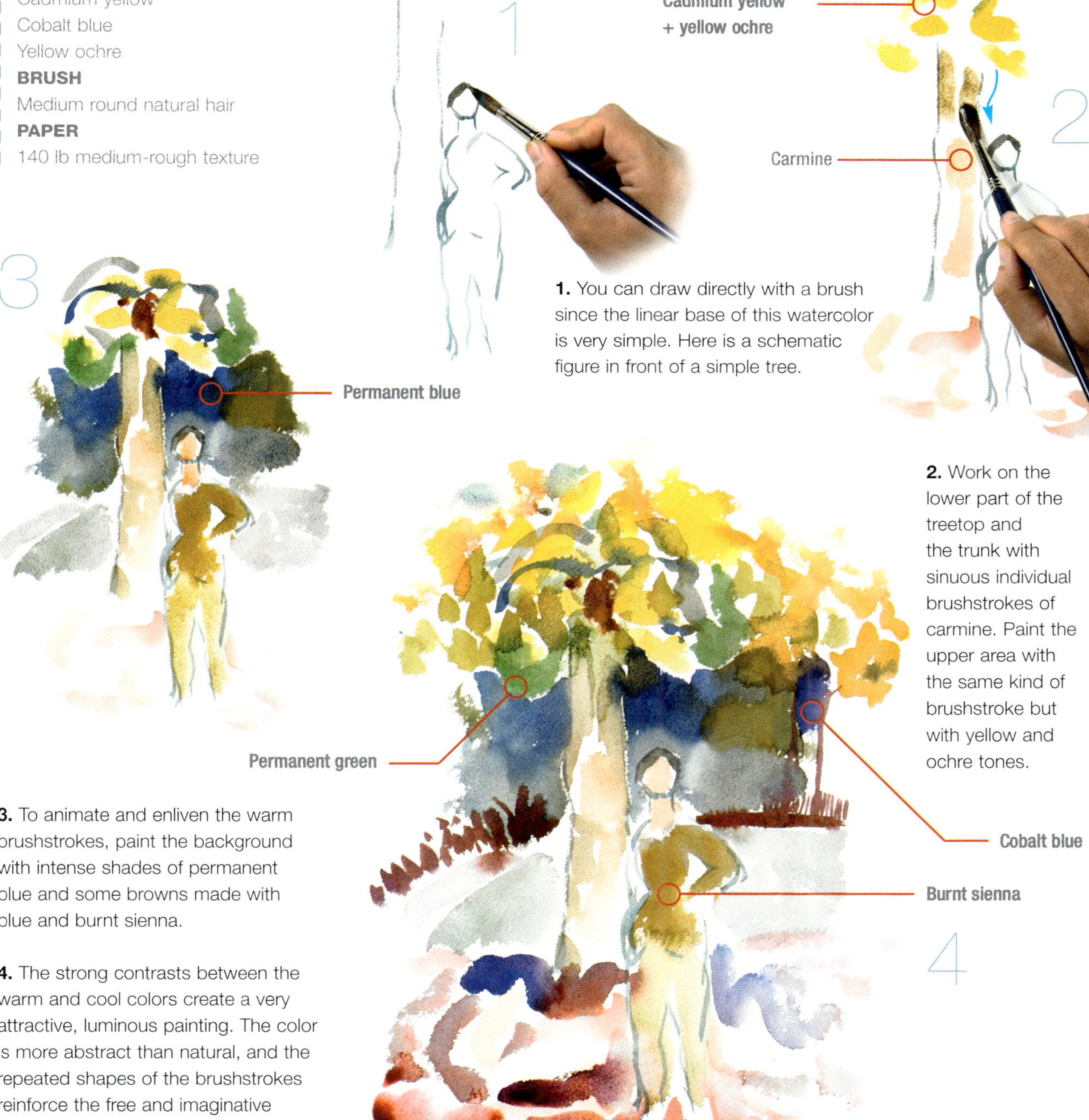

1. You can draw directly with a brush since the linear base of this watercolor is very simple. Here is a schematic figure in front of a simple tree.

2. Work on the lower part of the treetop and the trunk with sinuous individual brushstrokes of carmine. Paint the upper area with the same kind of brushstroke but with yellow and ochre tones.

3. To animate and enliven the warm brushstrokes, paint the background with intense shades of permanent blue and some browns made with blue and burnt sienna.

4. The strong contrasts between the warm and cool colors create a very attractive, luminous painting. The color is more abstract than natural, and the repeated shapes of the brushstrokes reinforce the free and imaginative character of the work.

LEVEL OF DIFFICULTY
★
COLORS
Sap green
Burnt sienna
Permanent blue
BRUSH
Medium round natural hair
PAPER
140 lb medium rough texture

Blues, violets, grays, and dark greens are the essential colors of the cool range. Using these tones here, you will develop a tonal watercolor (without contrasting color ranges). We have chosen the most discrete tones of the range to ensure the sober and harmonious unity required by this subject.

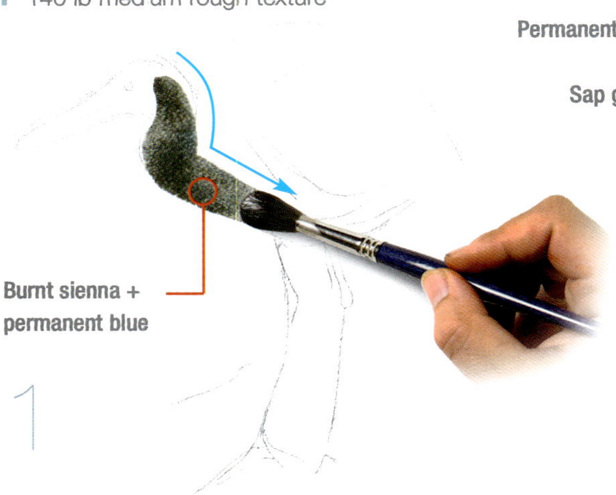

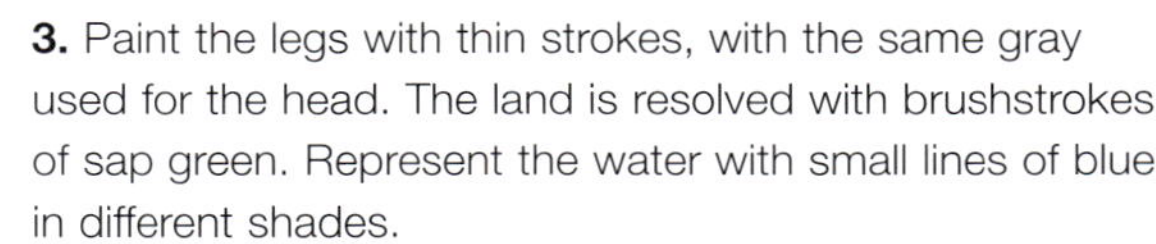

1. It is important to draw the body of the bird correctly, because after wetting the paper you will paint it with a single gray brushstroke, a mixture of burnt sienna and permanent blue.

2. Paint the head on dry paper, with a very saturated mixture of the gray used for the body, and the beak with diluted burnt sienna.

3. Paint the legs with thin strokes, with the same gray used for the head. The land is resolved with brushstrokes of sap green. Represent the water with small lines of blue in different shades.

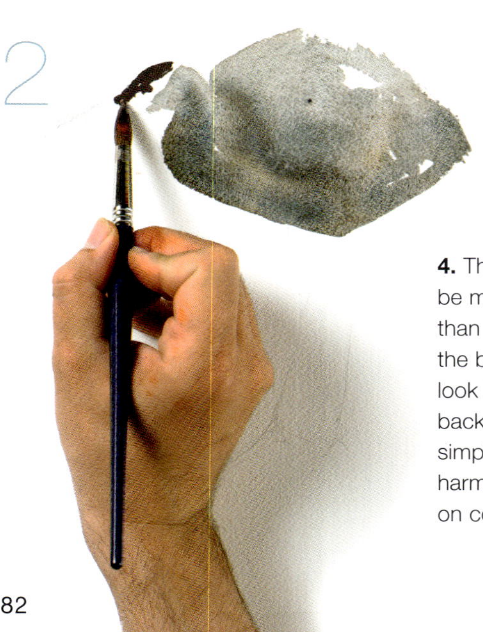

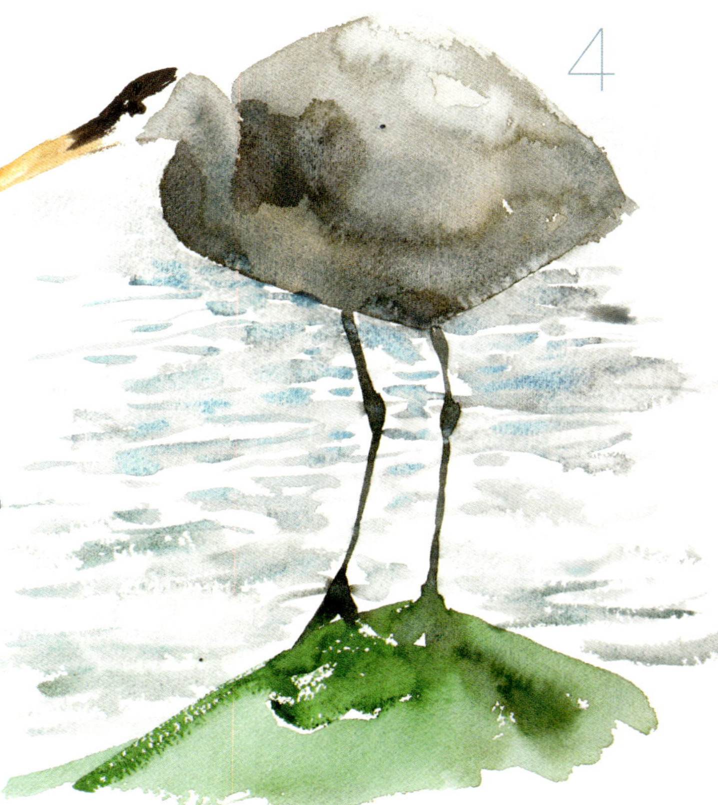

4. The water should be more toned down than the body of the bird, so it will look like it is in the background. This simple and sober harmony is based on cool tones.

Color Harmony / **Cool Chromatic Harmony**

LEVEL OF DIFFICULTY
★
COLORS
Emerald green
Cobalt violet
Permanent blue
BRUSH
Medium round natural hair
PAPER
140 lb medium-rough texture

In this approach you will use luminous colors to enrich a fundamentally cool range based on blues. The color is not natural; vibrant blues were chosen to achieve a cool harmony that includes hints of warmth in the light greens.

1. With no preliminary drawing, spread large colorful brushstrokes of blue and green. Use a large amount of water and reserve the side of the candle.

2. Make the drawing over the previously applied colors, highlighting the outlines that are not defined by the darkest masses of color. Paint the fruit with two large green washes on dry paper.

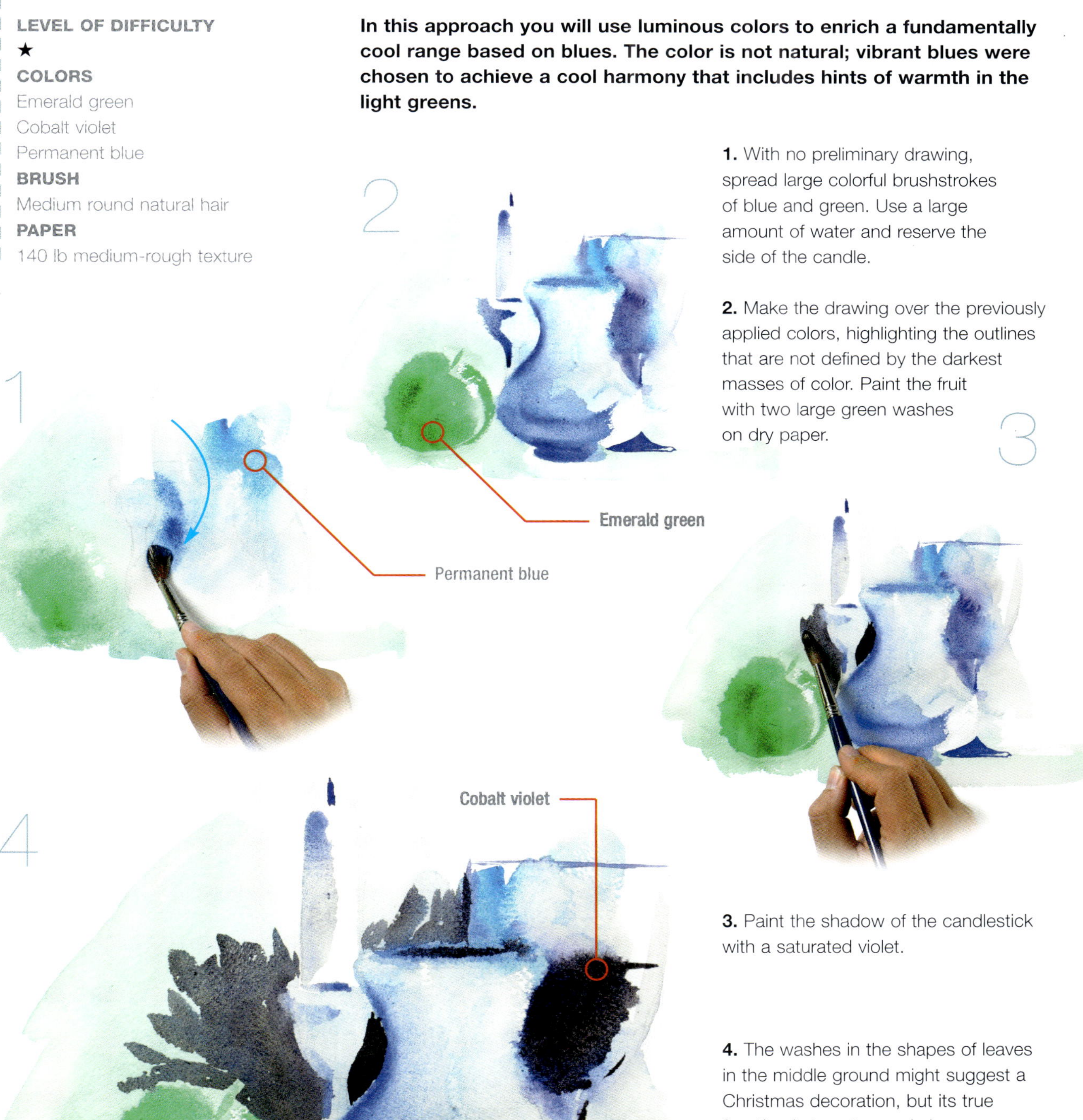

3. Paint the shadow of the candlestick with a saturated violet.

4. The washes in the shapes of leaves in the middle ground might suggest a Christmas decoration, but its true function is to act as a dark screen so that the most vibrant colors of the harmony are correctly shaded.

Color Harmony / **Combined Harmonies**

LEVEL OF DIFFICULTY
★★

COLORS
Permanent green
Burnt sienna
Cadmium orange
Carmine
Cobalt blue
Permanent blue

BRUSH
Medium round natural hair

PAPER
140 lb medium-rough texture

When you use colors from the warm range and the cool range without a clearly dominant color scheme, you must create contrasts and affinities among the colors. In this watercolor, you will use very different tones that will be carried to the most intense color vibration, because almost none of them will be mixed with each other.

1. It is important to draw a good outline, since the colors of the edges of the fish and the seaweed must be precise. Start by painting some seaweed with sienna mixed with a little orange.

2. Use permanent green to paint the seaweed that is not brown. The colors of some of the leaves and stems should be absorbed by the spongy paper to create a somewhat "rusty" texture that expresses the view through the surface of the water.

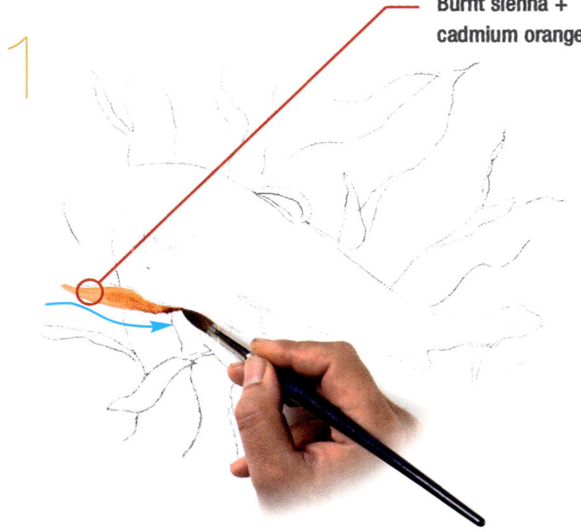

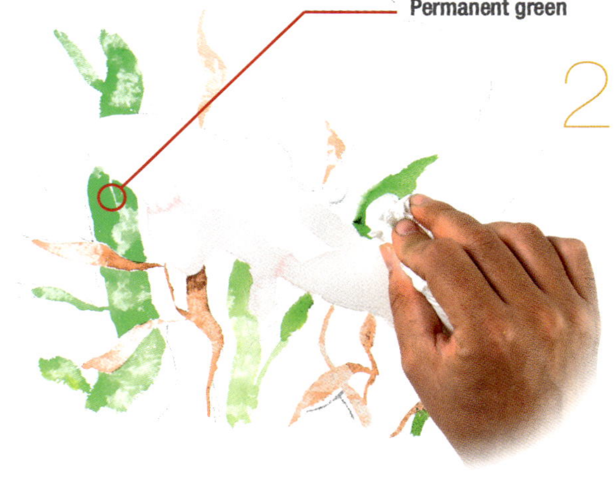

The well-known technique using absorbent paper can be used here to give the colors of the objects an irregular texture. The irregularity lets you represent the different texture of each object, or, as in this case, the distorted view caused by the water between you and the scene.

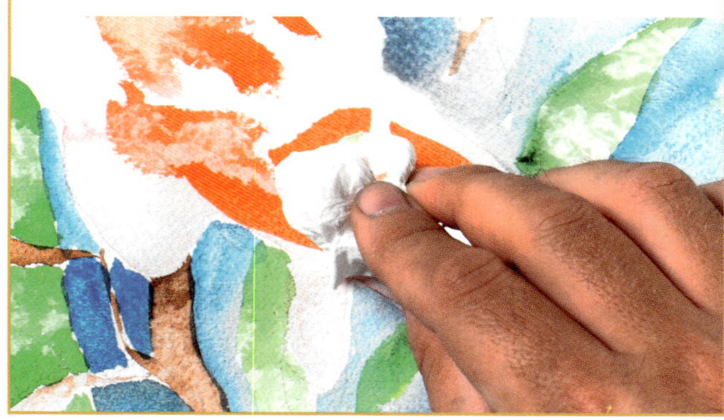

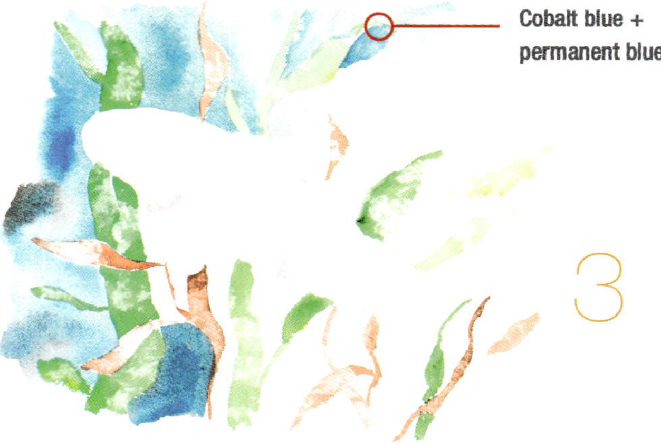

3. Wet the reserved areas between the seaweed before painting them with a mixture of permanent blue and cobalt blue. Also reserve the fish, carefully respecting its outline.

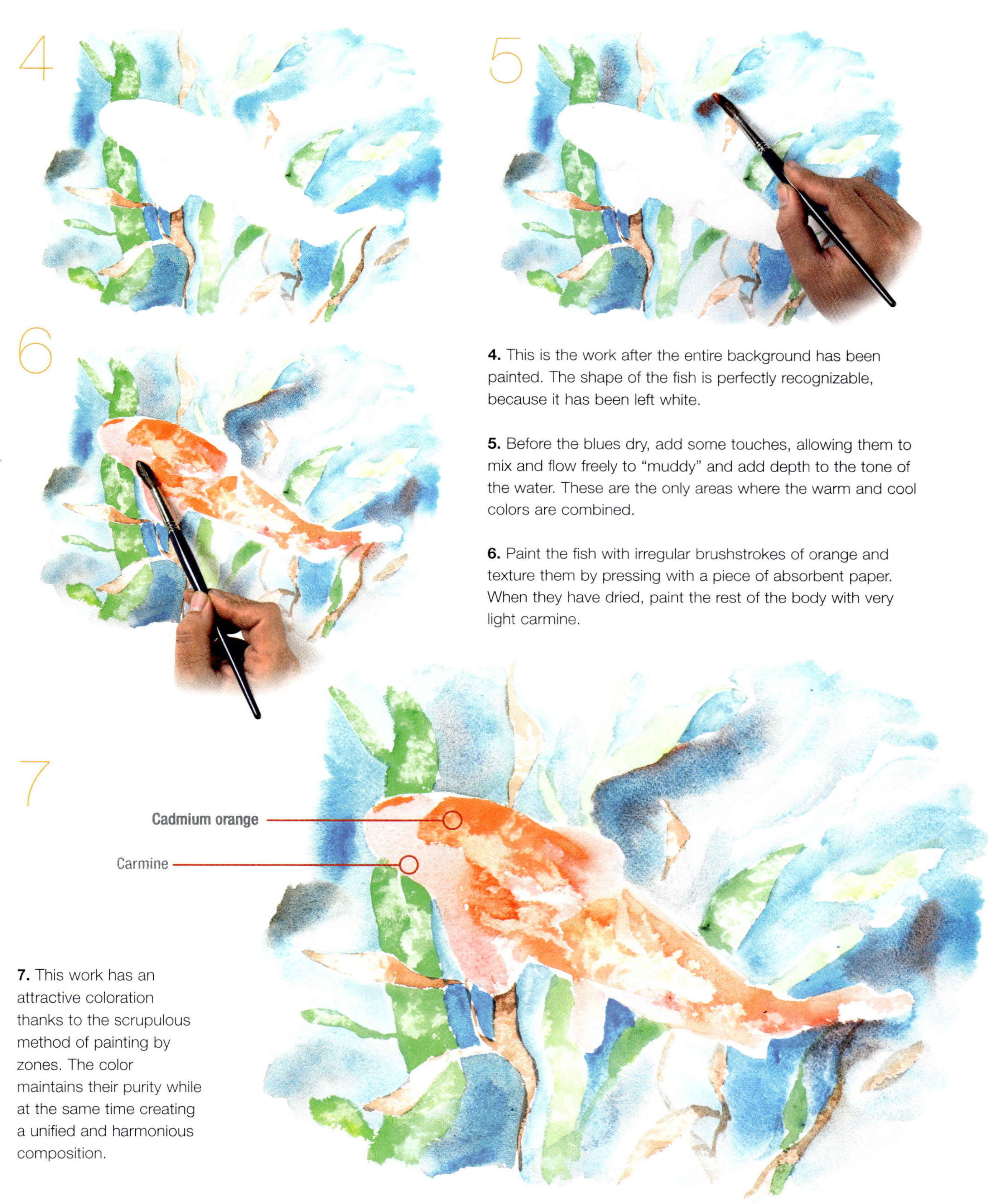

4. This is the work after the entire background has been painted. The shape of the fish is perfectly recognizable, because it has been left white.

5. Before the blues dry, add some touches, allowing them to mix and flow freely to "muddy" and add depth to the tone of the water. These are the only areas where the warm and cool colors are combined.

6. Paint the fish with irregular brushstrokes of orange and texture them by pressing with a piece of absorbent paper. When they have dried, paint the rest of the body with very light carmine.

7. This work has an attractive coloration thanks to the scrupulous method of painting by zones. The color maintains their purity while at the same time creating a unified and harmonious composition.

LEVEL OF DIFFICULTY
★★

COLORS
Burnt sienna
Ultramarine blue

BRUSH
Medium round natural hair

PAPER
140 lb medium-rough texture

Neutral colors are those that result from mixing cool tones with warm ones. This results in a brown or grayish color that can have a cool or warm tendency depending on the color that dominates the mixture. This watercolor will be painted with a single tone, made by mixing two colors: one warm (burnt sienna) and the other cool (ultramarine blue).

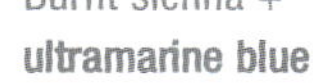

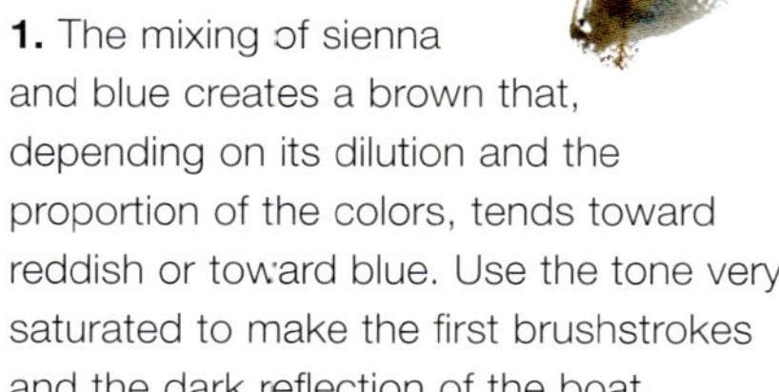

1. The mixing of sienna and blue creates a brown that, depending on its dilution and the proportion of the colors, tends toward reddish or toward blue. Use the tone very saturated to make the first brushstrokes and the dark reflection of the boat.

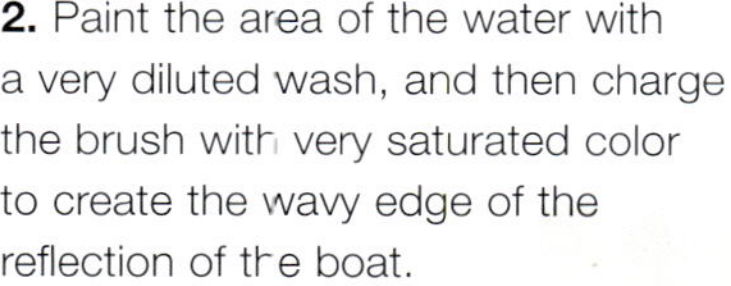

2. Paint the area of the water with a very diluted wash, and then charge the brush with very saturated color to create the wavy edge of the reflection of the boat.

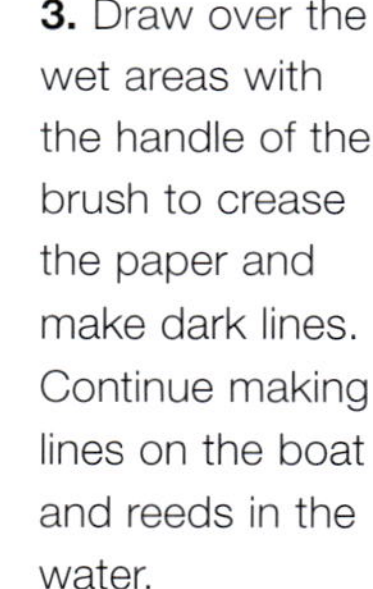

3. Draw over the wet areas with the handle of the brush to crease the paper and make dark lines. Continue making lines on the boat and reeds in the water.

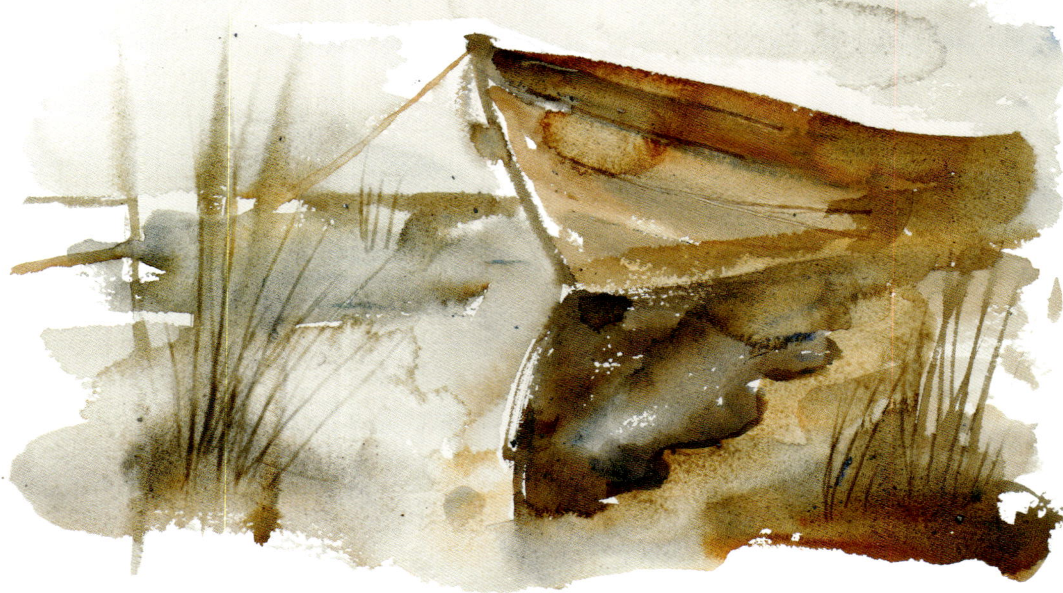

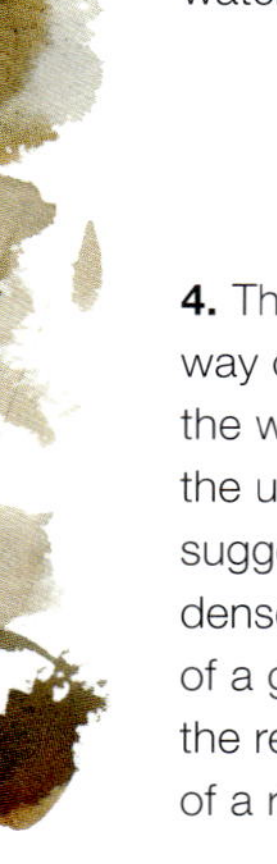

4. The informal way of applying the washes and the unity of color suggests the dense atmosphere of a gray day on the restless waters of a river.

59 Color Harmony / **Contrasting Neutral Harmony**

LEVEL OF DIFFICULTY
★
COLORS
Ultramarine blue
Burnt umber
BRUSH
Medium round natural hair
PAPER
140 lb medium-rough texture

You will not mix colors in this exercise, but the chromatic effect will have a neutral harmony. This is owed to the contrast between two tones that seem neutral, because the paint will run on the wet paper. This spreading will create a dull effect that will combine with the tints of the paint to create the impression of a gray atmosphere.

1. Wet the entire surface of the paper before staring to work. This will cause the paint to run as soon as the tip of the brush touches the paper.

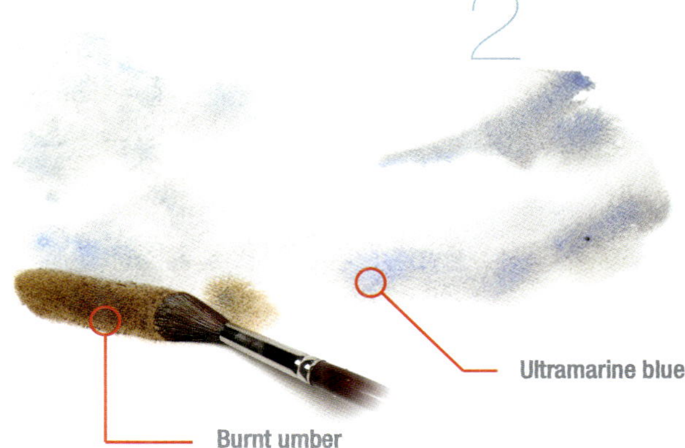

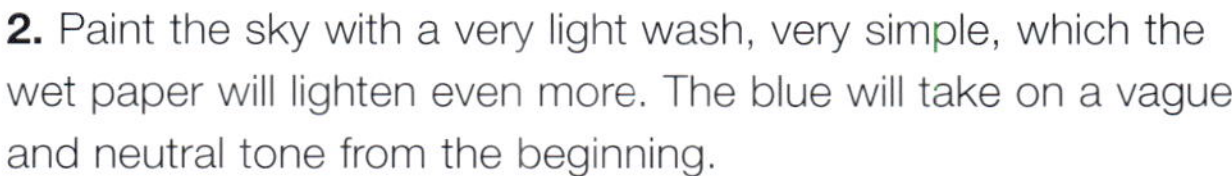

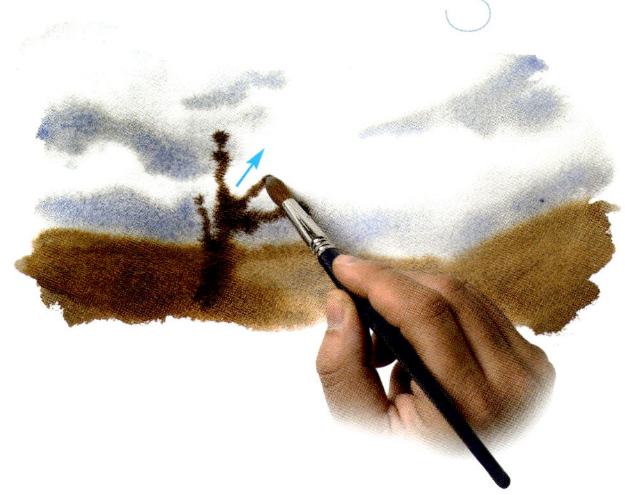

2. Paint the sky with a very light wash, very simple, which the wet paper will lighten even more. The blue will take on a vague and neutral tone from the beginning.

3. With the paper still a little wet, paint the lower part of the composition. Use a quite saturated burnt umber. Next, with the same color as saturated as possible, paint a tree whose branches blur against the background that is also damp.

4. Although you have not mixed the colors, the vague atmosphere that is always caused by painting on wet paper suggests a coloration that is halfway between a warm and a cool harmony: neutral tones.

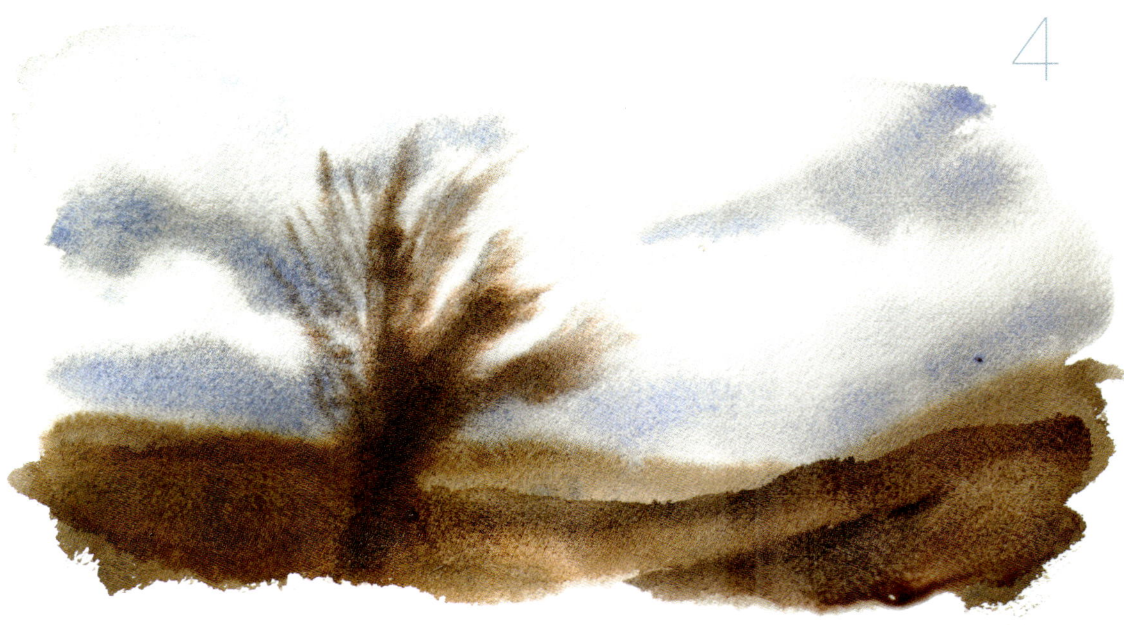

60 Color Harmony / **Cool Monochrome**

LEVEL OF DIFFICULTY
★
COLORS
Ultramarine blue
Burnt sienna
BRUSH
Medium round natural hair
PAPER
140 lb medium-rough texture

In this watercolor you will use the same colors that were used for the neutral harmony, but now the preponderance of blue over sienna makes the coloration decidedly cool. The cool colors are very appropriate for representing the soft shading of the gray fur of this cat.

1

Ultramarine blue + burnt sienna

2

1. Make a strong clear drawing, and over it paint large strokes of blue-gray color made from mixing the sienna and blue. The upper part of the head and the ears should have the darkest tones.

2. Two very dark gray strokes will define the pupils of the cat. If they are too dark apply a clean wet brush to lighten them.

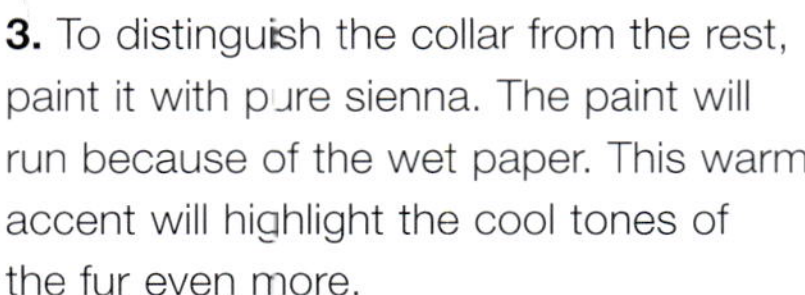

3. To distinguish the collar from the rest, paint it with pure sienna. The paint will run because of the wet paper. This warm accent will highlight the cool tones of the fur even more.

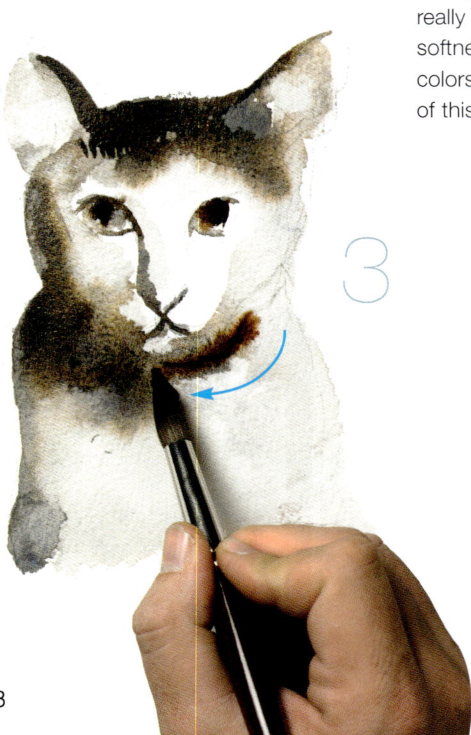

4. This monochrome painting is enriched by the presence of the warm shades. The gray tone really suggests the softness and the colors of the fur of this kitten.

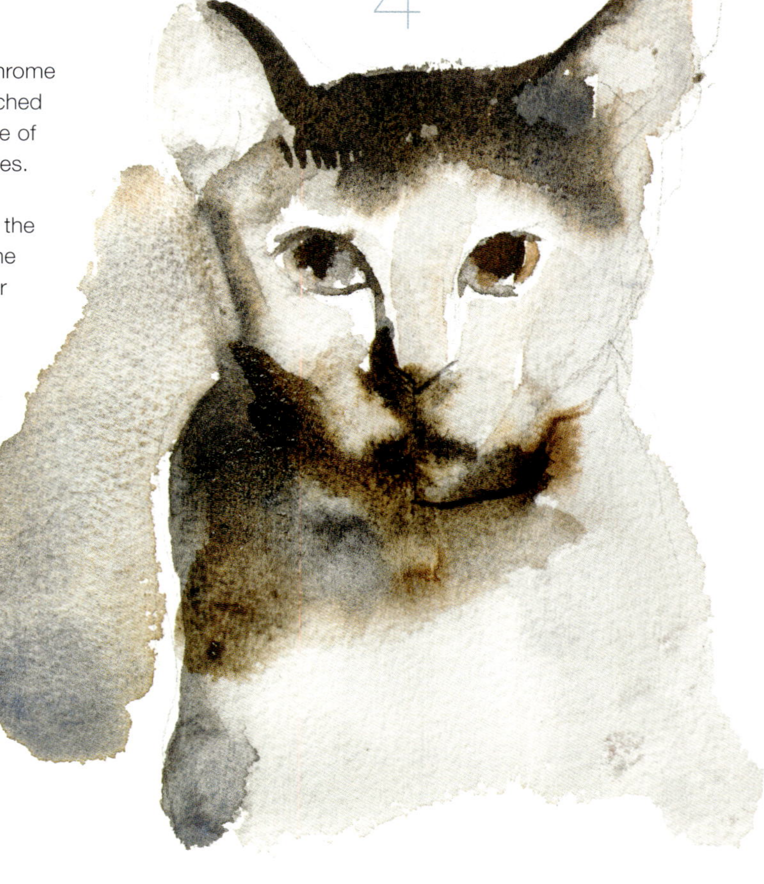

61 Color Harmony / **Warm Monochrome**

LEVEL OF DIFFICULTY
★
COLORS
Yellow ochre
Burnt sienna
BRUSH
Medium round natural hair
PAPER
140 lb medium-rough texture

Monochromes ensure total harmony among the tones precisely because the chromatic components of the work are tones, rather than colors. In this watercolor, you will use harmonious chestnut tones in accord with the autumn theme. Yellow ochre will be added to increase the tonal range of the palette dominated by burnt sienna.

1. Make a schematic drawing of the trunks, branches, and grasses of the subject, and add a very transparent wash of ochre and sienna. Then draw the branches with sienna, following the drawing with the tip of the brush.

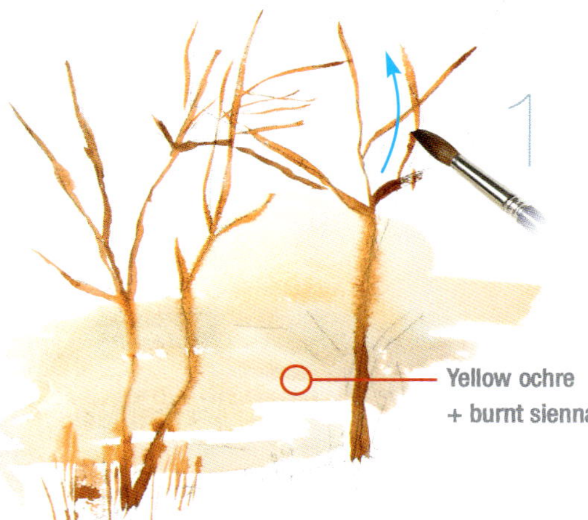

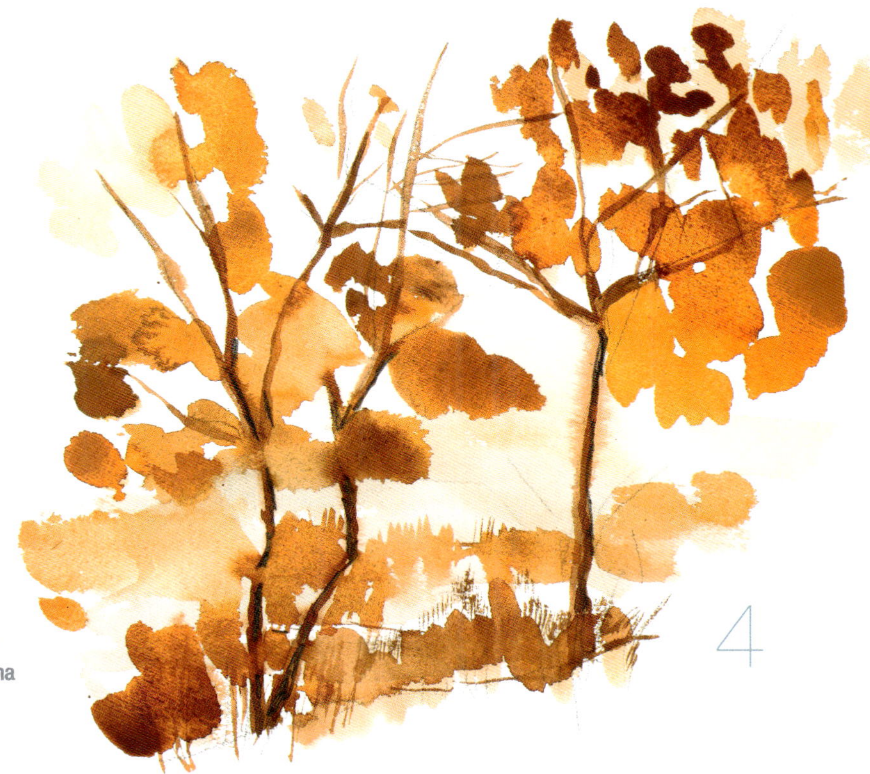

2. The foliage can be stylized with curved brushstrokes made by applying the brush flat against the paper. The colors are different intensities of sienna.

3. It is important to dilute the paint to create different planes in the foliage of the trees.

4. The foreground should be darker than the farther planes; the grass at the bottom is darker than the background. The rich tones animate and make up for the monochromatic colors.

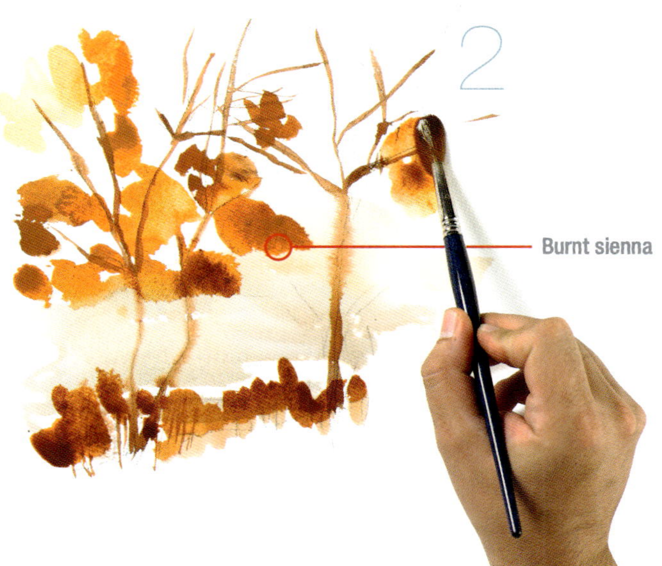

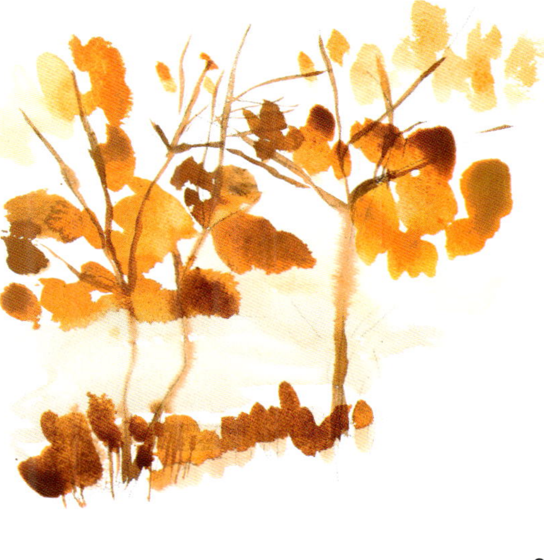

LEVEL OF DIFFICULTY
★★
COLORS
Ultramarine blue
Burnt sienna
Raw umber
BRUSHES
Fine round natural hair
Medium round natural hair
PAPER
140 lb medium-rough texture

Harmonizing cool and warm colors involves adjusting the values of both, in other words, making them lighter or darker so that the color contrast is appropriate for the tonal contrast. In this example, you will make these adjustments with a previously used method: absorbing the paint with an absorbent paper towel.

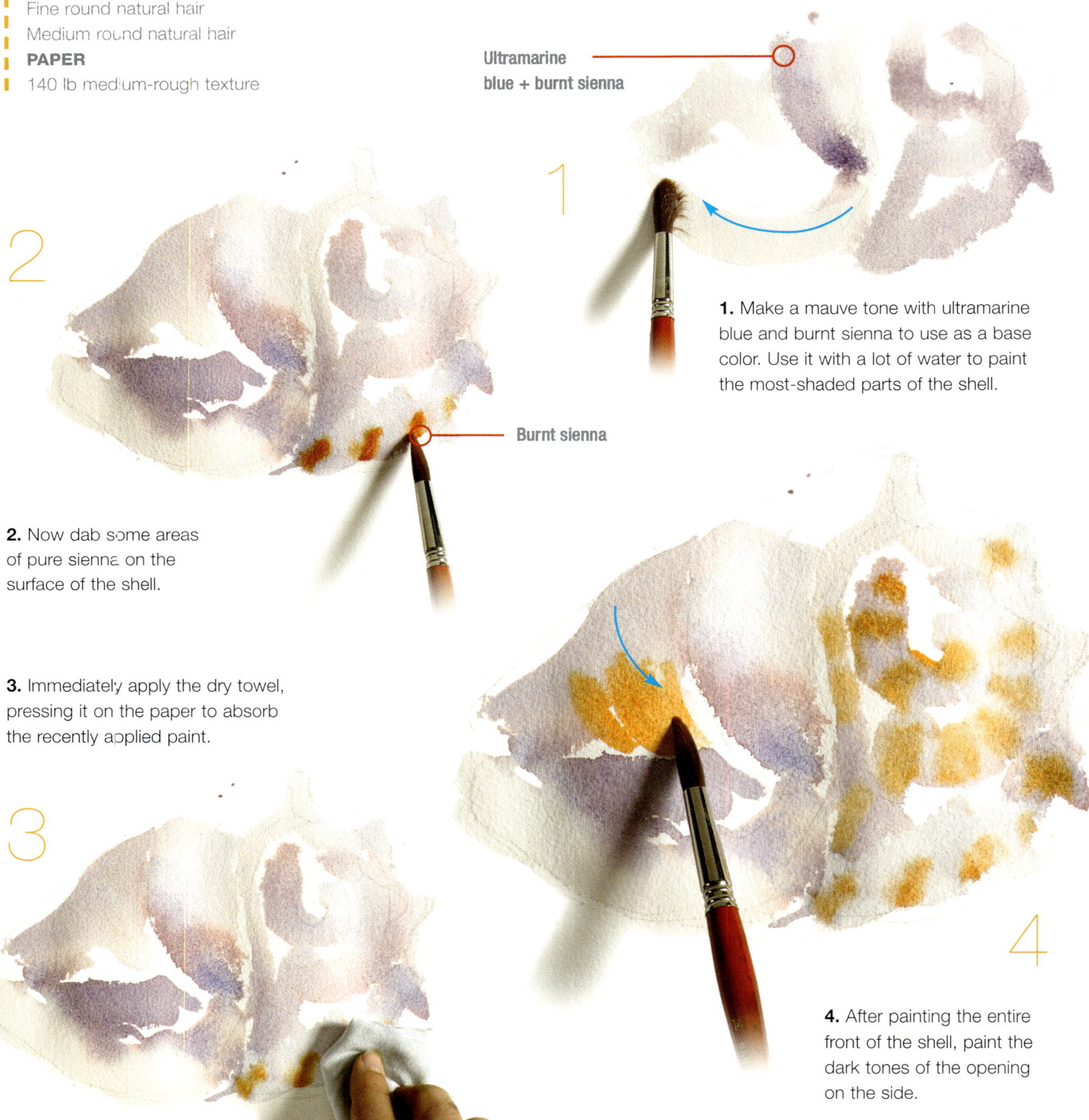

1. Make a mauve tone with ultramarine blue and burnt sienna to use as a base color. Use it with a lot of water to paint the most-shaded parts of the shell.

2. Now dab some areas of pure sienna on the surface of the shell.

3. Immediately apply the dry towel, pressing it on the paper to absorb the recently applied paint.

4. After painting the entire front of the shell, paint the dark tones of the opening on the side.

When you press a rag or paper towel on a recently painted area of dark color, you lighten the tone and create more-defined shading.

Afterward, the color is not as intense, but the shades have become more luminous.

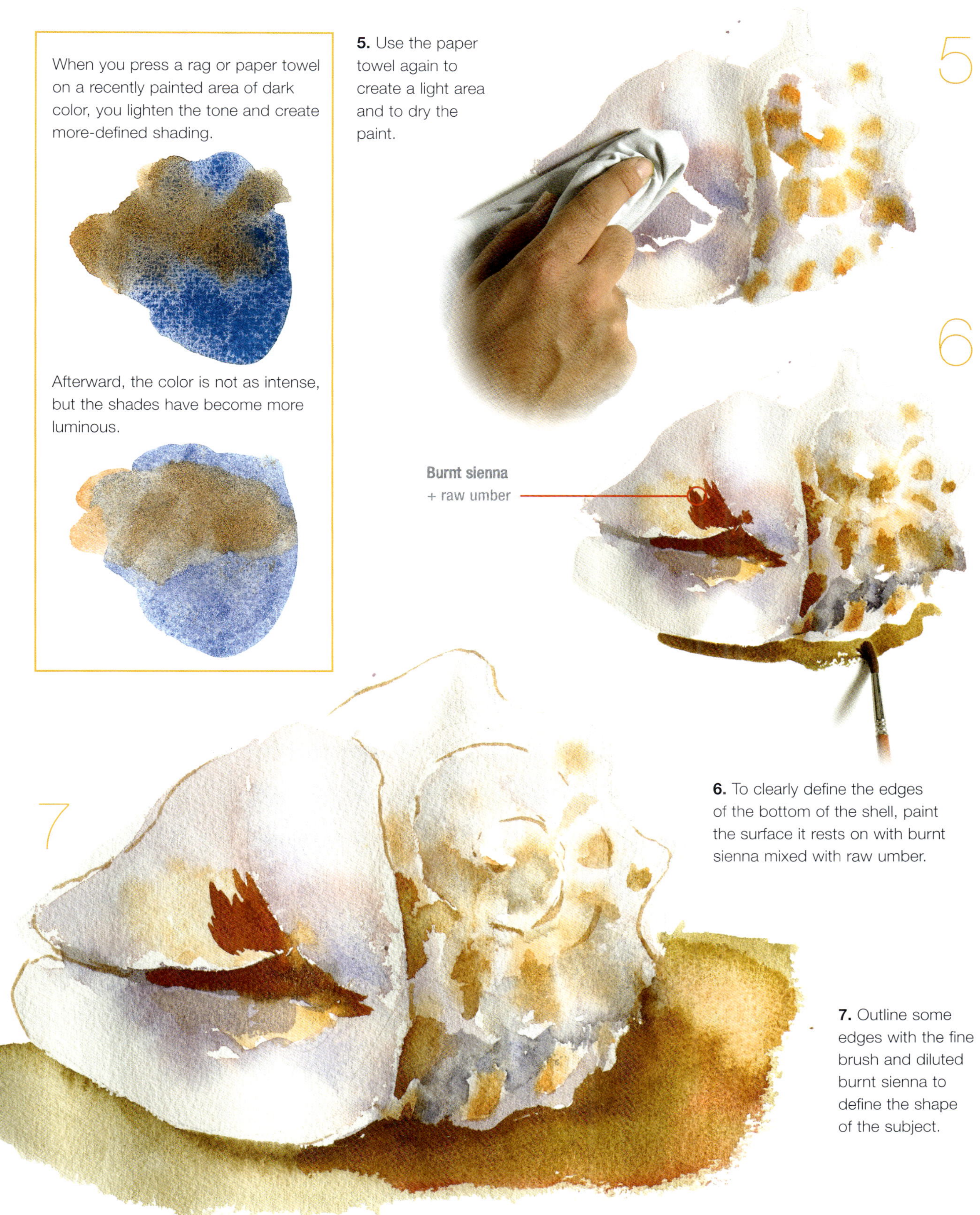

5. Use the paper towel again to create a light area and to dry the paint.

6. To clearly define the edges of the bottom of the shell, paint the surface it rests on with burnt sienna mixed with raw umber.

7. Outline some edges with the fine brush and diluted burnt sienna to define the shape of the subject.

Color Harmony / **Cool and Warm Overlaid Colors**

LEVEL OF DIFFICULTY

★

COLORS

Cerulean blue

Permanent red

Cobalt violet

BRUSH

Medium round natural hair

PAPER

140 lb medium-rough texture

Often the chromatic harmony of a watercolor is the result of the artist's intuitive approach rather than any previous planning. The resolute energy exhibited in this watercolor is the result of an attractive color harmony consisting of overlaying a very warm color over a decidedly cool background. A few neutral shades help unify the work.

1. A large wash of cerulean blue with a lot of water and paint will serve as the starting point. On it make a thick red brushstroke. There is no need for a preliminary drawing since the form will "appear" from among the colors of the wash.

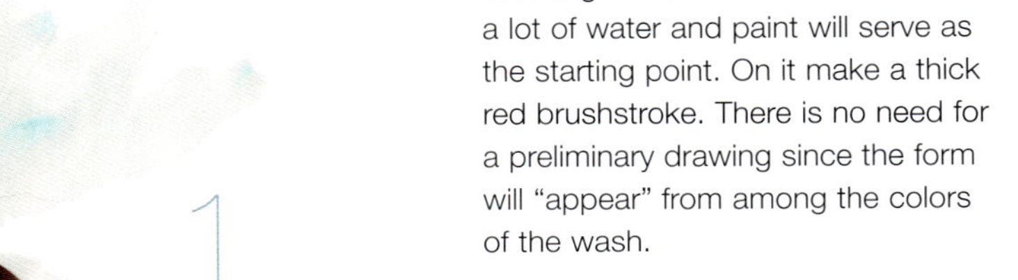

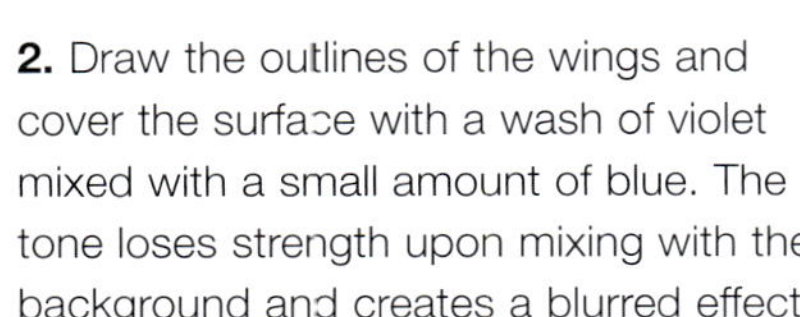

2. Draw the outlines of the wings and cover the surface with a wash of violet mixed with a small amount of blue. The tone loses strength upon mixing with the background and creates a blurred effect.

3. While the washes are still wet, define the body of the dragonfly with some lines made with the handle of the brush.

4. The combination of blurred washes and fine, precise lines creates the effect of movement that matches the nature of the subject. The color is imaginative, inspired by the peculiar colors of this insect.

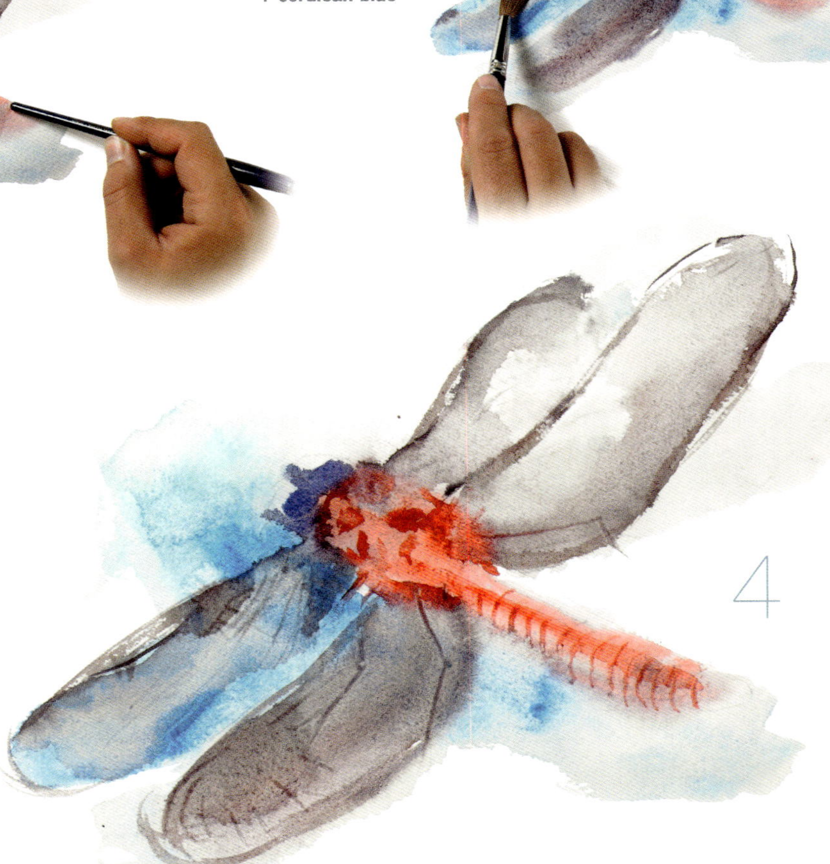

64 Color Harmony / **Contrasts with Cool and Warm Colors**

LEVEL OF DIFFICULTY
★★

COLORS
Cadmium yellow
Burnt sienna
Ultramarine blue
Carmine

BRUSH
Medium round natural hair

PAPER
140 lb medium-rough texture

The contrasts between warm and cool in clear, well-differentiated zones always produce clean and graphic effects. In this example, you will see how to create such effects while representing a subject that demands it. This ice cream, paradoxically represented with warm colors, contrasts with some well-defined cool colors.

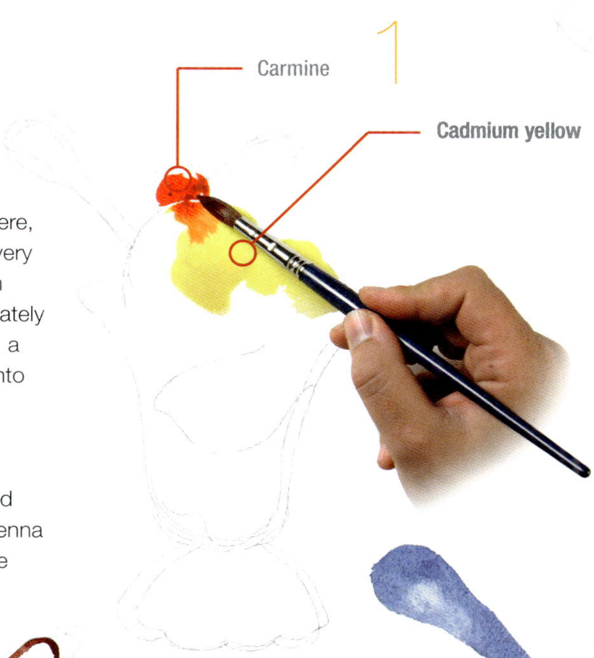

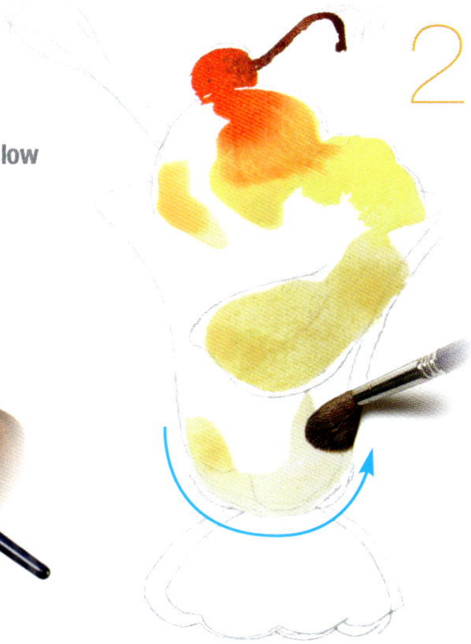

1. The drawing is very important here, because the colors must follow it very closely: the dish and the ice cream should be drawn correctly. Immediately begin to address the upper colors, a carmine cherry whose paint runs into the still-wet cadmium yellow.

1

Carmine

Cadmium yellow

2

2. Paint the areas that are occupied by vanilla first to ensure that the sienna will run over the yellow, and not the reverse.

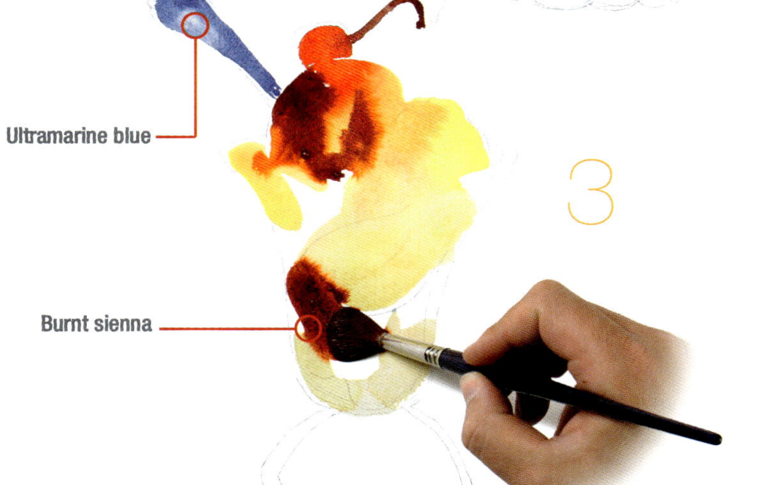

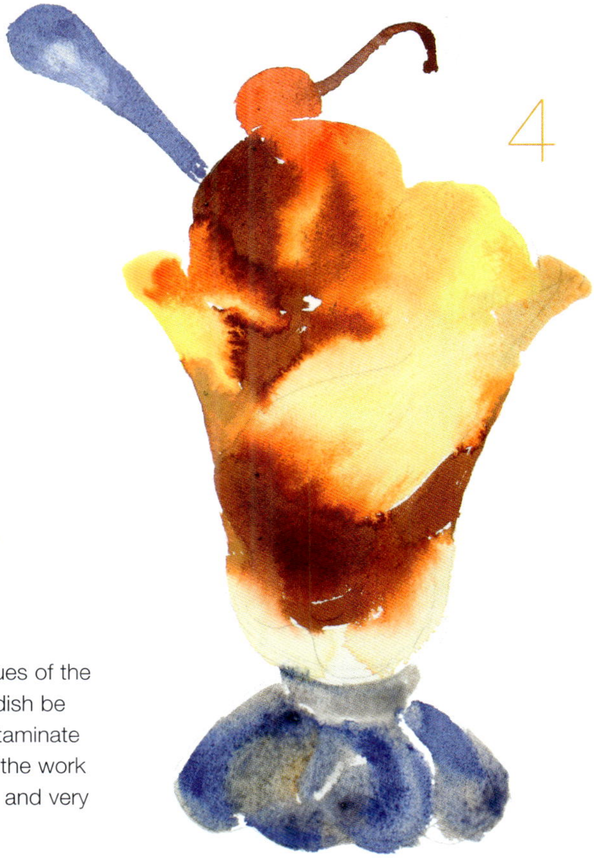

4

3. When painting the chocolate, the areas where the sienna and yellow come into contact create extensions of color that, curiously, are very similar to the typical effect of a large ice cream in this type of dish.

4. It is essential that the blues of the spoon and the foot of the dish be kept clean and do not contaminate the warm colors. This way the work has an attractive freshness and very clear colors.

65 Light and Shadow / **With Cool Colors**

LEVEL OF DIFFICULTY
★
COLORS
Burnt sienna
Cadmium orange
Cadmium yellow
Sap green
Ultramarine blue
BRUSH
Medium round natural hair
PAPER
140 lb medium-rough texture

According to Impressionist tradition, shadows should be painted with cool colors to contrast with the warm, more luminous colors. In this watercolor you will apply this norm almost to the letter. The contrast between the cool and warm colors is very evident; the blues appear in all the shaded areas while the illuminated areas have very warm tones.

1. After drawing the subject, paint the awning with orange very diluted with water, defining the fringe with the tip of the brush.

1

Cadmium orange

2. Paint the fruit with very saturated cadmium yellow and cadmium orange. Add shadows on the fruit with small touches of blue.

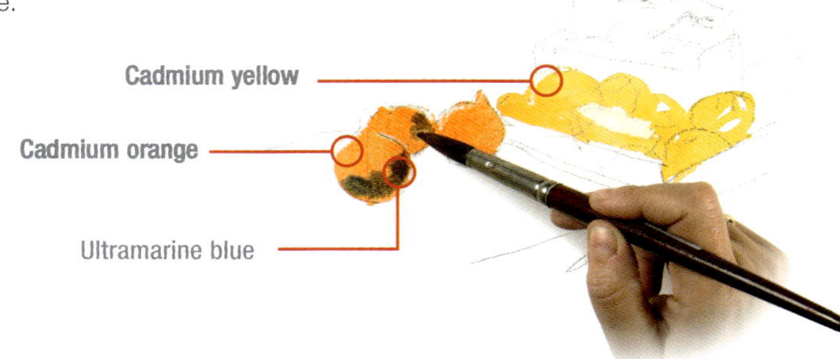

3. The warm colors are surrounded by cool colors making them stand out strongly. The shadows projected by the fruit are made with a somewhat more saturated blue.

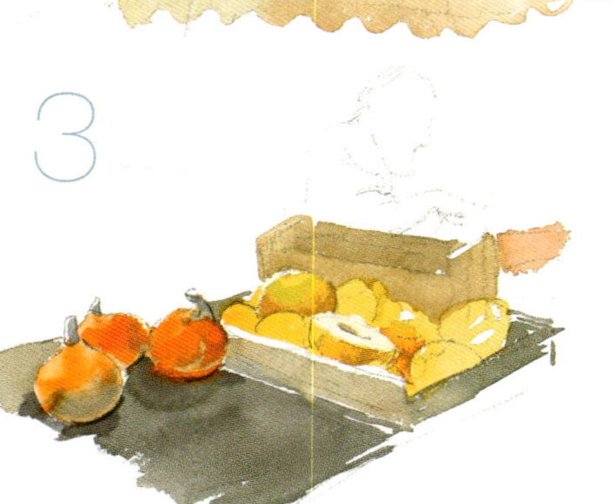

4. Cover the underside of the umbrella with blue painted on dry. The figure is orange shaded with sienna. Finally, emphasize the man's profile with pencil lines.

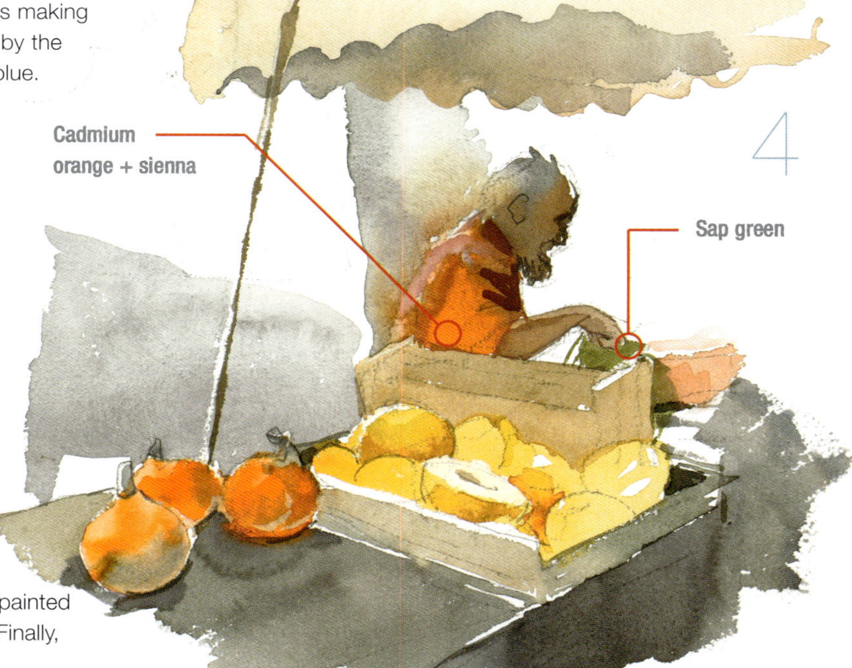

Light and Shadow / **With Warm Colors**

LEVEL OF DIFFICULTY
★
COLORS
Burnt sienna
Permanent red
Ultramarine blue
BRUSHES
Medium round natural hair
Wide flat synthetic hair
PAPER
140 lb medium-rough texture

Departing from the more usual approach, in many cases you can use warm colors to indicate the shaded areas. The figure in this watercolor has her back turned to the light and her face is in shadow. This shadow is warm and intense because of the warm reflection on the wall, and it contrasts with her back, which is exposed to full light and left in reserve.

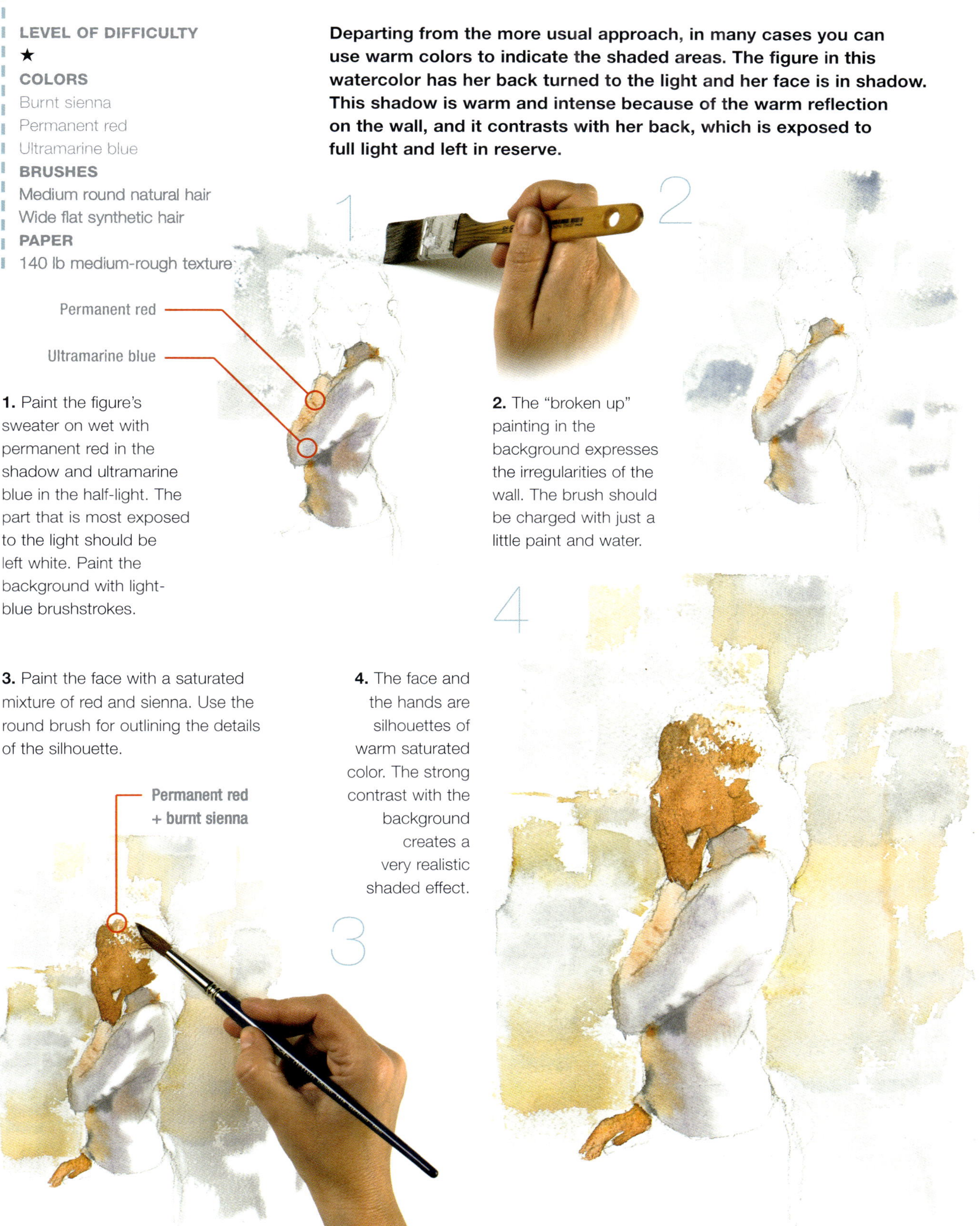

1. Paint the figure's sweater on wet with permanent red in the shadow and ultramarine blue in the half-light. The part that is most exposed to the light should be left white. Paint the background with light-blue brushstrokes.

2. The "broken up" painting in the background expresses the irregularities of the wall. The brush should be charged with just a little paint and water.

3. Paint the face with a saturated mixture of red and sienna. Use the round brush for outlining the details of the silhouette.

4. The face and the hands are silhouettes of warm saturated color. The strong contrast with the background creates a very realistic shaded effect.

67 Light and Shadow / **With Color Planes**

LEVEL OF DIFFICULTY
★★
COLORS
Burnt sienna
Carmine
Permanent green
Ultramarine blue
Cerulean blue
BRUSHES
Fine round natural hair
Medium round natural hair
Wide flat synthetic hair
PAPER
140 lb medium-rough texture

Successive contrasting planes of warm and cool colors can be used to create the effects of light and shadow. The planes refer to the objects and forms whose colors contrast with each other. In this watercolor, you will attempt to create these contrasts with areas of solid color to highlight the play of light and shadow.

1

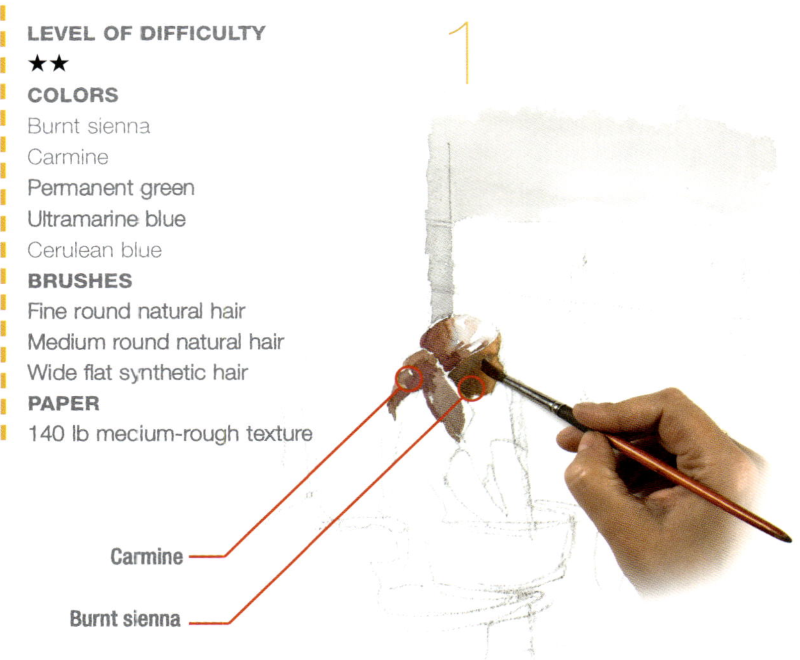

1. After drawing the subject, paint the head of the figure with carmine (for the headscarf) and apply burnt sienna to the face. Darken the color of the face by adding a little carmine.

2

2. Finish painting the figure's skin with burnt sienna. Use a combination of permanent green and a little cerulean blue for the hanging shirt. This is a luminous plane of flat color that contrasts with the warm tones of the figure.

Permanent green + cerulean blue

3

3. Here, paint the warm luminous pink tone against the dark cool blue of the tub.

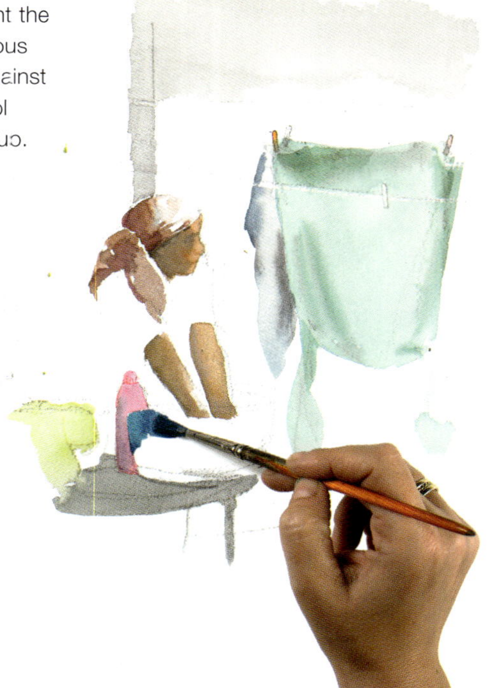

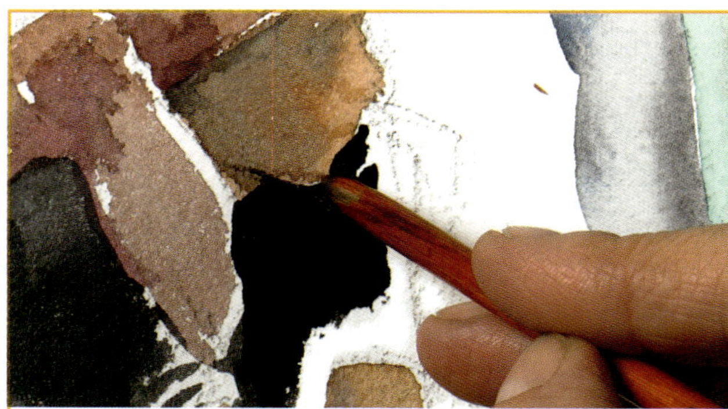

When you must paint the edge of an area that is touching the edge of another, you can use the handle of the brush. You can "push" the paint up to the edge of the drawing without leaving a white outline that will interrupt the continuity of the colors.

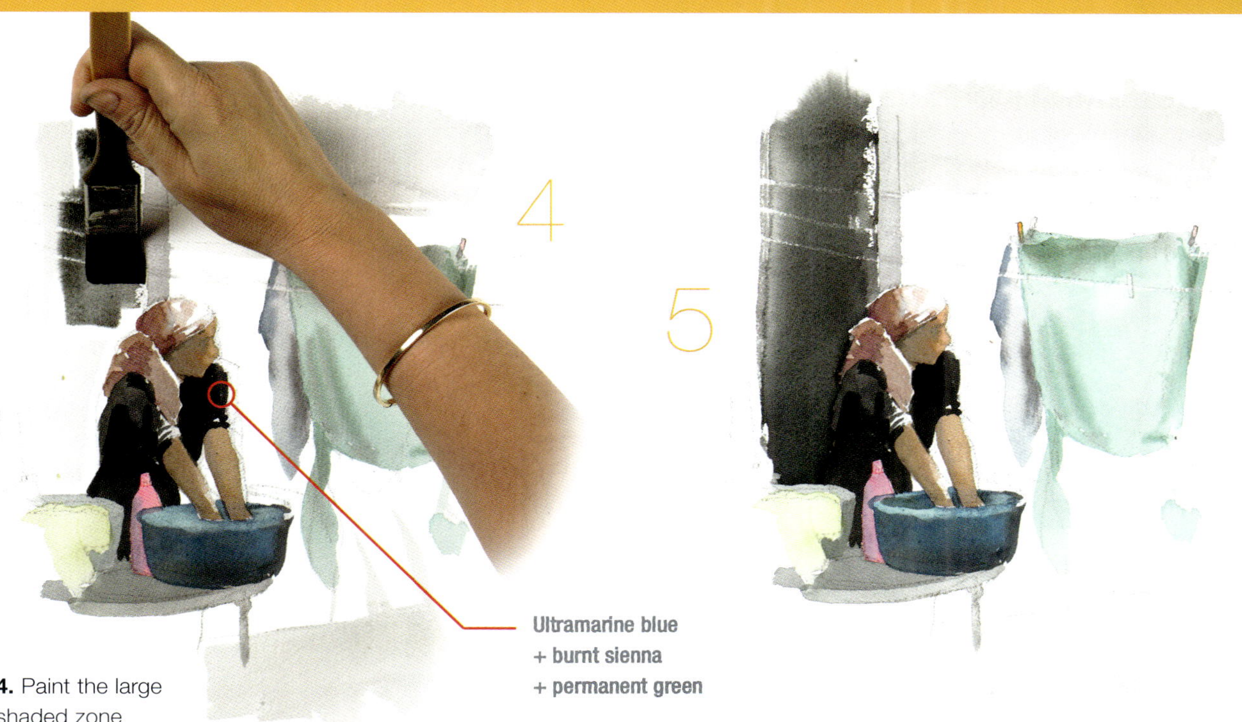

4. Paint the large shaded zone behind the figure, making large brushstrokes with the wide synthetic hair brush. Use the same color that is used for the woman's blouse.

5. Alternating zones of light and dark, warm and cool colors, creates a feeling of luminous, open air.

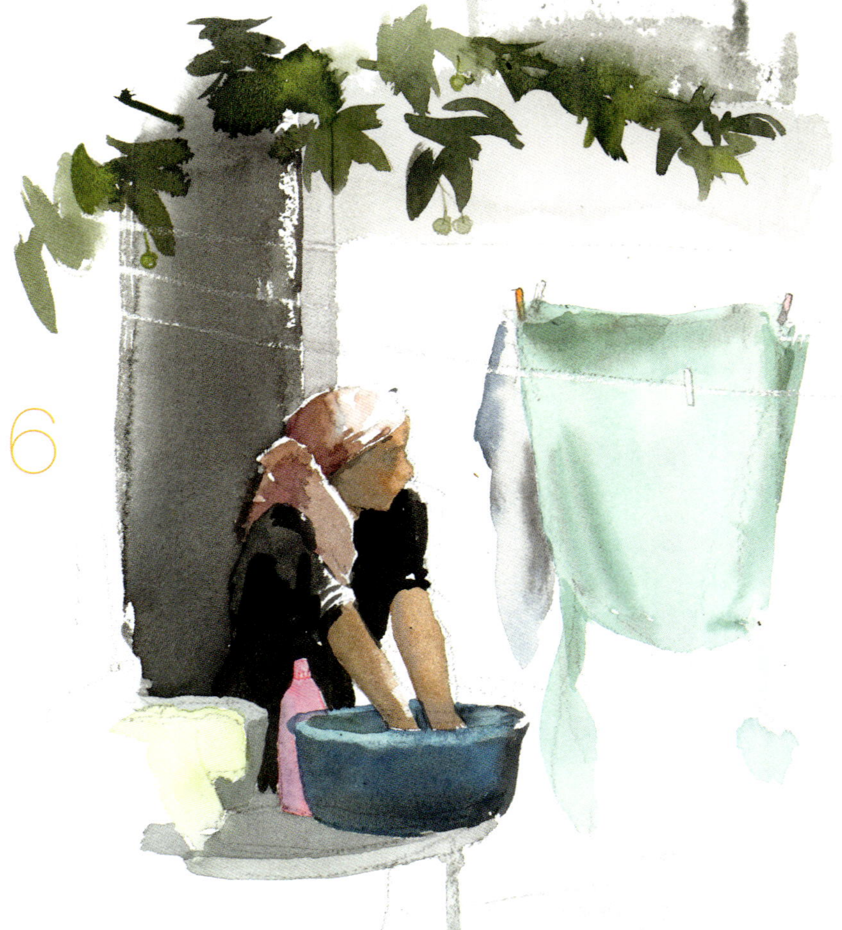

6. Adding the leaves in the foreground increases the feeling of space. Thanks to the white left around the colors, the space and the air flow among the forms.

Light and Shadow / **With Complementary Colors**

LEVEL OF DIFFICULTY
★
COLORS
Burnt sienna
Carmine
Sap green
Permanent red
Ultramarine blue
Cobalt violet
BRUSH
Medium round natural hair
PAPER
140 lb medium-rough texture

To create effects of modeling and volume, in other words, light and shadow, without using blended colors and preserving the purity of the colors as much as possible, you can make use of complementary tones. In this watercolor, the contrast will be between red and green.

Permanent red
Sap green
Burnt sienna + carmine

1

1. After making the drawing, paint the first piece of fruit permanent red, with a greenish shadow. The green piece of fruit (sap green) reinforces the contrast between the two.

2. The slices of melon are a very light and luminous red, applied after wetting the paper.

2

3. To heighten the contrast between the pure tones, paint the plate with ultramarine blue, a cool color that contrasts with the warm reds.

3

Ultramarine blue

4

4. Finally, paint the shadow of the plate with unmixed cobalt violet.

Cobalt violet

69 Light and Shadow / **With Neutral Colors**

LEVEL OF DIFFICULTY
★

COLORS
Burnt sienna
Permanent red
Cobalt blue

BRUSHES
Fine round natural hair
Medium round natural hair

PAPER
140 lb medium-rough texture

The subtlest effects of light and shadow, like the mist in this watercolor, are created with neutral colors. These colors are a mixture of warm and cool colors, or complementary colors. The result is a wide range of more or less cool grays dotted with accents of pure tones.

1

1. After sketching the scene and wetting the paper, make a very diluted wash of carmine mixed with cobalt blue. In the lower area, apply a somewhat more saturated wash of blue and sienna.

Burnt sienna + cobalt blue

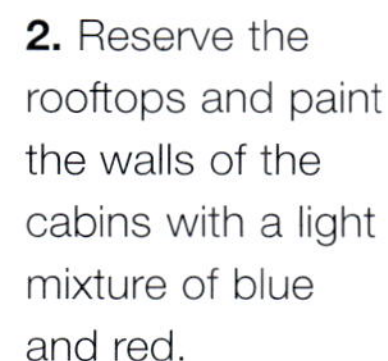

2. Reserve the rooftops and paint the walls of the cabins with a light mixture of blue and red.

3. After painting the fir trees with the gray used before, but much more saturated and on dry paper, apply some dabs of red in the highest branches.

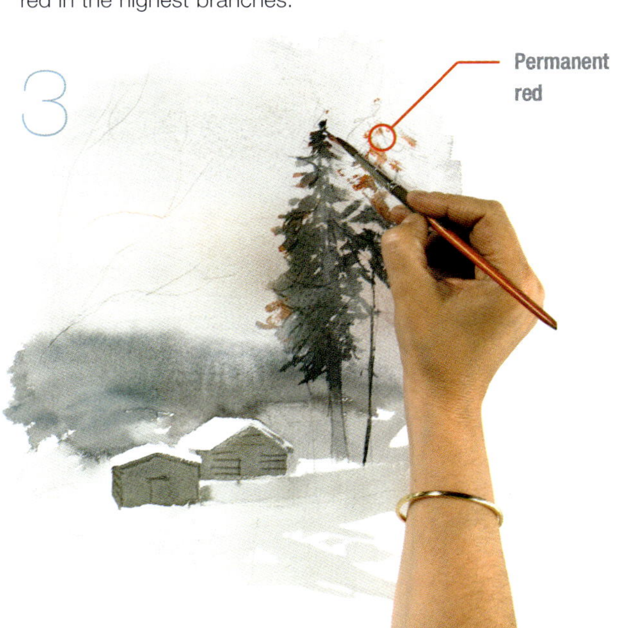

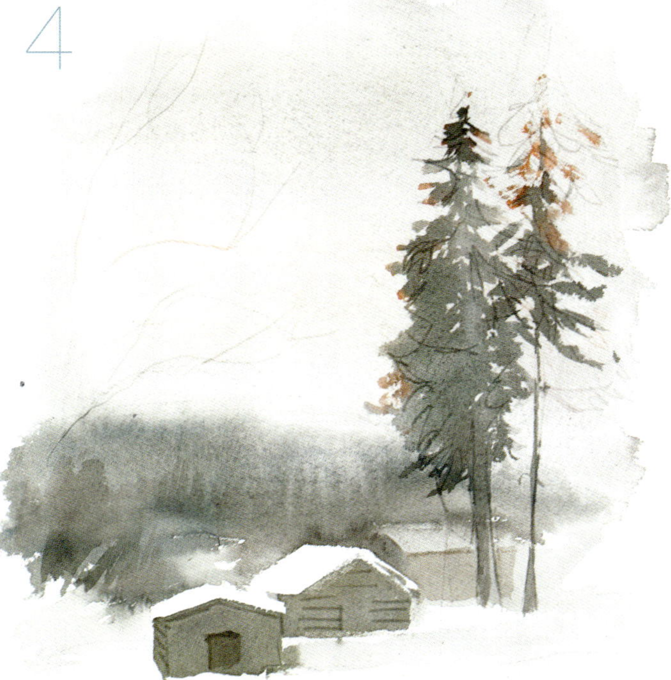

4. The warm and vibrant light in the tops of the trees shades and enlivens the faint and flat light of this misty landscape.

70 Light and Shadow / **Reflections**

LEVEL OF DIFFICULTY
★★

COLORS
Burnt sienna
Carmine
Burnt umber
Cobalt blue

BRUSHES
Wide flat synthetic hair
Fine round natural hair

PAPER
140 lb medium-rough texture

The reflection of a smooth wet surface is a typical effect in many watercolors: a landscape after rain. In this case, it is the seashore on a gray day. The reflection of the fisherman on the wet sand has a cool, limpid luminosity, reinforced by the somber warm colors in the foreground.

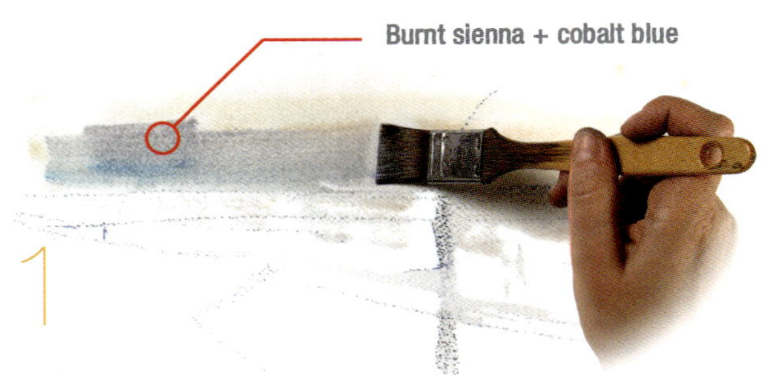

1. Make a very simple sketch of the subject. Apply a wash of burnt sienna and cobalt blue to the sky on dry paper.

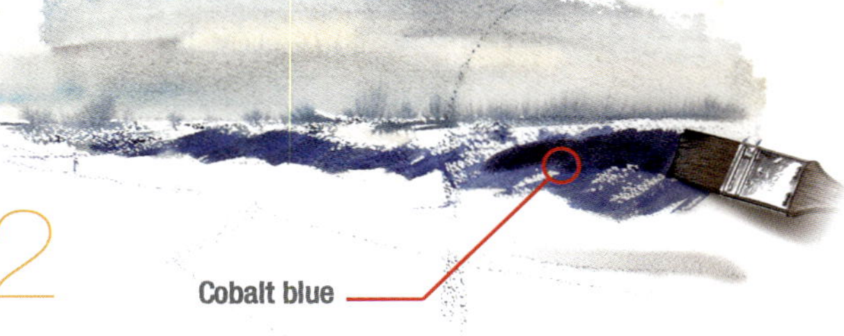

2. Paint the stormy sea with irregular brushstrokes of pure and saturated cobalt blue, leaving white reserves here and there. These whites represent the foamy crests of the waves.

3

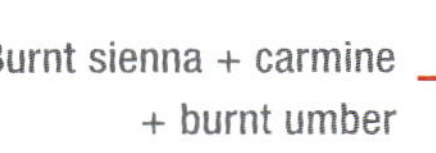

4

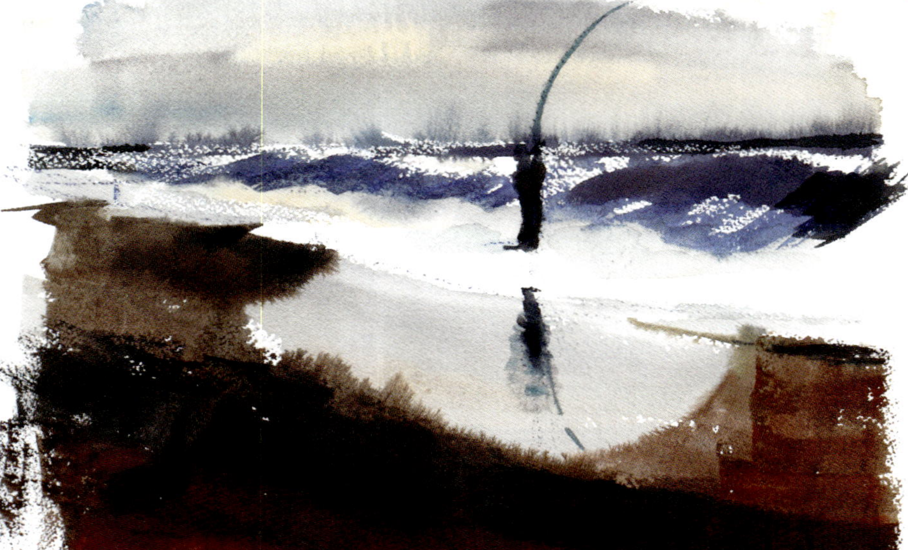

3. Cover the wet sand with a wash like that used for the sky. Between this wash and the sea leave a reserved band that suggests foam on the sand. Paint the foreground with a very saturated mix of burnt sienna, carmine, and burnt umber.

4. Finally, paint the reflection of the figure with the fine brush on wet so the paint will run lightly. You can also paint the silhouette of the fisherman, in this case on dry, with a saturated mixture of blue and burnt umber.

71 Light and Shadow / **Sky and Clouds**

LEVEL OF DIFFICULTY
★
COLORS
Burnt umber
Cobalt blue
BRUSH
Wide flat synthetic hair
PAPER
140 lb medium-rough texture

The direct luminosity of the sky is expressed much better if clouds are part of the representation. They shade the light and with their volume add depth and value to the celestial space. The secret of this effect is in the irregularity and spontaneity of the white reserves.

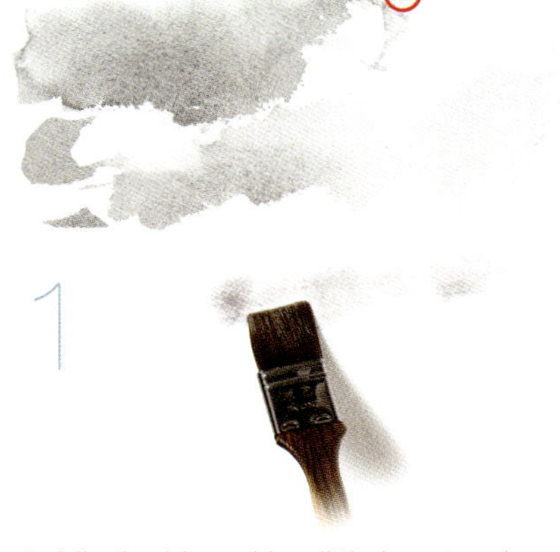

Burnt umber
+ cobalt blue

1

1. Mix the blue with a little burnt umber to make blue gray, and paint irregular washes leaving reserves between them. A drawing would hinder this process, because it is the spontaneity of the washes that creates the cloudy effect.

2

2. Paint the edges of the clouds with pure blue that is not very saturated, filling some of the spaces that were left white before.

Cobalt blue

4

Burnt umber
+ cobalt blue

3

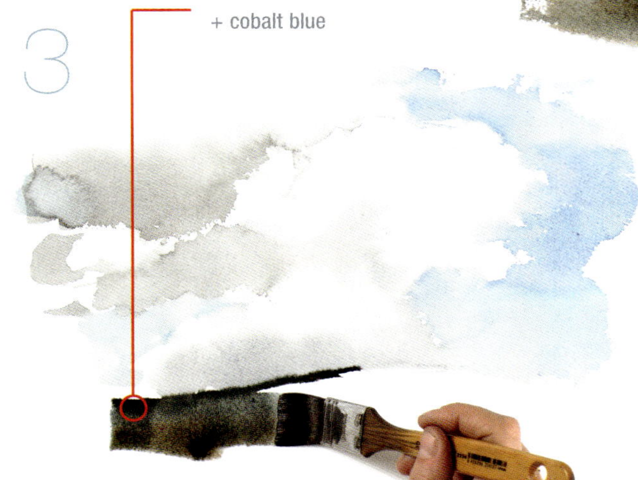

3. Paint the horizon with a very dense mixture of blue and umber. There is no need for details; it should just be a mass of color.

4. The wash of the landscape, in crude contrast with the pale tones of the sky, creates the weightless aerial luminosity of this watercolor.

LEVEL OF DIFFICULTY
★★

COLORS
Cadmium yellow
Cadmium orange
Permanent red
Cerulean blue
Burnt sienna

BRUSHES
Medium round natural hair
Wide flat synthetic hair

PAPER
140 lb medium-rough texture

Light on the water is a subject that all watercolorists return to again and again. The shadows and reflections on an undulating surface are fleeting, but the fluidity of watercolors makes it easy when you are trying to create irregular and transparent effects like those that this subject offers so abundantly.

1. First color the paper with a light wash of orange and yellow. At the bottom, add some touches of blue to the still-wet paint.

2. Now work on dry. Apply washes to the shaded parts of the bridge with a mixture of orange and permanent red.

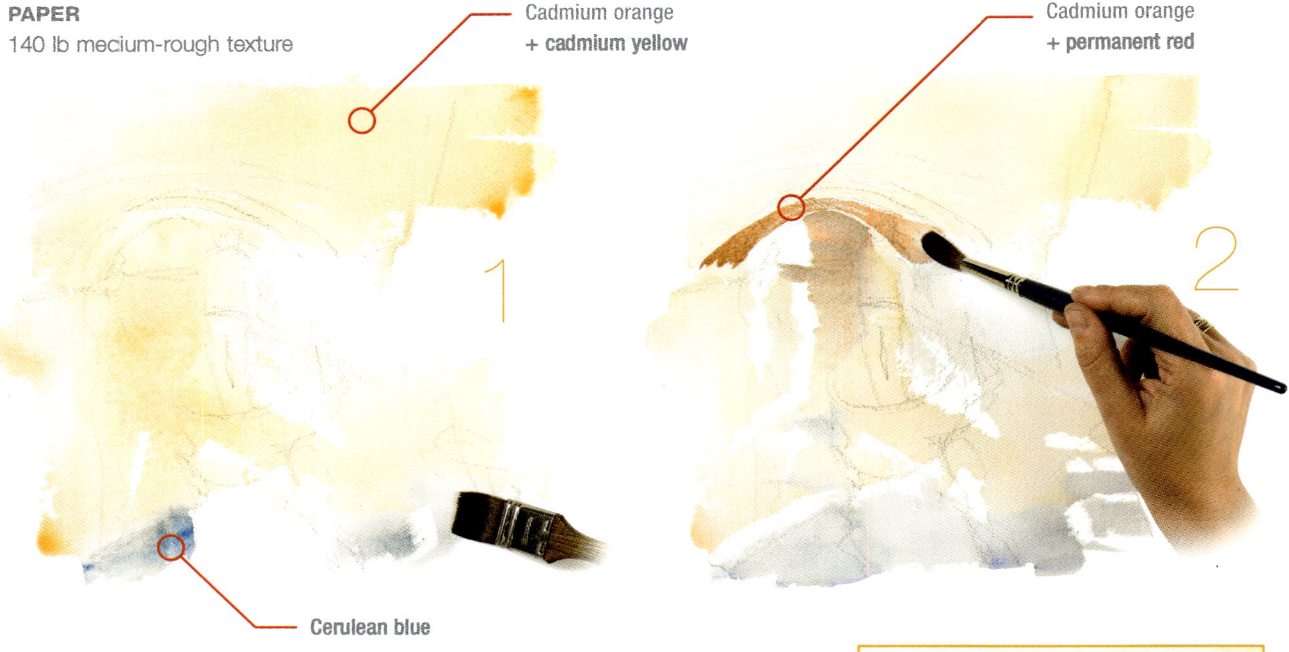

3. Paint the background with light washes of warm pinks and oranges. The color of the bridges incorporates a little blue to create cooler tones. Use saturated reds and yellows on the boat to emphasize the foreground.

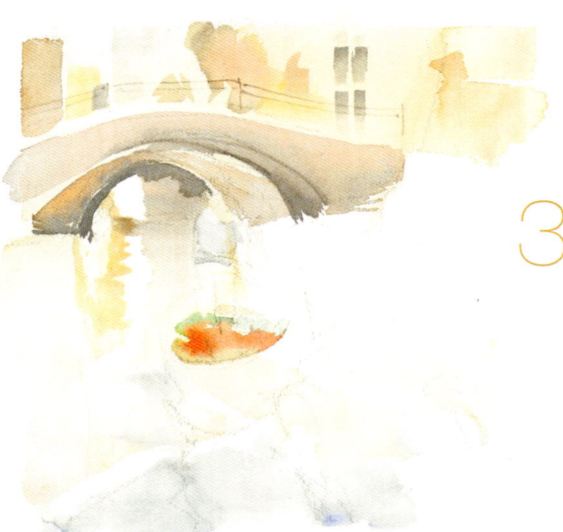

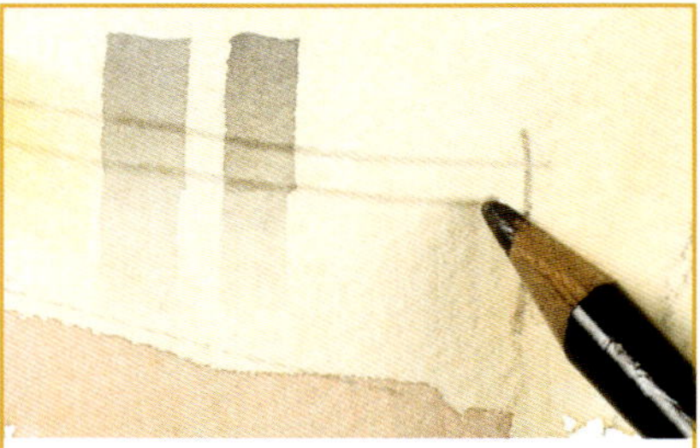

Pencil lines over the dried washes define forms and objects that do not need to be painted. The line itself is enough to represent everything that is important to the subject but is far away. This avoids an approach that could make the painting look overworked.

4. After the warm washes come the cool ones. Blue and sienna mixed make an excellent gray that the painter can use for the darkest shadows in the composition.

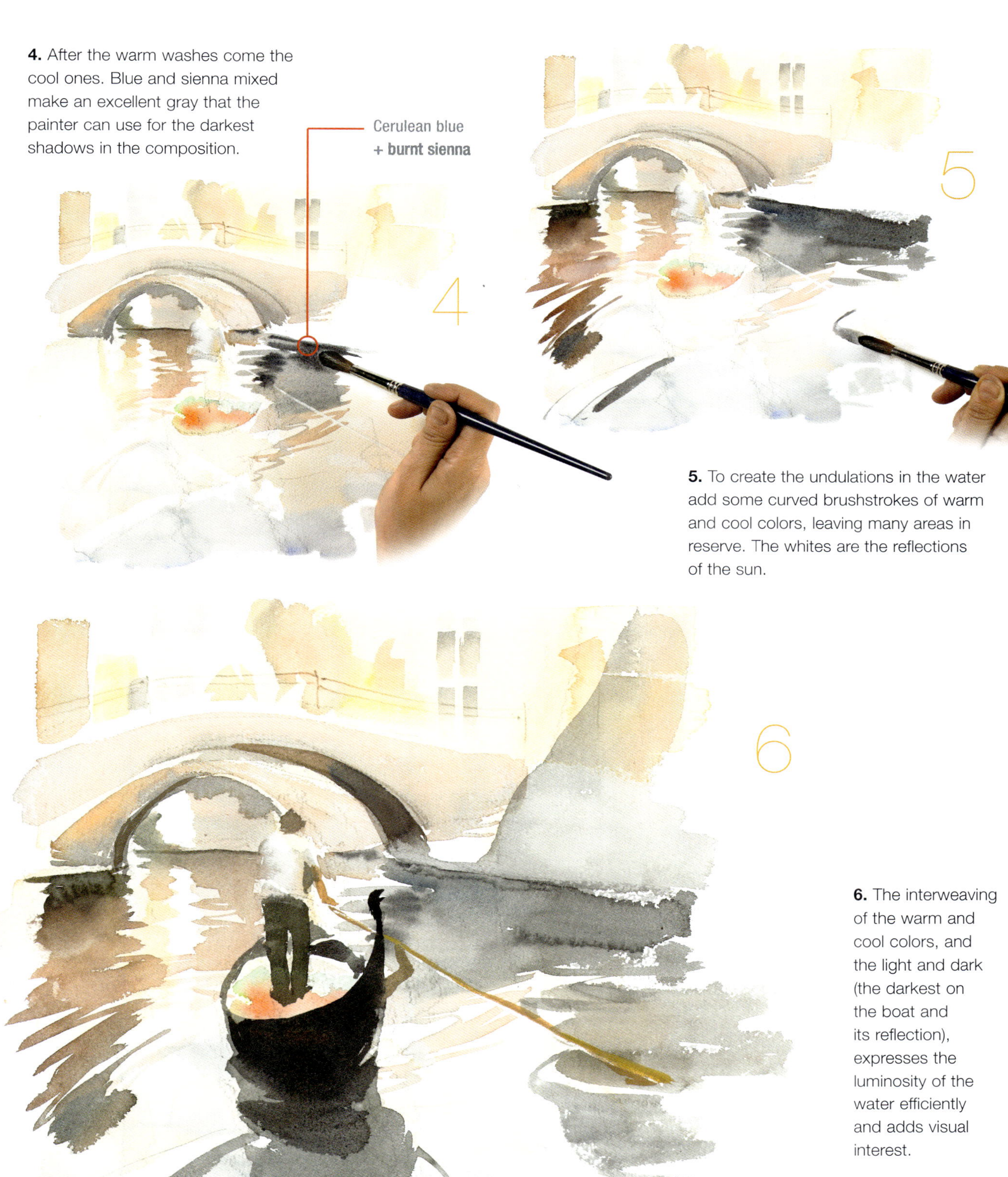

5. To create the undulations in the water add some curved brushstrokes of warm and cool colors, leaving many areas in reserve. The whites are the reflections of the sun.

6. The interweaving of the warm and cool colors, and the light and dark (the darkest on the boat and its reflection), expresses the luminosity of the water efficiently and adds visual interest.

73 Light and Shadow / **A Flash of Light**

LEVEL OF DIFFICULTY
★★
COLORS
Burnt sienna
Burnt umber
Permanent red
Cerulean blue
Ultramarine blue
BRUSH
Medium round natural hair
PAPER
140 lb medium-rough texture

The total and sharp contrast between light and shadow created by a "flash of sunlight" on objects is here expressed with a white reserve on the tablecloth on which only the shadows of the fold are shaded. The luminosity is very pronounced, in part thanks to the coloring of the child seated in the shadow.

1. A light wash of sienna on the table and a wash of ultramarine blue mixed with a little sienna over the wet background are enough to establish a general harmonious tone.

2. Paint the reds of the pants (permanent red) and the shadow of the tablecloth (burnt sienna) on dry paper.

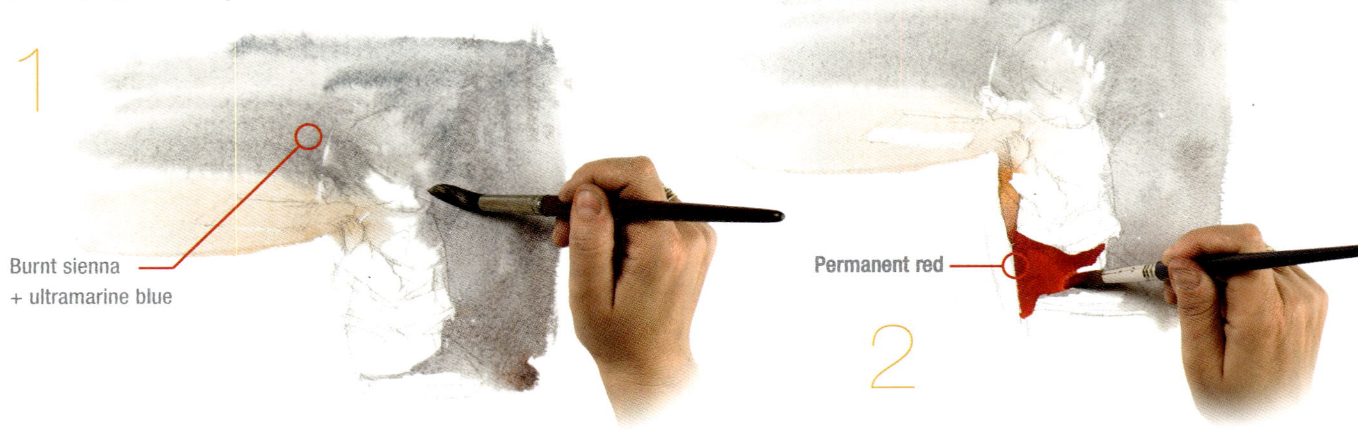

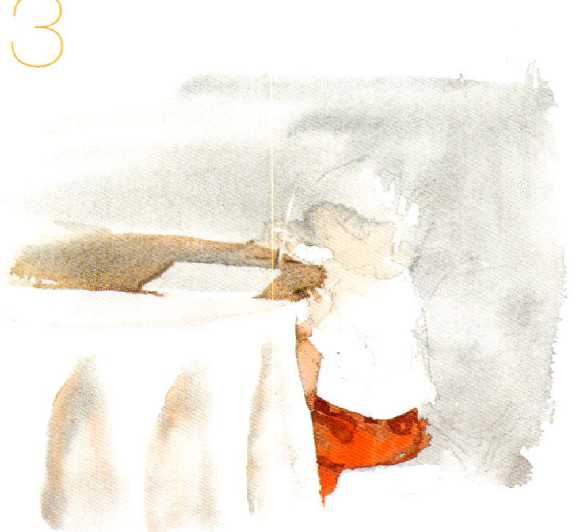

3. Reserve the paper that the child is drawing on to create a luminous area.

4. Paint the child's shirt with different shades of cerulean blue to express the folds and their shadows. Apply sienna to the hair, and burnt umber in the darkest areas. The folds of the tablecloth are light washes of burnt sienna.

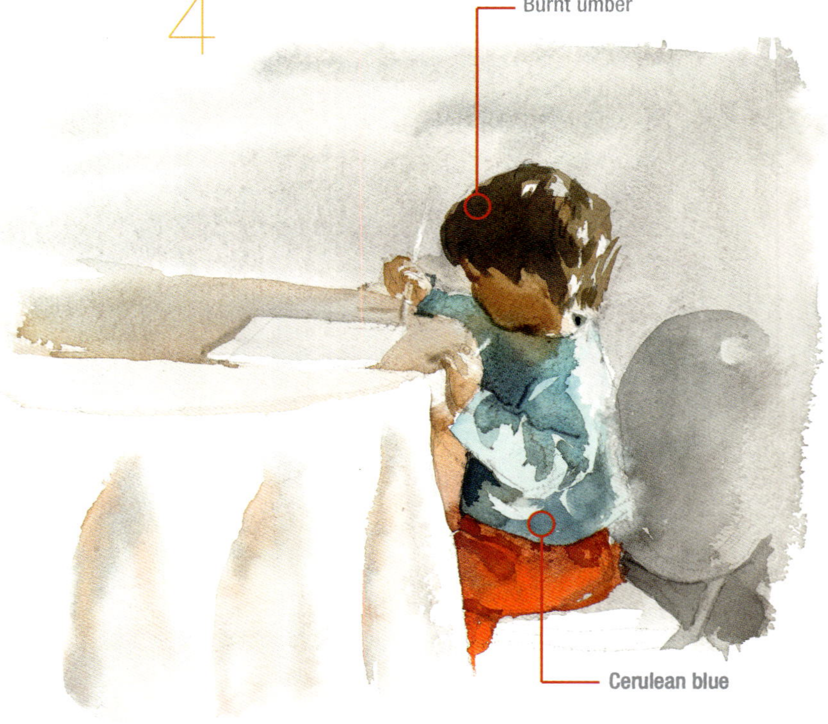

Light and Shadow / **Backlighting**

LEVEL OF DIFFICULTY
★
COLORS
Burnt sienna
Carmine
Ultramarine blue
Burnt umber
BRUSHES
Medium round natural hair
Wide flat synthetic hair
PAPER
140 lb medium-rough texture

A backlit figure looks like a dark cutout on a very light background. Because of the white plumage of this duck, its shadows are painted and blended against a much darker background, and the contrasting area is painted around the neck and head of the bird. Here the contrast between the gray tones creates the effect of luminosity.

1. Paint washes of blue mixed with sienna within the drawing, to make a neutral gray that tends toward cool, delineating the illuminated areas and the backlit areas.

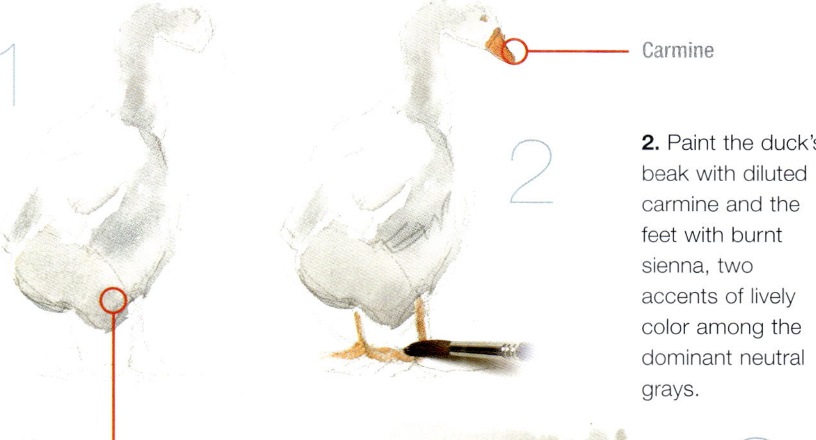

2. Paint the duck's beak with diluted carmine and the feet with burnt sienna, two accents of lively color among the dominant neutral grays.

Burnt sienna + ultramarine blue + burnt umber

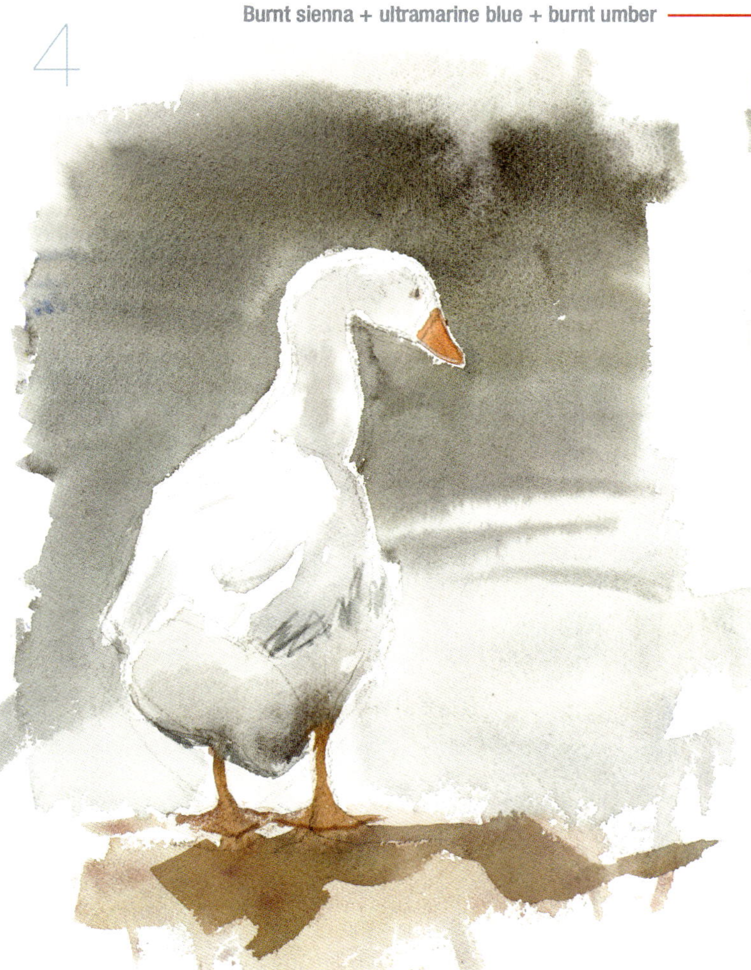

3. Mix saturated blue, sienna, and umber to make a very dark gray that is almost black, and use it to paint the background. Apply a light wash of sienna and carmine to the ground.

4. Add some dark brushstrokes to accentuate details of the feathers. The shadow cast by the duck on the ground (painted with saturated sienna) accentuates the luminous effect.

Twilight and Backlighting

LEVEL OF DIFFICULTY
★★

COLORS
Cadmium yellow
Burnt sienna
Carmine
Sap green
Permanent green
Permanent red
Ultramarine blue
Cerulean blue

BRUSHES
Medium round natural hair
Wide flat synthetic hair

PAPER
140 lb medium-rough texture

At twilight, spectacular lighting effects take place in the sky and the landscape. This watercolor illustrates one of those moments: some tree branches silhouetted against a fiery sunset. The great richness of color combined with the looseness of the painting creates a splendid watercolor effect full of strength and subtlety.

1

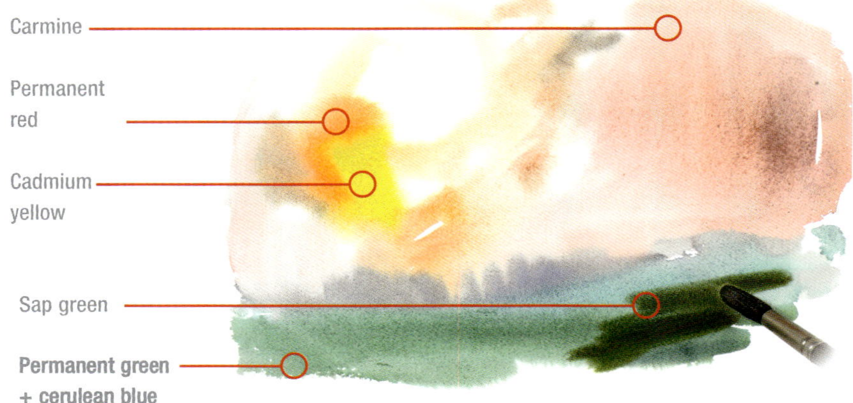

1. First wet the paper well so that the colors will spread and combine freely. Use diluted carmine as a base over which, later, you will apply reds and yellows that will create orange tones. Paint the lower area with permanent green and sap green.

2

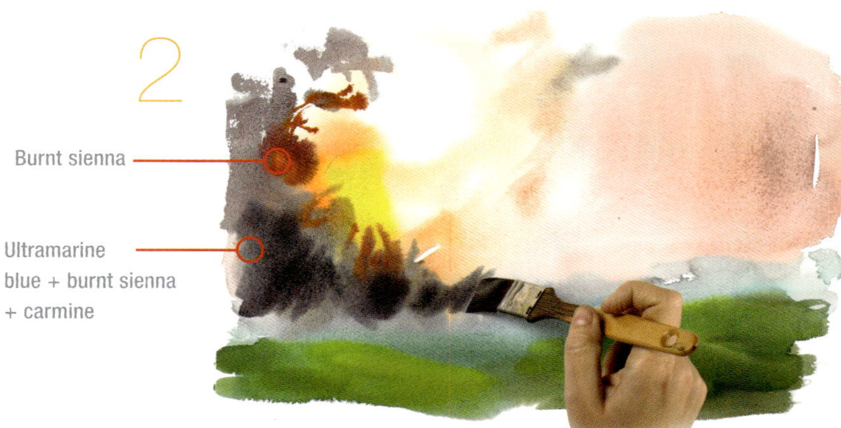

2. After they have dried, apply dark strokes of ultramarine blue, carmine, and sienna over the previous colors to create the dark masses of the tree.

3. Working with the edge of the wide brush, add straight brushstrokes of grays and reds in different directions. These brushstrokes represent the branches of the tree in silhouette.

3

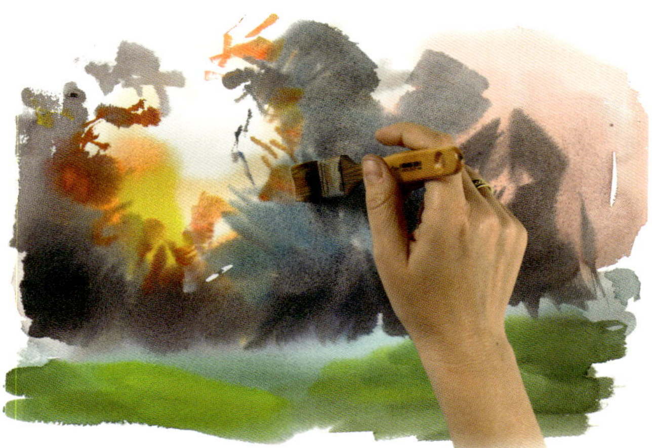

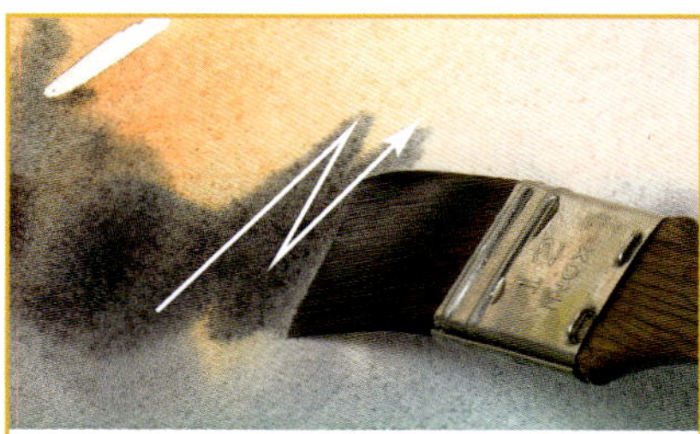

Move the flat brush in a zigzag to create wide indented lines that are very useful for expressing the irregularities of the tones in subjects based on large areas of color.

4

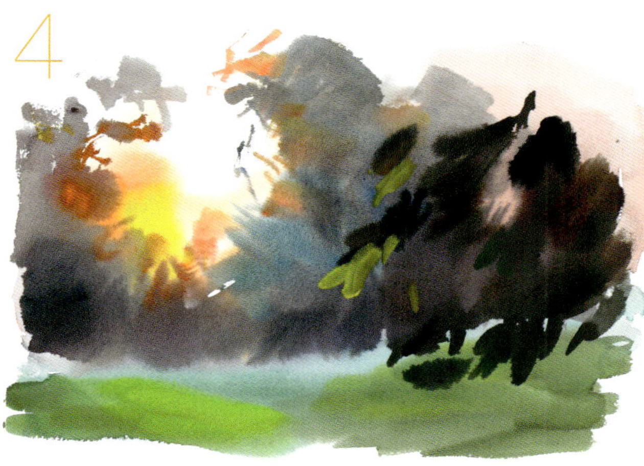

4. Now mix blue, sap green, and sienna to create the darkest and most-saturated color possible for painting the branches in the nearest plane.

5

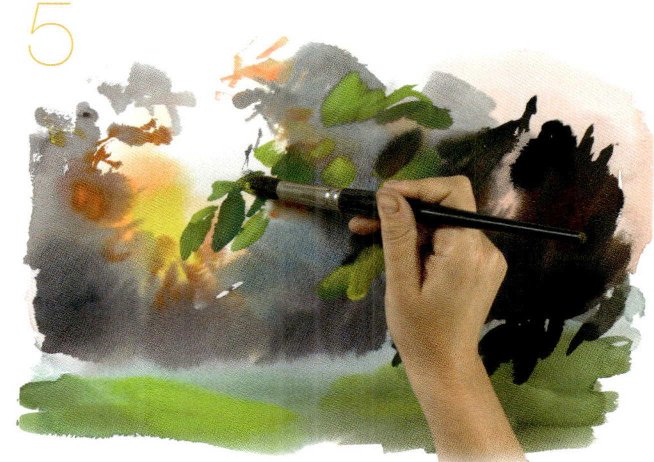

5. Using the round brush charged with the darkest sap green, paint some leaves to create the sense of the nearness of the dark foreground.

6. The contrast between the very light and very dark tones is reinforced by the contrast between the warm and cool colors. The feeling of depth is strengthened, and at the same time, reinforced by the luminous effect.

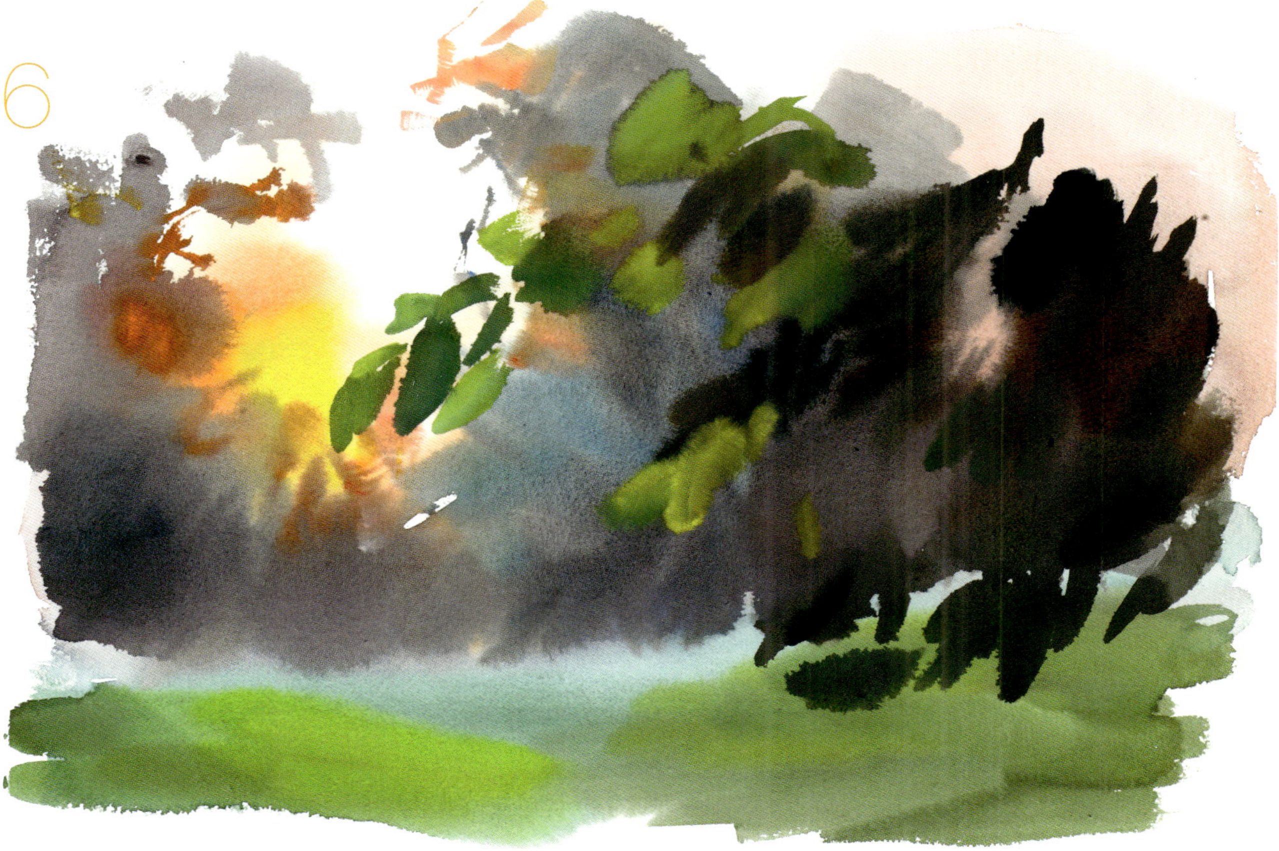

6

Dry Brush / **The Texture of the Paper**

LEVEL OF DIFFICULTY
★

COLORS
Cadmium yellow
Cadmium orange
Burnt sienna
Ultramarine blue

BRUSH
Medium round natural hair

PAPER
140 lb medium-rough texture

The dry brush technique consists of applying paint that is barely diluted with water so that the texture of the paper is revealed with each stroke of the brush. This creates textural effects that can be beneficial to subjects like this one, where the feathers of the chick are illustrated by the texture itself.

1. After drawing the small bird, paint the inside with very thick yellow. The brushstrokes are barely visible as an irregular texture appears in their place.

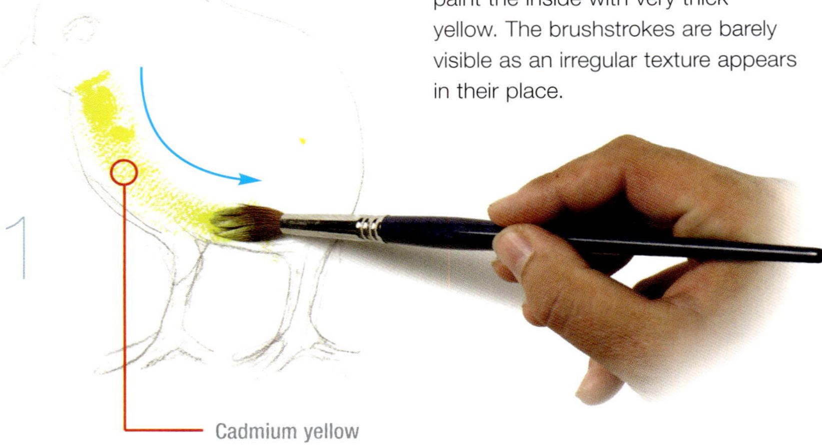

2. Paint over what has already been painted with "dry" brushstrokes of orange.

2

Cadmium orange

3. The execution is extremely simple, just like the subject matter.

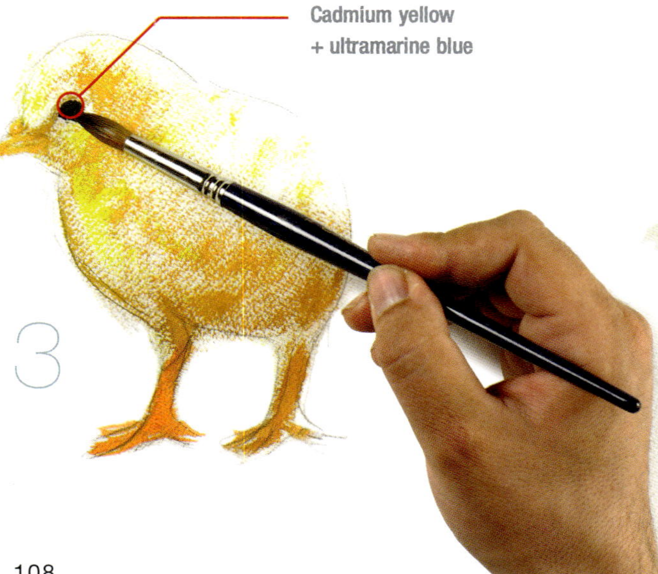

4

Burnt sienna + ultramarine blue

4. Apply a wash of diluted sienna and blue to the ground to create a shadow and to create a sense of a support for the chick.

77 Dry Brush / **The Effect of Transparency**

LEVEL OF DIFFICULTY
★

COLORS
Cadmium yellow
Carmine
Cerulean blue

BRUSHES
Medium round natural hair
Narrow flat synthetic hair

PAPER
140 lb medium-rough texture

In this exercise, the broken finish typical of the dry brush technique creates the sense of a transparent glass. The process is very simple: it is a matter of using barely diluted paint so that each brushstroke reveals the texture of the paper and small white areas appear among the painted zones.

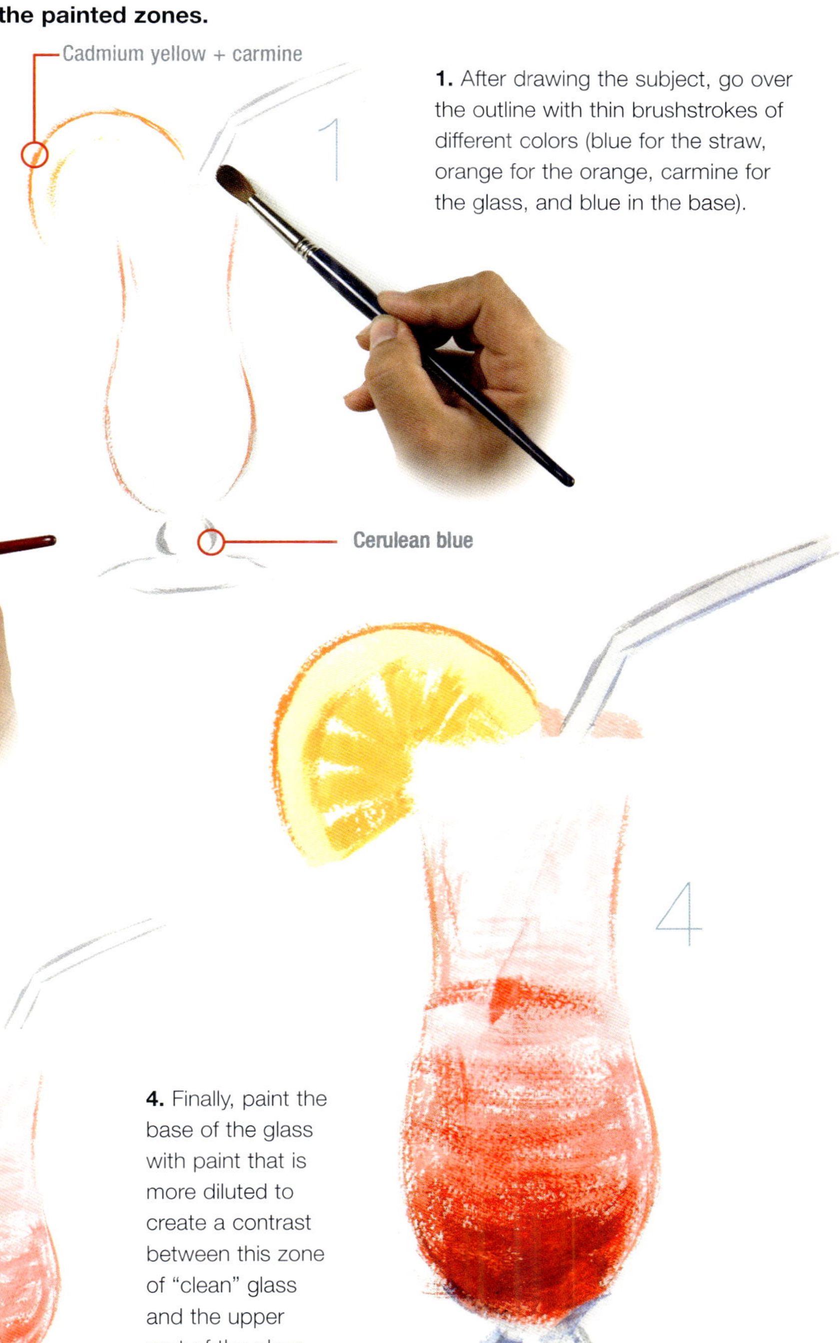

1. After drawing the subject, go over the outline with thin brushstrokes of different colors (blue for the straw, orange for the orange, carmine for the glass, and blue in the base).

2. The converging lines help represent the sections of the orange. In the glass, apply brushstrokes with the dry brush, lightly curving them to express its roundness.

3. Dilute the carmine more and more as you move up the glass. With each dilution, dry the hair of the brush so the stroke will create the appropriate marks.

4. Finally, paint the base of the glass with paint that is more diluted to create a contrast between this zone of "clean" glass and the upper part of the glass.

78 Dry Brush / **The Effect of Rain and Wind**

LEVEL OF DIFFICULTY
★★

COLORS
Raw umber
Cobalt violet
Cerulean blue
Carmine

BRUSHES
Fine round natural hair
Wide flat synthetic hair

PAPER
140 lb medium-rough texture

Dragging a wide and nearly dry brush across the paper, like you will do here, will create atmospheric effects that can evoke unpleasant weather. Rain, wind, fog, etc., can very easily be illustrated with this technique. To do it more efficiently, use a mixture of colors that will create a cool monochrome.

1. Use a wash mixed with blue, violet, and umber. The wide flat brush makes irregular streaks that will create the wet and windy atmosphere of the painting.

2. A very liquid wash of carmine creates the washed-out silhouette of an umbrella. Around it, distribute drier brushstrokes in the same direction.

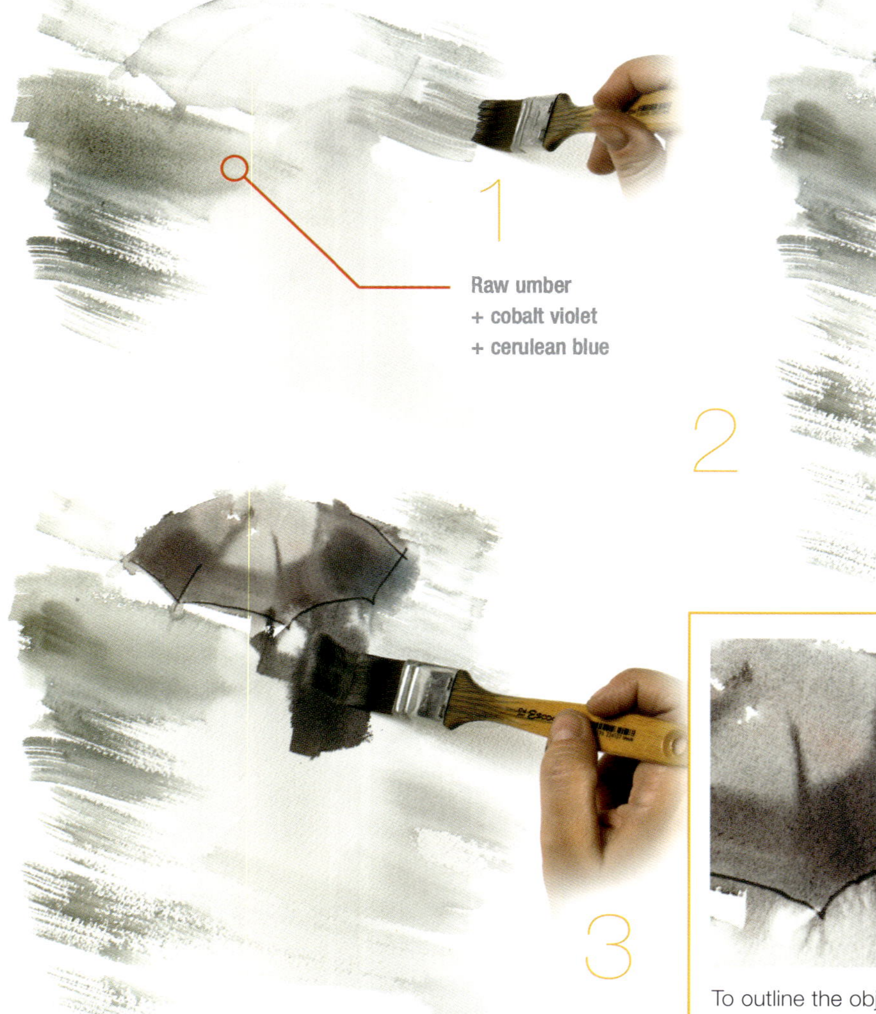

3. Paint the silhouette of a figure with a more-saturated wash without worrying about details or shading.

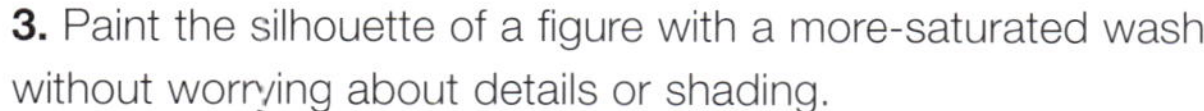

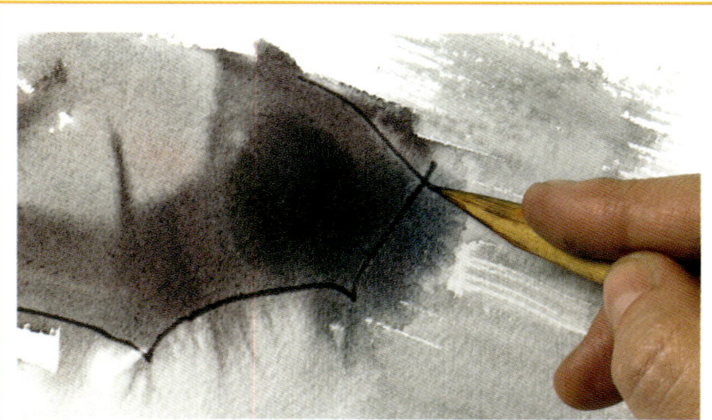

To outline the objects that require more definition, you can use the handle of the brush or a reed pen with a beveled tip. Creating outlines by indenting the paper will limit the expansion of the paint and make the profile clearer.

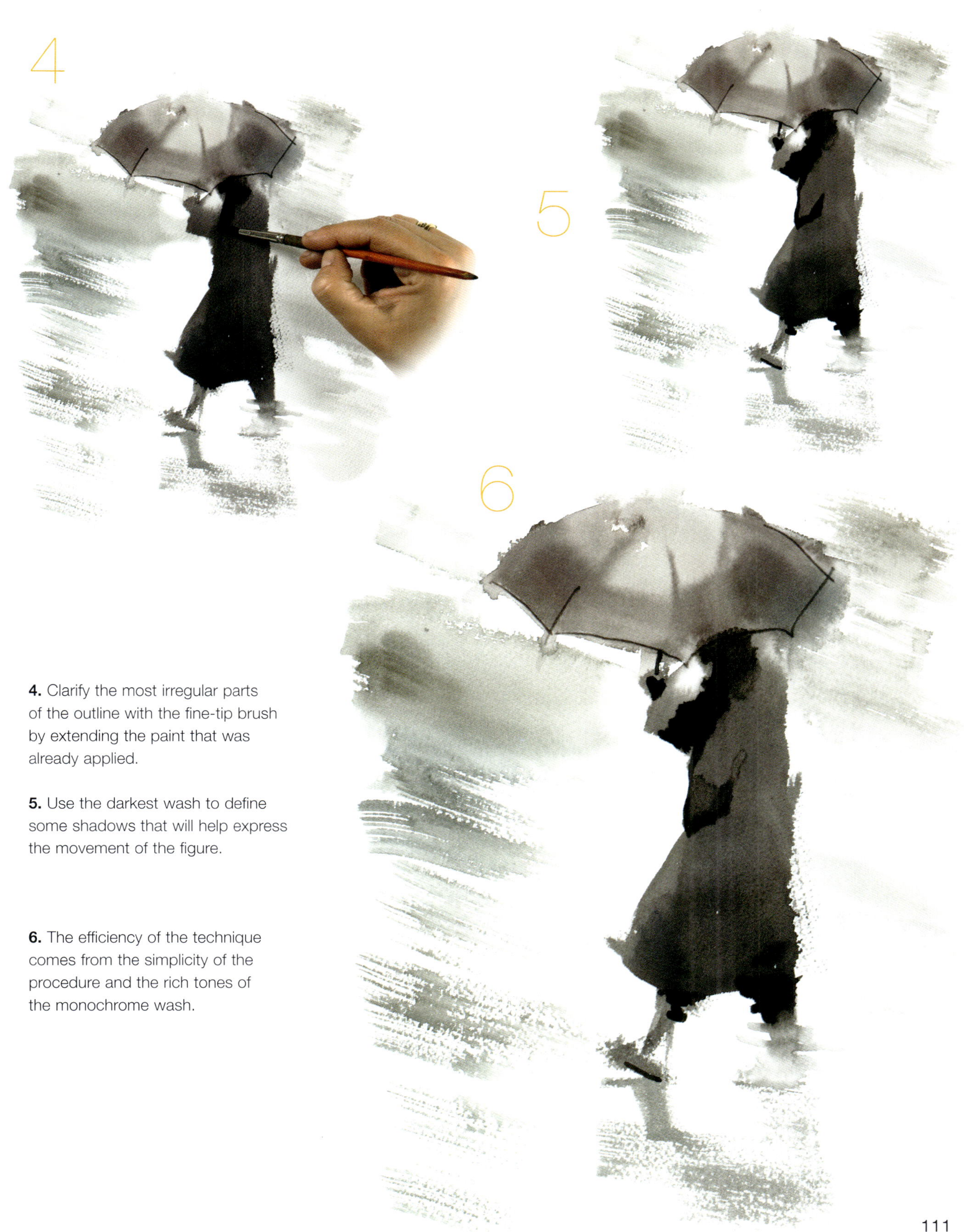

4. Clarify the most irregular parts of the outline with the fine-tip brush by extending the paint that was already applied.

5. Use the darkest wash to define some shadows that will help express the movement of the figure.

6. The efficiency of the technique comes from the simplicity of the procedure and the rich tones of the monochrome wash.

79 Dry Brush / **Plant Textures**

LEVEL OF DIFFICULTY
★
COLORS
Burnt sienna
Sap green
Permanent green
Ultramarine blue
Cerulean blue
BRUSHES
Narrow flat synthetic hair
Wide flat synthetic hair
PAPER
140 lb medium-rough texture

The texture of the paper combined with the dry brush technique creates many possibilities. One of them is suggesting the consistency of some plants, in this case a palm tree. You will make the trunk and the palm leaves using the dry brush technique, and the rest will be done in the conventional manner.

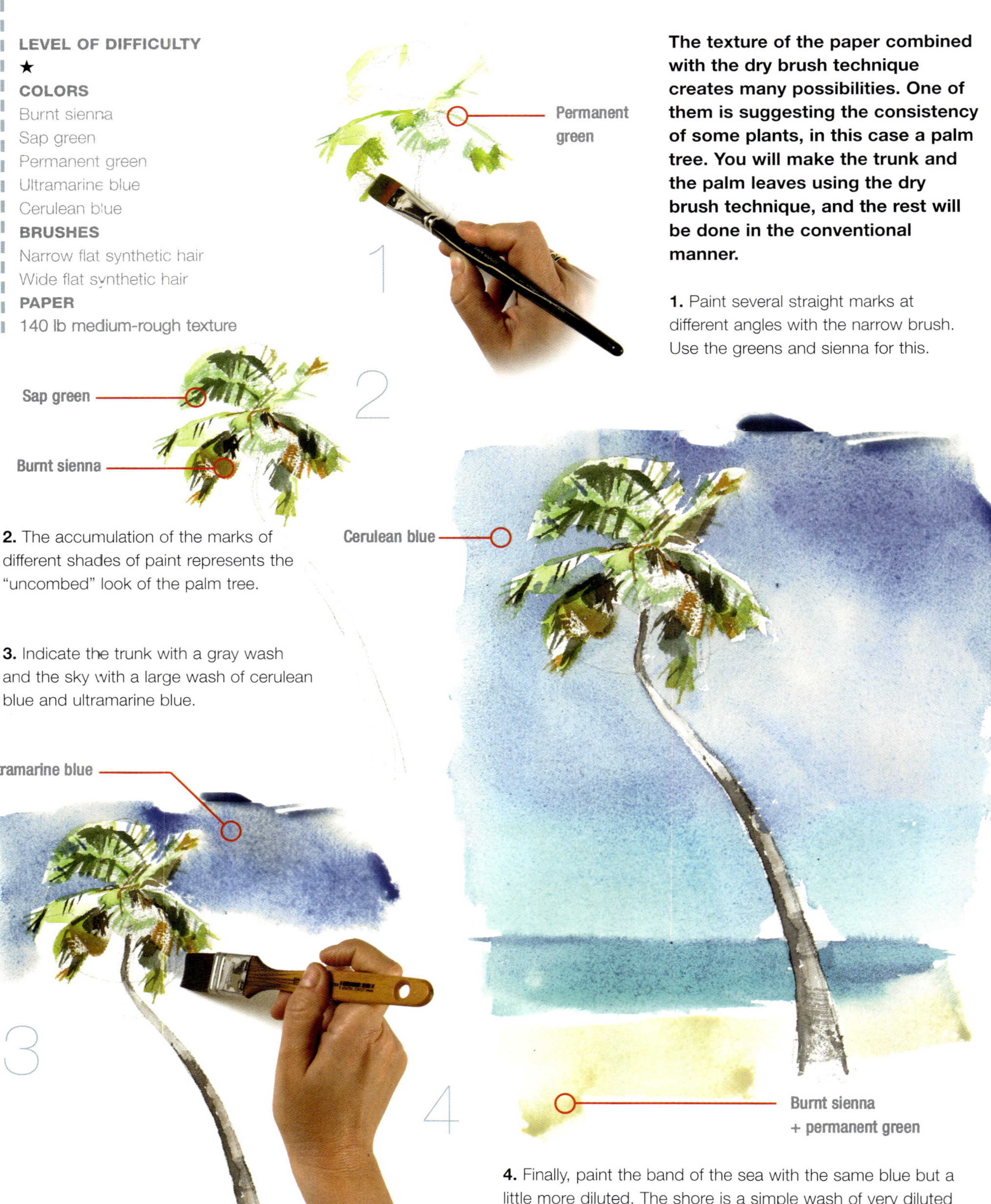

1. Paint several straight marks at different angles with the narrow brush. Use the greens and sienna for this.

2. The accumulation of the marks of different shades of paint represents the "uncombed" look of the palm tree.

3. Indicate the trunk with a gray wash and the sky with a large wash of cerulean blue and ultramarine blue.

4. Finally, paint the band of the sea with the same blue but a little more diluted. The shore is a simple wash of very diluted sienna mixed with a small amount of permanent green.

80 Dry Brush / **Free Brushstrokes**

LEVEL OF DIFFICULTY
★
COLORS
Cadmium orange
Burnt sienna
Ultramarine blue
BRUSH
Narrow flat natural hair
PAPER
140 lb medium-rough texture

This is a very illustrative example of the efficiency of dry brush with a very small range of colors and an economical use of color in the brushstroke. The strokes of the dry brush technique take watercolor closer to drawing. In this painting you will see how the brushstrokes are more important than the colors.

1

1. Draw the container and the brushes, and then paint or shade all the metallic parts with strokes of gray made from sienna and ultramarine blue.

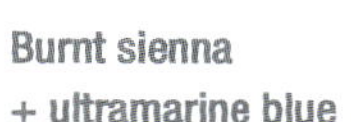

2. Paint the handles alternating the same gray with strokes of pure sienna. For the hair, use a mixture of orange and sienna. The dry brush clearly leaves its mark here.

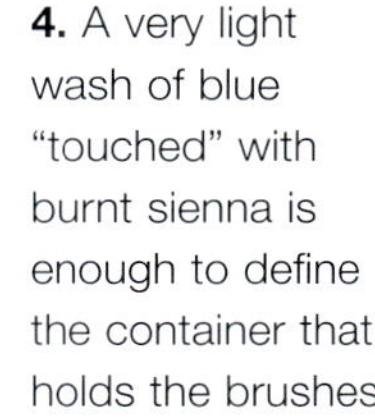

4. A very light wash of blue "touched" with burnt sienna is enough to define the container that holds the brushes.

3. There is no simpler representation of brushes: each stroke of color expresses a definite zone of each brush.

2

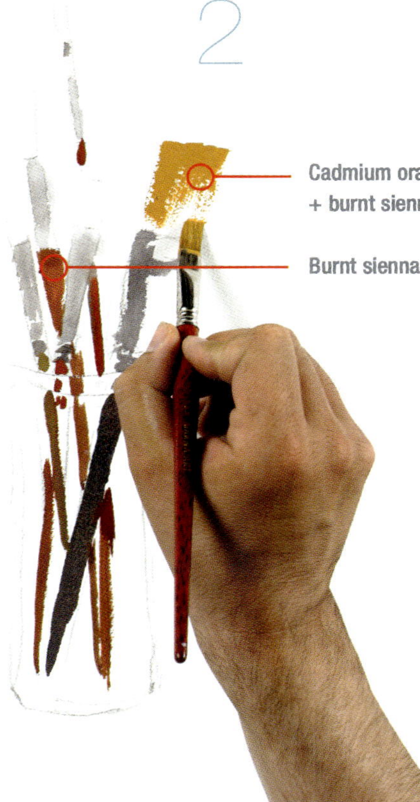

3

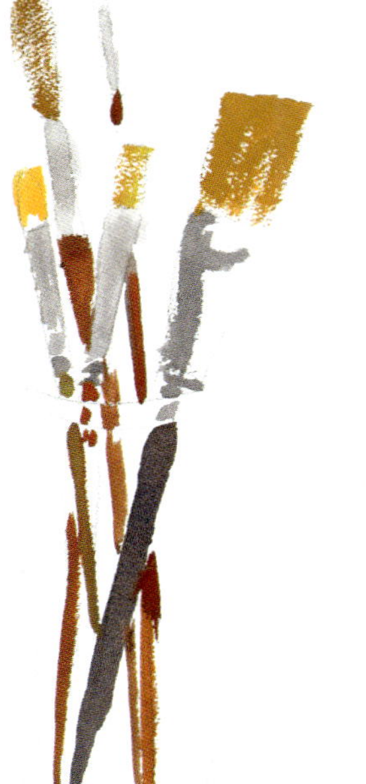

4

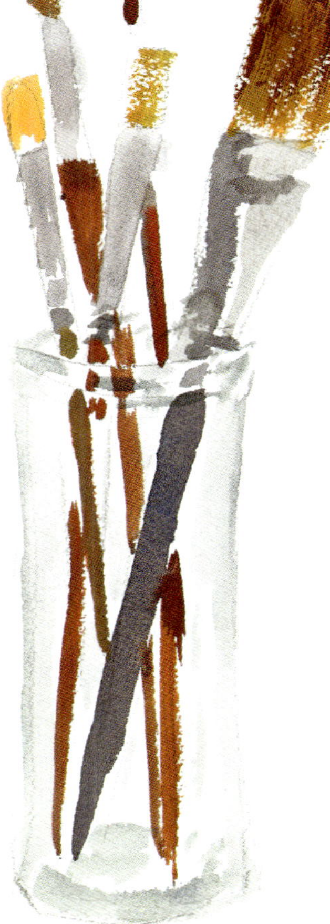

81 Dry Brush / **Opaque Color**

LEVEL OF DIFFICULTY
★★
COLORS
Burnt sienna
Carmine
Cobalt red
Ultramarine blue
Cobalt blue
BRUSH
Medium round natural hair
PAPER
140 lb medium-rough texture

When you charge the brush with very dense paint and you work with the dry brush technique, watercolor becomes an opaque medium, especially if you use dark colors. Here, the brush does not slide easily over the paper, and the paint has much more consistency than if you were working in the usual way.

1. Paint a first wash of cobalt blue to define the entire silhouette of the rooster, except for the head.

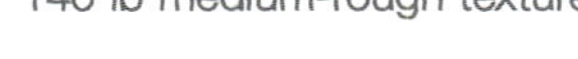

1

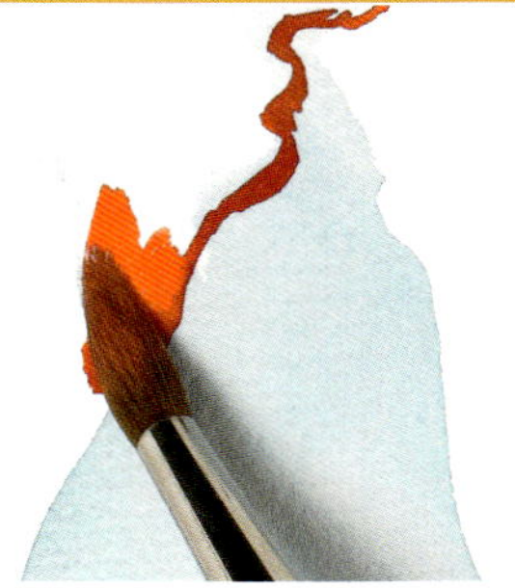

When using a very dense paint, you can very accurately outline a wash of color and with it achieve a surface of dense and saturated color.

2. Define the rooster's head exactly with a single wash of very saturated cobalt red.

3. Use a mixture of burnt sienna, carmine, and ultramarine blue to create darker tones on the body. Between these brushstrokes, add others of saturated sienna.

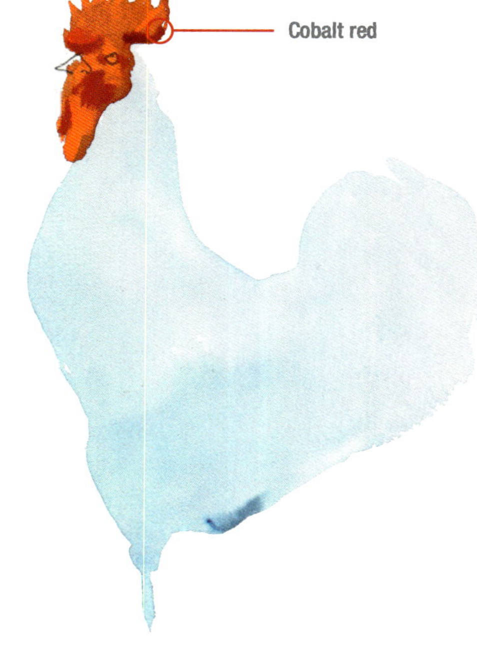

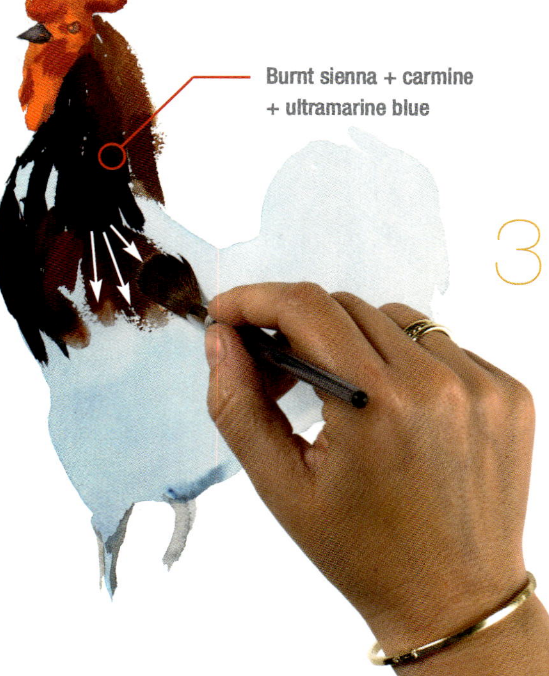

4. Each stroke of the brush creates a perfectly defined mark with rough edges, over the dry blue wash.

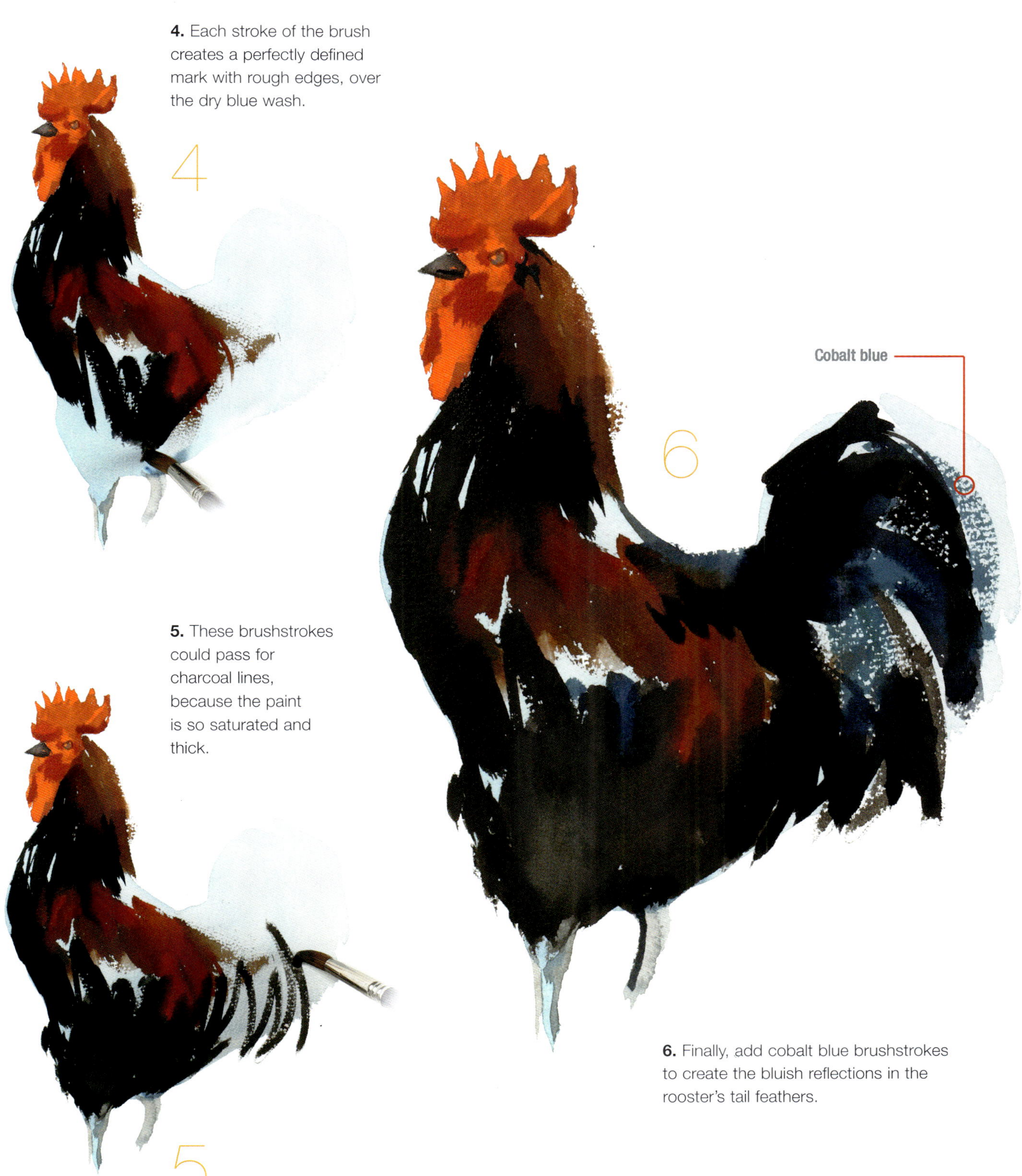

5. These brushstrokes could pass for charcoal lines, because the paint is so saturated and thick.

6. Finally, add cobalt blue brushstrokes to create the bluish reflections in the rooster's tail feathers.

Dry Brush / **Pointillist Effects**

LEVEL OF DIFFICULTY
★
COLORS
Cadmium yellow
Burnt sienna
Cadmium red
BRUSH
Medium round natural hair
PAPER
140 lb medium-rough texture

Marks made with a dry brush do not spread on the paper but stay where they have been applied. This favors the pointillist approach, which is based on small dabs or dots of paint and is very useful for defining the color and form of this tree in autumn.

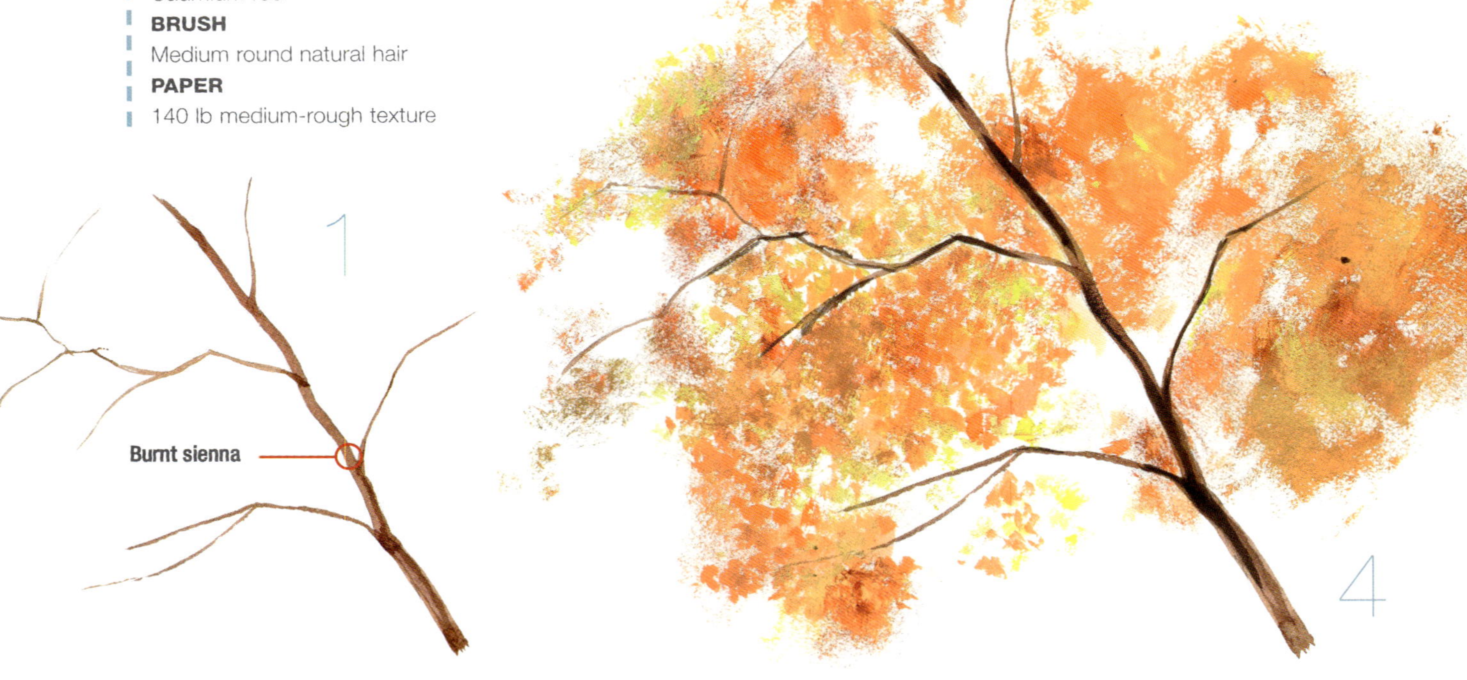

1. First paint the branches of the tree with burnt sienna. Use the tip of the brush to create the thinnest branches.

2. Paint an area with small dabs of yellow, and then go over it with cadmium red. The orange effect is created optically and not by really mixing.

3. To make smaller dots you can rub the brush on paper until it is very dry. The texture of the paper helps to create a blurred effect.

4. Use the mixture of red and yellow in different areas, rubbing the barely wet brush on the paper to achieve these results.

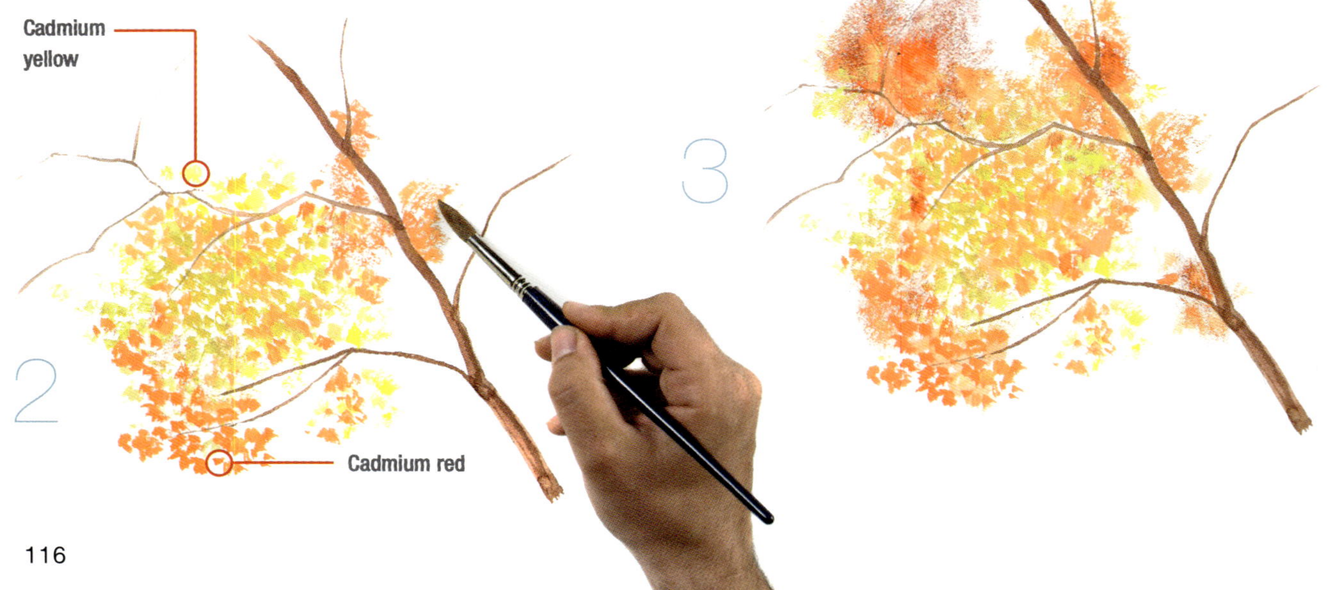

83 Dry Brush / **Suggested Forms**

LEVEL OF DIFFICULTY

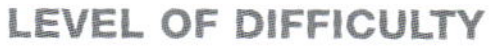

★

COLORS

Burnt sienna
Sap green
Permanent green
Permanent red
Ultramarine blue
Cerulean blue

BRUSHES

Medium round natural hair
Medium flat synthetic hair

PAPER

140 lb medium-rough texture

1

Sap green

Ultramarine blue

The line made with a dry brush is more a drawn line than a painted one. It allows you to create sketched effects similar to those seen in sketches from nature made with pencils, charcoal, and pastels. It is an agile and expeditious approach, where the most important thing is spontaneity in the general arrangement of the forms.

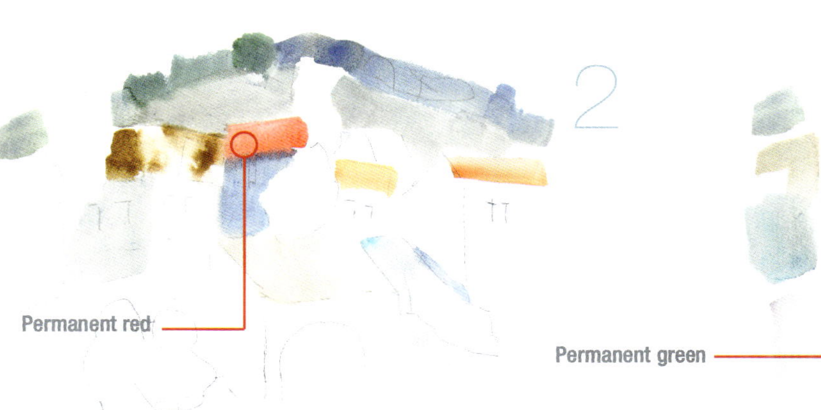

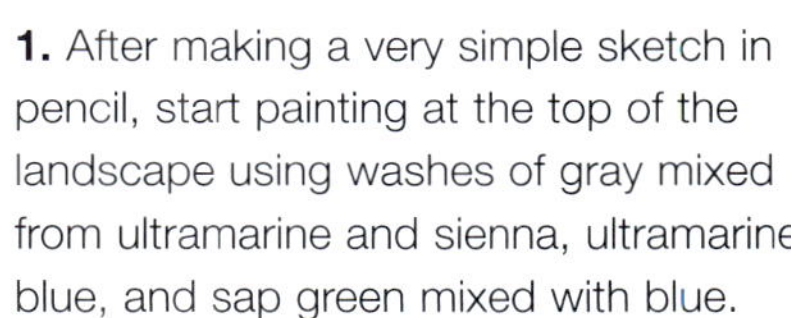

3

Permanent green

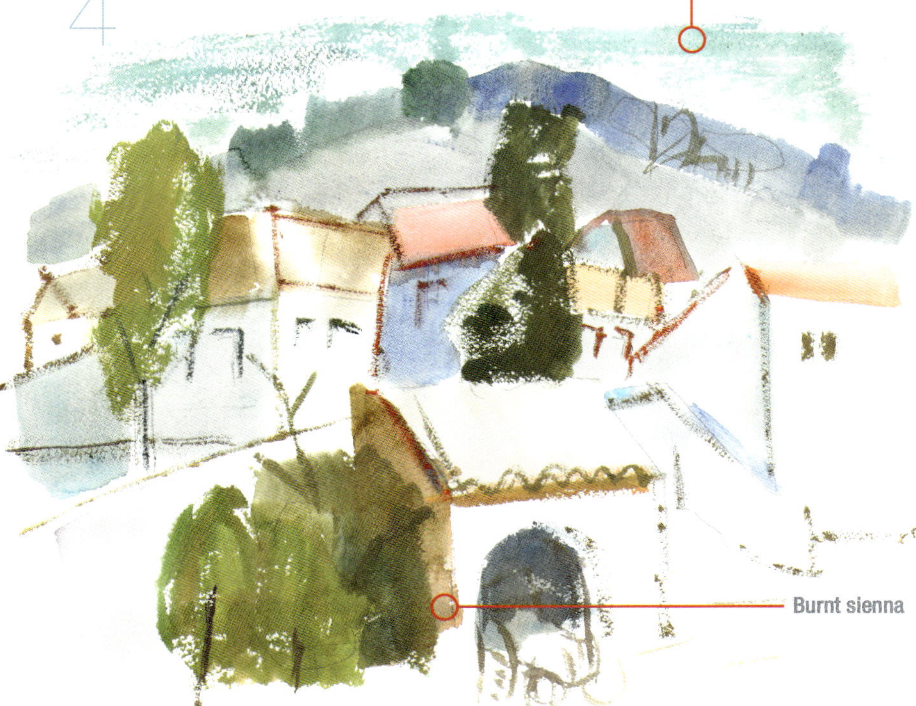

1. After making a very simple sketch in pencil, start painting at the top of the landscape using washes of gray mixed from ultramarine and sienna, ultramarine blue, and sap green mixed with blue.

2. Add cool washes between the warm washes on the rooftops and some of the shaded façades.

3. Paint the treetops with very "dry" permanent green, allowing the rough texture of the paper to show through.

4. Finally, add lines of different colors with the tip of the brush. These lines emphasize the feeling of a drawing and the look of a sketch typical of this style as opposed to a watercolor.

84 Dry Brush / **Wash and Dry Brush**

LEVEL OF DIFFICULTY
★★
COLORS
Burnt sienna
Ultramarine blue
Cerulean blue
BRUSHES
Fine round natural hair
Medium round natural hair
Wide flat synthetic hair
PAPER
140 lb medium-rough texture

The combination of a very light wash and a very textured dry brush technique is always attractive. On this occasion, the brush goes from wet to dry without anything in between. The contrast between the two effects suggests great freedom in the treatment, and it is a quick and direct way to define a form and color.

1

Burnt sienna
+ cerulean blue

1. Over a sketch of a cat, paint washes of cerulean blue mixed with a little sienna. Leave the areas that correspond to the lightest part of the fur white.

2

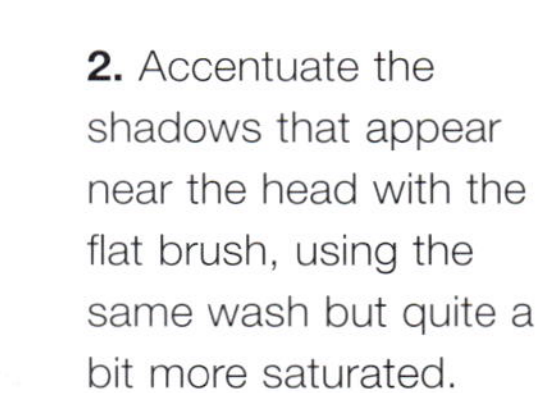

2. Accentuate the shadows that appear near the head with the flat brush, using the same wash but quite a bit more saturated.

3

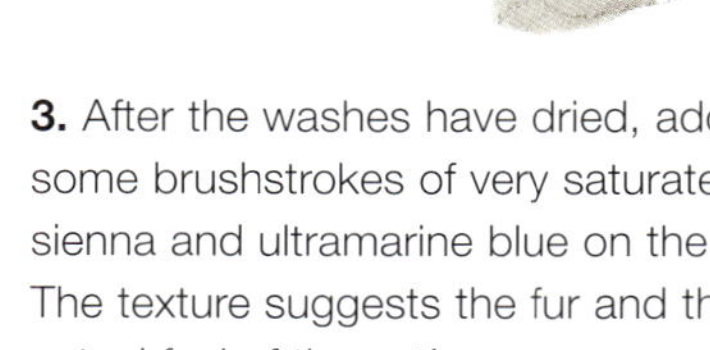

3. After the washes have dried, add some brushstrokes of very saturated sienna and ultramarine blue on the feet. The texture suggests the fur and the actual feel of the cat's paws.

4

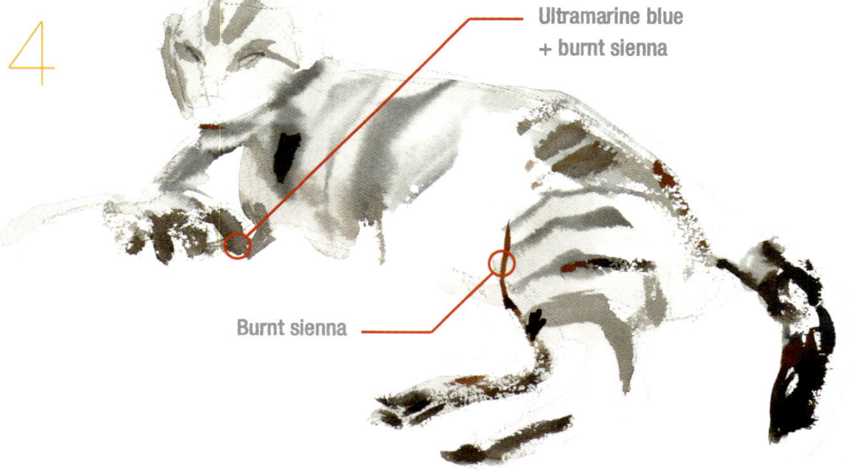

4. Using pure sienna, add some long thin brushstrokes with the round brush to define the outlines of the paws.

5. Using the same washes, carry the lines to the edges of the drawing.

6. This is a spectacular watercolor in the sureness of the layout and the determined and spontaneous resolution.

To define lines without drawing or painting, you can work on wet, marking the paper with the handle of the brush just like you were drawing. The wet paint will deposit there and make the details visible.

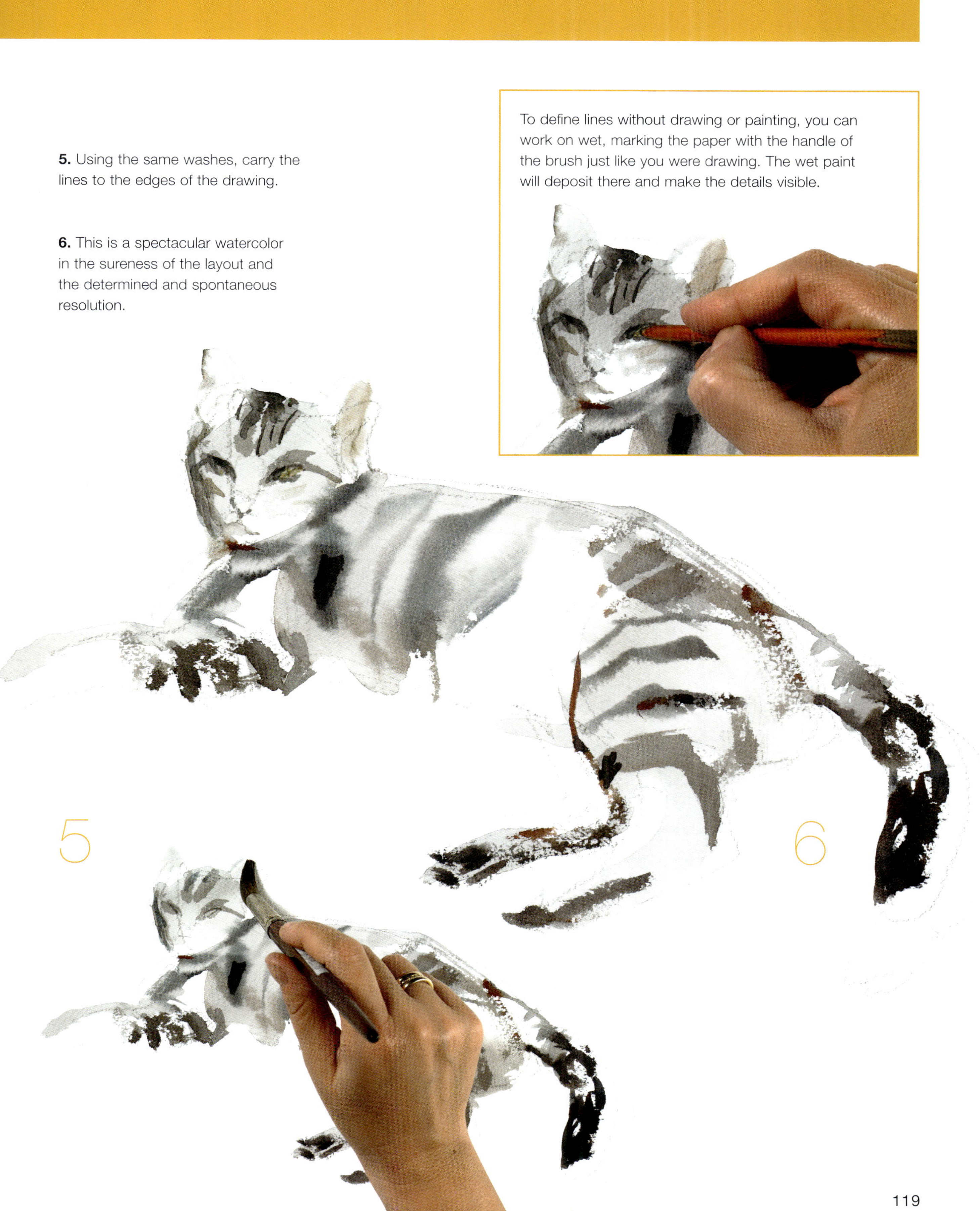

LEVEL OF DIFFICULTY
★★
COLORS
Burnt sienna
Permanent red
Ultramarine blue
Cobalt violet
Wax crayons
BRUSH
Medium round natural hair
PAPER
140 lb medium-rough texture

Wax is waterproof, and all wax marks in a watercolor will not be altered, will not come off, and the color will not be changed when they come into contact with the paint. In this watercolor you will apply color marks on the subject before it is painted. The colors will stay lively and precise, and they will create an interesting decorative effect that will emphasize the exotic subject matter.

1

1. Draw the figure with crayon, and then add the multicolored details that decorate the dress and hat.

Cobalt violet

Ultramarine blue

2. When the figure is painted, the water will not affect or cover the applications of wax colors. The gray wash, a mixture of blue and sienna, does not alter the drawing.

2

Ultramarine blue + burnt sienna

3

3. Adding dabs of blue and violet to the hat will cause the small wax marks to seem quite lively.

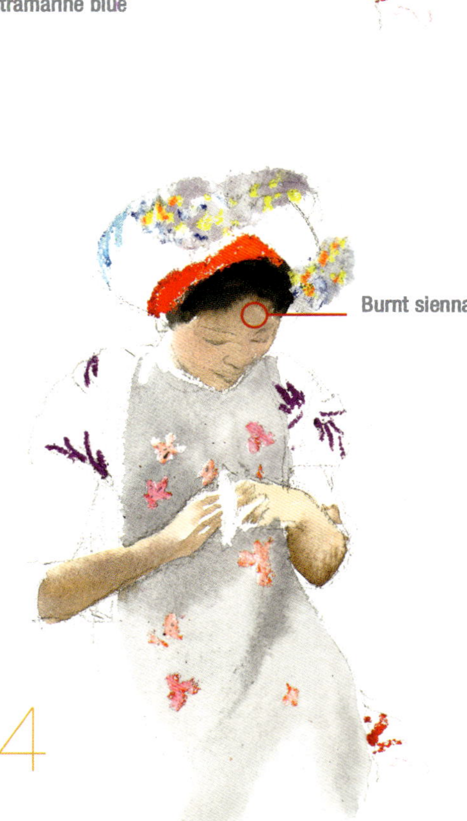

4

4. Paint the flesh tones wherever the skin is visible with a light wash of burnt sienna, which will make the coloring of the figure seem more natural.

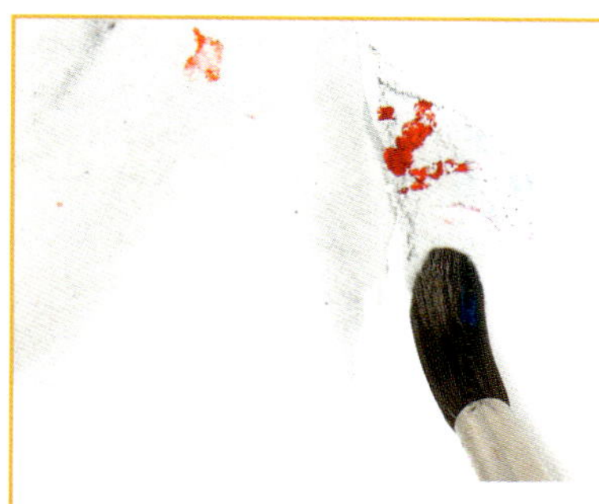

Marks made with wax crayons are, in reality, reserves made with pure colors. It would be very difficult to achieve results anywhere near this by reserving such small areas of the paper.

6

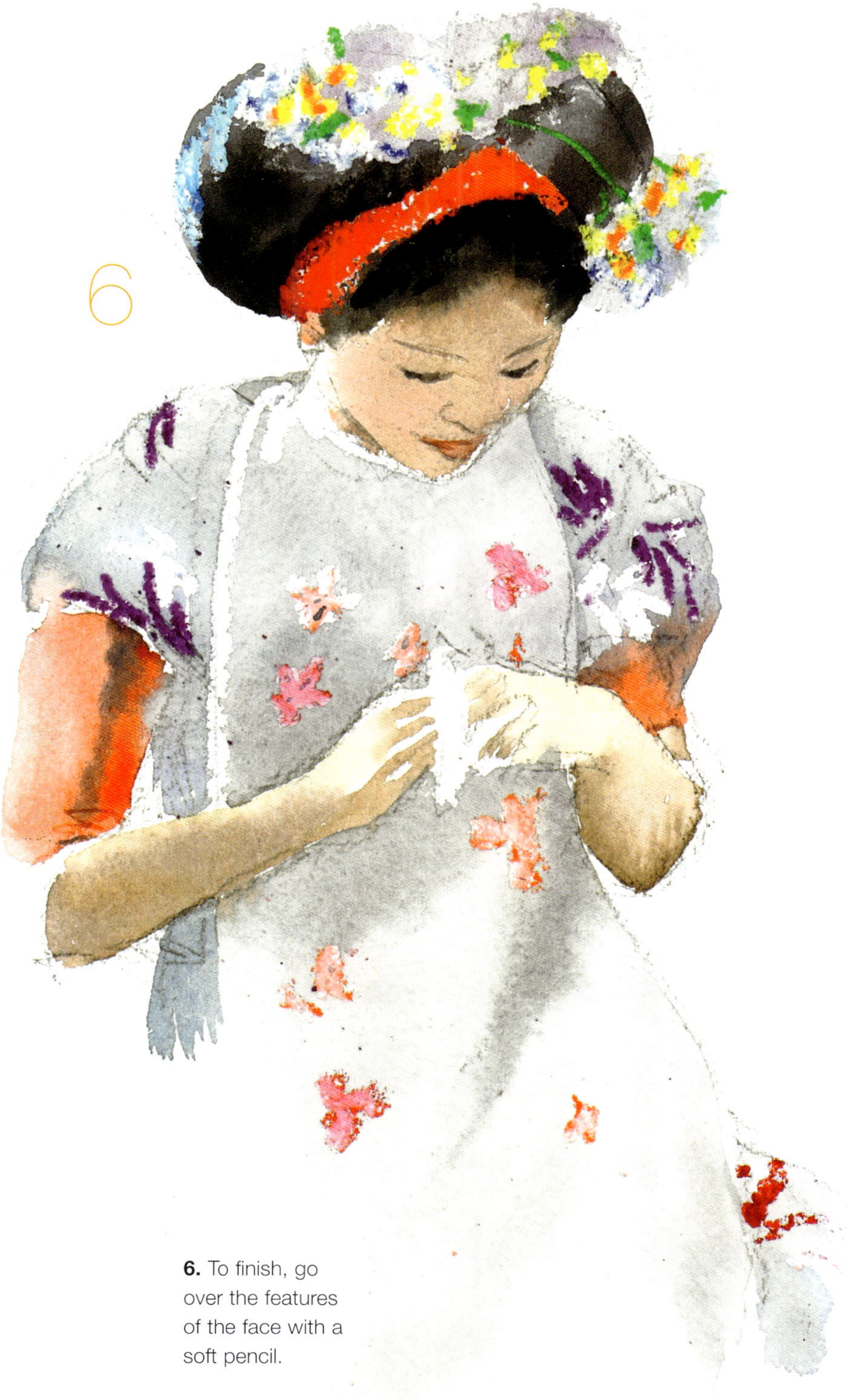

5

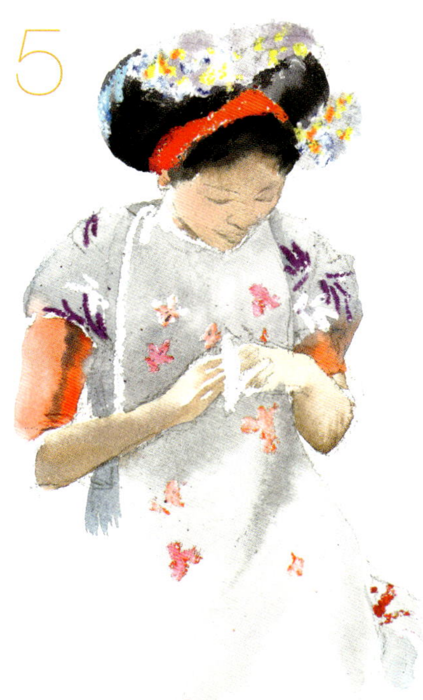

5. The vibrant and saturated tones of the crayons enliven the soft tones of the figure. The two complement and reinforce each other.

6. To finish, go over the features of the face with a soft pencil.

86 Effects and Textures / **White Wax Reserves**

LEVEL OF DIFFICULTY
★

COLORS
Burnt sienna
Sap green
Cobalt violet
Cerulean blue
White wax or oil color pencil

BRUSH
Medium round natural hair

PAPER
140 lb medium-rough texture

White wax allows you to create an effect similar to that of white reserves on the paper: a white area that is a detail in the overall picture and that, because of its size, would be very difficult to achieve by working with traditional techniques. Here you will use a white grease pencil (white wax), because with it you can draw more precise lines than you can with traditional wax crayons.

1. Right after completing the drawing, go over the feet of the dove with a few wax pencil strokes.

2. The darkest tones are a mixture of blue, sienna, and green. The result is a nearly black tone that highlights the light colors of the doves.

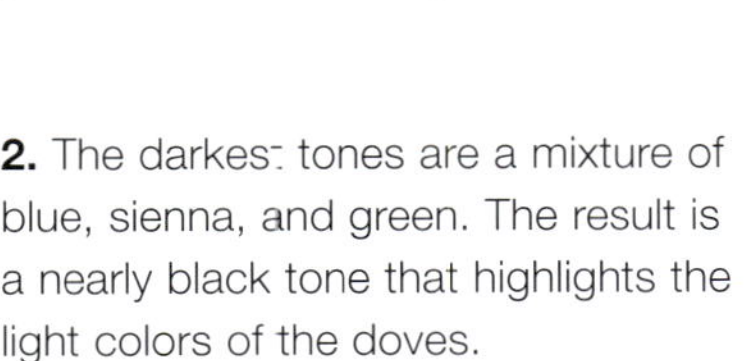

Burnt sienna + sap green + cerulean blue

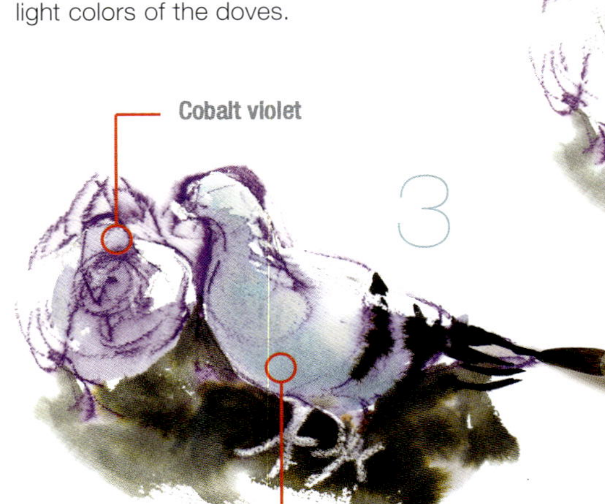

3. Go over the outlines of the doves with violet, and on the interior alternate strokes of blue with the original dark color.

4. The wax has not been altered during the entire process. The white feet of the dove stand out from the black.

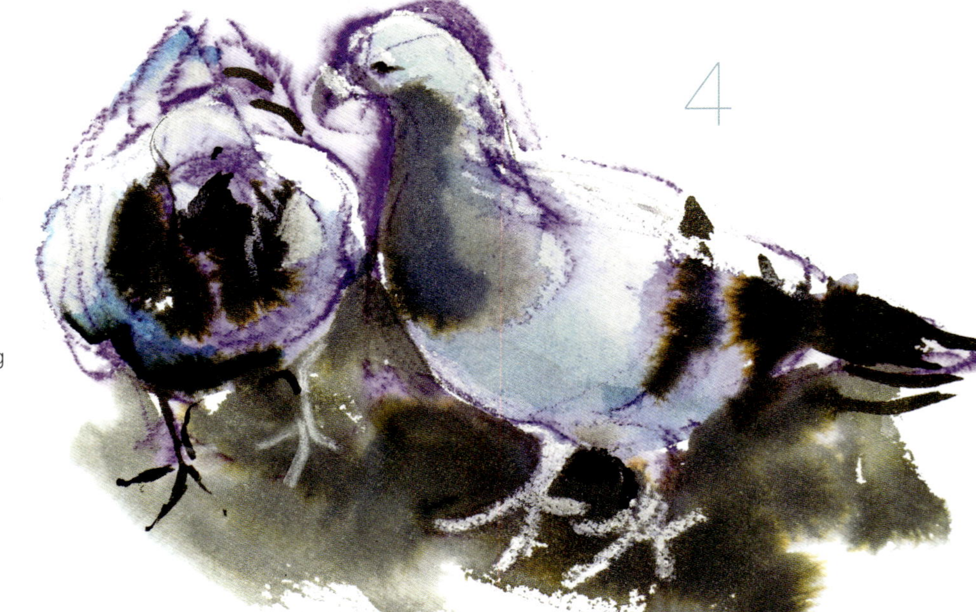

LEVEL OF DIFFICULTY
★

COLORS
Cadmium yellow
Permanent green
Permanent red
Ultramarine blue
White wax crayon
Orange wax crayon

BRUSH
Medium round natural hair

PAPER
140 lb medium-rough texture

Wax crayons can also be used to reinforce the contrasts and colors of the watercolor paint. When you cover large areas with the wax, it does not completely cover the surface of the paper and leaves small open areas. The watercolor collects in these zones and highlights the color of the wax crayon, creating an interesting effect.

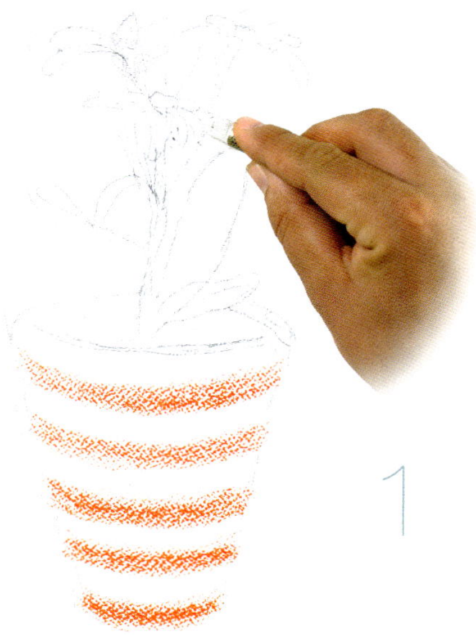

1

1. Draw the planter and add stripes with the orange wax crayon. Color the flower petals with the white crayon to create a small reserve of the white paper there.

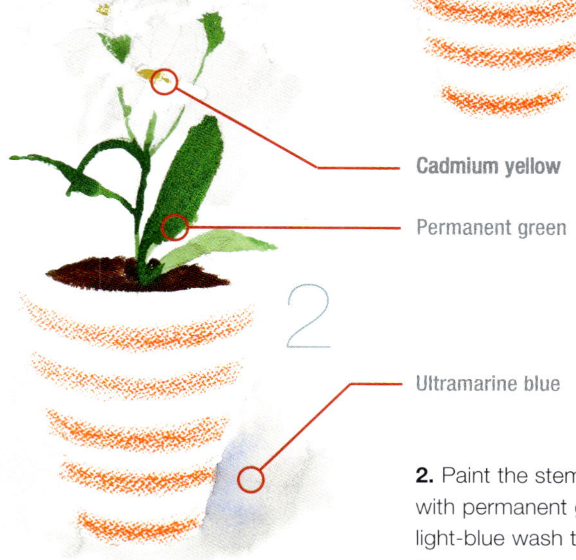

2

Cadmium yellow

Permanent green

Ultramarine blue

2. Paint the stems and the leaves with permanent green, and use a light-blue wash to make the white flowers stand out.

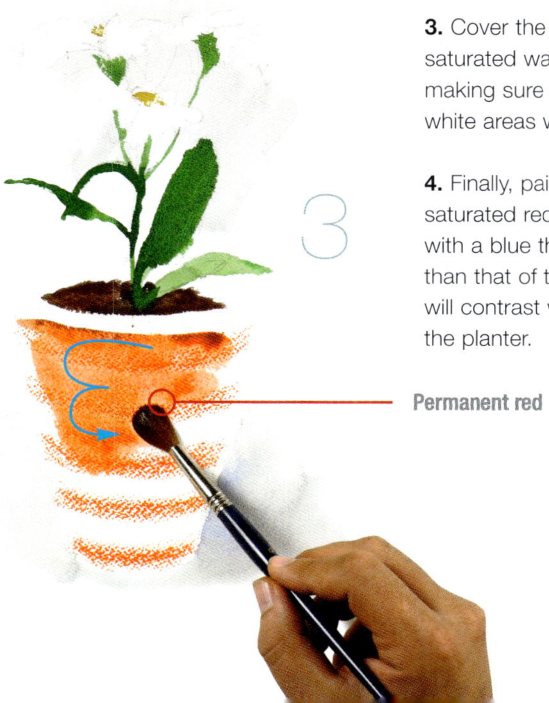

3

3. Cover the entire planter with a saturated wash of permanent red, making sure the paint penetrates the white areas within the wax lines.

Permanent red

4. Finally, paint the stripes with a saturated red and the top of the table with a blue that is somewhat darker than that of the background so that it will contrast with the warm colors of the planter.

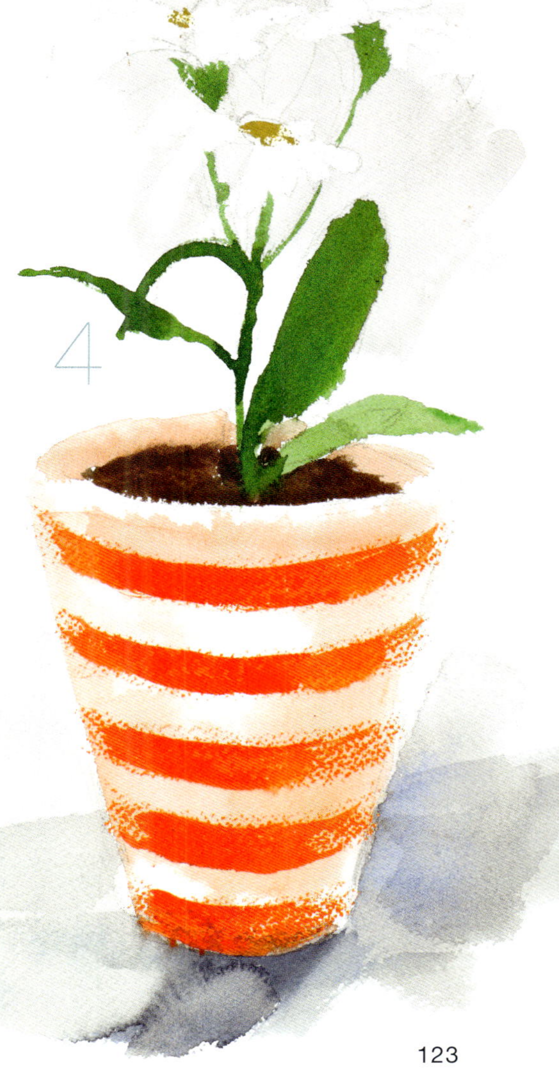

LEVEL OF DIFFICULTY
★★

COLORS
Yellow ochre
Burnt sienna
Sap green
Permanent red
Cobalt blue

BRUSHES
Medium round natural hair
Wide flat synthetic hair

PAPER
140 lb medium rough texture, prepared with gesso

Gesso is a thick white liquid that is used for preparing the surface of a canvas before painting with an oil or water-base paint. This preparation usually has an acrylic base, and it can be drawn and painted on by many different media. Cover the paper used for this watercolor with a layer of gesso, and allow it to dry before beginning work.

1. Use a wide flat brush to spread a layer of gesso diluted with a little water. When the paper is dry, draw the horse. Begin painting the background pure cobalt blue while leaving the horse as a white reserve.

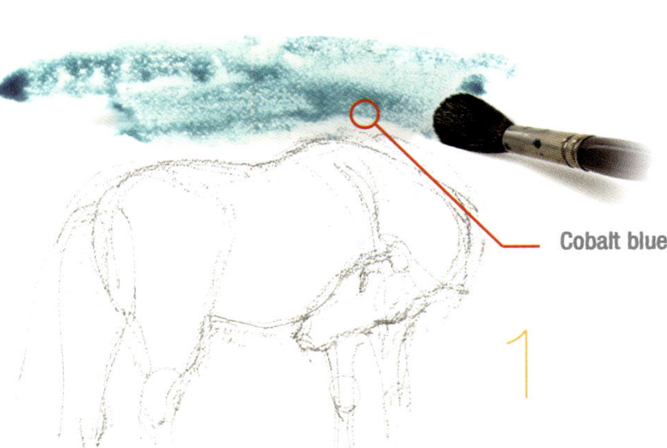

2. The paint will puddle, and if you add brushstrokes of ochre to the lower part, interesting effects of partial mixing of the wet paint will result. The effect is very atmospheric.

2

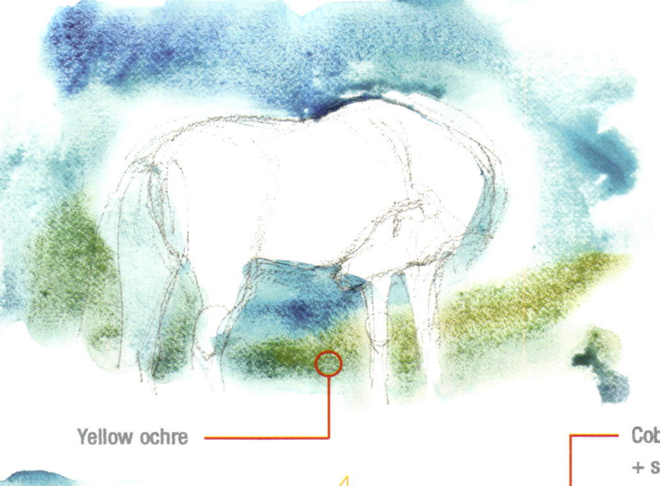

3. Paint the tail with red mixed with ochre using the dry brush technique. Begin painting the horse with a mixture of blue, sienna, and green.

3

Yellow ochre + permanent red

4. The dark mixture is not absorbed in the usual manner either; it creates puddles and mottling that suggest the coloring of the horse.

4

Cobalt blue + burnt sienna + sap green

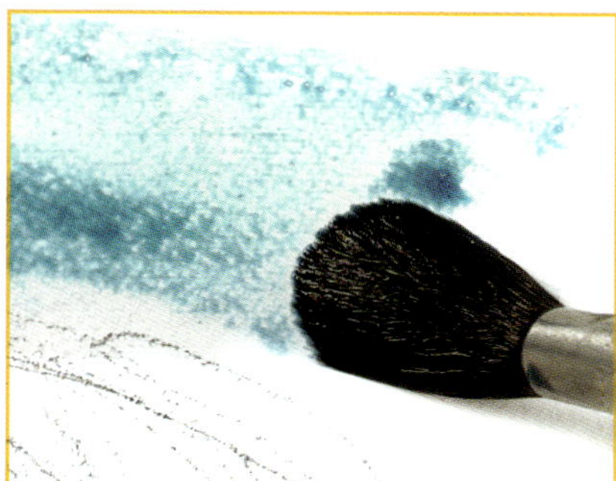

The watercolor responds in a very different manner when it is applied over gesso. The paint is not absorbed in a regular way by the paper; it creates bubbles and puddles that produce a special mottled look when dry. The resulting texture is very suggestive and the colors are bright and lively.

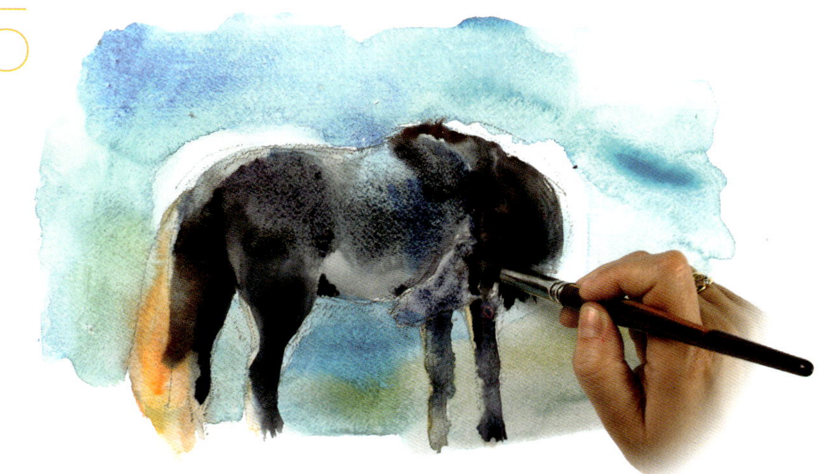

5. To create the darkest accents on the hooves and mane, increase the amount of blue and sienna in the mixture to make an opaque saturated color.

6. Chance plays an important part in the distribution of the colors. The absorbency of the paper is diminished, and the puddled colors, when dry, are darker and irregular.

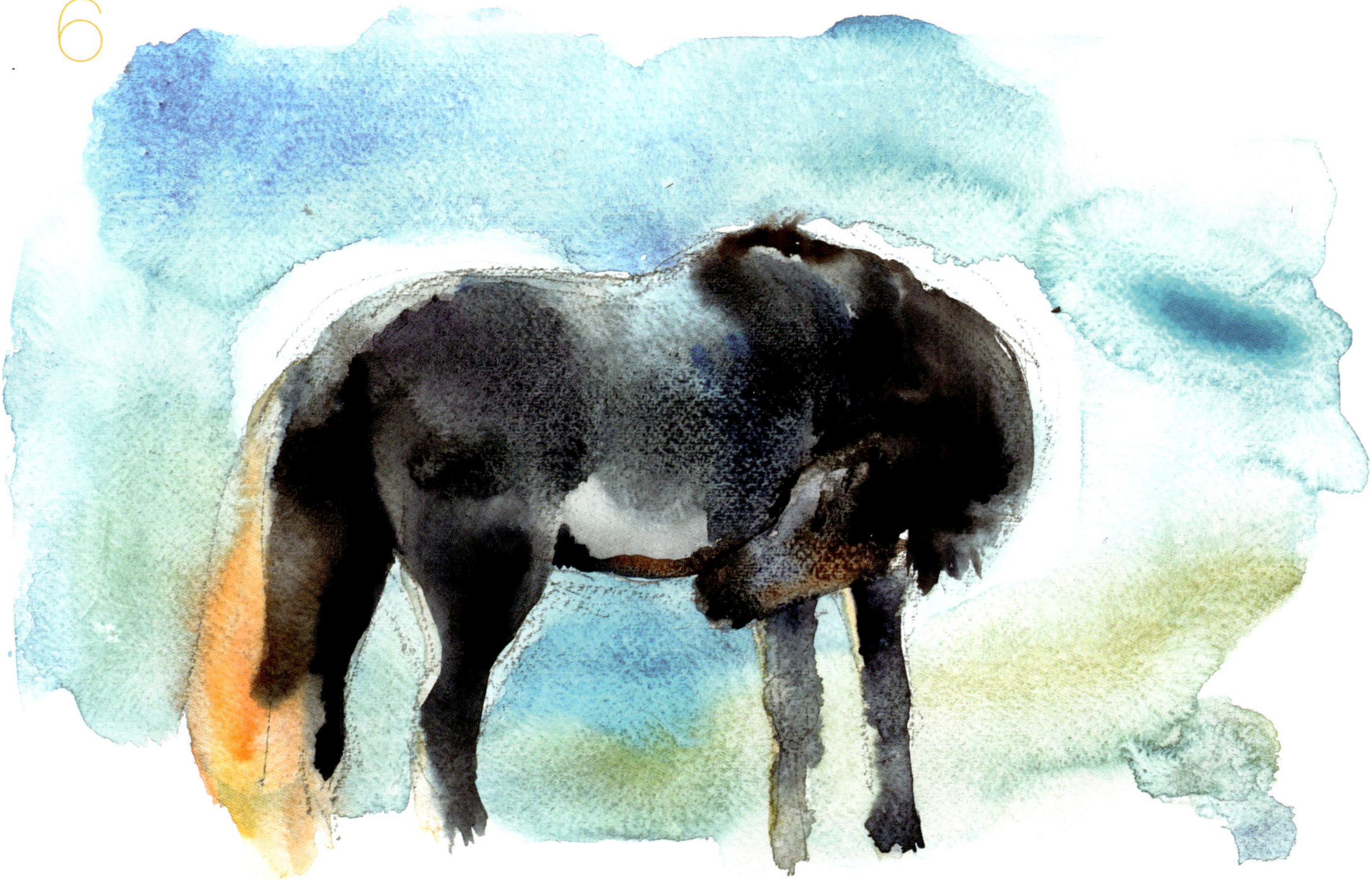

LEVEL OF DIFFICULTY
★
COLORS
Burnt sienna
Ultramarine blue
Cerulean blue
Sanguine, blue, and black pastels
BRUSH
Wide flat synthetic hair
PAPER
140 lb medium-rough texture

Unlike wax crayons, pastels will become partially diluted in water and tint the brushstrokes, because the pigment is not completely agglutinated. This semi-dilution is responsible for the broken irregular effect in this watercolor. There are very few colors used here, because the shades will be created by the partial mixing with the pastels.

1. First draw the landscape with three colors in pastel, using the side of the sticks. Then draw distinct lines to define the branches.

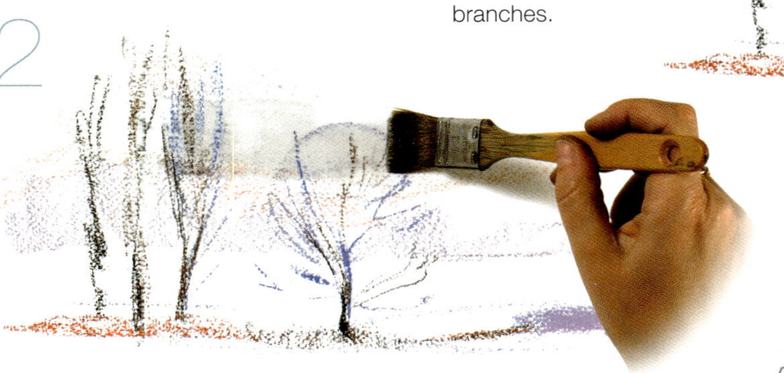

2. When the brush charged with clean water passes over the lines, part of the pigment will tint the water and create a blue-gray wash that is very appropriate for the sky.

3. The reserves in the background suggest mountains in the distance. Paint the foreground with cerulean blue mixed with burnt sienna.

Cerulean blue + burnt sienna

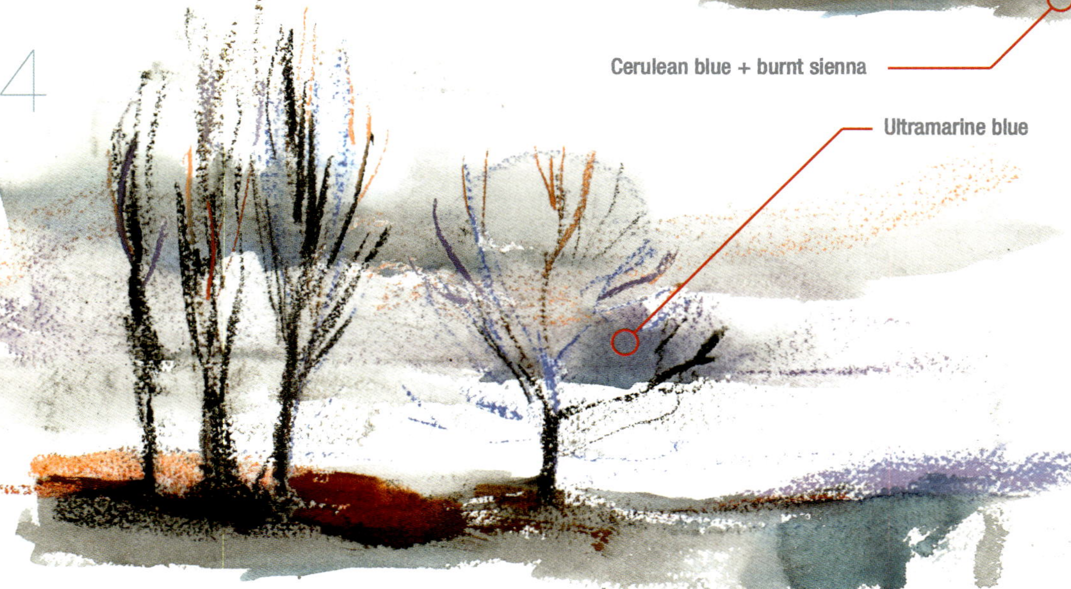

4. Go back over the wet areas with the pastels to make darker marks that will emphasize the contrasts. This watercolor was painted in a very short time and has a fresh and lively feeling.

LEVEL OF DIFFICULTY
★★

COLORS
Yellow ochre
Burnt sienna
Permanent green
Cerulean blue
Colored wax crayons

BRUSHES
Fine round natural hair
Medium round natural hair

PAPER
140 lb medium rough texture, prepared with white glue

The paper used for this watercolor will first be covered with a layer of white glue using a stiff brush. The marks of the brush will remain on the surface after the glue has dried, and they will be partially visible under the paint, creating a rough and irregular texture.

1. After drawing the subject and highlighting some details with wax crayons, paint various strokes of cerulean blue and sienna, allowing them to mix as they spread on the paper. The pigment will settle in the irregular lines of the preparation.

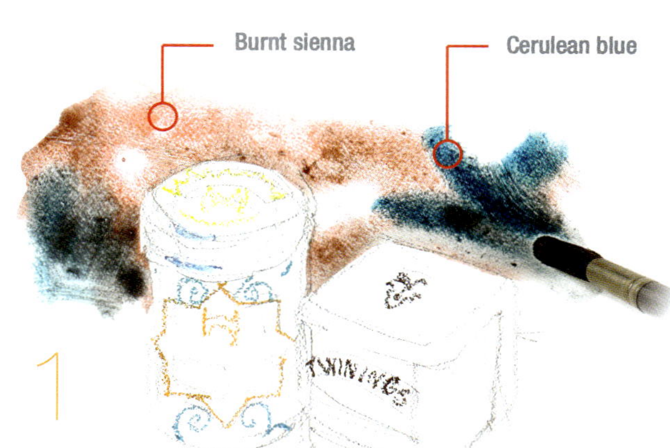

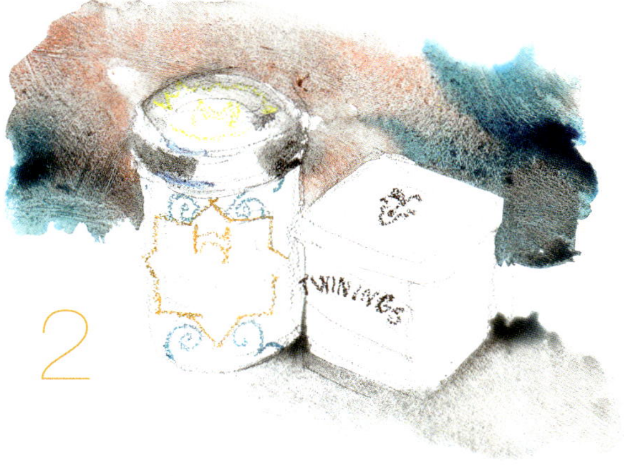

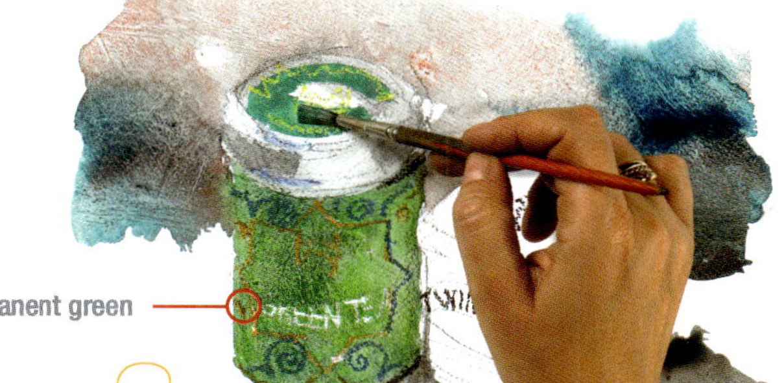

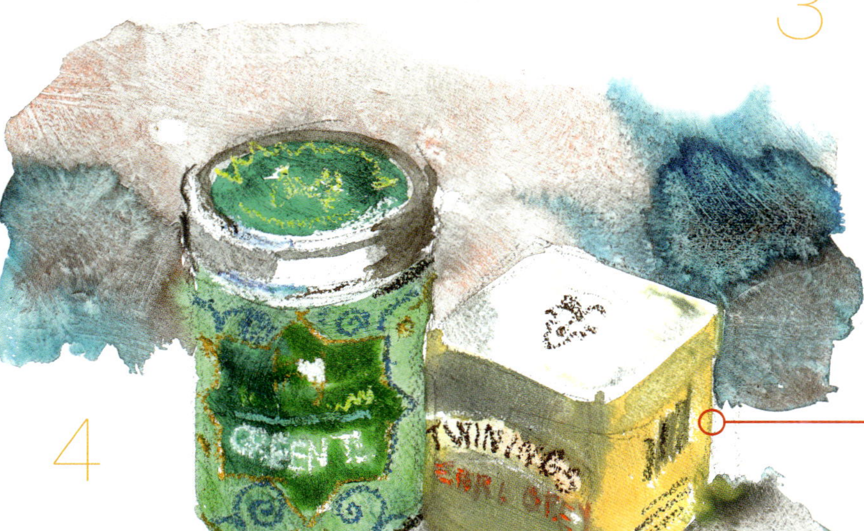

2. As the paint is drying, the texture created with the white glue will become more visible.

3. When you paint the container green, the white wax lines will continue to be plainly visible.

4. The colors will be irregular and flow into each other. This will create chromatic unity and an atmospheric feeling to the watercolor, which is already very rich in textures and shades.

Effects and Textures / **Applying Turpentine**

LEVEL OF DIFFICULTY
★
COLORS
Carmine
Cadmium red
Sap green
Cerulean blue
Green and blue wax crayons
BRUSHES
Medium round natural hair
Fat round natural hair
PAPER
140 lb medium-rough texture

Turpentine is an organic solvent that is used in oil painting. When used in combination with watercolors it makes the paint run, because it repels water in the areas where it is used. In this painting you will use turpentine to cause the paint to run in the darkest parts of the work.

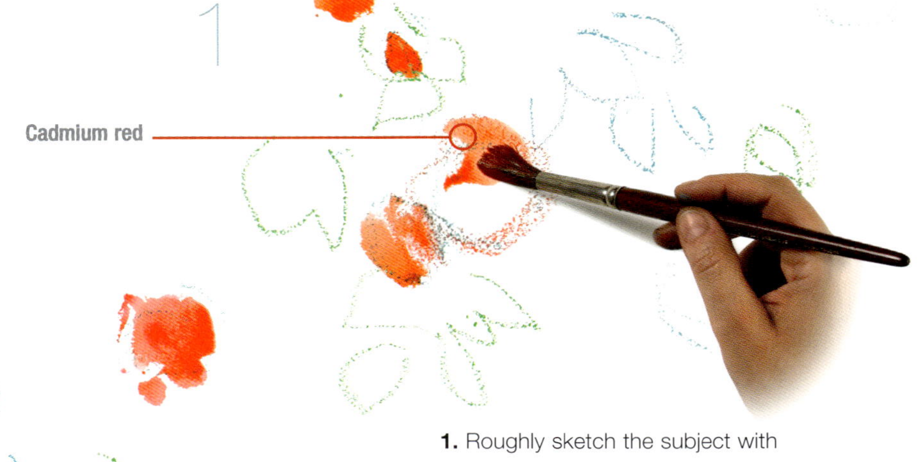

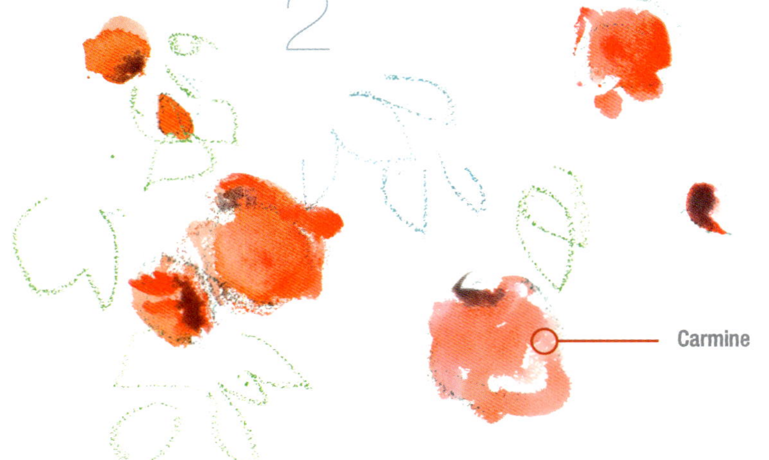

1. Roughly sketch the subject with colored wax crayons. This way the outlines will stay clear and strong during the whole process.

2. Paint the roses with similar brushstrokes of cadmium red and carmine paint diluted with water.

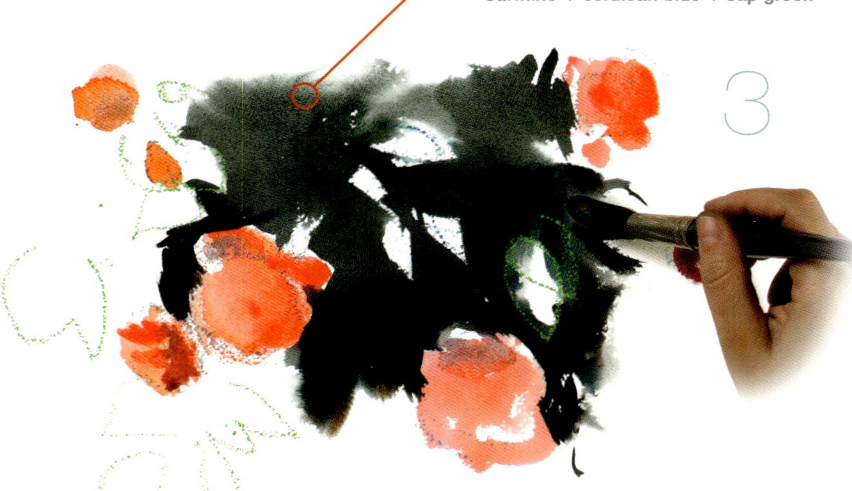

3. The dark background of the leaves is a mixture of carmine, cerulean blue, and sap green. Leave some white areas in reserve to later color in some leaves.

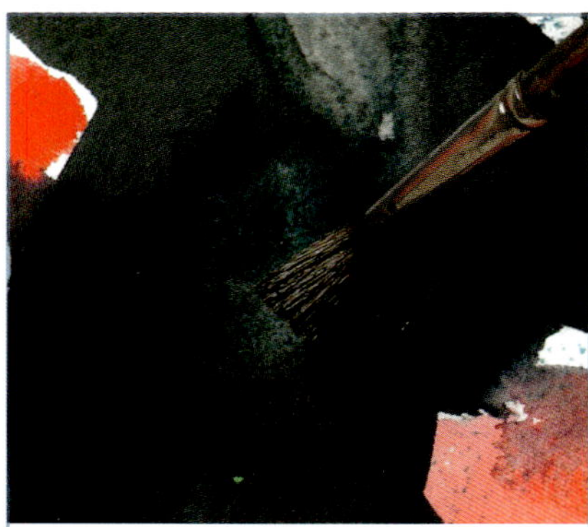

When you apply turpentine over wet paint, the water (and with it the paint) will run toward the outside. This way you will create a muddy shade that is somewhat lighter than the base color, which will make the darkest tones richer.

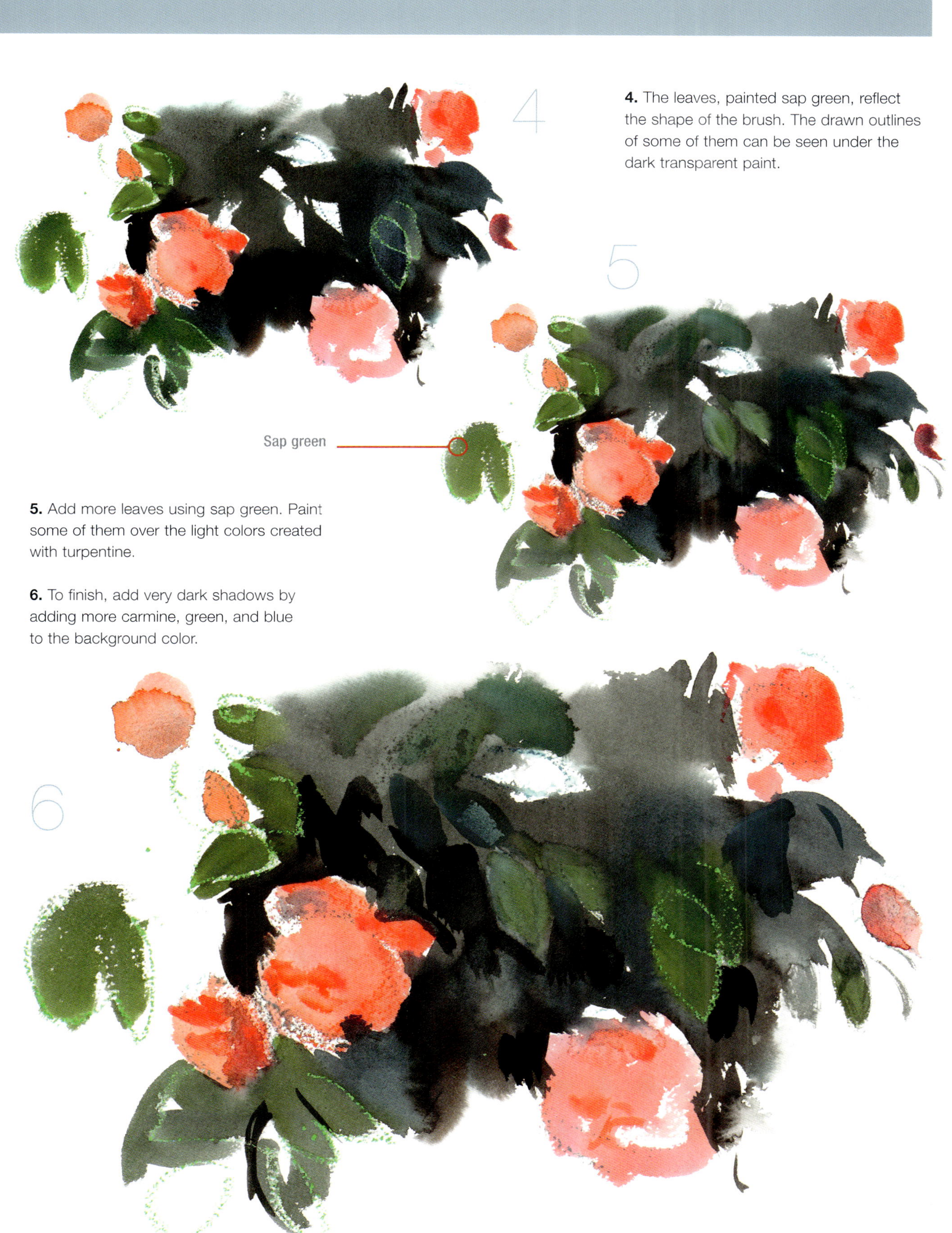

4. The leaves, painted sap green, reflect the shape of the brush. The drawn outlines of some of them can be seen under the dark transparent paint.

5. Add more leaves using sap green. Paint some of them over the light colors created with turpentine.

6. To finish, add very dark shadows by adding more carmine, green, and blue to the background color.

LEVEL OF DIFFICULTY
★
COLORS
Burnt sienna
Raw umber
Cerulean blue
India ink
BRUSHES
Medium round natural hair
Wide flat synthetic hair
PAPER
140 lb medium-rough texture

India ink applied with a nib pen allows you to draw during the working process and at the end. When the ink is dry, it is waterproof, so highlights created with it can be permanent if you wish. In this watercolor you will use a nib pen to add light lines and some important details.

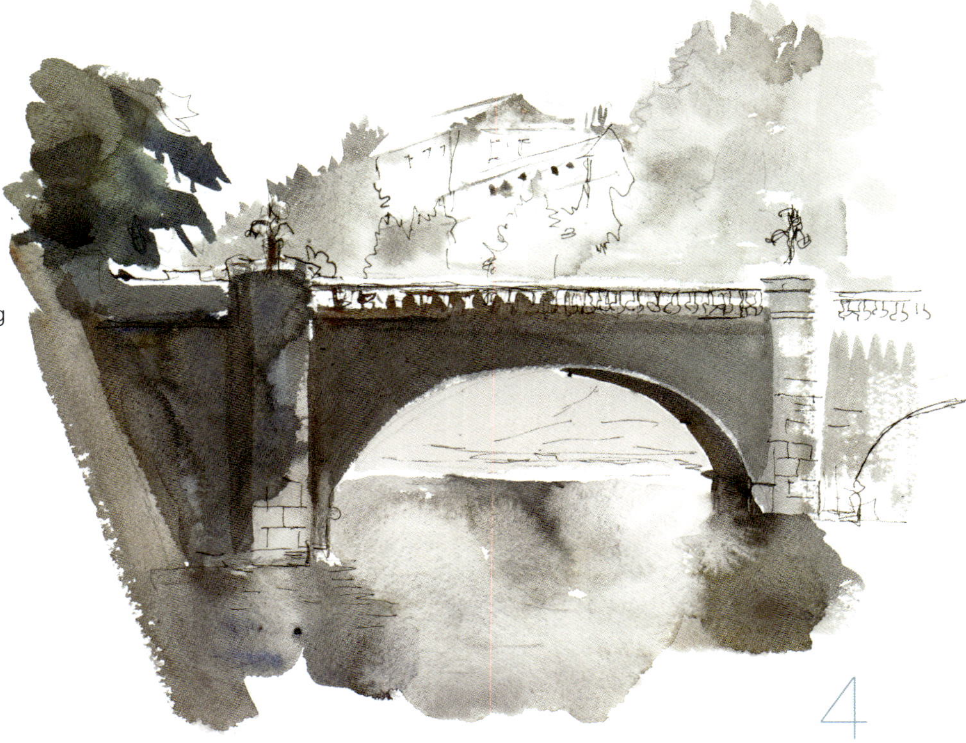

1. After making the pencil drawing, begin painting with a flat brush, applying large washes with a mix of blue and burnt sienna, which makes a cool gray that will dominate the watercolor.

2. During the process, you can emphasize some aspects of the bridge that are too detailed to be attempted with a brush.

3. Vary the proportions of the colors in the mixture, also changing the amount of water to create many different shades of the dominant gray. Work now with the round brush.

4. Add most of the drawing, lines, and details in India ink at the end, enriching the lightest areas of the painting with all manner of details.

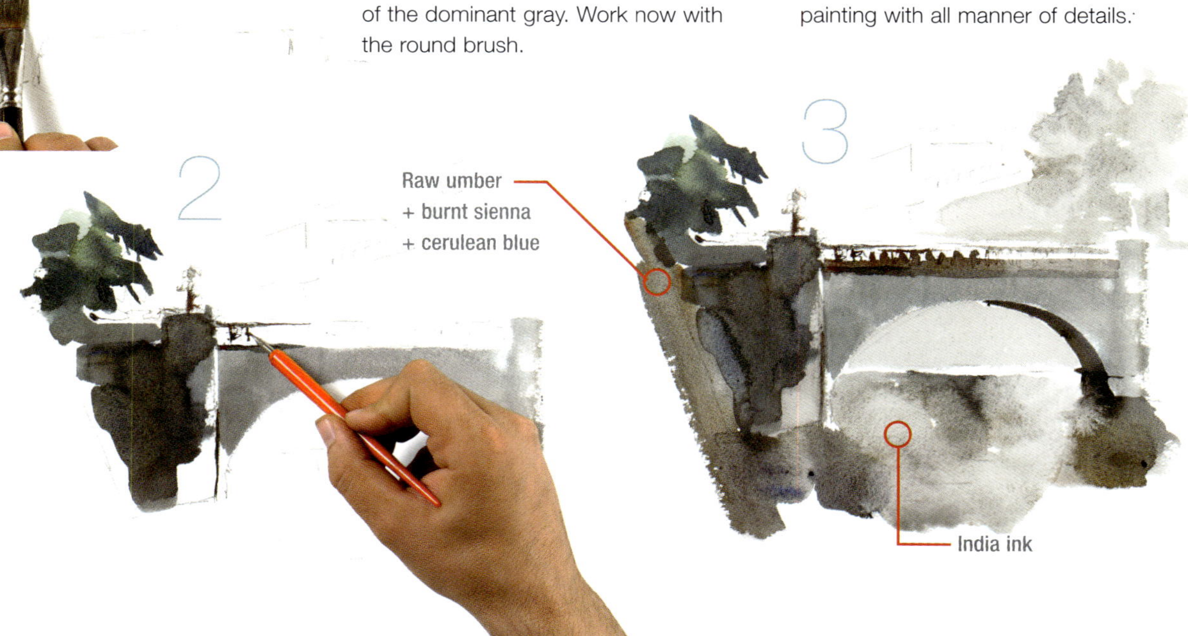

93 Effects and Textures / **Ink and Watercolor Combined**

LEVEL OF DIFFICULTY
★
COLORS
Carmine
Burnt sienna
Ultramarine blue
India ink
BRUSH
Medium round natural hair
PAPER
140 lb medium-rough texture

India ink can be diluted with water, so it can combine fairly well with watercolors as long as there is plenty of water and much less ink is used than paint. In this exercise, the ink lines of the drawing partially "contaminate" the colors to create interesting shades.

1

2

3

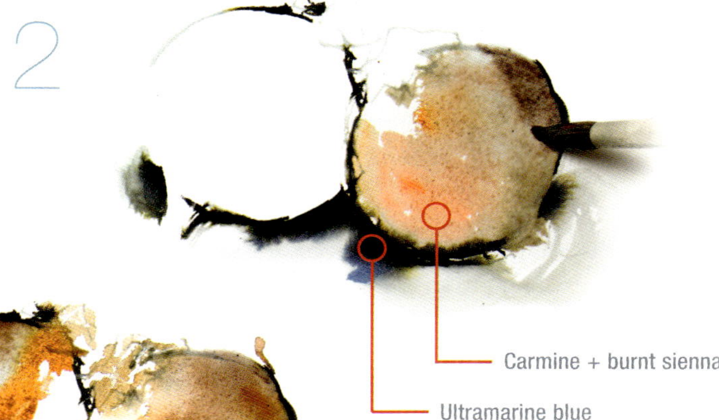

1. Before starting to paint, go over the pencil drawing of these onions with ink lines.

2. Create the color of the onions based on a mixture of carmine diluted with a little sienna. The paint will mix slightly when it contacts the India ink lines to produce more somber tones.

3. Paint the bases of the onions by wetting the ink lines with the brush and allowing them to flow outward.

4

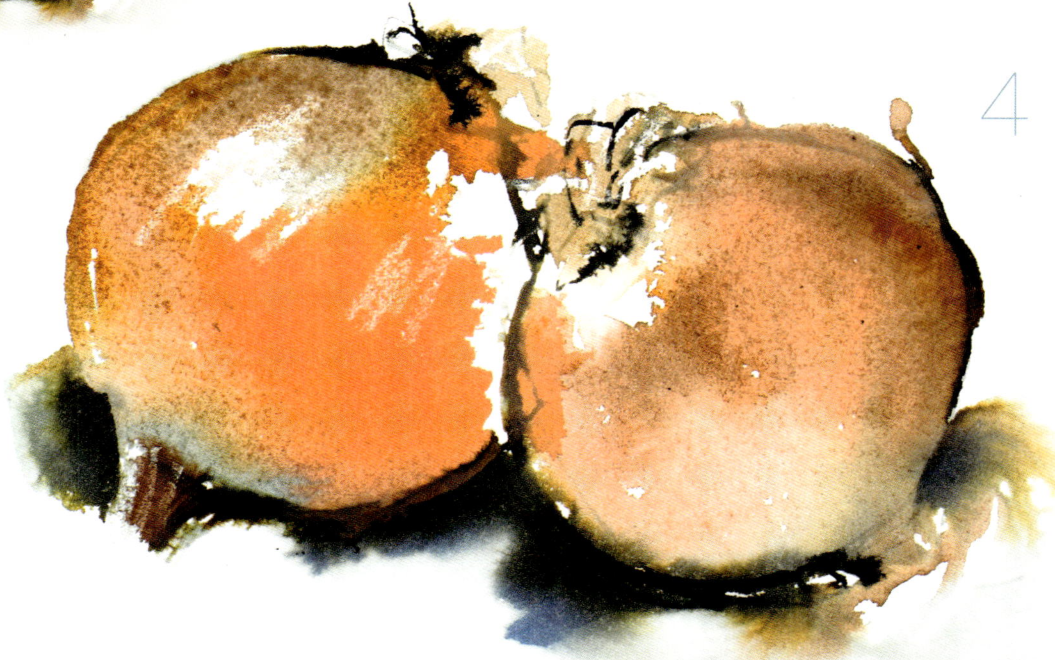

4. Finally, slightly darken the pinkish tones by adding a little more diluted carmine.

94 Effects and Textures / **Effects with Salt**

LEVEL OF DIFFICULTY
★★

COLORS
Yellow ochre
Burnt sienna
Raw umber
Permanent green
Permanent red
Ultramarine blue
White pencil

BRUSHES
Fine round natural hair
Medium round natural hair
Wide flat synthetic hair

PAPER
140 lb medium rough texture

When you sprinkle salt on wet paint the grains absorb the water and create a uniquely rough and granulated mottling, visible after removing the salt when the watercolor has completely dried. Here you will apply this texture in the background of this waterscape.

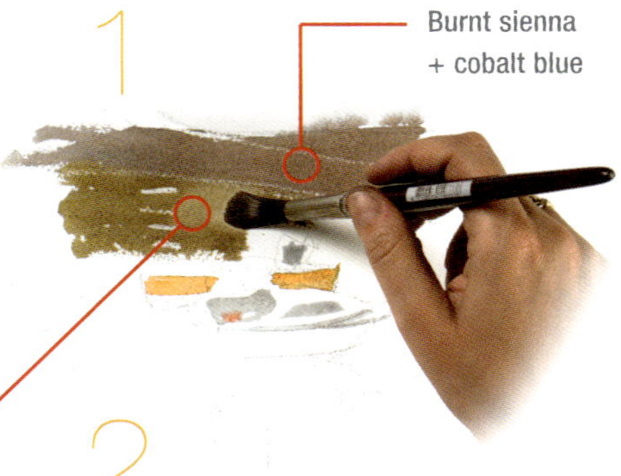

1. Go over some of the lines of the drawing with a white pencil to create a dividing line between the colors of the background and some white reserves in the water.

2. Sprinkle a large amount of salt on the wet paint; much of it will adhere to the surface of the paper. You must not remove it until the watercolor is completely dry.

3. The neutral colors in the background (raw umber and red mixed with blue and sienna) contrast with the bright colors of the shore, where the unmixed permanent red stands out on the hull of the boat.

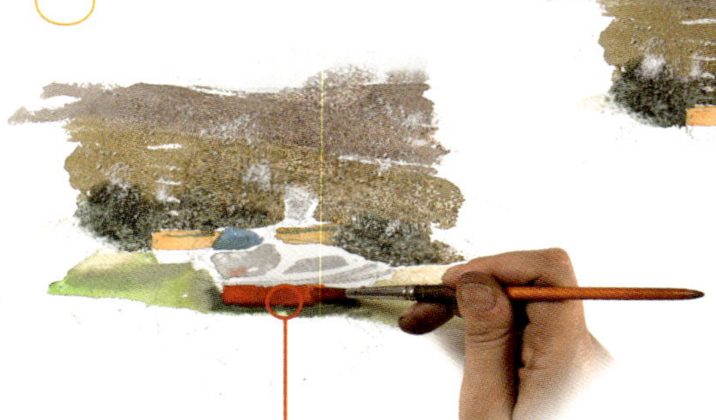

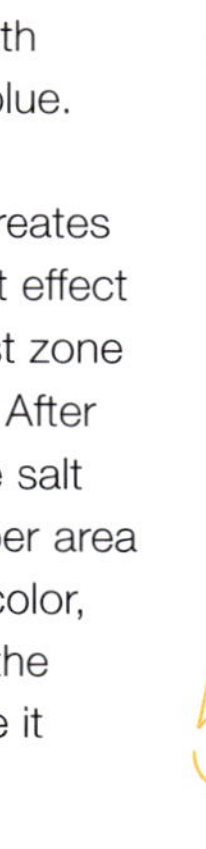

4. After wetting the lower part of the paper, paint the area of the reflection with red and the lower part of the surface of the sea with ultramarine blue.

5. The salt creates a transparent effect in the darkest zone of the water. After removing the salt from the upper area of the watercolor, you will see the rough texture it creates.

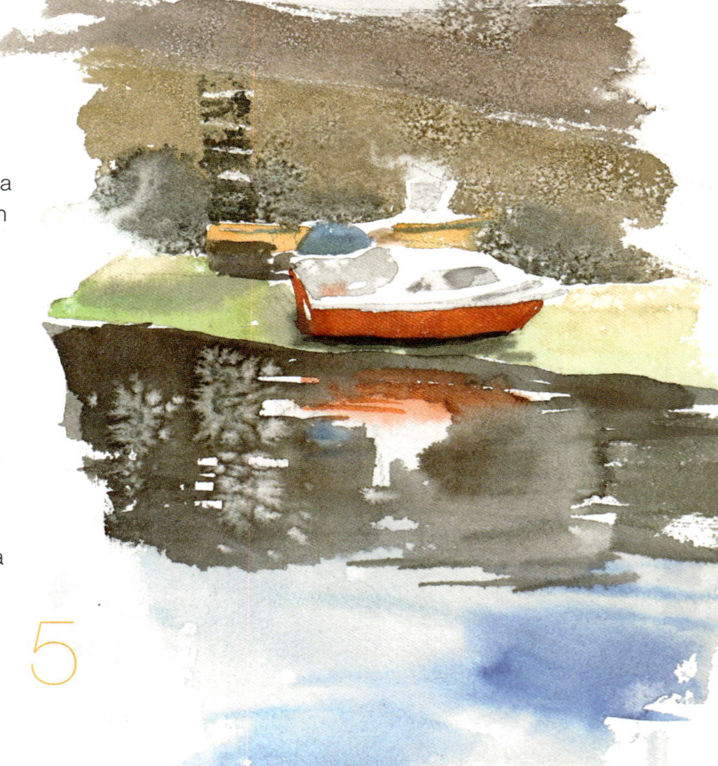

95 Effects and Textures / **Watercolor Applied with a Reed Pen**

LEVEL OF DIFFICULTY
★
COLORS
Cadmium yellow
Cadmium red
Ultramarine blue
BRUSH
Medium round natural hair
PAPER
140 lb medium-rough texture

The reed pen, just like the nib pen, is used for drawing with India ink. But the consistency of the ink is very similar to that of watercolors; therefore it is possible to use the reed pen to draw with watercolor paints. You just have to dilute a little paint with water in a small container to the proper consistency for making lines with the drawing pen.

1
Cadmium yellow
Cadmium red
Ultramarine blue + cadmium red

1. After drawing the apple, apply a wash of blue mixed with red around it. Dip the tip of the pen in diluted paint, and draw some lines on the upper part of the fruit, marking the roundness of the form.

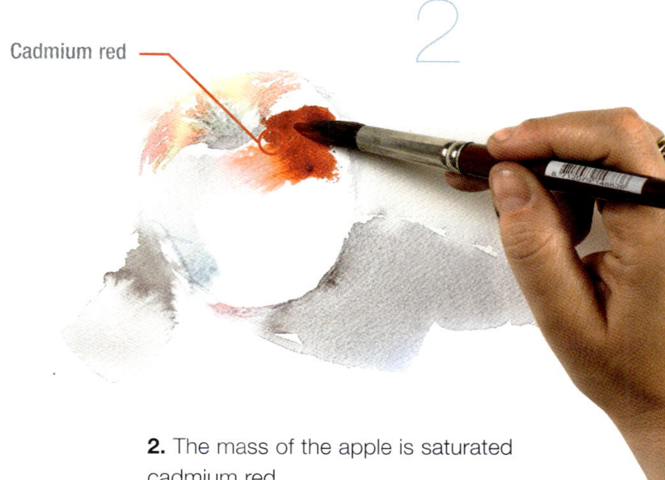

2. The mass of the apple is saturated cadmium red.

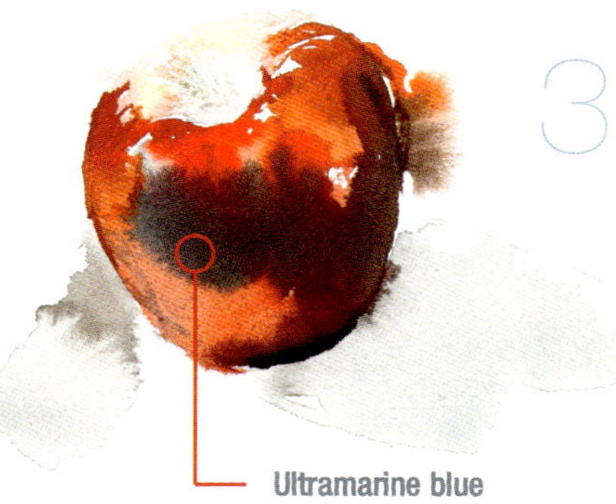

3. In the center of the fruit, add some blue to create the dark tone of the shadow.

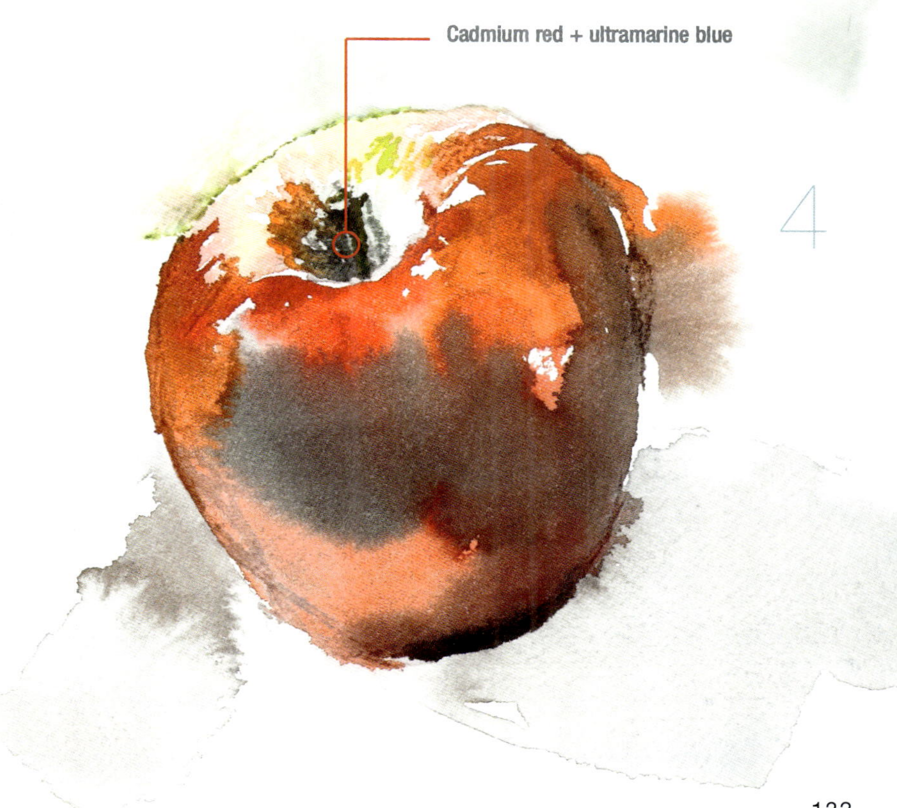

4. Use the reed pen again, charged with a mixture of red and blue, to draw the stem of the apple and thus finish the painting.

LEVEL OF DIFFICULTY
★
COLORS
Raw umber
Burnt sienna
Carmine
BRUSHES
Medium round natural hair
Medium flat synthetic hair
PAPER
140 lb medium-rough texture

If a painted wash is very saturated and opaque, the teeth of a comb will leave very well-defined marks on it. This is not a common approach, but it renders unexpected and interesting results that help illustrate the texture of the mouse's fur. It is not necessary to press very hard. It is best if the teeth are not very far apart nor too close together to create this effect.

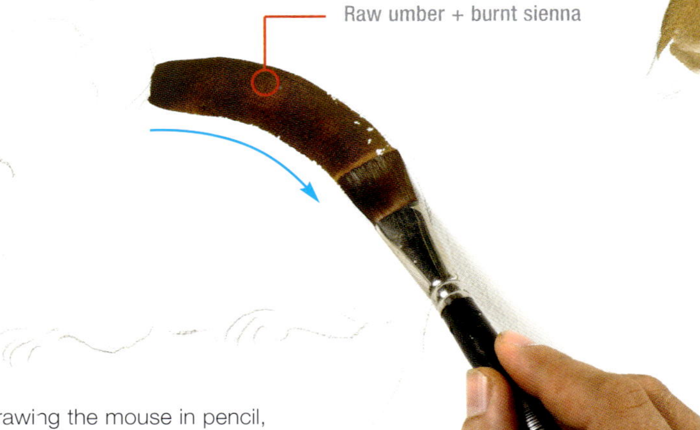

1. After drawing the mouse in pencil, paint the inside with a very saturated mixture of raw umber and burnt sienna.

2. The mouse is now partially covered with a richly colored wash. It is time to apply the comb.

3. Press the comb to the paper, making sure that the marks of the teeth are clearly visible The texture should be made by dragging the comb in a curve from top to bottom.

4. Add different applications of the comb to the body and head of the mouse. They are more than enough to suggest the mouse's characteristic fur.

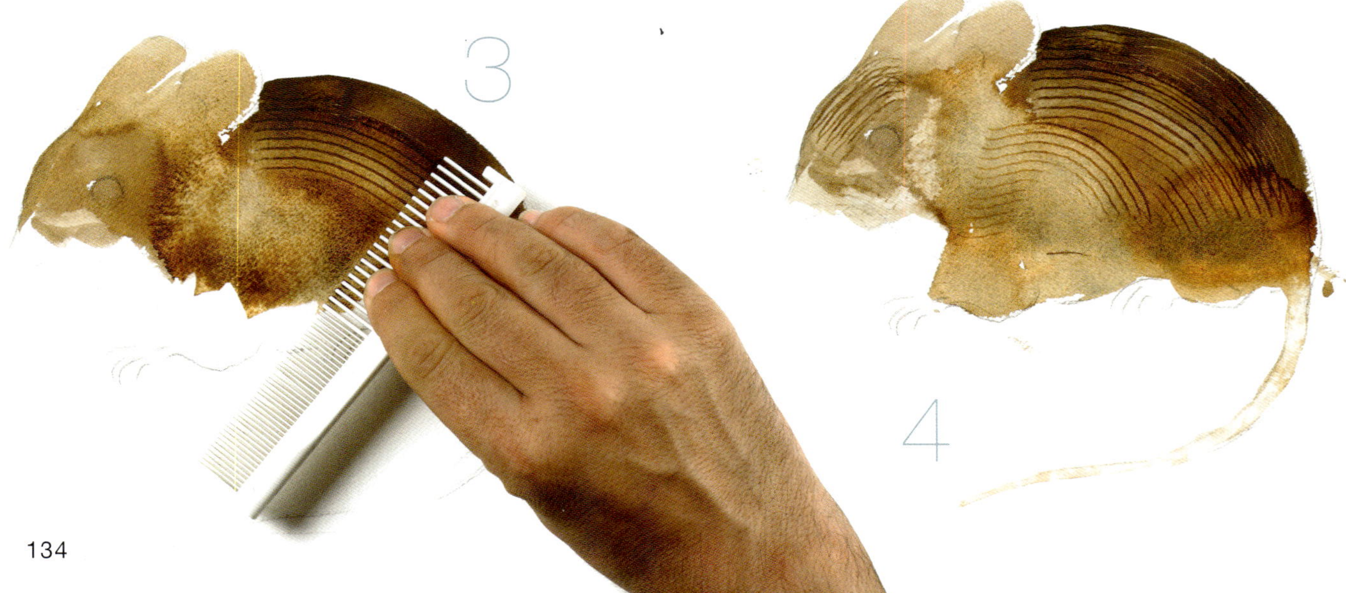

Textures created by sharp or pointed objects are always precise and well defined. It is important to work carefully so as not to puncture or tear the paper, especially when the texture is applied while the paint is wet.

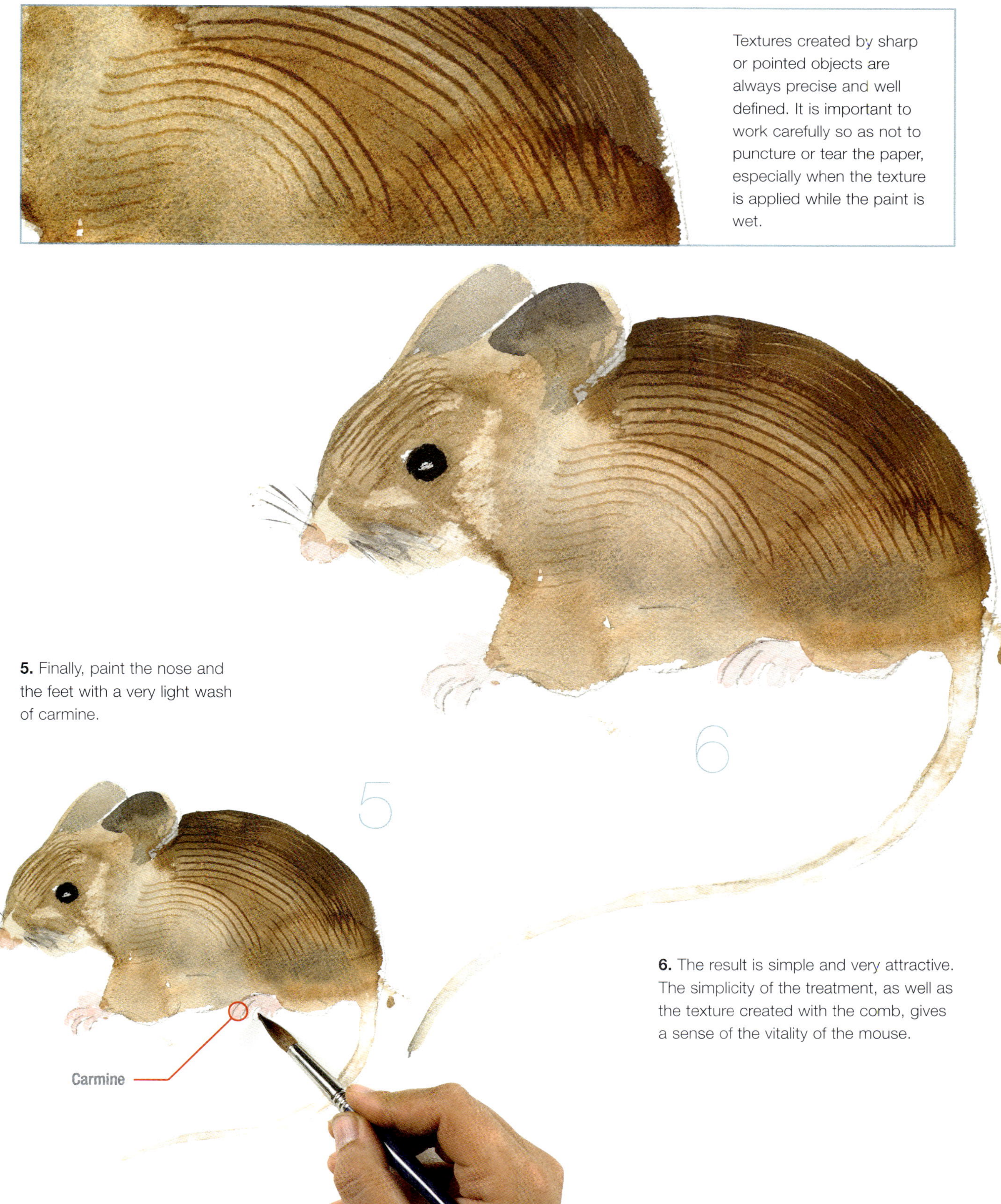

5. Finally, paint the nose and the feet with a very light wash of carmine.

6. The result is simple and very attractive. The simplicity of the treatment, as well as the texture created with the comb, gives a sense of the vitality of the mouse.

97 Special Papers / **On Hot Press Paper**

LEVEL OF DIFFICULTY
★★

COLORS
Cerulean blue
Ultramarine blue
Cobalt violet
Raw umber
Permanent red

BRUSHES
Medium round natural hair
Medium flat synthetic hair

PAPER
140 lb hot press

Hot press is the smoothest variety of watercolor papers. Its texture is imperceptible, and it absorbs water faster than medium- and rough-texture papers. Every shade and mark can be seen on it, and it is quite a demanding support for the beginning watercolorist. It allows you to work with a very wide tonal range, even when you are using a very limited palette.

1. After drawing the sailboat, cover its sails with a very light wash of ultramarine blue. Nearly every pass of the brush is visible on the surface of the hot-press paper.

2. Now add a little raw umber to the blue from the previous wash. This will make a neutral gray tone that you can use to paint the values of the shadows of the boat.

Washes on hot-press paper require more water than usual to keep the brushstrokes from drying on the paper and leaving many gaps and areas of broken color in the wash.

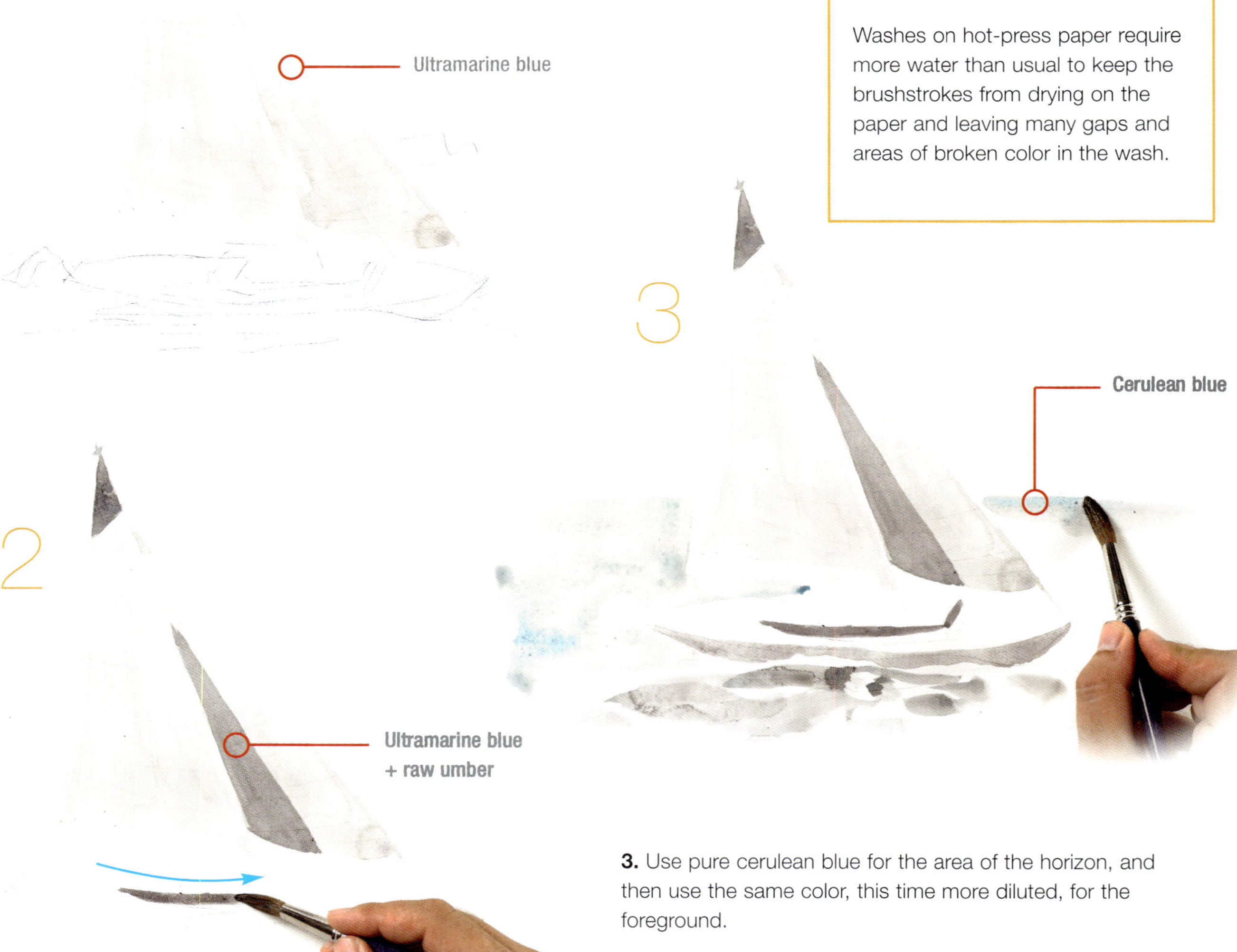

3. Use pure cerulean blue for the area of the horizon, and then use the same color, this time more diluted, for the foreground.

4. Paint the trees on the horizon with cerulean blue mixed with a very small amount of raw umber. The vertical brushstrokes perfectly represent the line of the trees. Add cobalt violet to the boat.

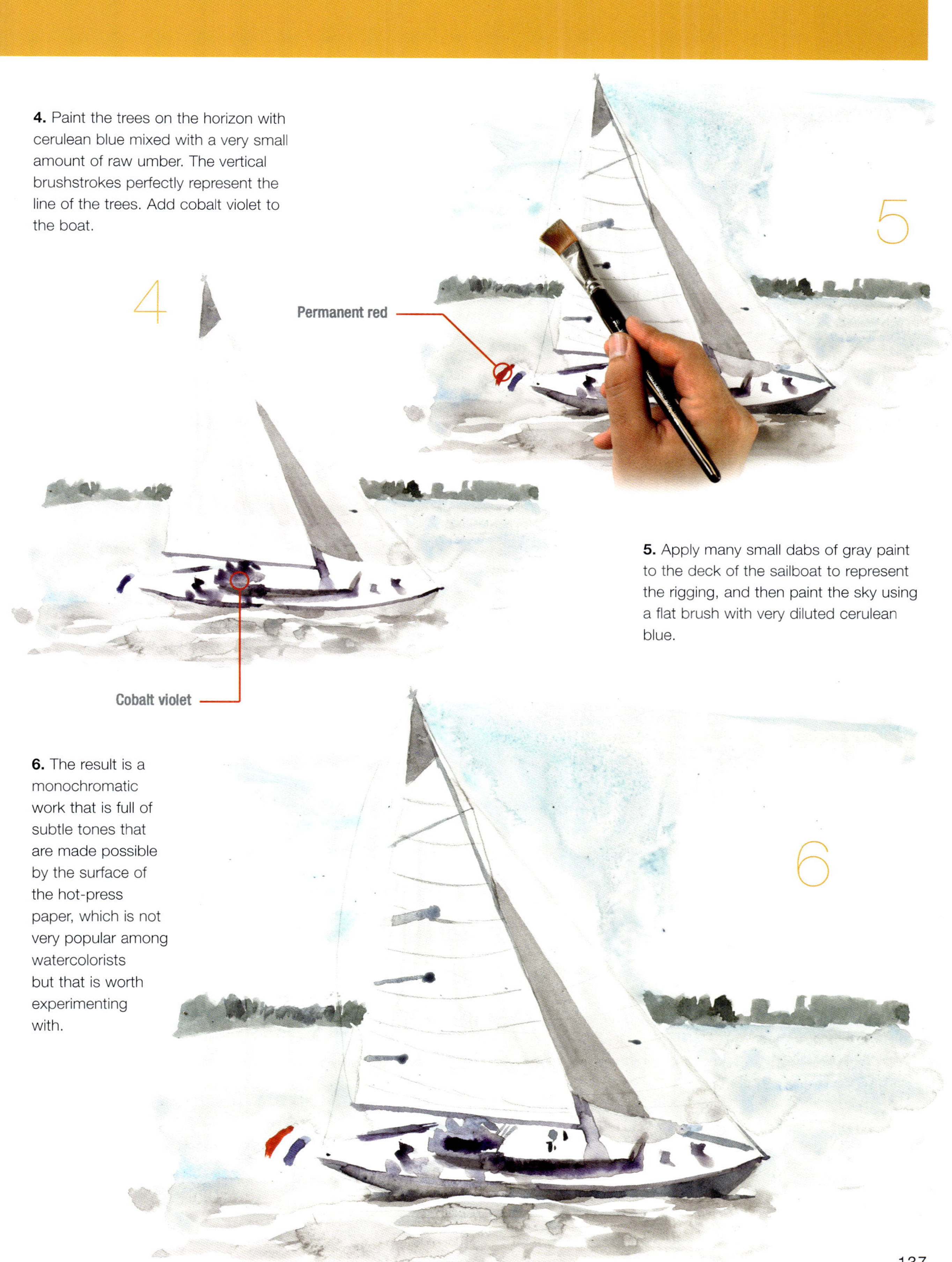

5. Apply many small dabs of gray paint to the deck of the sailboat to represent the rigging, and then paint the sky using a flat brush with very diluted cerulean blue.

6. The result is a monochromatic work that is full of subtle tones that are made possible by the surface of the hot-press paper, which is not very popular among watercolorists but that is worth experimenting with.

LEVEL OF DIFFICULTY
★
COLORS
Raw umber
Burnt sienna
Permanent green
BRUSH
Medium round natural hair
PAPER
Rice paper (Japanese paper)

Japanese paper is made from rice fiber, and despite its extremely fine and delicate appearance, it is very durable. In this watercolor, you will use it after first soaking it with water until it is nearly adhered to the worktable (which should be of some waterproof material). Despite the water, the lines maintain their shapes.

1
Permanent green

1. After dampening the paper and smoothing it on the surface of the board or table, start painting the chameleon without a previous sketch. A single line is enough to define its back and tail.

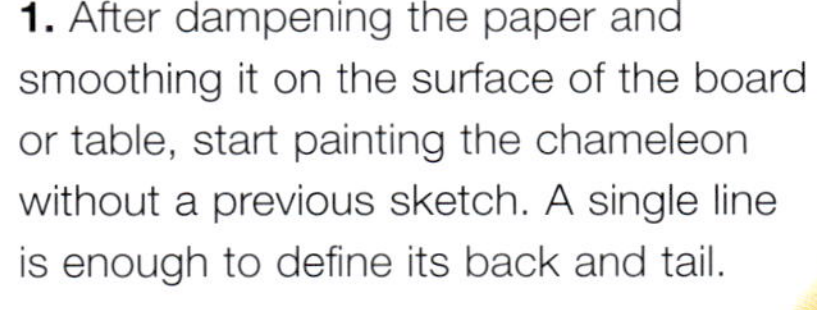

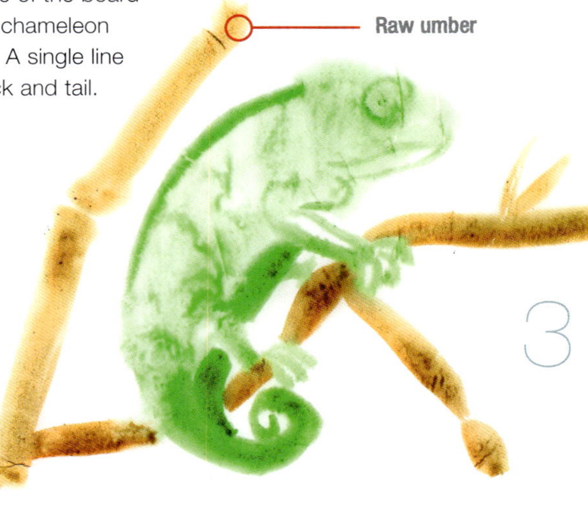

2. Paint the whole body with diluted permanent green. Add detail to the head and feet. One of the advantages of this support is that the brushstrokes do not lose their shapes even when the paper is very wet.

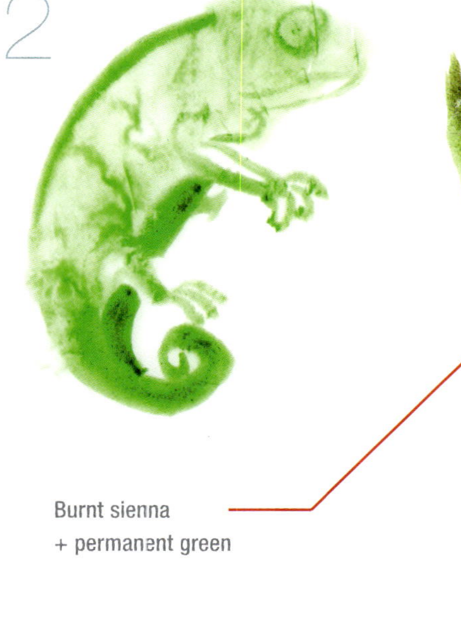

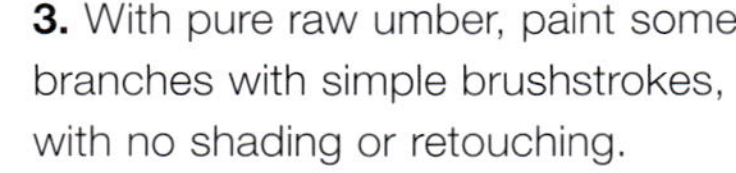

3. With pure raw umber, paint some branches with simple brushstrokes, with no shading or retouching.

Burnt sienna
+ permanent green

4

4. Outline some details on the head, and paint some leaves with a mixture of burnt sienna and green, with quick simple brushstrokes. That is all.

99 Special Papers / On *Sumi-e* Paper

LEVEL OF DIFFICULTY

★

COLORS

Permanent green

Carmine

BRUSH

Medium round natural hair

PAPER

Sumi-e watercolor paper

This type of paper is very similar to the previous one; it is also made from rice fiber, but this time you will be painting on dry paper in the Japanese wash style called *Sumi-e*. The secret of this is, in simplicity, each brushstroke counts, and you must never add even one extra stroke. Synthesis is the ideal that should guide each movement of the brush.

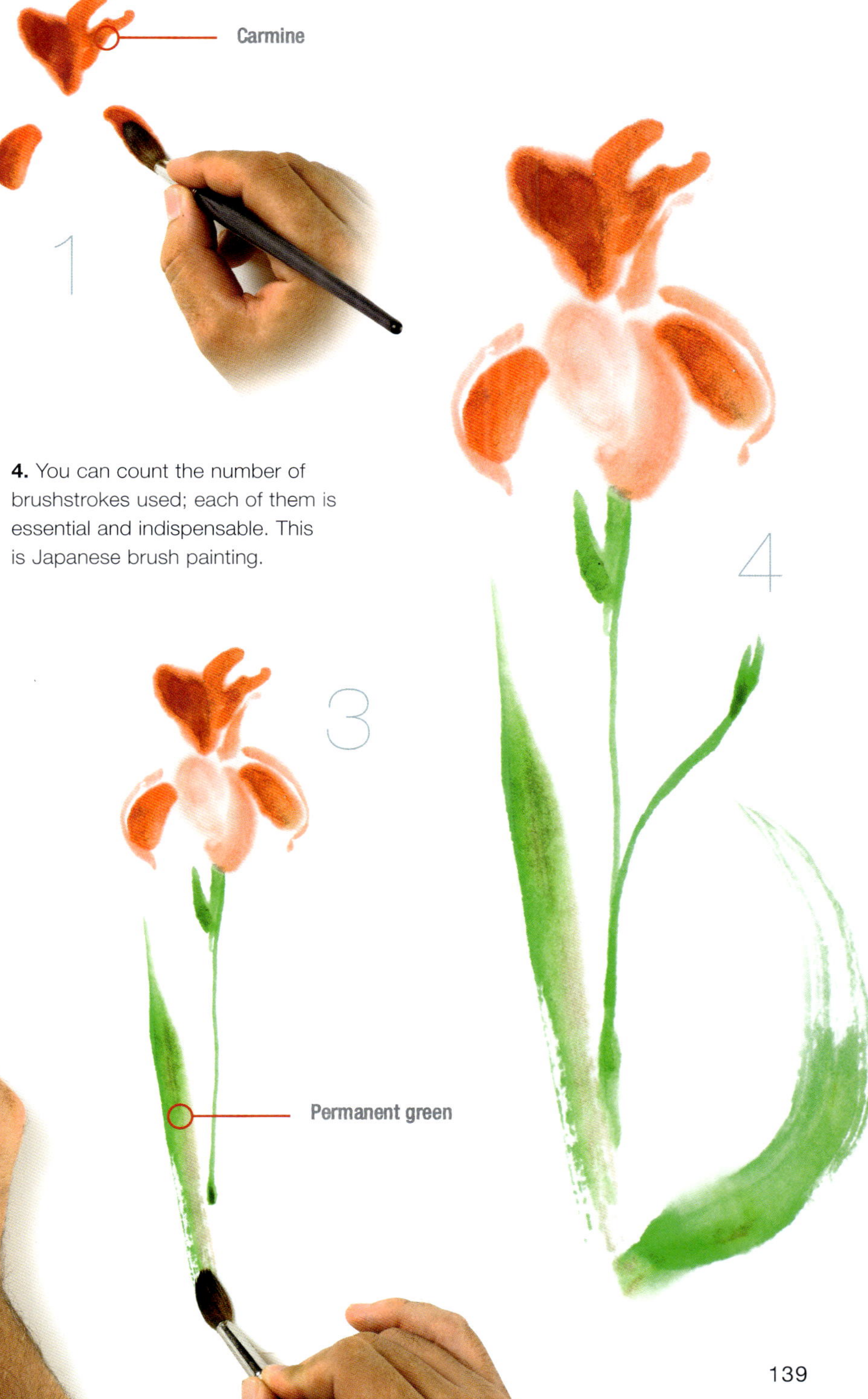

1. You do not have to make any preliminary drawing, because in this style the drawing is defined by the brushstrokes themselves. The first applications of saturated carmine will form the darkest petals.

2. Paint the lighter petals with more-diluted carmine.

3. A very thin brushstroke made with the brush held nearly vertical to the paper defines the stem. Use a wide straight brushstroke to represent the leaf.

4. You can count the number of brushstrokes used; each of them is essential and indispensable. This is Japanese brush painting.

100 Special Papers / **On Handmade Paper**

LEVEL OF DIFFICULTY
★★
COLORS
Raw umber
Burnt sienna
Carmine
Cobalt violet
Permanent green
BRUSHES
Medium round natural hair
Medium flat synthetic hair
PAPER
140 lb handmade

Handmade paper follows a totally artisanal manufacturing process. Its fibers are more irregular and its surface is rougher than machine-made paper. And because the surface of the sheet has less glue or sizing, it is much more absorbent. In this case, the support is nearly as absorbent as blotter paper.

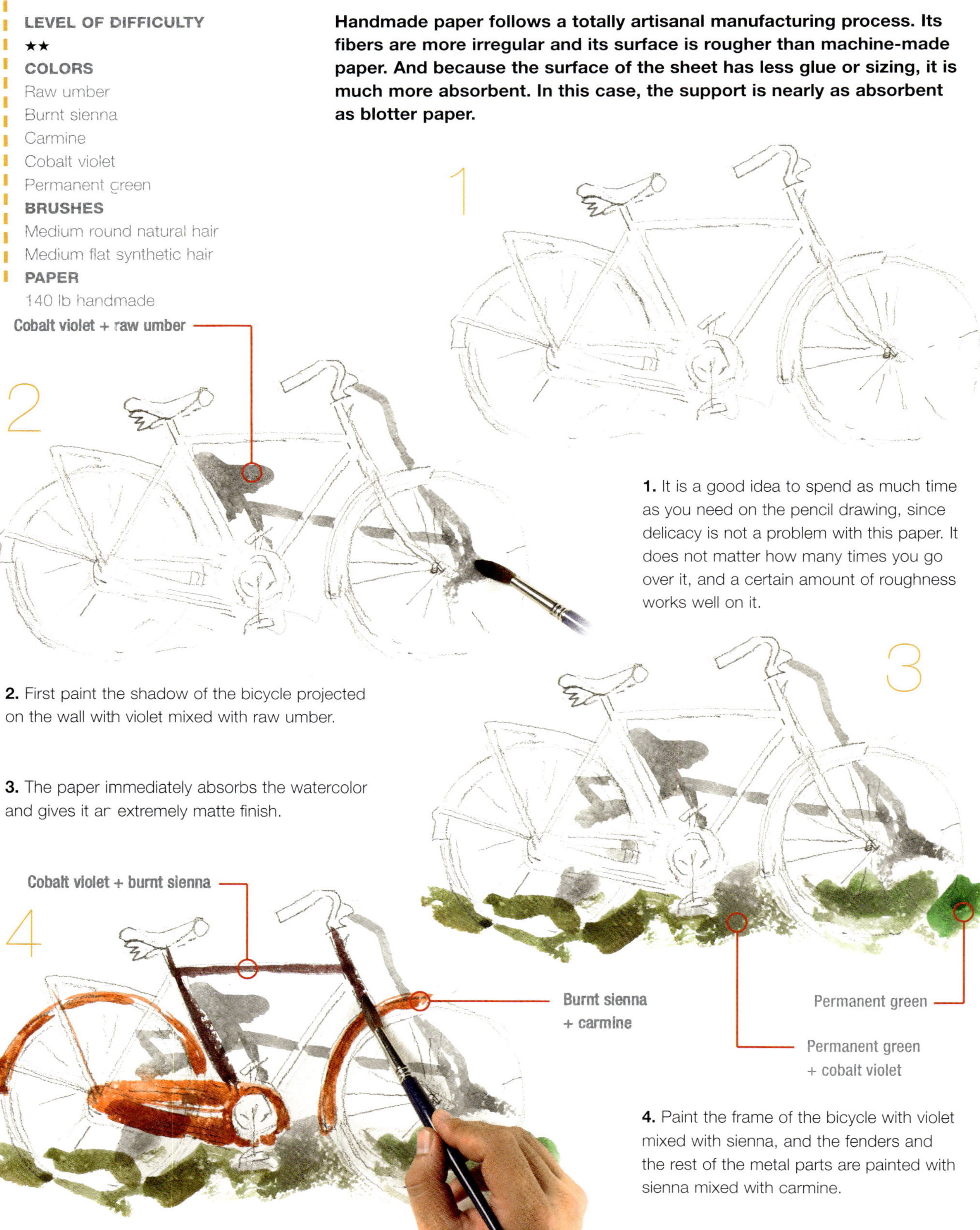

1. It is a good idea to spend as much time as you need on the pencil drawing, since delicacy is not a problem with this paper. It does not matter how many times you go over it, and a certain amount of roughness works well on it.

2. First paint the shadow of the bicycle projected on the wall with violet mixed with raw umber.

3. The paper immediately absorbs the watercolor and gives it an extremely matte finish.

4. Paint the frame of the bicycle with violet mixed with sienna, and the fenders and the rest of the metal parts are painted with sienna mixed with carmine.

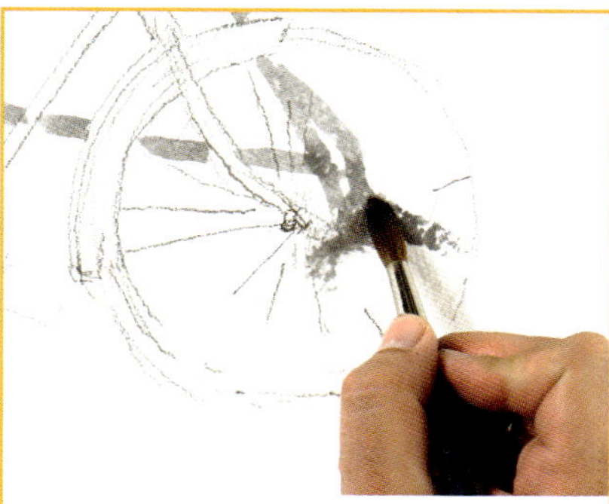

When working on very absorbent paper, the brush loses its paint right away and creates dry brush effects. This can be used to advantage in a watercolor with a rustic and irregular finish.

5. Apply the brushstrokes without trying to achieve precise and delicate effects. The colors will run and flow over each other.

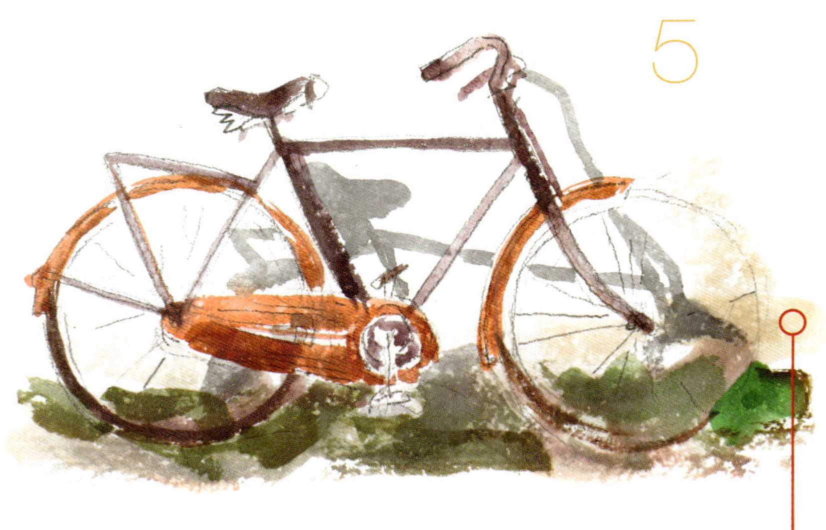

Raw umber

6. After painting the tires with violet mixed with sienna, you will have created a very spontaneous and natural-looking work.

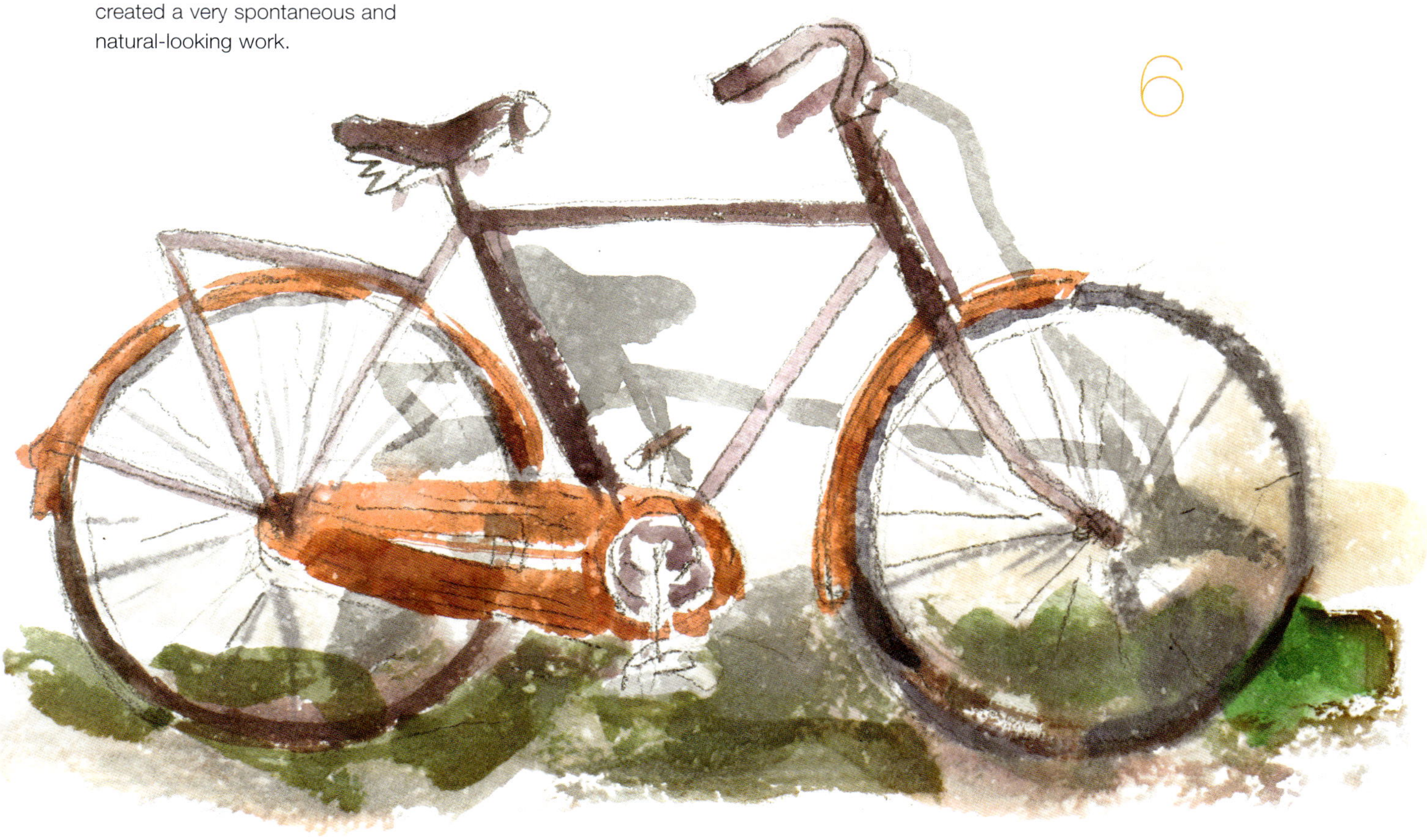

6

101 Special Papers / **On Paper with Long Fibers**

LEVEL OF DIFFICULTY
★

COLORS
Carmine
Cobalt violet
Cobalt blue
Cadmium red
Cadmium yellow
Permanent green
Sap green

BRUSHES
Medium round natural hair
Medium flat synthetic hair

PAPER
Vegetable-fiber paper

Today there are a great variety of papers for painting and for crafts that are worth exploring. In this case, you will use a rice paper with long vegetable fibers that create a very unique sinuous design. Work in a relaxed and uninhibited manner, striving for an effect that is more decorative than descriptive.

1. Draw some lines in pencil that suggest plants and insects. Immediately begin to create multicolor effects, using the purest tones possible.

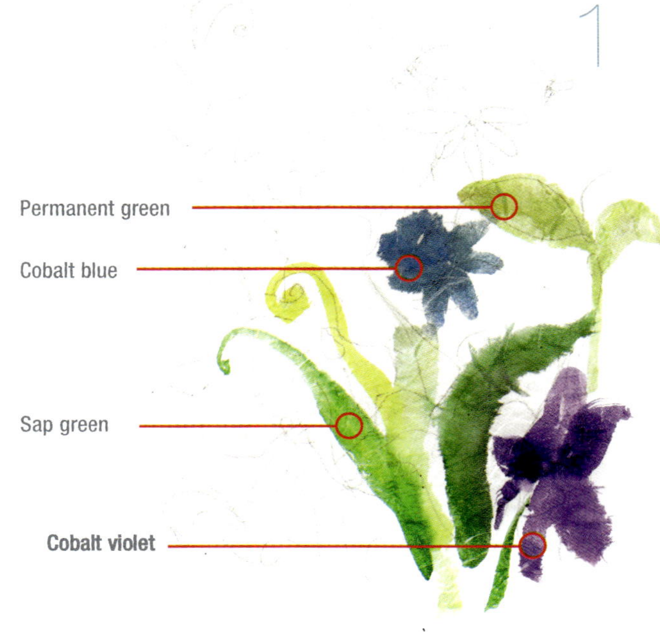

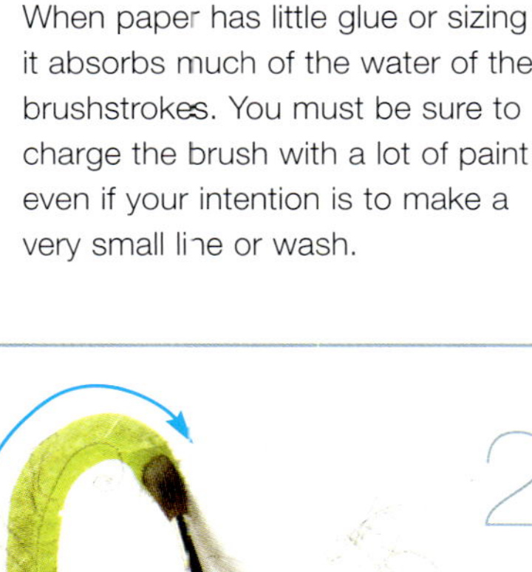

When paper has little glue or sizing it absorbs much of the water of the brushstrokes. You must be sure to charge the brush with a lot of paint even if your intention is to make a very small line or wash.

2

2. Following the Japanese brush painting approach, try to make each stem and each flower with simple direct brushstrokes.

3. Alternate wide brushstrokes with others made with the tip of the brush to add variety to the lines and forms of the painting.

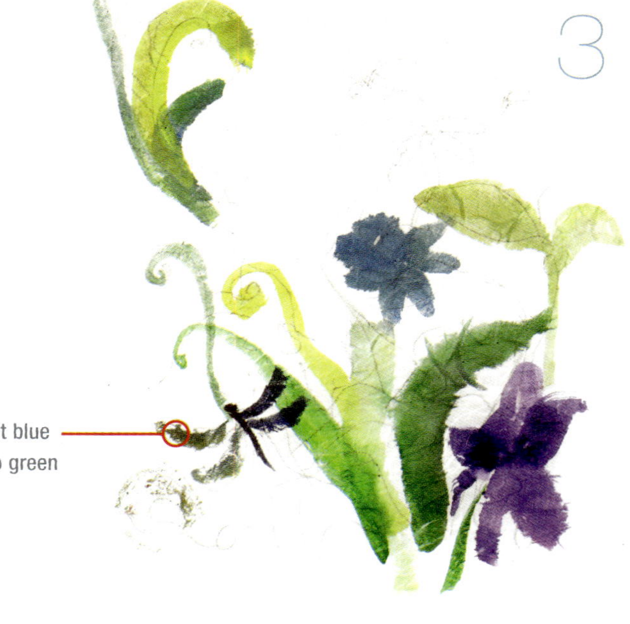

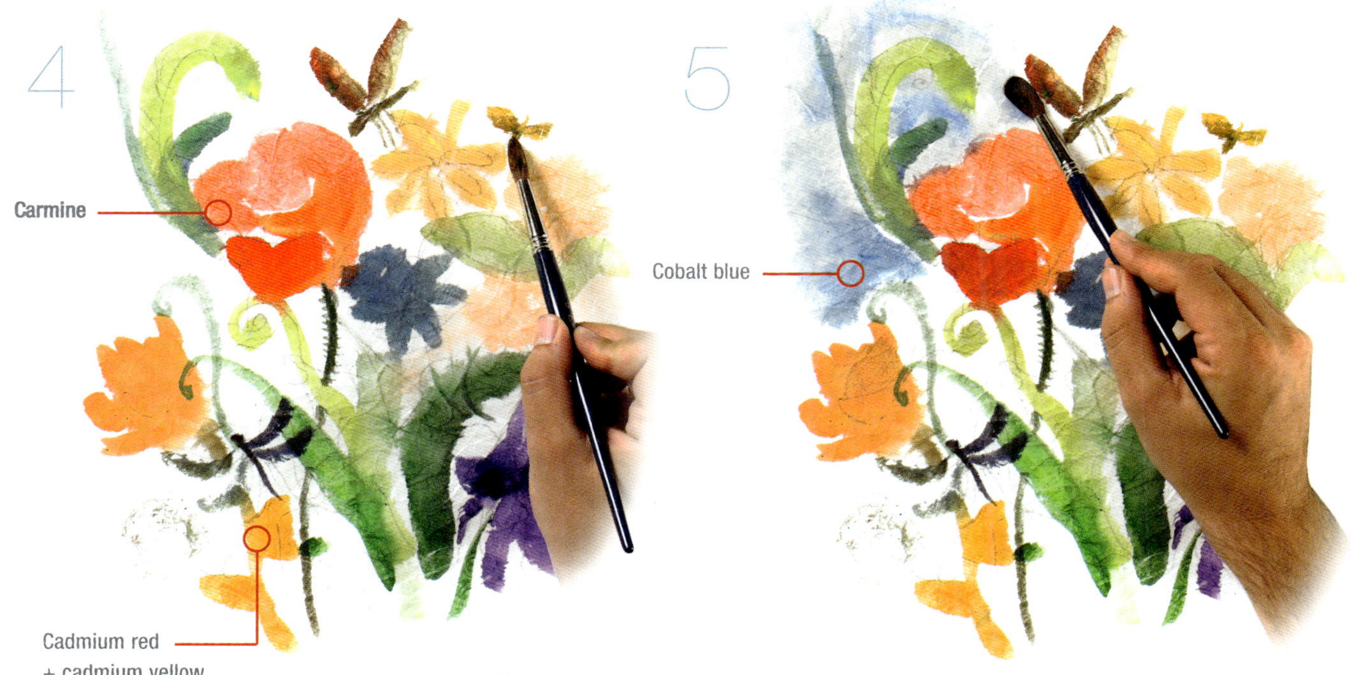

4. You can create each insect with three or four simple brushstrokes that will represent the wings, the body, and the legs.

5. Paint large areas of the background with diluted cobalt blue. Work quickly because this paper absorbs water immediately.

6. The resulting watercolor is festive, colorful, and free, in accordance with the original and somewhat extravagant nature of this paper.

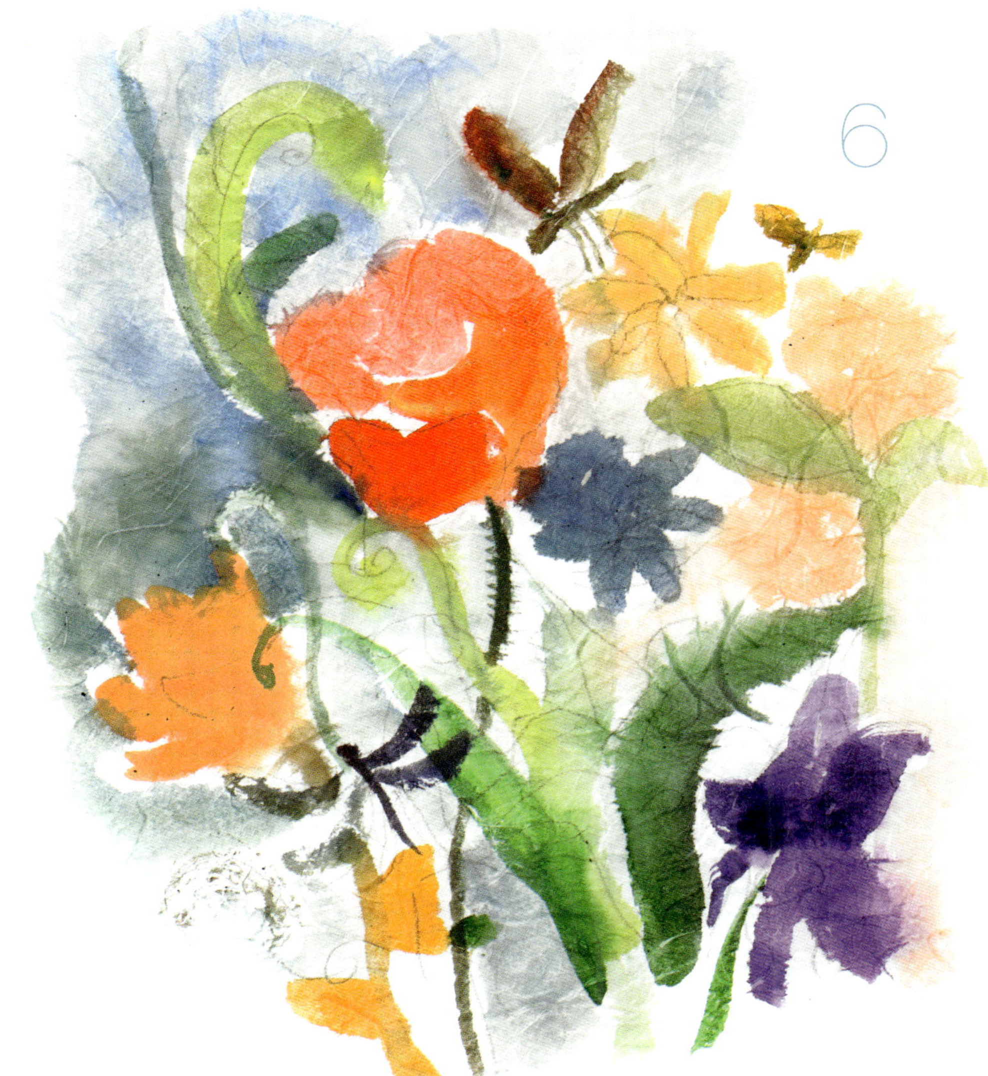

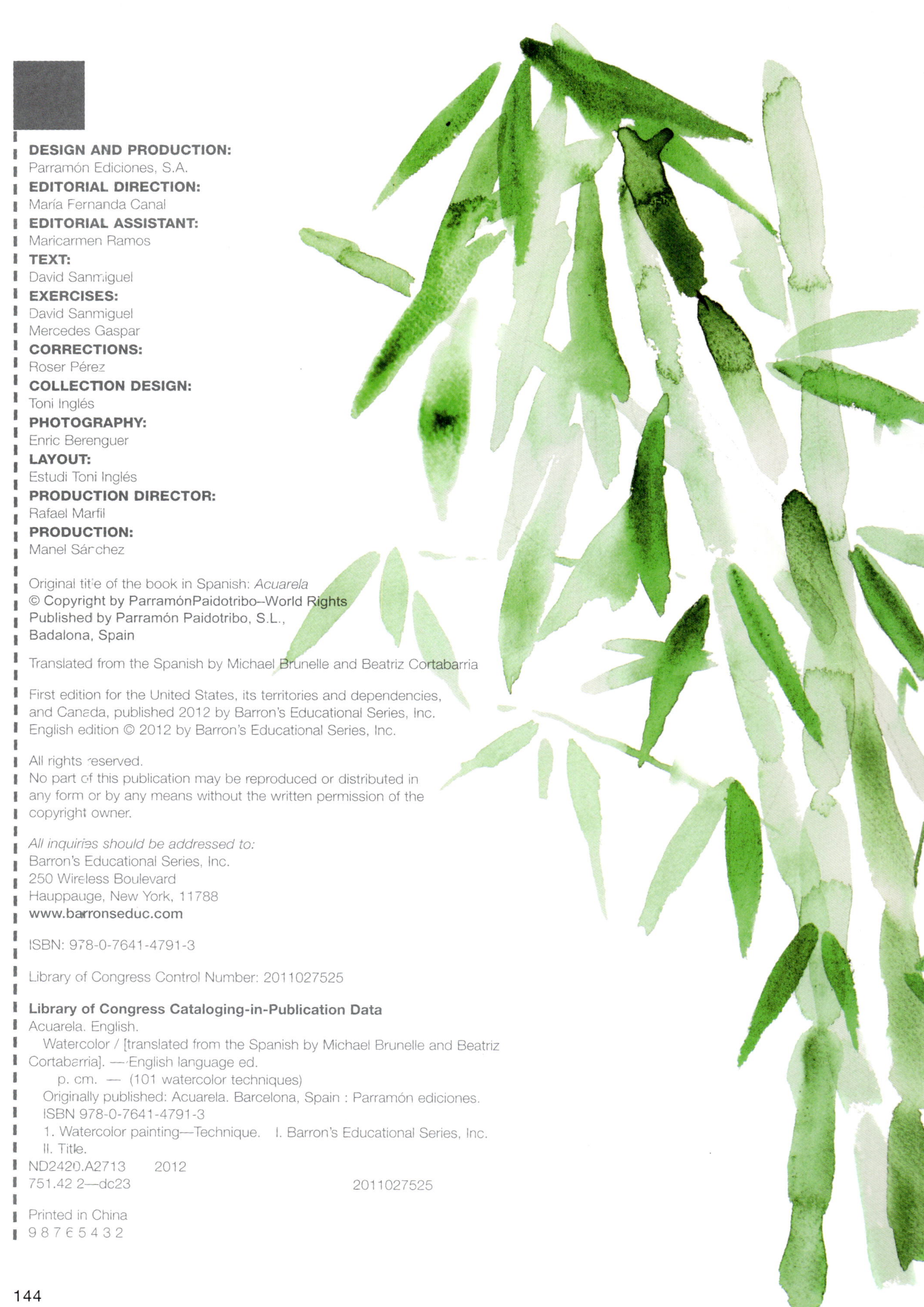

DESIGN AND PRODUCTION:
Parramón Ediciones, S.A.
EDITORIAL DIRECTION:
María Fernanda Canal
EDITORIAL ASSISTANT:
Maricarmen Ramos
TEXT:
David Sanmiguel
EXERCISES:
David Sanmiguel
Mercedes Gaspar
CORRECTIONS:
Roser Pérez
COLLECTION DESIGN:
Toni Inglés
PHOTOGRAPHY:
Enric Berenguer
LAYOUT:
Estudi Toni Inglés
PRODUCTION DIRECTOR:
Rafael Marfil
PRODUCTION:
Manel Sánchez

Original title of the book in Spanish: *Acuarela*

Published by Parramón Paidotribo, S.L.,
Badalona, Spain

Translated from the Spanish by Michael Brunelle and Beatriz Cortabarria

First edition for the United States, its territories and dependencies, and Canada, published 2012 by Barron's Educational Series, Inc.

All inquiries should be addressed to:
Barron's Educational Series, Inc.
250 Wireless Boulevard
Hauppauge, New York, 11788
www.barronseduc.com

ISBN: 978-0-7641-4791-3

Library of Congress Control Number: 2011027525

Library of Congress Cataloging-in-Publication Data
Acuarela. English.
Watercolor / [translated from the Spanish by Michael Brunelle and Beatriz Cortabarria]. —English language ed.
p. cm. — (101 watercolor techniques)
Originally published: Acuarela. Barcelona, Spain : Parramón ediciones.
ISBN 978-0-7641-4791-3
1. Watercolor painting—Technique. I. Barron's Educational Series, Inc. II. Title.
ND2420.A2713 2012
751.42 2—dc23 2011027525

Printed in China
9 8 7 6 5 4 3 2